# The Art of Mathematics in Business

# The Art of Mathematics in Business

## Analyzing Facts and Figures for Smart Business Decisions

Dr Jae K Shim

**GLOBAL**
professional
*publishing*

Global Professional Publishing

Random Acres
Slip Mill Lane
Hawkhurst
Cranbrook
Kent

Email: publishing@gppbooks.com

ISBN 978-1-906403-32-4

Printed in the United Kingdom by Good News Press

For full details of Global Professional Publishing titles in

Finance and Banking see our website at:

www.gppbooks.com

# Contents

# Preface

*The Art of Mathematics in Business* provides managers and entrepreneurs with the information, analysis, and insights necessary to analyze and calculate the consequences of a wide range of business financial strategies and problems. The ability to select the right operational technique is vital if the business is to survive, profit, and grow in today's uncertain economic environment. The manager and entrepreneur of a business must be able to make the right financial decision based on sound mathematical reasoning in order to run the business efficiently. He or she must understand the problem, and then apply math skills to solve it.

This book is a comprehensive, one-stop desk reference for managers and owners of businesses who must use quantitative calculations to make daily operating and investing decisions. Its purpose is to provide the fundamentals of business math techniques that can be quickly applied to real-word problems. This unique resource will save countless hours of research time by making sound financial planning truly easy. It provides analyses as well as clear and understandable explanations of complex business problems. Basic mathematical techniques are presented in a step-by-step fashion that takes the reader through each stage of the problem-solving process. The examples in this book provide an invaluable and effective operating tool. This book also contains user-friendly personal computer techniques. The examples enable the businessperson to measure results and to report the data in an easy-to-understand format.

Each section begins with an overview of the mathematics necessary to solve the problem under discussion. The presentation of the data will enable the business owner to select and use the appropriate statistical method to make cost-effective and profitable business decisions. The language associated with the mathematical techniques can also be adopted by the manager when circumstances require communication with investors, lenders, vendors, customers, employees, and other parties associated with the enterprise. Each business math tool is illuminated in the following, step by step fashion:

◆ Introduction

◆ How is it computed?

◆ Can a computer help?

◆ How is it used and applied?

The objectives and methods illustrated in this book cover a wide range of areas, including management, marketing, accounting, taxes, finance, operations, insurance, and economics. This book provides solutions to traditional as well as new operating and financial problems created by today's uncertain economic environment. It also advises the business manager and/or business consultant about ways to respond to sudden and unexpected problems. Complex business problems are broken down into smaller ones for easier solution.

This book is divided into parts, each of which covers an area that is important in starting and running a business. Part topics include managing cash and inventory, evaluating loans and credit, researching the market and competition, and preparing financial statements. Each part is broken down into sections. For example, budgeting and profit planning is made up of sections that discuss such important areas as predicting sales and costs, cash flow analysis, the allocation of financial resources, and finding the payback period. This book also contains illustrative and practical mathematical formulas, equations, models, ratios, and other statistical techniques that can be used to make sound and profitable business decisions. The examples in each section focus on financial problems and highlight the importance of using mathematical and financial management principles.

Other topics covered in *The Art of Business Math* include the methods used to find the correct level of inventory, determining the amount and rate of production, computing profits, finding the rate of return, monitoring and controlling costs, allocating financial resources, analyzing the financial position of the business, identifying trends, comparing performance to that of competitors, evaluating supervisors and employee productivity, using human and physical resources efficiently, determining how much and when to reorder, computing the necessary amount of merchandise safety stock, whether to offer a discount to customers, computing the cost of financing, determining cash requirements, computing the breakeven point, calculating the debt level, finding the variances between budgeted and actual revenues and/or costs, forecasting sales accurately, calculating adequate insurance coverage, finding the tax liability, computing the potential cash flows for projects, analyzing floor space, evaluating the effects of inflation, appraising customer relationships and transactions such as average order size and the number of backorders, computing the value of the business, and identifying potential bankruptcy so steps may be taken to avoid it. The business operator will also learn am how to use a computer to assemble data and perform rapid calculations which will promote the effective use of the mathematical procedures. There are also in-depth discussions of both simple and complex mathematical applications that may be applicable to a particular problem. Each quantitative approach is described clearly and concisely. In some cases, the reader will be directed to the use of financial calculators, spreadsheet programs such as Excel, Lotus 1-2-3 add-ins, stand-alone specialized computer software, accounting software, and cash management software.

The author does not assume that the reader has any mathematical expertise. Thus both the novice and the experienced businessperson will profit from the methodology contained in this action-oriented book. The applications will make the business manager competent in the use of the most up-to-date managerial tools. The presentation is easy to understand and is user-friendly. This book shows what the mathematical technique measures, why it is important, when it should be used, how it should be used, and what the numbers mean.

The field of financial management has recently witnessed a dangerous period of rapid change, stagnation, and contraction. Uncertainty about the future growth of the economy has forced the business operator to be more prudent and sophisticated in the allocation of financial resources. It is therefore imperative that business owners employ new mathematical and financial management techniques to aid their decision making. The author is aware of these vital and complex techniques and cover them in clear and concise detail.

The business manager must also be aware of both the usefulness and the limitations of the particular mathematical technique employed to solve a problem. This book points out, when required, that a particular technique may be appropriate in one situation but not in others. This book also contains hundreds of filled-in examples, illustrations, practical applications, measures, procedures, rules of thumb, statistical data, exhibits, tables, graphs, and diagrams. They are presented to aid in the comprehension and successful solution of a particular problem. The reader will also learn when and how to use the appropriate computational method, why it is used, when computer techniques such as spreadsheets should be used, and how to read and analyze the computer printout. Typical questions of concern to business managers are answered, such as: How much sales are needed to justify the cost of a proposed advertising program? How many factory workers are required to meet production needs? Is the business growing, and how does it compare to competition?

In today's marketplace, economic downturns force business managers to face new challenges. This book will minimize the effects of these potentially disastrous periods. It is designed to maximize both the profits and the value of the firm for its owners. This is a central objective of this book, and each financial procedure discussed is linked to the impact it has on the value of the firm. The reader will find this book useful, practical, comprehensive, and profitable. Keep it handy as an easy-to-use reference. There is cross-referencing of topics and mathematical techniques. The index can be used to find a specific area of interest. The glossary defines important mathematical terms.

In summation, this book is an invaluable addition to any library and will provide quick and accurate answers to the business entrepreneur and manager. It will make an individual "savvy," comfortable, and proficient in both the business math and the financial applications required for the successful operation of any business.

Jae K Shim

Los Alamitos, California

# Acknowledgments

I wish to express my deep gratitude to Mike Jeffers of Glenlake for this edition. The input and efforts are much recognized and appreciated. Many thanks also go to Lana Murillo and Christina Ramos of California State University, Long Beach for their excellent editorial contribution in the production stage.

# Part I

# Evaluating the Cost of Bank Loans, Business Loans, Trade Credit, and Other Financing

## 1. Understanding Simple Interest

### Introduction

The fee charged for the use of money, or principal, is called interest. It is the amount charged by a lender to a borrower. The interest rate is usually stated on an annual basis. The sum of the principal and the interest due is called the *accumulated value*, *amount due*, or *maturity value*. Compound interest is discussed in Sec. 60, How Do You Calculate Future Values? How Money Grows?

### How is it Computed?

The amount of interest due is based on three factors: the principal, the rate of interest, and the time period during which the principal is used. One year is generally used as the time period. Simple interest is calculated on original principal only. The formula for simple interest is:

**Interest = principal x rate x time**

$$I = Prt$$

The maturity value $S$ is given as:

**Maturity value = principal + interest**

Although the time span of a loan may be given in days, months, or years, the rate of interest is an annual rate. Thus, when the duration of a loan is given in months or days, the time must be converted to years. When the time is given in months, the formula is:

$$t = \frac{\textbf{Number of months}}{12}$$

## Example 1

A business owner obtains a 2-year loan of $10,000 from the Amalgamated Bank. The bank charges an annual simple interest rate of 10 percent. The rate of interest charged for 1 year is $1,000, calculated as follows:

$$\$10,000 \times 10\% \times 1 \text{ year} = \$1,000$$

The total simple interest for the 2-year period is $2,000, calculated as follows:

$$\$1,000 \times 2 \text{ years} = \$2,000$$

The maturity value (S) of the loan is $12,000, calculated as follows:

$$I = Prt$$

$$S = P + I = \$10,000 + \$2,000 = \$12,000$$

## Example 2

A business owner obtains a 3-month loan of $10,000 from Fidelity Bank. The bank charges an annual simple interest rate of 10 percent. The interest charged for the 3-month period is $250, and the maturity value of the loan is $10,250, calculated as follows:

$$P = \$10,000 \qquad r = 10\% \text{ or } 0.10 \qquad t = 3/12 \text{ month}$$

$$I = Prt$$

$$\$10,000 \times 0.10 \times 3/12 \text{ month} = \$250$$

The maturity value of the loan is

$$S = P + I$$

$$\$10,000 + \$250 = \$10,250$$

## How is it used and applied?

The owner must know how to determine the cost of money in a debt or lease agreement. By knowing the cost of borrowing, the owner can better plan a business strategy to obtain an adequate return on his or her money and to provide sufficient funds to pay principal and interest.

The business owner who seeks a loan should shop around to obtain the best interest terms possible. Excessive interest rates, although they are tax deductible, are a drain on an owner's profits. Large outstanding loans, coupled with high interest rates, can substantially reduce an owner's profits and impair a business' credit rating. A balance sheet showing high interest-bearing loans can also result in lenders charging even higher rates of interest because of the possibility of default and even bankruptcy if the loans are not paid at their maturity date.

See Sec. 2, Real (Effective) Interest Rate.

# 2. Real (Effective) Interest Rate

## Introduction

The stated rate of interest does not tell the whole story: you need to be sure you understand all the fees and charges that might affect the real interest rate. The real rate of interest on a loan is expressed as an annual percentage applicable for the life of the loan.

## How is it computed?

$$\text{Real interest rate} = \frac{\text{nominal interest on face of loan}}{\text{net proceeds of loan}}$$

For a discounted loan, which is a common form of loan, interest is deducted immediately in arriving at the net proceeds – which increases the effective interest rate. A bank may require a compensating balance, i.e., a deposit that offsets the unpaid loan. In this case, no interest is earned on the compensating balance, which is stated as a percentage of the loan. A compensating balance also increases the effective interest rate.

## *Example*

A business takes out a $10,000, 1-year, 10% discounted loan. The compensating balance is 5 percent. The effective interest rate is:

$$\frac{\$1,000}{\$10,000 - \$1,000 - \$500} = \frac{1,000}{8,500} = 11.8\%$$

## How is it used and applied?

Business owners compute the effective interest rate to determine the true cost of borrowing.

See Sec. 3, The Cost of Credit: Annual Percentage Rate.

# 3. The Cost of Credit: Annual Percentage Rate

## Introduction

The annual percentage rate (APR) is a true measure of the effective cost of credit. It is the ratio of the finance charge to the average amount of credit in use during the life of the loan, and is expressed as a percentage rate per year.

## How is it computed?

We present below a discussion of the way the effective APR is calculated for various types of loans.

## *Single-Payment Loans*

The single-payment loan is paid in full on a given date. There are two ways of calculating APR on single-payment loans: the simple interest method and the discount method.

## *1. Simple interest method*

Recall from Sec. 1 that, under the simple interest method, interest is calculated only on the amount borrowed (proceeds):

$$\text{APR} = \frac{\text{average annual finance charge}}{\text{amount borrowed or proceeds}}$$

## Example 1

A business owner took out a single-payment loan of $1000 for 2 years at a simple interest rate of 15 percent. The interest charge is: $300 ($1,000 x 0.15 x 2 years). Hence the APR is:

$$APR = \left(\frac{150}{1,000}\right) = 15\%$$

Under the simple interest method, the stated simple interest rate and the APR are always the same for single-payment loans.

## Discount method

Under the discount method, interest is determined and then deducted from the amount of the loan. The difference is the actual amount the borrower receives. In other words, the borrower prepays the finance charges.

## Example 2

Using the same figures as in Example 1, the actual amount received $700 ($1,000 - $300), not $1,000. The APR is:

$$APR = \left(\frac{150}{700}\right) = 21.43\%$$

The rate the lender must quote on the loan is 21.43 percent, not 15 percent.

The discount method always gives a higher APR than the simple interest method for single-payment loans at the same interest rates because the proceeds received are less.

## Installment Loans

Most consumer loans are the add-on method. One popular method of calculating the APR for add-on loans is the *constant-ratio method*. The constant-ratio formula is:

$$APR = \frac{2MC}{P(N + 1)}$$

where   $M$ = number of payment period in 1 year

$N$ = number of scheduled payments

$C$ = finance charges in dollars (dollar cost of credit)

$P$ = original proceeds

## Example 3

Assume that a business owner borrows $1,000 to be repaid in 12 equal monthly installments of $93 each for a finance charge of $116. The APR under the constant-ratio method is computed as follows:

$$APR = \frac{2MC}{P(N+1)}$$

$$= \frac{2 \times 12 \times 116}{1,000(12+1)} = \frac{2,784}{13,000} = 21.42\%$$

Note that some lenders charge fees for a credit investigation, a loan application, or for life insurance. When these fees are required, the lender must include them in addition to the finance charge in dollars as part of the APR calculations.

## How is it used and applied?

The lender is required by the Truth in Lending Act (Consumer Credit Protection Act) to disclose to a borrower the effective annual percentage rate (APR) as well as the finance charge in dollars.

Banks often quote their interest rates in terms of dollars of interest per hundred dollars. Other lenders quote in terms of dollars per payment. This leads to confusion on the part of borrowers. Fortunately, APR can eliminate this confusion. By comparing the APRs of different loans, a borrower can determine the best deal.

## Example 4

Bank A offers a 7 percent car loan if a business owner puts down 25 percent. That is, if the owner buys a $4,000 auto, she will finance $3,000 over a 3-year period with carrying charges that amount to $630 (0.07 x $3,000 x 3 years). The owner will make equal monthly payments of $100.83 for 36 months.

Bank B will lend $3,500 on the same car. In this case the business owner must pay $90 per month for 48 months.

Which of the two quotes offers the best deal?

The APR calculations (using the constant-ratio formula) follow.

$$\text{Bank A:} \quad APR = \frac{2 \times 12 \times 630}{3,000(36+1)} = \frac{15,120}{111,000} = 13.62\%$$

$$\text{Bank B:} \quad APR = \frac{2 \times 12 \times 820}{3,500(48+1)} = \frac{19,680}{171,500} = 11.48\%$$

In the case of Bank B, it is necessary to multiply $90 x 48 months to arrive at a total cost of $4320. Therefore, the total credit cost is $920 ($4,320 – $3,500).

Based on the APR, the business owner should choose Bank B over Bank A.

# 4. Calculating Due Dates

## Introduction

The *due date*, also called maturity date, is the exact date when a loan must be repaid.

## How is it computed?

Some loans specify the maturity date while other loans state the period of the loan in days or months. When the maturity date is given in days, the date is determined by counting the days from the day the loan was secured. The day on which the loan is procured is not counted. For example, a 120-day loan obtained on October 17, 20x7, is due on February 15, 20x8. When the period is given in months, the loan's maturity date falls on the same day of the month as the date the loan is issued. For example a 6-month loan dated March 15 matures on September 15. If the due date of the loan falls on a nonbusiness day, the maturity date is the next business day, with an additional day(s) added to the period for which interest is charged.

## *Example*

Motor Parts, Inc., obtained a 90-day loan dated March 16, 20x7. The maturity date of the loan is June 15, 20x7, as determined below.

To determine the maturity date, calculate forward for the exact number of days in the loan period. Do not count the day on which you actually received the loan. Remember that some months have 30 days and some have 31.

| Time period of loan | | | | 90 days |
|---|---|---|---|---|
| | March | 31 | | |
| Issuance date | | <u>16</u> | 15 days | |
| | April | | 30 days | |
| | May | | <u>31</u> days | |
| Total | | | | <u>76</u> days |
| Maturity date | June | | | <u>14</u> days |

## How is it used and applied?

Due dates are not approximations; they are precise and final. On that date, you must be prepared to make full payment. Failure to do so means that you have defaulted on a loan and that can have disastrous consequences for your business.

It is critical, therefore, that you know the exact date well in advance so you can make certain you will have the funds available.

# 5. Promissory Notes and Bank Discounts

## Introduction

A business may both make a promissory note and receive one. Notes receivable and notes payable are formal arrangements promising payment. Often a debtor signs a *promissory note*, which serves as evidence of a debt. The promissory note is a written promise to pay principal with interest at a maturity date. A business owner might discount a note if cash is needed quickly and he or she does not wish to hold the note until its maturity date.

## How is it computed?

As with loans, some notes specify the maturity date, while others state the period of the note, in days or months. When the maturity value is given in days, the maturity date is determined by counting the days from issue. Interest is usually computed on the basis of a 360-day year (12 months x 30 days per month.) Recall from Sec. 1 that the following formula is used:

### Interest = principal x interest rate x time

For example, the maturity date of a 90-day note issued May 6, 20x8, is August 4, 20x8, computed as follows:

| Time period of loan | | | | 90 days |
|---|---|---|---|---|
| | May | 31 | | |
| Issuance date | | _6_ | 25 days | |
| | June | | 30 days | |
| | July | | 31 days | |
| Total | | | | 86 days |
| Maturity date | August | | | _4_ days |

When the period is given in months, the note's maturity date falls on the same day of the month as the date of the note is issued. For example a 6-month note dated January 15 matures on July 15. If the due date of the note falls on a nonbusiness day, the maturity date is the next business day, with the additional day(s) added to the period for which interest is charged.

If you are holding a promissory note from a supplier or other party, you may find yourself in the position of needing more money before the due date, in which case you may discount the note receivable at a bank or finance company.

The proceeds received by the holder at the time the note is discounted are equal to the maturity value less the bank discount (interest charge). The bank discount is based on the period of time the bank will hold the note and the note's interest rate. The interest rate charged by the bank need not be the same as the interest rate on the marker's note. In fact, it is usually higher, because the bank generally charges a higher interest rate. The rate may also be different because of changes in the going interest rate since the note was originally written. The maturity value of the note is found as follows:

**Maturity value = face value of note + interest income**

The bank discount is:

**Bank discount = maturity value x bank discount x period of time held by bank**

## Example 1

On June 30, 20xx, Susan Ray, a business owner, issued a 180-day, 18 percent note to the Denmark Company to pay a short-term business loan. The note's interest rate 6 months later will be $900, calculated as follows:

**Principal x rate of interest x time = interest**

$$\$10,000 \times 18\% \times 6 \text{ months} = \$900$$

## Example 2

The Solvay Tool Company received the following notes:

| Date | Term | Interest Rate (%) | Face Amount |
|------|------|-------------------|-------------|
| (a) Aug. 2 | 4 months | 6 | $1,000 |
| (b) Aug. 11 | 60 days | 8 | 7,500 |
| (c) Sept. 9 | 45 days | 9 | 2,000 |
| (d) May 20 | 90 days | 12 | 5,000 |

The due date and amount of interest on each note is:

| Due Date | Interest Rate (%) | Face Amount |
|---|---|---|
| (a) Nov. 30 | $ 20 ($1,000 x $^4/_{12}$ x 6%) | $1,020.00 |
| (b) Oct. 10 | 100 ($7,500 x $^{60}/_{360}$ x 8%) | 7,600.00 |
| (c) Oct. 24 | 22.50 ($7,200 x $^{45}/_{360}$ x 9%) | 2,022.50 |
| (d) Aug. 18 | 150 ($5,000 x $^{90}/_{360}$ x 12%) | 5,150.00 |

## Example 3

On June 20, 20x8, the Bunyan Grass Seed Company received a 90-day, 12 percent note receivable for $5,000. On August 5 the company, in need of cash, discounts the note at its bank. The bank charges a discount rate of 15 percent. The proceeds from the discounted note are 5,077.04 calculated as follows:

Bank discount = maturity value x discount rate x period note is held by bank

| | |
|---|---|
| Face value of note dated June 20 | $5,000.00 |
| Add: Interest on note ($5,000 x 12% x $^{90}/_{360}$) | $150.00 |
| Maturity value of note due Sept. 18 | $5,150.00 |
| Bank discount on maturity value ($5,000 x 12% x $^{90}/_{360}$) | $72.96 |

The net proceeds received by the payee at the time of discounting are:

### Net proceeds = maturity value – bank discount

| | |
|---|---|
| Maturity value of note dated Sept. 18 | $5,150.00 |
| Less: Discount period (Aug. 5 – Sept. 18 = 34 days) | |
| Discount on maturity value (34 days at 15%) | $72.96 |
| Net proceeds of note after discounting | $5,077.04 |

## How is it used and applied?

When a note receivable is sold or discounted to a bank or other financial institution, the seller (business owner) of the note remains *contingently liable* until the maker pays at maturity. If the original maker of the note does not pay the note at its maturity, the bank will seek payment from the seller of the note. The party who originally discounted the note will not be forced to pay and must seek reimbursement from the original maker of the note.

# 1.6  Trade Credit

## Introduction

When you buy supplies or materials on credit, you are agreeing to pay the supplier within a certain period after receiving the goods. This is called *trade credit*, because it is a sale within the trade (as opposed to a sale to the public at large), and it is in effect a form of loan: you get the materials now and pay for them later. Many suppliers also offer a discount if you pay early.

## How is it computed?

Trade credit is usually extended for a specific period of time; 30 days is common. This means that payment is due 30 days after you receive the merchandise. If a supplier offers a discount, there is also a specific period during which the discount may be taken. One very common arrangement is 2/10, net 30, sometimes written 2/10, n/30, which means that if you pay the invoice within 10 days, you can take a 2 percent discount; otherwise, the full amount is due within 30 days. The cost of *not* taking the discount is referred to as the *opportunity cost of credit*; it can be substantial.

The cost of credit if a cash discount is not taken is:

$$\text{Credit cost} = \frac{\text{percent discount}}{100 - \text{percent discount}}$$

$$\times \quad \frac{360}{\text{Credit period} - \text{discount period}}$$

## *Example 1*

Suppose that a supplier has extended \$900 of trade credit to a business owner on terms of 2/10, net 30. The owner can either pay \$900 x 0.98 = 822 at the end of the 10-day period, or wait for the full 30 days and pay the full \$900. By waiting the full 30 days, the owner effectively borrows \$882 for an additional 20 days, paying \$900 - \$882 or \$18 in interest. Now, \$18 may not seem like much of a savings, but if you can it in annual terms, it is significant.

This information can be used to compute the credit cost of borrowing this money:

$$\text{Credit cost} = \frac{\text{percent discount}}{100 - \text{percent discount}}$$

$$x \quad \frac{360}{\text{Credit period} - \text{discount period}}$$

$$= \frac{2}{100 - 2} \times \frac{360}{30 - 10}$$

$$= \frac{2}{98} \times \frac{360}{20}$$

$$= 36.73\%$$

It is important for a buyer to take advantage of all available discounts, even though it may be necessary to borrow the money to make the payment.

## Example 2

Andover Supply receives a $2,000 invoice, discount terms 2/10, n/30, for goods purchased from Czar Wholesalers. Andover borrows the money for the remaining 20 days of the discount period at an annual interest rate of 12% and saves $26.93, computed as follows:

| | |
|---|---:|
| Discount of 2% on $2,000 | $40.00 |
| Interest for 20 days, at a rate of 12% on $1,960 ($2,000 - $40) | $13.07 |
| Savings effect by borrowing | $26.93 |

## How is it used and applied?

Computing the cost of credit is an essential part of doing business. You should always be weighing the savings gained by paying early against the benefit of holding onto your money longer. Which is more advantageous to you: paying a smaller amount sooner, or paying more later by having the use of the funds in the meantime? The only way to answer those questions is to work through the numbers both ways, and compare the results.

If you do not take the discount, you are losing the savings; the amount lost is the true cost of the credit. However, that cost may be of secondary importance to you if other forms of finance are not available. On the other hand, if bank credit is not a problem, you may be better to forgo the discount and invest the money short term in something that generates revenue.

Doing this now/later analysis is a continual process. Your decisions may change from one month to the next, as your cash flow changes. You should also be aware that the amounts of discount offered to you will often change to reflect the overall economic climate. Thus the cost of not taking trade credit usually declines as discount terms are reduced. Also, you may be available to negotiate with your major suppliers for a more favorable discount, especially if you have a strong record with them or they are particularly eager for cash.

# 7. Receivables and Inventory Financing

## Introduction

You may be able to improve your business' cash flow by using receivables or inventory as collateral for loans. Both these assets represent important financing sources because they are significant in amount and relate to recurring business activities.

## 1 Receivable Financing

Receivable financing is the use of short-term financing backed by financing backed by receivables, under either a *factoring* or an *assignment* arrangement. The financing of accounts receivable is facilitated if customers are financially strong, sales returns are minimal, and title to the goods is received by the buyer at shipment.

## Factoring of Accounts Receivable

*Factoring* is the outright sale of accounts receivable to a third party *without recourse*; the purchaser assumes all credit and collection risks. The factor will usually advance you up to 80 percent, meaning that the factor buys the receivables for 80 percent of face value. The factor collects the full amount from the customer and keeps the difference. The proceeds you receive equal face value minus commission, fee and discount. The amount the factor will advance depends on the quality of the accounts receivable. The cost of factoring includes the factor's commission for credit investigation of the customer, interest charges, and the discount from the face value of the receivables. The factor's total fee depends on the volume of business you give the factor and the credit-worthiness of your customers. Billing and collection are done by the factor.

## How is it computed?

The cost of a factoring agreement is computed as follows:

**Factor fee + cost of borrowing = total cost**

## Example 1

You have $10,000 per month in accounts receivable that a factor will buy, advancing you up to 75 percent of the receivables for an annual charge of 15 percent and a 1.0 percent fee on receivables purchased. The cost of this factoring arrangement is:

| | |
|---|---|
| Factor fee [0.01 x ($10,000 x 121)] | $1,200 |
| Cost of borrowing [0.15 x ($10,000 x 0.751)] | 1,125 |
| Total cost | **$2,375** |

## Assignment of Accounts Receivable

*Assignment* is the transfer of accounts receivable to a finance company *with recourse*: if the customer does not pay, you (as borrower) have to pay. The accounts receivable act as collateral, and new receivables substitute for receivables collected. Ownership of accounts receivable is not transferred. Customer payments continue to be made directly to you.

## How is it computed?

The finance company usually advances between 50 and 85 percent of the face value of the receivables in cash. You incur a service charge and interest on the advance, and you absorb any bad debt losses. The cost is computed as follows:

**Service charge + interest + bad debt = total cost**

## 2 Inventory Financing

*Inventory financing* is the use of inventory as collateral for a loan. This typically occurs when you have fully exhausted your borrowing capacity on receivables.

Inventory financing requires the existence of marketable, nonperishable, standardized goods with fast turnover. Inventory should preferably be stable in price; expenses associated with its sale should be minimal.

## How is it computed?

The cost of inventory financing is computed as:

**Interest + warehouse cost = total cost**

## Example 2

You want to finance $250,000 of inventory. Funds are required for 2 months. An inventory loan may be taken out at 14 percent with an 80 percent advance against the inventory's value. The warehousing cost is $2,000 for the 2-month period. The cost of financing the inventory is:

| | |
|---|---|
| Interest (0.14 x 0.80 x $250,000 x $^2/_{12}$) | $4,667 |
| Warehousing cost | 2,000 |
| Total cost | $6,667 |

## How is it used and applied?

The advantages of receivables financing are that it (1) avoids the need for long-term financing and (2) provides needed cash flow. Its major disadvantage is its high administrative cost if the business has many small accounts.

The advantages of factoring are that (1) you receive immediate cash, (2) overhead is reduced because credit investigation is no longer needed, (3) you can obtain advances as needed on a seasonal basis, and (4) there are no loan restrictions or required account balances. Disadvantages are that factoring involves (1) high cost, (2) possible negative customer reaction and (3) possible antagonism from customers who are past due and who are subject to pressure from the factor.

Advantages of assignment are that (1) cash is immediately available, (2) cash advances are received on a seasonal basis, and (3) it avoids negative customer reaction. Its disadvantages are (1) its high cost, (2) the continued credit function, and (3) significant credit risks.

The advance on inventory financing is usually higher for readily marketable goods. A bank will typically lend about 50 percent of the market value of merchandise at an interest rate about 3 to 50 points over the prime interest rate.

Disadvantages of inventory financing include its high interest rate and the restrictions often placed on the inventory.

# 8. Estimating the Cost of Debt and Equity Financing

## Introduction

The business owner should observe that if she invests money today to receive benefits in the future, she must be absolutely certain that the business earns at least as much as it costs to acquire the funds for the business. This amount is called the *minimum acceptable return*. If funds cost the business 10 percent, the owner must be sure that she is earning at least this rate of return. To satisfy this test, the business must determine the cost of its funds, or, more properly stated, the cost of capital.

The business owner must ascertain which combination of debt and equity will result in the lowest cost of capital.

## How is it computed?

The best way to calculate a business' cost of capital is to examine each element of its capital structure. The capital structure of a business may be based on long-term debt, preferred stock and common stock. (Stock may only be issued by a corporation.) Capital structure is the mix of long-term debt and equity used by the business to finance.

The cost of debt is the interest rate paid to noteholders. The simplest case would be a $1,000 note paying $100 annually and thus costing the business 10 percent. The holder of the note would then say that the note's *yield* is 10 percent. The after-tax cost of the debt to the business is the yield to maturity times 1 minus the tax rate. The formula is:

$$\textbf{Cost of debt} = \textbf{Y (1 – tax)}$$

where Y is the yield.

The cost of preferred stock is similar to the cost of debt in that a constant annual payment is made only if the stock pays dividends. Note, however, that preferred stock has no maturity date, so the business owner merely has to divide the annual dividend by the current price to calculate the annual percentage cost of the preferred stock. Costs are converted to percentages so that they may be compared. The formula is:

$$\text{Cost of preferred stock} \quad = \quad \frac{\text{annual dividend}}{\text{price of preferred stock}}$$

The cost of common stock is similar to the cost of preferred stock in that an annual dividend payment may exist. Like preferred stock, common stock has no maturity date, so the business owner merely has to divide the annual dividend by the current price to calculate the annual cost of the common stock. The formula is:

$$\text{Cost of common stock} \quad = \quad \frac{\text{annual dividend}}{\text{price of common stock}}$$

A business corporation that issues notes, preferred stock, and common stock would combine all elements to arrive at a weighted-average cost of capital. It would be calculated as follows:

| | (1)<br>Cost<br>(after tax) | (2)<br>Percentage<br>of capital<br>structure | (3)<br>Weighted cost |
|---|---|---|---|
| Debt | | | |
| Preferred stock | | | |
| Common stock | | | _____ |
| Weighted average cost of capital | | | ========== |

## Example 1

The Max Clothing Company signed a note for $10,000 at 10 percent. The business is in the 15 percent corporate tax bracket. The after-tax cost of the note is 8.5 percent, calculated as follows:

$$
\begin{aligned}
\text{Cost of debt} &= Y(1 - \text{tax}) \\
&= 10\%(1 - 0.15) \\
&= 10\%(0.85) \\
&= 8.5\%
\end{aligned}
$$

## Example 2

The Palo Wire Company sold 100 shares of preferred stock for $100 a share to an investor. The preferred stock will pay a guaranteed annual dividend of $9 per share. The cost of the stock is 9 percent annually, calculated as follows:

$$
\text{Cost of preferred stock} = \frac{\text{annual dividend}}{\text{price of preferred stock}}
$$

$$
= \frac{\$9}{\$100} = 9\%
$$

## Example 3

The Rex Photo Development Company sold 100 shares of its common shares for $100 a share to an investor. All common shareholders expect a guaranteed annual dividend of $7.50 per share. The cost of the common stock is 7.5 percent annually, calculated as follows:

$$\text{Cost of common stock} = \frac{\text{annual dividend}}{\text{price of common stock}}$$

$$= \frac{\$7.50}{\$100} = 7.5\%$$

## Example 4

The Halo Paint Company raised capital by issuing a $20,000 bond at 11 percent; selling $20,000 of $100-par-value, 8 percent preferred stock, and selling $10,000 of 6 percent common stock. The company is in the 25 percent tax bracket and estimates that it will earn 10 percent on its capital. The company's weighted-average cost of capital is 7.7 percent, and it is earning 2.3 percent more than its cost of financing. Halo's weighted-average cost of capital is determined as follows:

Cost of $20,000 bond:

Cost of $20,000 in preferred stock:

$$\text{Cost of debt} = Y(1 - \text{tax})$$
$$= 11\%(1 - 0.25)$$
$$= 11\%(0.75)$$
$$= 8.25\%$$

$$\text{Cost of preferred stock} = \frac{\text{annual dividend}}{\text{price of preferred stock}}$$

$$= \frac{\$8}{\$100} = 8\%$$

Cost of $10,000 common stock:

$$\text{Cost of common stock} = \frac{\text{annual dividend}}{\text{price of common stock}}$$

$$= \frac{\$6}{\$100} = 6\%$$

|  | (1)<br>Cost<br>(after tax) | (2)<br>Percentage<br>of capital<br>structure | (3)<br>Weighted<br>cost |
|---|---|---|---|
| Debt | 8.25% | ($20,000) 40% | $3.30 |
| Preferred stock | 8.00 | ($20,000) 40% | $3.20 |
| Common stock | 6.00 | ($10,000) 20% | $1.20 |
| Weighted average cost of capital |  |  | $7.70 |

## How is it used and applied?

The weighted-average cost of capital is compared to the business' return on capital to see whether the business owner is at least earning the cost of financing his/her operations.

A business owner may need a certain amount of money to develop a new product and in so doing has to weigh the costs of various funding sources.

The minimum expected rate of return of any business must exceed its cost of capital if the business is to survive. While debt is usually the easiest form of financing because it merely entails borrowing money, excessive debt may increase the financial risk of the business and drive up the costs from all sources of financing.

# Part 2
# Budgeting and Profit Planning

## 9. Establishing a Budgeting System for Profit Planning

### Introduction

Business managers should adopt a budgeting procedure almost immediately after they start in business. Deviations from what has been budgeted enable business managers to anticipate potential serious financial problems early enough to take corrective action. A comprehensive (master) budget is a formal statement of management's expectations regarding sales, expenses, volume, and other financial transactions of an organization for the coming period. Simply put, a budget is a set of pro forma (projected or planned) financial statements.

### How is it computed?

The budget is classified broadly into two categories:

1.  Operating budget, reflecting the results of operating decisions.
2.  Financial budget, reflecting the financial decisions of the firm.

The operating budget consists of:
- Sales budget
- Production budget
- Direct materials budget
- Direct labor budget
- Factory overhead budget

◆ Selling and administrative expense budget

◆ Pro forma income statement

The financial budget consists of:

◆ Cash budget

◆ Pro forma balance sheet

The major steps in preparing the budget are:

1. Prepare a sales forecast.

2. Determine expected production volume.

3. Estimate manufacturing costs and operating expenses.

4. Determine cash flow and other financial effects.

5. Formulate projected financial statements.

Figure 9.1 shows a simplified diagram of the various parts of the comprehensive (master) budget, the master plan of the company.

## Illustration

To illustrate how all these budgets are put together, we will focus on a *manufacturing* company called the Putnam Company, which produces and markets a single product. We will make the following assumptions:

◆ The company uses a single material and one type of labor in the manufacture of the product.

◆ It prepares a master budget on a *quarterly* basis.

◆ Work in process inventories at the beginning and end of the year are negligible and are ignored.

◆ The company uses a single cost driver—direct labor hours (DLH)---as the allocation base for assigning all factory overhead costs to the product.

## The Sales Budget

The sales budget is the starting point in preparing the master budget, since estimated sales volume influences nearly all other items appearing throughout the master budget. The sales budget should show total sales in quantity and value. The expected total sales can be break-even or target income sales or projected sales. It may be analyzed further by product, by territory, by customer and, of course, by seasonal pattern of expected sales.

Generally, the sales budget includes a computation of expected cash collections from credit sales, which will be used later for cash budgeting.

# Figure 9.1: A Master (Comprehensive) Budget

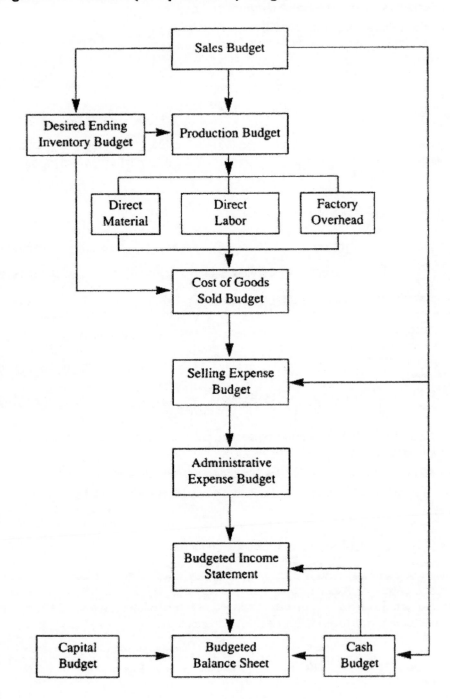

## Schedule 1
## The Putnam Company – Sales Budget

For the Year Ended December 31, 20B

| | QUARTER | | | | |
|---|---|---|---|---|---|
| | 1 | 2 | 3 | 4 | Year as A Whole |
| Expected sales in units* | 1,000 | 1,800 | 2,000 | 1,200 | 6,000 |
| Unit sales price* | x $150 | x$150 | x$150 | x$150 | x$150 |
| Total sales | $150,000 | $270,000 | $300,000 | $180,000 | $900,000 |

*Given.

### Schedule of Expected Cash Collections

| | | | | | |
|---|---|---|---|---|---|
| Accounts receivable, 12/31/20A | 100,000+ | | | | $100,000 |
| 1st quarter sales ($150,000) | 60,000++ | $ 90,000+++ | | | 150,000 |
| 2nd quarter sales ($270,000) | | 108,000 | $162,000 | | 270,000 |
| 3rd quarter sales ($300,000) | | | 120,000 | $180,000 | 300,000 |
| 4th quarter sales ($180,000) | | | | 72,000 | 72,000 |
| Total cash collections | $160,000 | $198,000 | $282,000 | $252,000 | $892,000 |

+ All of the $100,000 accounts receivable balance is assumed to be collectible in the first quarter.

++ 40 percent of a quarter's sales are collected in the quarter of sale.

+++ 60 percent of a quarter's sales are collected in the quarter following.

## Monthly Cash Collections from Customers

Frequently, there are time lags between monthly sales made *on account* and their related monthly cash collections. For example, in any month, credit sales are collected as follows: 15% in month of sale, 60% in the following month, 24% in the month after, and the remaining 1 percent are uncollectible.

| | April-Actual | May-Actual | June-Budgeted | July-Budgeted |
|---|---|---|---|---|
| Credit sales | $320 | $200 | $300 | $280 |

The budgeted cash receipts for June and July are computed as follows:

For June:

| | | |
|---|---|---|
| From April sales | $320 x .24 | $ 76.80 |
| From May sales | 200 x .60 | 120.00 |
| From June sales | 300 x .15 | 45.00 |
| Total budgeted collections in June | | $241.80 |

For July:

| | | |
|---|---|---|
| From May sales | $200 x .24 | $ 48 |
| From June sales | 300 x .60 | 180 |
| From July sales | 280 x .15 | 42 |
| Total budgeted collections in July | | $270 |

## The Production Budget

After sales are budgeted, the production budget can be determined. The production budget is a statement of the output by product and is generally expressed in units. It should take into account the sales budget, plant capacity, whether stocks are to be increased or decreased and outside purchases. The number of units expected to be manufactured to meet budgeted sales and inventory requirements is set forth in the production budget.

**Expected Production Volume** **=** **Planned sales** **+** **Desired Ending Inventory** **−** **Beginning inventory**

The production budget is illustrated as follows:

**Schedule 2**
**The Putnam Company – Production Budget**

For the Year Ended December 31, 20B

| | QUARTER | | | | |
|---|---|---|---|---|---|
| | 1 | 2 | 3 | 4 | Year as a Whole |
| Planned sales (Schedule 1) | 1,000 | 1,800 | 2,000 | 1,200 | 6,000 |
| Desired ending inventory* | 180 | 200 | 120 | 300 ** | 300 |
| Total Needs | 1,180 | 2,000 | 2,120 | 1,500 | 6,300 |
| Less: Beginning inventory | 200 ** | 180 *** | 200 | 120 | 200 |
| Units to be produced | 980 | 1,820 | 1,920 | 1,380 | 6,100 |

\*     10 percent of the next quarter's sales. (For example, 180 = 10% x 1,800).
\*\*    Given.
\*\*\*   The same as the previous quarter's ending inventory.

25

## Inventory Purchases – Merchandising Firm

Putnam Company is a manufacturing firm, so it prepares a production budget, as shown in Schedule 2. If it were a *merchandising* (retailing or wholesaling) firm, then instead of a production budget, it would develop a *merchandise purchase budget* showing the amount of goods to be purchased from its suppliers during the period. The merchandise purchases budget is in the same basic format as the production budget, except that it shows *goods to be purchased* rather than goods to be produced, as shown below:

| | |
|---|---|
| Budgeted cost of goods sold   (in units or dollars) | $560,000 |
| Add: Desired ending merchandise inventory | 120,000 |
| Total needs | $680,000 |
| Less: Beginning merchandise inventory | (80,000) |
| Required purchases (in units or in dollars) | $600,000 |

*Note:*

1. Cost of goods sold = beginning inventory + purchases - ending inventory.

   Hence, purchases = cost of goods sold + ending inventory - beginning inventory

2. Gross profit (margin) = sales – cost of goods sold (or cost of sales). For example, percentagewise, 30% = 100% - 70%. For example, sales is $800,000, then the cost of goods sold is $800,000 x 70% = $560,000

## *The Direct Material Budget*

When the level of production has been computed, a direct material budget should be constructed to show how much material will be required for production and how much material must be purchased to meet this production requirement.

The purchase will depend on both expected usage of materials and inventory levels. The formula for computation of the purchase is:

| **Purchase in units** | = | **Usage** + | **Desired ending material inventory units** | - | **Beginning inventory units** |
|---|---|---|---|---|---|

The direct material budget is usually accompanied by a computation of expected cash payments for materials.

## Schedule 3
## The Putnam Company – Direct Material Budget

For the Year Ended December 31, 20B

| | QUARTER | | | | |
|---|---|---|---|---|---|
| | 1 | 2 | 3 | 4 | Year as a Whole |
| Units to be produced (Sch.2) | 980 | 1,820 | 1,920 | 1,380 | 6,100 |
| Material needs per unit (lbs)* | x 2 | x 2 | x 2 | x 2 | x 2 |
| Production needs (usage) | 1,960 | 3,640 | 3,840 | 2,760 | 12,200 |
| Desired ending inventory of materials** | 910 | 960 | 690 | 520 *** | 520 |
| Total needs | 2,870 | 4,600 | 4,530 | 3,280 | 12,720 |
| Less: Beginning inventory of materials | (490)** | 910 **** | 960 | 690 | 490 |
| Materials to be purchased | 2,380 | 3,690 | 3,570 | 2,590 | 12,230 |
| Unit price* | x $5 | x $5 | x $5 | x $5 | x $5 |
| Purchase cost | $11,900 | $18,450 | $17,850 | $12,950 | $61,150 |

\*  Given

\*\*  25 percent of the next quarter's units needed for production. For example, the 2$^{nd}$ quarter production needs are 3,640 lbs. Therefore, the desired ending inventory for the 1st quarter would be 25% x 3,640 lbs. = 910 lbs. Also note: 490 lbs = 25% x 1,960 = 490 lbs.

\*\*\*  Assume that the budgeted production needs in lbs. for the 1$^{st}$ quarter of 20C = 2,080 lbs. So, 25% x 2,080 lbs. = 520 lbs.

\*\*\*\*  The same as the prior quarter's ending inventory.

## Schedule of Expected Cash Disbursements

| | | | | | |
|---|---|---|---|---|---|
| Accounts payable, 12/31/20A | $6,275 + | | | | $6,275 |
| 1st quarter purchases($11,900) | 5,950 ++ | 5,950 ++ | | | 11,900 |
| 2nd quarter purchases($18,450) | 9,225 | 9,225 | | | 18,450 |
| 3rd quarter purchases($17,850) | | 8,925 | | 8,925 | 17,850 |
| 4th quarter sales ($12,950) | | | | 6,475 | 6,475 |
| Total disbursements | $12,225 | $15,175 | $18,150 | $15,400 | $60,950 |

\+  All of the $6,275 accounts payable balance (from the balance sheet, 20A) is assumed to be paid in the first quarter.

++  50 percent of a quarter's purchases are paid for in the quarter of purchase; the remaining 50% are paid for in the following quarter.

## The Direct Labor Budget

The production requirements as set forth in the production budget also provide the starting point for the preparation of the direct labor budget. To compute direct labor requirements, expected production volume for each period is multiplied by the number of direct labor hours required to produce a single unit. The direct labor hours to meet production requirements is then multiplied by the (standard) direct labor cost per hour to obtain budgeted total direct labor costs.

### Schedule 4 4
### The Putnam Company – Direct Labor Budget

For the Year Ended December 31, 20B

|  | QUARTER | | | | |
|---|---|---|---|---|---|
|  | 1 | 2 | 3 | 4 | Year as a Whole |
| Units to be produced (Sch.2) | 980 | 1,820 | 1,920 | 1,380 | 6,100 |
| Direct labor hours per unit* | x 5 | x 5 | x 5 | x 5 | x 5 |
| Total hours | 4,900 | 9,100 | 9,600 | 6,900 | 30,500 |
| Direct labor cost per hour* | x $10 | x $10 | x $10 | x $10 | x $10 |
| Total direct labor cost | $49,000 | $91,000 | $96,000 | $69,000 | $305,000 |

\* Both are given.

## The Factory Overhead Budget

The factory overhead budget should provide a schedule of all manufacturing costs other than direct materials and direct labor. We must remember that depreciation does not entail a cash outlay and therefore must be deducted from the total factory overhead in computing cash disbursement for factory overhead.

To illustrate the factory overhead budget, we will assume that

- ◆ Total factory overhead budgeted = $18,300 fixed (per quarter), plus $2 per hour of direct labor. This is one example of a cost-volume (or flexible budget) formula ($y = a + bx$), developed via the *least-squares method* with a high $R^2$.
- ◆ Depreciation expenses are $4,000 each quarter.
- ◆ Overhead costs involving cash outlays are paid for in the quarter incurred.

## Schedule 5
## The Putnam Company – Factory Overhead Budget

For the Year Ended December 31, 20B

| | QUARTER | | | | |
|---|---|---|---|---|---|
| | 1 | 2 | 3 | 4 | Year as a Whole |
| Budgeted direct labor hrs. | 4,900 | 9,100 | 9,600 | 6,900 | **30,500** |
| Variable overhead rate | x $2 | x $2 | x $2 | x $2 | x $2 |
| Variable overhead budgeted | 9,800 | 18,200 | 19,200 | 13,800 | 61,000 |
| Fixed overhead budgeted | 18,300 | 18,300 | 18,300 | 18,300 | 73,200 |
| **Total budgeted overhead** | 28,100 | 36,500 | 37,500 | 32,100 | **134,200** |
| Less: Depreciation* | 4,000 | 4,000 | 4,000 | 4,000 | 16,000 |
| **Cash disbursements for Factory overhead** | $24,100 | $32,500 | $33,500 | $28,100 | $118,200 |

\* Depreciation does not require a cash outlay.

# The Ending Finished Goods Inventory Budget

The ending finished goods inventory budget provides us with the information required for the construction of budgeted financial statements. After completing Schedules 1-5, sufficient data will have been generated to compute the per-unit manufacturing cost of finished product. This computation is required for two reasons: (1) to help compute the cost of goods sold on the budgeted income statement; and (2) to give the dollar value of the ending finished goods inventory to appear on the budgeted balance sheet.

## Schedule 6
## The Putnam Company – Ending Finished Goods Inventory Budget

*Ending inventory*

| Units | Unit Product Cost | Total |
|---|---|---|
| 300 units (Sch. 2) | $82* | $24,600 |

\* The unit product cost of $82 is computed as follows

| | Unit cost | Units | Total |
|---|---|---|---|
| Direct Materials | $5 per lbs. | 2 pounds | $10 |
| Direct labor | 10 per hr. | 5 hours | 50 |
| Factory overhead** | 4.40 per hr. | 5 hours | 22 |
| Unit product cost | | | $82 |

\*\* Predetermined factory overhead applied rate = Budgeted annual factory overhead/budgeted annual activity units = $134,200/30,500 DLH = $4.40 (see Chapter 3; Accumulation of Costs – Job Order Costing).

29

# The Selling and Administrative Expense Budget

The selling and administrative expense budget lists the operating expenses involved in selling the products and in managing the business. Just as in the case of the factory overhead budget, this budget can be developed using the coat-volume (*flexible budget*) formula in the form of $y = a + bx$.

If the number of expense items is very large, separate budgets may be needed for the selling and administrative functions.

## Schedule 7
## The Putnam Company – Selling & Administrative Expense Budget

For the Year Ended December 31, 20B

|  | QUARTER | | | | |
|---|---|---|---|---|---|
|  | 1 | 2 | 3 | 4 | Year as a Whole |
| Expected sales in units | 1,000 | 1,800 | 2,000 | 1,200 | 6,000 |
| Variable selling and administrative expense per unit* | x $3 | x $3 | x $3 | x $3 | x $3 |
| Budgeted variable expense | $3,000 | $5,400 | $6,000 | $3,200 | $18,000 |
| Fixed selling and administrative expense**: | | | | | |
| Advertising | 20,000 | 20,000 | 20,000 | 20,000 | 80,000 |
| Insurance | | 12,600 | | | 12,600 |
| Office salaries | 40,000 | 40,000 | 40,000 | 40,000 | 160,000 |
| Taxes | | | | 7,400 | 7,400 |
| Total budgeted selling and Administrative expenses*** | $63,000 | $78,000 | $66,000 | $71,000 | $278,000 |

\*      Assumed. It includes sales agents' commissions, shipping, and supplies.

\*\*    Scheduled to be paid.

\*\*\*  Paid for in the quarter incurred.

## *The Cash Budget*

The cash budget is prepared for the purpose of cash planning and control.   It presents the expected cash inflow and outflow for a designated time period. The cash budget helps management keep cash balances in reasonable relationship to its needs.  It aids in avoiding unnecessary idle cash and possible cash shortages.   The cash budget consists typically of four major sections:

1. The *cash receipts* section, which is cash collections from customers and other cash receipts such as royalty income and investment income.

2. The *cash disbursements* section, which comprises all cash payments made by purpose.

3. The *cash surplus* or *deficit* section, which simply shows the difference between the total cash available and the total cash needed including a *minimum cash balance* if required. If there is surplus cash, loans may be repaid or temporary investments made.

4. The *financing* section, which provides a detailed account of the borrowings, repayments , and interest payments expected during the budgeting period.

5. The *investments* section, which encompasses investment of excess cash and liquidation of investment of surplus cash.

## Schedule 8

To illustrate, we will make the following assumptions:

- ◆ Putnam Company has an open line of credit with its bank, which can be used as needed to bolster the cash position.

- ◆ The company desires to maintain a $10,000 minimum cash balance at the end of each quarter. Therefore, borrowing must be sufficient to cover the cash shortfall and to provide for the minimum cash balance of $10,000

- ◆ All borrowings and repayments must be in multiples of $1,000 amounts, and interest is 10 percent per annum.

- ◆ Interest is computed and paid on the principal as the principal is repaid.

- ◆ All borrowings take place at the beginning of a quarter, and all repayments are made at the end of a quarter.

- ◆ No investment option is allowed in this example. The loan is *self-liquidating* in the sense that the borrowed money is used to obtain resources that are combined for sale, and the proceeds from sales are used to pay back the loan.

*Note*: To be useful for cash planning and control, the cash budget must be prepared on a *monthly* basis.

# The Putnam Company – Cash Budget

For the Year Ended December 31, 20B

| | From Schedule | 1 | 2 | 3 | 4 | Year as a Whole |
|---|---|---|---|---|---|---|
| | | | | QUARTER | | |
| Cash balance, beginning | | $19,000* | 10,675 | 10,000 | 10,350 | 19,000 |
| Add: **Receipts**: | | | | | | |
| Collections from customers | 1 | 160,000 | 198,000 | 282,000 | 252,000 | 892,000 |
| Total cash available (a) | | | 208,675 | 292,000 | 262,350 | 911,000 |
| Less: **Disbursements**: | | | | | | |
| Direct materials | 3 | 12,225 | 15,175 | 18,150 | 15,400 | 60,950 |
| Direct labor | 4 | 49,000 | 91,000 | 96,000 | 69,000 | 305,000 |
| Factory overhead | 5 | 24,100 | 32,500 | 33,500 | 28,100 | 118,200 |
| Selling and Admin. | 7 | 63,000 | 78,000 | 66,000 | 71,000 | 278,000 |
| Equipment purchase | Given | 30,000 | 12,000 | 0 | 0 | 42,000 |
| Dividends | Given | 5,000 | 5,000 | 5,000 | 5,000 | 20,000 |
| Income tax | 10 | 15,000 | 15,000 | 15,000 | 15,000 | 60,000 |
| Total disbursements (b) | | 198,325 | 248,675 | 233,650 | 203,500 | 884,150 |
| Minimum cash balance | | 10,000 | 10,000 | 10,000 | 10,000 | 10,000 |
| Total cash needed (c) | | 208,325 | 258,675 | 243,650 | 213,500 | 894,150 |
| Cash surplus (deficit) (a) – (c) | | (29,325) | (50,000) | 48,350 | 48,850 | 16,850 |
| Financing: | | | | | | |
| Borrowing | | 30,000** | 50,000 | 0 | 0 | 80,000 |
| Repayment | | 0 | 0 | (45,000) | (35,000) | (80,000) |
| Interest | | 0 | 0 | (3,000)*** | (2,625)+ | (5,625) |
| Total effects of financing (d) | | 30,000 | 50,000 | (48,000) | (37,625) | (5,625) |
| Cash balance, ending [(a) – (b) + (d)] | | $10,675 | 10,000 | 10,350 | 21,225 | $21,225 |

\* $19,000 (from the balance sheet 20A).

\*\* The company desires to maintain a $10,000 minimum cash balance at the end of each quarter. Therefore, borrowing must be sufficient to cover the cash shortfall of $19,325 and to provide for the minimum cash balance of $10,000, for a total of $29,325.

\*\*\* The interest payments relate only to the principal being repaid at the time it is repaid. For example, the interest in quarter 3 relates only to the interest due on the $30,000 principal being repaid from quarter 1 borrowing and on the $15,000 principal being repaid from quarter 2 borrowing. Total interest being paid is $3,000, shown as follows:

$30,000 \times 10\% \times 3/4 = \$2,250$

$15,000 \times 10\% \times 2/4 = \underline{750}$

# The Budgeted Income Statement

The budgeted income statement summarizes the various component projections of revenue and expenses for the budgeting period. However, for control purposes the budget can be divided into quarters or even months depending on the need.

## Schedule 9
## The Putnam Company – Budgeted Income Statement

For the Year Ended December 31, 20B

| | From Schedule | | |
|---|---|---|---|
| Sales (6,000 units @$150) | 1 | | $900,000 |
| Less: Cost of goods sold | | | |
| Beginning finished goods inventory | 10 | $16,400 | |
| Add: Cost of goods manufactured | | | |
| (6,100 units @$82)* | 6 | 500,200 | |
| Cost of goods available for sale | | 516,600 | |
| Less: Ending finished goods inventory | 6 | (24,600) | 492,200 |
| Gross margin | | | 408,000 |
| Less: Selling and administrative expenses | 7 | | 278,000 |
| Operating income | | | 130,000 |
| Less: Interest expense | 8 | | 5,625 |
| Net income before taxes | | | 124,375 |
| Less: Income taxes | | | 60,000** |
| Net income after taxes | | | $64,365 |

\* Cost of goods manufactured = total manufacturing cost + beginning work in process inventory - ending work in process inventory. Since there are no work in process inventories in this illustration, cost of goods manufactured = total manufacturing cost. Thus cost of goods manufactured = direct materials used + direct labor + factory overhead = $61,000 (12,200 lbs. @$5 per lbs.—Schedule 3) + $305,000 (Schedule 4) + $134,200 (Schedule 5) = $500,200

\*\* Estimated

## The Budgeted Balance Sheet

The budgeted balance sheet is developed by beginning with the balance sheet for the year just ended and adjusting it, using all the activities that are expected to take place during the budgeting period. Some of the reasons why the budgeted balance sheet must be prepared are:

- ◆ It could disclose some unfavorable financial conditions that management might want to avoid.
- ◆ It serves as a final check on the mathematical accuracy of all the other schedules.
- ◆ It helps management perform a variety of ratio calculations.
- ◆ It highlights future resources and obligations.

We can construct the budgeted balance sheet by using:

- ♦ The December, 20A balance sheet (Schedule 10)
- ♦ The cash budget (Schedule 8)
- ♦ The budgeted income statement (Schedule 9).

Putnam's budgeted balance sheet for December 31, 20B, is presented below. Supporting calculations of the individual statement accounts are also provided. To illustrate, we will use the following balance sheet for the year 20A.

## Schedule 10
## The Putnam Company – Balance Sheet

| December 31, 20A | | |
|---|---|---|
| **Assets** | | |
| | | |
| Current assets: | | |
| Cash | $ 19,000 | |
| Accounts receivable | 100,000 | |
| Materials inventory (490 lbs.) | 2,450 | |
| Finished goods inventory (200 units) | 16,400 | |
| Total current assets | | $137,850 |
| Plant and equipment: | | |
| Land | 30,000 | |
| Buildings and equipment | 250,000 | |
| Accumulated depreciation | (74,000) | |
| Plant and equipment, net | | 206,000 |
| Total assets | | $343,850 |

| Liabilities and Stockholders' Equity | | |
|---|---|---|
| Current liabilities | | |
| Accounts payable (raw materials) | $ 6,275 | |
| Income tax payable | 60,000 | |
| Total current liabilities | | $66,275 |
| Stockholders' equity: | | |
| Common stock, no par | $200,000 | |
| Retained earnings | 77,575 | |
| Total stockholders' equity | | 277,575 |
| Total liabilities and stockholders' equity | | $343,850 |

## The Putnam Company – Balance Sheet

December 31, 20B

| Assets | | |
|---|---|---|
| Cash | $ 21,225 | (a) |
| Accounts receivable | 108,000 | (b) |
| Materials inventory (520 lbs.) | 2,600 | (c) |
| Finished goods inventory (300 units) | 24,600 | (d) |
| Total current assets | | $156,425 |
| Plant and equipment: | | |
| Land | 30,000 | (e) |
| Buildings and equipment | 292,000 | (f) |
| Accumulated depreciation | (90,000) | (g) |
| Plant and equipment, net | | 232,000 |
| Total assets | | $388,425 |
| **Liabilities and Stockholders' Equity** | | |
| Current liabilities | | |
| Accounts payable (raw materials) | $ 6,475 | (h) |
| Income tax payable | 60,000 | (i) |
| Total current liabilities | | $66,475 |
| Stockholders' equity: | | |
| Common stock, no par | $200,000 | (j) |
| Retained earnings | 121,950 | (k) |
| Total stockholders' equity | | 321,950 |
| Total liabilities and stockholders' equity | | $388,425 |

Supporting computations:

a. From Schedule 8 (cash budget).

b. $100,000 (Accounts receivable, 12/31/20A) + $900,000 (Credit sales from Schedule 1) - $892,000(Collections from Schedule 1) = $108,000, or 60% of 4th quarter credit sales, from Schedule 1 ($180,000 x 60% = $108,000).

c. Direct materials, ending inventory = 520 pounds x $ 5 = $2,600 (From Schedule 3)

d. From Schedule 6 (ending finished goods inventory budget).

e. From the 20A balance sheet and Schedule 8 (no change).

f. $250,000 (Building and Equipment, 12/31/20A) + $42,000 (purchases from Schedule 8) = $292,000.

g. $74,000 (Accumulated Depreciation, 12/31/20A) + $16,000 (depreciation expense from Schedule 5) = $90,000.

h. Note that all accounts payable relate to material purchases. $6,275 (Accounts payable, 12/31/20A) + $61,150 (credit purchases from Schedule 3) - $60,950 (payments for purchases from Schedule 3) = $6,475, or 50% of 4th quarter purchase = 50% ($12,950) = $6,475.

i. From Schedule 9.

j. From the 20A balance sheet and Schedule 8 (no change).

k. $77,575 (Retained earnings, 12/31/20A) + $64,375 (net income for the period, Schedule 9) − $20,000 (cash dividends from Schedule 8) = $121,950.

## How is it used and applied?

A budget is a tool for both planning and control. At the beginning of the period, the budget is a plan or standard; at the end of the period, it serves as a control device to help the business manager measure performance against the plan so that future performance may be improved.

The major objectives of a budgeted system are to:

1. Set acceptable targets for revenues and expenses.
2. Increase the likelihood that targets will be reached.
3. Provide time and opportunity to formulate and evaluate options should obstacles arise.
4. Evaluate a variety of "what-if" scenarios (especially with the aide of computer software) in an effort to find the best possible course of action.

It is important to realize that with the aide of computer technology, budgeting can be used as an effective device for evaluation of "what-if" scenarios. This way managers should be able to move toward finding the best course of action among various alternatives through simulation. If the manager does not like what he sees in analyzing the budgeted financial statements in terms of various financial ratios such as liquidity, activity (turnover), leverage, profit margin, and market value ratios, he can always alter the contemplated decision and planning set. A ratio is a relationship of one amount to another. It relates financial statement components to each other.

# 10. What Is The Cost Structure?

## Introduction

The ratio of variable costs to fixed costs measures the relationship between costs that change with volume and costs that do not change within the short term.

## How is it computed?

$$\frac{\text{Total variable costs}}{\text{Total fixed costs}}$$

Examples of variable costs are direct materials and direct labor used in producing a product. Examples of fixed costs are rent, insurance and property taxes.

## Example

A business reports total variable costs of $800,000 and total fixed costs of $8,000,000. The ratio is 0.10. This in unfavorable, because it is difficult to reduce the fixed costs in the short run when business falls off.

## How is it used and applied?

When there is idle capacity, additional volume may be produced but total fixed costs remains constant. However, fixed cost per unit decreases because total fixed cost is spread over more units. Total variable cost increases as more units are produced, but the variable cost per unit remains the same. In a nonmanufacturing environment, service hours are substituted for units produced.

The cost structure of the business indicates what costs may be cut if needed, as in a recessionary environment (e.g., the early 1990's). The owner can more readily control and adjust variable costs than fixed costs.

See Sec. 54, Cost-Volume-Profit Analysis; Sec. 55, Contribution Margin Analysis; and Sec. 107, Operating Leverage.

# 11. Using Budgeting to Control Cash

## Introduction

The *cash budget* presents the amount and timing of the expected cash inflows and out flows for a specified time period. It is a tool for cash planning and control and should be detailed enough that you know how much is required to run your business. If you can estimate cash flows reliably, you will be able to keep cash balances near a target level using fewer transactions.

The cash budget should be prepared for the shortest time period for which reliable financial information can be obtained. In the case of many businesses, this may be one week. However, it is also possible to predict major cash receipts and cash payments for a specific day.

## How is it prepared?

The cash budget usually consists of four major sections:

1.  The *receipts sections*, which is the beginning cash balance, cash collections from customers, and other receipts

2.  The *disbursements sections*, which comprises all cash payments that are expected for the budgeting period

3.  The *cash surplus* or *deficit section*, which shows the difference between the cash receipts section and the cash disbursements section

4.  The financing section, which provides a detailed account of the borrowings and repayments anticipated during the budgeting period

If further financing is needed, the cash budget projections allow adequate lead-time for the necessary arrangements to be made.

Cash budgets are often prepared monthly, but there are no general, it should be long enough to show the effects of your business policies, yet short enough so that estimates can be made with reasonable accuracy. Table 11.1 shows the major elements of a cash budget.

The basis for predicting cash receipts is *sales*, whether from cash sales or collections from customer balances. An incorrect sales estimate will result in erroneous cash estimates. The sales prediction also influences the projected cash outlays for manufacturing cost, since production is tied to sales. The projection of operating expenses may be tied to the supplier's payment terms.

## Table 11.1: Important Components of a Cash Budget

| | |
|---|---|
| **Cash inflows** | |
| Operating: | Cash sales, collections from customer on account |
| Non-operating: | Investment income (dividend income, interest income), rental income, sales of assets, amount received from debt incurrence, royalty income |
| **Cash outflows** | |
| Operating: | Salaries expense, rent expense, purchase of materials and supplies, payments to vendors utilities expense |
| Non-operating: | Purchases of fixed assets, repayments of loans, tax expense, purchases of stock and bonds in other companies |

## *Example*

### FRED'S SPORTS CENTER
### Cash Budget
### January 20x8

| | |
|---|---:|
| Cash balance, Jan. 1 | $50,000 |
| Add: Cash receipts from customers | 150,000 |
| Cash available | $ 200,000 |
| Less: Cash payments | |
| For inventory | $ 40,000 |
| Rent | 10,000 |
| Insurance | 5,000 |
| Utilities | 3,000 |
| Purchase of equipment | 2,000 |
| Salaries | 12,000 |
| Taxes | 10,000 |
| Total cash payments | $ 90,000 |
| Cash balance, Jan. 31 | $110,000 |

## How is it used and applied?

The cash budget allows you to review future cash receipts and cash payments to identify possible *patterns of cash flows*. In this way, you can examine your collection and disbursement efforts to ascertain if you are maximizing your net cash flows. Further, the cash budget reveals when and how much to borrow and when you will be able to pay the money back. For instance, if your cash budget indicates that a large cash outlay will be needed to purchase assets such as store fixtures, you may have to borrow money and determine a debt repayment schedule. In order to obtain a credit line lenders usually required you to submit a cash budget, among with your financial statements.

Comparing estimated and actual cash figures allows you to study the reasons for any major discrepancies and to take any corrective action. *Variance analysis* gives you an idea of your cash position and provides insight in improving cash estimates in the next budgeting period. It also aids in the periodic revision of projections. This updating usually occurs at the beginning of each budget segment (e.g., the first day of a quarter, or the first day of a month). Budgets should be modified immediately for significant changes. Table 11.2 shows a format that may be used for variance analysis.

Variance analysis is important for a business, whether it be a retailer, wholesaler, manufacturer, or service concern. Evaluation of cash variances may be performed yearly, quarterly, monthly, or daily. If theft is suspected, variance analysis should be done frequently. After all, cash is the easiest asset to steal.

**Table 11.2: Variance Analysis Report for Cash Budgeting**

| | Budget | Actual | Percentage | Change | Reason |
|---|---|---|---|---|---|
| Cash balance, Jan 1 | | | | | |
| Add: Cash receipts | | | | | |
| Cash sales | | | | | |
| Collections on account | | | | | |
| Cash available | | | | | |
| Less: Cash payments | | | | | |
| Wages | | | | | |
| Utilities | | | | | |
| Rent | | | | | |
| Insurance | | | | | |
| Purchase assets | | | | | |
| Miscellaneous | | | | | |
| Taxes | | | | | |
| Total cash paid | | | | | |
| Cash balance, Jan. 31 | | | | | |

# 12. Forecasting Cash Collections

## Introduction

A forecast of cash collections and potential bad debts is an essential part of cash budgeting. The critical step in making such a forecast is estimating the cash collection and bad debt *percentages* and applying them to sales or accounts receivable balances.

## How is it computed?

The historical trend in cash collections relative to sales should be examined for the past three years. An example illustrates the technique.

### Example 1

Assume that an analysis by Mr. Jones, the owner of a clothing store, of collection experience for August sales revealed the following collection data:

| Description | | Percent of total credit sales |
|---|---|---|
| Collected in | August | 2.3 |
| | September | 80.2 |
| | October | 9.9 |
| | November | 5.1 |
| | December | 0.5 |
| Cash discounts | | 1.0 |
| Bad debt losses | | 1.0 |
| Total | | 100.0 |

If next year's August sales are expected to fall into the same pattern, then the calculated percentage for August credit sales can be used to determine the probable monthly distribution of collections. The same analysis applied to each month of the year will give a reasonably reliable basis for collection forecasting. The worksheet (August column) for cash collections might look as follows:

| Month of sales | Percent of total | Net sales | August collections |
|---|---|---|---|
| April | 0.5 | $168,000 | $840 |
| May | 4.2 | 192,000 | 8,064 |
| June | 8.9 | 311,100 | 27,688 |
| July | 82.1 | 325,600 | 267,318 |
| August | 2.3 | | 7,820 |
| Total collections | | | $ 311,730 |
| Cash discounts | 1.0 | 325,600 | (3,256) |
| Losses | 1.0 | 340,000 | (3,400) |
| Total | | | $ 305,074 |

The following example illustrates how cash collection rates are used to generate a forecast of the cash collection porting of the cash budget.

## Example 2

The following data are given for Sharpe's Clothing Store:

|  | September actual | October actual | November actual | December actual |
|---|---|---|---|---|
| Cash sales | $ 7,000 | $ 6,000 | $8,000 | $6,000 |
| Credit sales | 50,000 | 48,000 | 62,000 | 80,000 |

Past experience based on the aging of accounts receivable indicates that collections normally occur in the following pattern:

◆ No collections are made in the month of sales.

◆ 80 percent of the sales are collected in the second following month.

◆ 19 percent of sales are collected in the second following month.

◆ 1 percent of sales are uncollectible.

The total cash receipts for November and December are computed as follows:

|  | November | December |
|---|---|---|
| Cash receipts |  |  |
| Cash sales | $ 8,000 | $ 6,000 |
| Cash collections |  |  |
| September sales |  |  |
| $50,000 x 19% | 9,500 |  |
| October sales |  |  |
| $48,000 x 80% | 38,400 |  |
| $48,000 x 19% |  | 9,120 |
| November sales |  |  |
| $62,000 x 80% |  | 49,600 |
| Total cash receipts | $55,900 | $64,720 |

## How is it used and applied?

The forecasting of cash collections is important in predicting whether sufficient cash will be available to meet expenditure needs. Further, the more quickly cash is received from customers, the less is the risk of noncollection. In addition, a return can be earned on the cash received early.

# 13. "What-if" Analysis

## Introduction

Managers make decisions in the fact of uncertainty or risk. The environments in which they operate are subject to change without notice. It is therefore advisable to set up "what-if: scenarios and analyze them with the aid of computer software.

## How is it computed?

Many "what-if" scenarios can be evaluated using the concepts of contribution margin as a tool for profit planning. *Contribution margin* is the difference between sales and the variable cost of a product or service; it is the amount of money available to cover fixed costs and generate profits.

## Example 1

To illustrate a 'what-if: analysis, consider the following data for the Allison Toy Store:

|  | Total | Per unit | Percentage |
|---|---|---|---|
| Sales (1,500 units) | $37,500 | $25 | 100% |
| Less: Variable costs | 15,000 | 10 | 40 |
| Contribution | $22,000 | $15 | 60% |
| Less: Fixed Cost | 15,000 |  |  |
| Net income | $ 7,500 |  |  |

Let us suppose that, in an effort to stimulate sales, the owner is considering cutting the unit price by $5 and increasing the advertising budget by $1000. If these two steps be taken? To answer the question, you may construct a proposed income statement as follows:

|  | (A) Present (1,500 units) | | (B) Proposed (2,400 units) | | (B-A) Difference |
|---|---|---|---|---|---|
| Sales | $37,500 | (@ $25) | $484,000 | (@ $20) | $10,500 |
| Less: Variable | 15,000 | (@ $10) | 24,000 | (@ $10) | 9,000 |
| Contribution margin | $22,500 | | $24,000 | | $ 1,500 |
| Less: Fixed costs | 15,000 | | 16,000 | | 1,000 |
| Net income | $ 7,500 | | $ 8,000 | | $ 500 |

The answer is yes, since these two steps will increase net income by $500.

## Example 2

Delta Gamma Manufacturing wishes to prepare a 3-year projection on net income using the following information:

1.    20x8 base-year amounts are as follows:

| | |
|---|---|
| Sales revenues | $4,500,000 |
| Cost of sales | 2,900,000 |
| Selling and administrative expenses | 800,000 |
| Net income before taxes | 800,000 |

2.    Using the following "what-if: assumptions:

   ◆    Sales revenues increase by 6 percent in 20x9, 7 percent in 20x10, and 8 percent in 20x11.

   ◆    Cost of sales increases by 5 percent each year.

   ◆    Selling and administrative expenses increase only 1 percent in 20x9 and will remain at the 20x9 level thereafter.

   ◆    The income tax rate is 46 percent.

Figure 13.1 shows a spreadsheet for the pro forma income statement for the next 3 years. Using a spreadsheet program such as Excel allows managers to evaluate various "what-if" scenarios.

### Figure 13.1: Delta Gamma Manufactures: three-year income projections (20x8-20x11)

| | 20x8 | 20x9 | 20x10 | 20x11 |
|---|---|---|---|---|
| Sales | $4,500,000 | $4,770,000 | $5,103,900 | $5,512,212 |
| Cost of sales | $2,900,000 | $3,045,000 | $3,197,250 | $3,357,113 |
| Gross profit | $1,600,000 | $1,725,000 | $1,906,650 | $2,155,100 |
| Selling & adm. exp. | $ 800,000 | $ 808,000 | $ 816,080 | $ 824,241 |
| Earning before tax | $ 800,000 | $ 917,000 | $1,090,570 | $1,330,859 |
| Tax | $ 368,000 | $ 421,820 | $ 501,662 | $ 612,195 |
| Earning after tax | $ 432,000 | $ 495,180 | $ 588,908 | $ 718,664 |

## Can a Computer Help?

Performing "what-if: analyses without the aid of a computer is almost impossible. "What-if" software includes:

1.  Spreadsheet programs such as: Lotus 1-2-3, Microsoft's Excel, and Quattro Pro.

2.  Cash management and accounting software such as Quicken and Up Your Cash Flow.

3.  Decision-support and budgeting software such as: Adaptive Planning, ®Risk, and BudgetMaestro.

## How is it used and applied?

The cash budget would be incomplete if it were based on only one set of estimated cash inflows and cash outflows. These figures may well be *expected* cash flows or even *most likely* estimates, but we need to consider the possibility of errors or variability in cash flow estimates. Table 13.2 lists the principal known and uncertain cash flows.

The variability in cash flows can be handled by 'what-if" analysis or by optimistic/ pessimistic forecasts. For example, what if your cash sales were, say, 10 percent higher, or lower, than originally expected? A cash budget prepared for a worst-case scenario might be quite useful. It may also allow you to plan better for difficult times.

**Table 13.1: Certain and Uncertain Cash Flows**

| Known cash flow | Uncertain cash flow |
|---|---|
| Interest receipts | Cash sales |
| Rent | Collections |
| Payroll | Payable payments |
| Tax Payments | |
| Interest Payments | |
| Loan repayments | |
| Purchase of long-term assets | |

# 14. Budget Accuracy Ratios

## Introduction

The accuracy of a budget may be evaluated by comparing budget figures to actual figures. The closer the actual amounts are to the estimates, the better is the budget process and the greater is the reliance that may be placed on future projections.

## How is it computed?

$$\text{Budget sales accuracy} = \frac{\text{actual sales}}{\text{budget sales}}$$

$$\text{Budget cost compliance} = \frac{\text{actual costs}}{\text{budgeted costs}}$$

$$\text{Budget profit reliability} = \frac{\text{actual profit}}{\text{budgeted profits}}$$

## Example

An owner budgeted profit for $800,000, but the business actually earned $1,000,000. The reasons for this favorable result might be one or more of the following:

◆ Higher revenue and/or fewer expenses than predicted. The higher revenue might be due to excellent salesperson efforts. The lower expenses might have risen from a cost-reduction program.

◆ The intentional underestimation of the budgeted profits, so that when actual sales exceed budgeted sales the manager looks good.

◆ Poor planning due to the failure to properly take historical and current factors into account when making up the budget.

## How is it used and applied?

There is no assurance that a plan designed to increase earnings will in fact do so. However, if actual profits exceeds budgeted profits, the owner has achieved the profit goal. This may arise because of greater revenue than expected, or better control over costs than anticipated.

By comparing actual to budgeted amounts, the owner can determine whether the business plans are sound. If not, improvements in the planning process are needed. Perhaps the planning is over-optimistic or unrealistic. On the other hand, the problem may lie with an inclination to overspend and/or waste. The expense deviation should be related to that of sales. Perhaps all that has happened is simply that expenses went up because sales revenue increased. In that case, the result is expected and no negative sign exists.

# Part 3

# Business Forecasting Methods

## 15. Projecting Financing Needs

### Introduction

Forecasts of the future sales and their related expenses provide the firm with the information needed to project its future needs for financing. Percentage of sales is the most widely used method for projecting a company's financing needs. This method involves estimating the various expenses, assets, and liabilities for a future period as a percent of the sales forecast and then using these percentages, together with the projected sales, to construct pro-forma balance sheets.

### How is it computed?

The basic steps involved in projecting financing needs are as follows:

1. Project the first firm's sales. The sales forecast is the most important initial step. Most other forecasts (budgets ) follow the sales forecast.

2. Project additional variables such as expenses.

3. Estimate the level of investment in current and fixed assets required to support the projected sales.

4. Calculate the firm's financing needs.

The following example illustrates ,how to develop a pro-forma balance sheet and determine the amount of external financing needed.

## Example

Assume that sales for 20x7=$20, projected sales for 20x8 = $24, net income = 5 percent of sales, and the dividend payout ratio = 40 percent. The steps for the computations are outlined as follows, with the results shown in Exhibit 15.1:

*Step 1:* Express those balance sheet items that vary directly with sales as a percentage of sales. Any item such as long term debt that does not vary directly with sales is designed "n.a.," or "not applicable."

*Step 2:* Multiply these percentages by the 20x8 projected sales = $24 to obtain the projected amounts as shown in the last column.

*Step 3:* Insert figures for long-term debt, common stock, and paid-in-capital from the 20x1 balance sheet.

*Step 4:* Compute 20x8 retained earnings as shown in Note *b*.

*Step 5:* Sum the asset accounts, obtaining total projected assets of 47.2, and also add projected liabilities and equity to obtain $7.12, the total financing provided. Since there is a short fall of $0.08 "external financing needed." Any external financing needed may be raised by issuing notes payable, bonds, stocks, or any combination of these financing sources.

## Figure 15.1: Pro Forma Balance Sheet in Millions of Dollars

|  | Present (20x7) | % of Sales (20x7 Sales=$20) | Projected (20x8 Sales=$24) | |
|---|---|---|---|---|
| Assets |  |  |  | |
| Current assets | 2 | 10 | 2.4 | |
| Fixed assets | 4 | 20 | 4.8 | |
| Total assets | 6 |  | 7.2 | |
| Liabilities and Stockholders' equity |  |  |  | |
| Current liabilities | 2 | 10 | 2.4 | |
| Long-term debt | 2.5 | n.a. | 2.5 | |
| Total liabilities | 4.5 |  | 4.9 | |
| Common stock | 0.1 | n.a. | 0.1 | |
| Paid-in-capital | 0.2 | n.a. | 0.2 | |
| Retained earnings | 1.2 |  | 1.92 | |
| Total equity | 1.5 |  | 2.22 | |
| Total liabilities and stockholders' equity | 6 |  | 7.12 | Total financing provided |
|  |  |  | 0.08 | External financing needed |
|  |  |  | 7.2 | Total |

20x8 retained earnings = 20x7 retained earnings + projected net income – cash dividends paid = $1.2 + 5%($24) - 40%[5%($24)] = $1.2 + $1.2 - $0.48 = $2.4 - $0.48 = $1.92

External financing needed projected total assets - (projected total liabilities + projected equity) = $7.2  -  ($4.9 + $2.22) = $7.2 - $7.12 = $0.08

## How is it used and applied?

Financial officers and business owners need to determine the portion of the next year's funding requirements that has to be raised externally. By doing so, they can get a head start in arranging a least-cost financing plan.

The major advantage of the percent-of-sales method of financial forecasting is that it is simple and inexpensive to use. To obtain a more precise projection of the firm's future financing needs, however, the preparation of a cash budget is required. One important assumption behind the use of the method is that the firm is operating at full capacity. This means that the business has no production capacity to absorb a projected increase in sales, and thus requires an additional investment in assets.

# 16. Naive Forecasting Models

## Introduction

Naive forecasting models are based exclusively on historical observation of sales or other variables such as earnings and cash flows being forecast. They do *not* attempt to explain the underlying causal relationships that produce the variables being forecast. Naive models may be classified into two groups. One group consists of simple projection models. These models require inputs of data from recent observations, but no statistical analysis is performed. The second group is comprised of models that, while naive, are complex enough to require a computer. Traditional methods such as classical decomposition, moving average, and exponential smoothing models are some examples. (See Sec. 17, Moving Averages, and Sec. 18, Exponential Smoothing.)

The advantages of naive forecasting models are that they are inexpensive to develop, store data, and operate. The disadvantages are that they do not consider possible causal relationships that underlie the forecasted variable.

## How is it computed?

A simple example of a naive model type is to use the actual sales of the current period as the forecast for the next period. Let us use F as the forecast value and the symbol $A_t$ as the actual value. Then:

$$F = A_t$$

If trends are considered, then:

$$F = A_t + (A_t - A_{t-1})$$

This model adds the latest observed absolute period-to-period change to the most recent observed level of the variable.

If it is desirable to incorporate the rate of change rather than the absolute amount, then:

$$F = A_t = \left( \frac{A_t}{A_{t-1}} \right)$$

## *Example*

Consider the following monthly sales data for 20x7:

| Month | Monthly sales of product |
|-------|--------------------------|
| 1 | $5,504 |
| 2 | 5,810 |
| 3 | 6,100 |

Forecasts will be developed for the fourth month of 20x7, using the three models:

$$F = A_t = \$6,100$$

$$F = A_t + (A_t - A_{t-1}) = \$6,100 + (\$6,100 - \$5,810) = \$6,100 + \$290 = \$6,390$$

$$F = A_t \left( \frac{A_t}{A_{t-1}} \right) = \$6100 \left( \frac{\$6,100}{\$5810} \right) = \$6,100(1.05) = \$6,405$$

## How is it used and applied?

Naive models can be applied, with very little need of a computer, to develop forecasts for sales, earnings, and cash flows. These models, however, must be used in conjunction with more complex naive models such as classical decomposition and exponential smoothing and more sophisticated models such as regression analysis. The object is to pick the model (or models) that will best forecast performance.

# 17. Moving Averages

## Introduction

A moving average is an average that is updated as new information is received. A manger employs the most recent observations to calculate an average, which is used as the forecast for the next period.

## How is it computed?

For a moving average, simply take the most recent observations and calculate an average. Moving averages are updated continually as new data are available.

## *Example*

Assume that the manager of Drake Hardware Store has the following sales data:

| Month | Sales (000) |
|-----------|-------------|
| April | 20 |
| May | 21 |
| June | 24 |
| July | 22 |
| August | 26 |
| September | 25 |

Using a 5-month average, predicted sales for October are computed as follows:

$$\frac{21 + 24 + 22 + 26 + 25}{5} = \frac{118}{5} = 23.6 \text{ or } \$23,600$$

## How is it used and applied?

Moving averages are used, for example, to project future sales. Once sales are projected, needed financing for production and inventory may be planned. Business owners can choose the number of periods to use on the basis of the relative importance attached to old versus current date.

For example, one can compare two possibilities, a 5-month and a 3-month period. In terms of the relative importance of new versus old data, the old data receive a weight of ⁴/₅ and current data ¹/₅. In the second possibility, the old data receive a weight of ²/₃, while current observation receives a ¹/₃ weight. This is a special case of the exponential smoothing method, in which a smoothing constant is in effect the weight given to the most recent data. See Sec.18, Exponential Smoothing.

Sales forecast can be fairly accurate if the right number of observations to be averaged is picked. In order to pick the right number, the business manager may have to experiment with different moving-average periods. Measures of forecasting accuracy, such as the *mean absolute deviation* (MAD), can be used to pick the optimal number of periods. See Sec, 24, Measuring Accuracy of Forecasts.

# 18. Exponential Smoothing

## Introduction

Exponential smoothing is a popular technique for short run business forecasting. It uses a weighted average of past data as the basis for a forecast. The procedure gives heaviest weight to recent information and smaller weights to observations in the more distant past. The reason for this is that the future is more dependent on the recent past than on the distant past.

## How is it computed?

(The formula for exponential smoothing is

$$\hat{y}_{t+1} = \alpha y_t + (1-\alpha)\hat{y}_t$$

or

$$\hat{y}_{new} = \alpha y_{old} + (1-\alpha)\hat{y}_{old}$$

where $\hat{y}_{new}$ = exponentially smoothed average to be used as the forecast

$y_{old}$ = most recent actual data

$\hat{y}_{old}$ = most recent smoothed forecast

$\alpha$ = smoothing constant

The higher the $\alpha$, the greater is the weight given to the more recent information.

## Example

The following data on sales are given for an appliance business:

| Time period, t | Actual sales (1000), $y_t$ |
|:---:|:---:|
| 1 | $60.00 |
| 2 | 64.0 |
| 3 | 58.0 |
| 4 | 66.0 |
| 5 | 70.0 |
| 6 | 60.0 |
| 7 | 70.0 |
| 8 | 74.0 |
| 9 | 62.0 |
| 10 | 74.0 |
| 11 | 68.0 |
| 12 | 66.0 |
| 13 | 60.0 |
| 14 | 66.0 |
| 15 | 62.0 |

To initialize the exponential smoothing process, it is necessary to have the initial forecast. The first smoothed forecast to be used can be

1. First actual observations.
2. An average of the actual data for a few periods

For illustrative purposes, let us use a six-period average as the initial forecast y, with a smoothing constant of $\alpha = 0.40$. Then

$$\hat{y}_7 = \frac{Y_1 + Y_2 + Y_3 + Y_4 + Y_5 + Y_6}{6}$$

$$= \frac{60+64+58+66+70+60}{6} = 63$$

Note that $y_7 = 70$. Then $\hat{y}_8$ is computed as follows:

$$\hat{y}_8 = \alpha y_7 + (1 - \alpha)\hat{y}_7$$
$$= (0.40)(70) + (0.60)(63)$$
$$= 28.0 + 37.80 = 65.80$$

Similarly,

$$\hat{y}_9 = \alpha y_8 + (1 - \alpha)\hat{y}_8$$
$$= (0.40)(74) + (0.60)(65.80)$$
$$= 29.60 + 39.48 = 69.08$$

and

$$\hat{y}_{10} = \alpha y_9 + (1 - \alpha)\hat{y}_9$$
$$= (0.40)(62) + (0.60)(69.08)$$
$$= 24.80 + 41.45 = 66.25$$

By using the same procedure, the values of $\hat{y}_{11}$, $\hat{y}_{12}$, $\hat{y}_{13}$, $\hat{y}_{14}$ and $\hat{y}_{15}$ can be calculated. Table 18.1 shows a comparison between the actual sales and predicted sales using the exponential smoothing method.

**Table 18.1: Comparison of Actual Sales and Predicted Sales**

| Time period, t | Actual sales, $y_t$ | Predicted sales, $\hat{y}_t$ | Difference $y_t - \hat{y}_t$ | Difference² $(y_t - \hat{y}_t)_2$ |
|---|---|---|---|---|
| 1 | 60 | | | |
| 2 | 64 | | | |
| 3 | 58 | | | |
| 4 | 66 | | | |
| 5 | 70 | | | |
| 6 | 60 | | | |
| 7 | 70 | 63 | 7 | 49.00 |
| 8 | 74 | 65.8 | 8.2 | 67.24 |
| 9 | 62 | 69.08 | -7.08 | 50.13 |
| 10 | 74 | 66.25 | 7.75 | 60.06 |
| 11 | 68 | 69.35 | -1.35 | 1.82 |
| 12 | 66 | 68.81 | -2.81 | 7.90 |
| 13 | 60 | 67.69 | -7.69 | 59.14 |
| 14 | 66 | 64.61 | 1.39 | 1.93 |
| 15 | 62 | 65.17 | -3.17 | 10.05 |
| | | | | 307.27 |

Because of the negative and positive differences between actual sales and predicted sales, the forecaster can use a higher or lower smoothing constant, $\alpha$, in order to adjust the prediction as quickly as possible to large fluctuations in the data aeries. For example, if the forecast is slow in reacting to increased sales (that is, if the difference is negative), the forecaster may want to try a higher value of $\alpha$. For practical purposes, the optimal $\alpha$ may be picked by minimizing the mean squared error (MSE), defined as:

$$MSE = \frac{(y_t - \hat{y}^t)^2}{n - i}$$

where i = the number of observations used to determine the initial forecast

In our example, i = 6, so the mean squared error is

$$MSE = \frac{307.27}{15 - 6} = \frac{307.27}{9} = 34.14$$

The idea is to select the $\alpha$ that minimizes MSE, which is the average sum of the variations between the historical sales data and the forecast values for, the corresponding periods.

## Can a Computer Help?

A manager will sometimes be confronted with complex problems requiring large sample data, necessitating trial of many different values of a for exponential smoothing. Excel has a routine for exponential smoothing.

## How is it used and applied?

The exponential smoothing method is effective when there is randomness but no seasonal fluctuations in the data. The forecaster can use a higher or lower smoothing constant $\alpha$ in order to adjust the prediction as quickly as possible to large fluctuations it the data series. For example, if the forecast is slow in reacting to increases sales (that is, if the difference is negative), the forecaster may want to try a higher value. Finding the best $\alpha$ is the key to success in using this method.

The method is simple and effective, since it does not require a lot of data other than for the variable involved. One disadvantage of the method, however, is that it does not include industrial or economic factor such as market conditions, prices, or the effects of competitors' actions.

# 19. Regression Analysis

## Introduction

Regression analysis is a statistical procedure for estimating mathematically the average relationship between the dependent variable and the independent variable(s). The least-squares method is widely used in regression analysis for estimating the parameter values in a regression equation. *Simple regression* involves one independent variable, price or advertising in a demand function, whereas *multiple regression* involves two or more variables, that is price and advertising together.

## How is it computed?

We will assume a simple (linear) regression to illustrate the least-squares method, which means that we will assume the $Y = a + bX$ relationship, where a = intercept and b = slope. The regression method includes all the observed data and attempts to find a line of best fit. To find this line, a technique called the least-squares method is used.

### The Least-Squares Method

To explain the least-squares method, we define the error as the difference between the observed value and the estimated one and denote it with u.   Symbolically,

$$u = Y - Y'$$

where   Y = observed value of the dependent variable

$Y'$ = estimated value based on $Y' = a + bX$

The least-squares criterion requires that the line of best fit be such that the sum of the squares of the errors (or the vertical distance in Figure 19.1 from the observed data points to the line) is a minimum, i.e.,

Minimum: $\Sigma u^2 = \sum(Y - Y')^2 = \Sigma(Y-a-bX)^2$

Using differential calculus we obtain the following equations, called normal equations:

$$\Sigma Y = na + b\Sigma X$$

$$\Sigma XY = a\Sigma X + b\Sigma X^2$$

Solving the equations for b and a yields

$$b = \frac{n\sum XY - (\sum X)(\sum Y)}{n\sum X^2 - (\sum X)^2}$$

$$a = \overline{Y} - b\overline{X}$$

$$\text{where } \overline{Y} = \frac{\sum Y}{n} \text{ and } \overline{X} = \frac{\sum X}{n}$$

**Figure 19.1: Y AND Y¢**

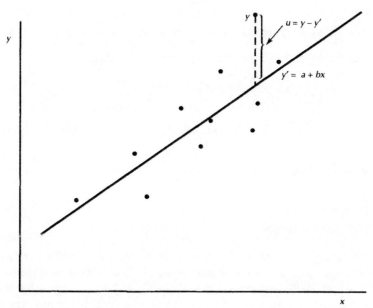

## Example I

To illustrate the computations of b and a, we will refer to the data in Table 19.1. All the sums required are computed and shown in Table 19.1.

**Table 19.1: Computed Sums**

| Adv.(X)<br>(in $000s) | Sales (Y)<br>(in $000s) | XY | X² |
|---|---|---|---|
| 9 | 15 | 135 | 81 |
| 19 | 20 | 380 | 361 |
| 11 | 14 | 154 | 121 |
| 14 | 16 | 224 | 196 |
| 23 | 25 | 575 | 529 |
| 12 | 20 | 240 | 144 |
| 12 | 20 | 240 | 144 |
| 22 | 23 | 506 | 484 |
| 7 | 14 | 98 | 49 |
| 13 | 22 | 286 | 169 |
| 15 | 18 | 270 | 225 |
| 17 | 18 | 306 | 289 |
| 174 | 225 | 3,414 | 2,792 |

From the table:

$$\Sigma X = 174; \quad \Sigma Y = 225; \quad \Sigma XY = 3,414; \quad \Sigma X^2 = 2,792.$$

$$\overline{X} = \Sigma X/n = 174/12 = 14.5; \quad Y = \Sigma Y/n = 225/12 = 18.75.$$

Substituting these values into the formula for b first:

$$b = \frac{n\Sigma XY - (\Sigma X)(\Sigma Y)}{n\Sigma X^2 - (\Sigma X)^2} = \frac{(12)(3,414) - (174)(225)}{(12)(2,792) - (174)2} = \frac{1,881}{3,228} = 0.5632$$

$$a = \overline{Y} - b\overline{X} = 18.75 - (0.5632)(14.5) = 18.75 - 8.1664 = 10.5836$$

Thus,

$$Y' = 10.5836 + 0.5632\,X$$

## Can a computer help?

Spreadsheet programs such as Excel include a regression routine which can be used without any difficulty. As a matter of fact, in reality, you do not compute the parameter values a and b manually. Table 19.2 shows an Excel regression output that contains the statistics we discussed so far. Other statistics that appear are discussed in Sec. 20, Regression Statistics.

### Table 19.2: Excel regression output

SUMMARY OUTPUT

| Regression Statistics | |
| --- | --- |
| Multiple R | 0.77998 |
| R Square | 0.60837 ($r^2$) |
| Adjusted R Square | 0.56921 |
| Standard Error | 2.34362 ($S_e$) |
| Observations | 12 |

ANOVA

| | df | SS | MS | Significance F |
| --- | --- | --- | --- | --- |
| Regression | 1 | 85.32434944 | 85.3243 | 0.002769 |
| Residual | 10 | 54.92565056 | 5.49257 | |
| Total | 11 | 140.25 | | |

| | Coefficients | Standard Error (S$_b$) | t Stat | Lower 95% | Upper 95% |
|---|---|---|---|---|---|
| Intercept | 10.5836(a) | 2.17960878 | 4.85575 | 5.727171 | 15.4401 |
| Advertising | 0.5632(b) | 0.142893168 | 3.94139 | 0.244811 | 0.88158 |

(1) R-squared ($r^2$) = .608373 = 60.84%
(2) Standard error of the estimate (S$_e$) = 2.343622
(3) Standard error of the coefficient (S$_b$) = 0.142893
(4) t-value = 3.94

Note that all of the above are the same as the ones manually obtained.


## How is it used and applied?

Before attempting a least-squares regression approach, it is extremely important to plot the observed data on a diagram, called the scattergraph (See Figure 19.3). The reason is that you might want to make sure that a linear (straight-line) relationship existed between Y and X in the past sample. If for any reason there was a nonlinear relationship detected in the sample, the linear relationship we assumed -- Y = a + bX -- would not give us a good fit.


## *Example 2*

Assume that the advertising of $10 is to be expended for next year; the projected sales for the next year would be computed as follows:

$$Y' = 10.5836 + 0.5632 X$$

$$= 10.5836 + 0.5632 (10)$$

$$= \$16.2156$$

In order to obtain a good fit and achieve a high degree of accuracy, you should be familiar with statistics relating to regression such as r-squared ($R^2$) and t-value, which are discussed later.

**Figure 19.3: Scatter diagram**

# 20. Regression Statistics

## Introduction

Regression analysis is a statistical procedure for estimating mathematically the average relationship between the dependent variable (e.g., sales) and the independent variable(s) (e.g., price, advertising, or both). It uses a variety of statistics to convey the accuracy and reliability of the regression results.

## How is it computed?

Regression statistics include:

1.    Correlation coefficient ($r$) and coefficient of determination ($r^2$)
2.    Standard error of the estimate ($S_e$)
3.    Standard error of the regression coefficient ($S_b$) and $t$ statistics

## 1. Correlation Coefficient (r) and Coefficient of Determination (r²)

The correlation coefficient $r$ measures the degree of correlation between $Y$ and $X$. The range of values it takes on is between -1 and +1. More widely used, however, is the coefficient of determination, designated $r^2$ (read as r-squared). Simply put, $r^2$ tells the level of quality of the estimated regression equation--a measure of "goodness of fit" in the regression. Therefore, the higher the $r^2$, the more confidence can be placed in the estimated equation.

More specifically, the coefficient of determination represents the proportion of the total variation in Y that is explained by the regression equation. It has the range of values between 0 and 1.

## Example 1

The statement "Sales is a function of advertising dollars with $r2 = 70$ percent," can be interpreted as "70 percent of the total variation of factory overhead is explained by regression equation or the change in advertising and the remaining 30 percent is accounted for by something other than advertising."

The coefficient of determination is computed as

$$r^2 = 1 - \frac{\sum(Y - Y')^2}{\sum(Y - \overline{Y})^2}$$

where Y = actual values

$\quad$ Y' = estimated values

$\quad$ $\overline{Y}$ = average (mean) value of Y

In a simple regression, however, there is a shortcut method available:

$$r^2 = \frac{[n\sum XY - (\sum X)(\sum Y)]^2}{[n\sum X^2 - (\sum X)^2][n\sum Y^2 - (\sum Y)]}$$

where $n$ = number of observations

$\quad$ X = value of independent value

## Example 2

To illustrate the computations of various regression statistics, use the same data used in Sec. 19, Regression Analysis. All the sums required are computed and shown below. Note that the $Y^2$ column is added in Table 20.1 to be used for $r^2$.

## Table 20.1: Computed Sums

| Adv.(X) (in $000s) | Sales (Y) (in $000s) | XY | X² | Y² |
|---|---|---|---|---|
| 9 | 15 | 135 | 81 | 225 |
| 19 | 20 | 380 | 361 | 400 |
| 11 | 14 | 154 | 121 | 196 |
| 14 | 16 | 224 | 196 | 256 |
| 23 | 25 | 575 | 529 | 625 |
| 12 | 20 | 240 | 144 | 400 |
| 12 | 20 | 240 | 144 | 400 |
| 22 | 23 | 506 | 484 | 529 |
| 7 | 14 | 98 | 49 | 196 |
| 13 | 22 | 286 | 169 | 484 |
| 15 | 18 | 270 | 225 | 324 |
| 17 | 18 | 306 | 289 | 324 |
| 174 | 225 | 3,414 | 2,792 | 4,359 |

From this table,

$$\Sigma X = 174 \quad \Sigma Y = 225 \quad \Sigma XY = 3414 \quad \Sigma X2 = 2792$$

$$\bar{X} = \frac{\Sigma X}{n} = \frac{174}{12} = 14.5 \quad \bar{Y} = \frac{\Sigma Y}{n} = \frac{225}{12} = 18.75$$

Using the shortcut method for $r^2$,

$$r^2 = \frac{(1818)^2}{(3228)[(12)(4,359)-(225)^2]} = \frac{3,305,124}{(328)(52,308-50,625)} = \frac{3,305,124}{(3,228)(1,683)}$$

$$= \frac{3,305,124}{5,432,724} = 0.6084 = 60.84\%$$

This means that about 60.84 percent of the total variation in total sales is explained by advertising and the remaining 39.16 percent is still unexplained. A relatively low $r^2$ indicates that there is a lot of room for improvement in the forecasting equation ($Y^2 = \$10.5836 + \$0.5632X$). Advertising or a combination of price and advertising might improve $r^2$.

Note: A low $r^2$ is an indication that the model is inadequate for explaining the y variable. The general causes for this problem are:

1. Use of a wrong functional form.
2. Poor choice of an x variable as the predictor.
3. Omission of some important variable or variables from the model.

## 2. Standard Error of the Estimate (Se)

The standard error of the estimate, designated Se, is defined as the standard deviation of the regression. It is computed as

$$Se = \sqrt{\frac{\sum(Y-Y')^2}{n-2}} = \sqrt{\frac{\sum Y^2 - a\sum Y - b\sum XY}{n-2}}$$

Statistics can be used to gain some idea of accuracy of these predictions.

Since, t = 3.94 > 2, we conclude that the b coefficient is statistically significant. As was indicated previously, the table's critical value (cut-off value) for 10 degrees of freedom is 2.228 (from Table 8 in the Appendix).

*Rule of thumb*: Any t value greater than +2 or less than 2 is acceptable. The higher the t value, the greater the confidence we have in the coefficient as a predictor. Low t values are indications of low reliability of the predictive power of that coefficient.

## Example 3

Returning to our example data, Se is calculated as

$$Se\sqrt{\frac{4359 - (10.5836)(225) - (0.5632)(3414)}{12 - 2}} = \sqrt{\frac{54.9252}{10}} = 2.3436$$

Suppose you wish to make a prediction regarding an individual Y value--such as a prediction about the sales when an advertising expense = $10. Usually, we would like to have some objective measure of the confidence we can place in our prediction, and one such measure is a *confidence (or prediction) interval* constructed for Y.

*Note*: t is the critical value for the level of significance employed. For example, for a significant level of 0.025 (which is equivalent to a 95% confidence level in a two-tailed test), the critical value of t for 10 degrees of freedom is 2.228 (See Table A.2 in the Appendix). As can be seen, the confidence interval is the linear distance bounded by limits on either side of the prediction.

## Example 4

If you want to have a 95 percent confidence interval of your prediction, the range for the prediction, given an advertising expense of $10 would be between $10,595.10 and $21,836.10, as determined as follows: Note that from Example 4.2, Y' = $16.2156

The confidence interval is therefore established as follows:

$$\$16.2156 \pm (2.228)(2.3436)$$

$$= \$16.2156 \pm (2.228)(2.3436)$$

$$= \$16.2156 \pm 5.2215$$

which means the range for the prediction, given an advertising expense of $10 would be between $10.5951 and $21.8361. Note that $10.9941 = $16.2156 - 5.2215 and $21.4371 = $16.2156 + 5.2215.

## 3. Standard Error of the Regression Coefficient ($S_b$) and the t Statistic

The standard error of the regression coefficient , designated s, and the t statistic are closely related. $S_b$ is calculated as:

$$S_b = \frac{Se}{\sqrt{\sum(X - \overline{X})^2}}$$

or, in short-cut form,

$$S_b = \frac{Se}{\sqrt{\sum X^2 - \overline{X}\sum X}}$$

$S_b$ gives an estimate of the range where the true coefficient will "actually" fall.

The t statistics (or t value) is a measure of the statistical significance of an independent variable X in explaining the dependent variable Y. It is determined by dividing the estimated regression coefficient b by its standard error $S_b$. It is then compared with the table t value (see Table 7 in the appendix). Thus, the t statistic measures how many standard errors the coefficient is away from zero. Low t values are indicators of low reliability of that coefficient.

## Example 5

The $S_b$ for our example is:

$$s_b = \frac{2.3436}{\sqrt{2792 - (14.5)(174)}}$$

$$= \frac{2.346}{\sqrt{2792 - 2523}} = \frac{2.346}{\sqrt{269}} = 0.143$$

Thus,

$$\text{t-statistic} = \frac{b}{S_b} = \frac{0.5632}{0.143} = 3.94$$

Since t - 3.94 > 2, the conclusion is that the b coefficient is statistically significant.

## How is it used and applied?

The least-squares method is used to estimate both simple and multiple regressions, although in reality managers will confront multiple regression more often than simple regression. Computer software is used to estimate *b*'s. A spreadsheet program such as Excel can be used to develop a model and estimate most of the regression statistics discussed thus far. Table 20.1 shows the relevant statistics.

Regression analysis is a powerful statistical technique that is widely used by businesspersons and economists. In order to obtain a good fit and to achieve a high degree of accuracy, analysts must be familiar with statistics relating to regression, such as $r^2$ and the *t* value, and be able to make further tests that are unique to multiple regression.

See also Sec. 19, Regression Analysis; Sec. 21, Simple Regression.

### Table 20.1: Excel regression output

SUMMARY OUTPUT

| *Regression Statistics* | | |
|---|---|---|
| Multiple R | 0.77998 | |
| R Square | 0.60837 | ($r^2$) |
| Adjusted R Square | 0.56921 | |
| Standard Error | 2.34362 | ($S_e$) |
| Observations | 12 | |

ANOVA

| | df | SS | MS | Significance F |
|---|---|---|---|---|
| Regression | 1 | 85.32434944 | 85.3243 | 0.002769 |
| Residual | 10 | 54.92565056 | 5.49257 | |
| Total | 11 | 140.25 | | |

| | Coefficients | Standard Error ($S_b$) | t Stat | Lower 95% | Upper 95% |
|---|---|---|---|---|---|
| Intercept | 10.5836(a) | 2.17960878 | 4.85575 | 5.727171 | 15.4401 |
| Advertising | 0.5632(b) | 0.142893168 | 3.94139 | 0.244811 | 0.88158 |

(1) R-squared ($r^2$) = .608373 = 60.84%
(2) Standard error of the estimate ($S_e$) = 2.343622
(3) Standard error of the coefficient ($S_b$) = 0.142893
(4) t-value = 3.94

Note that all of the above are the same as the ones manually obtained. Note the following:

(1)   t-statistic is more relevant to multiple regressions which have more than one b's.

(2)   $r^2$ tells you how good the forest (overall fit) is while t-statistic tells you how good an individual tree (an independent variable) is.

In summary, the table t value, based on a degree of freedom and a level of significance, is used:

1.   To set the prediction range—upper and lower limits—for the predicted value of the dependent variable.

2.   To set the confidence range for regression coefficients.

3.   As a cutoff value for the t-test.

# 21.  Simple Regression

## Introduction

Simple regression is a type of regression analysis that involves one independent (explanatory) variable.

## How is it computed?

Simple regression takes the form:

**Y = a + bX**

Where Y = dependent variable

X = independent variable

a = constant

b = slope

The least-squares estimation method is typically used to estimate the parameter values *a* and *b*.

## *Example*

Assume that data on DVD sales and advertising expenditures have been collected over the past seven periods.  The linear regression equation can be estimated using the least-squares method.  For example, the sales/advertising regression for DVDs is estimated to be:

DVD sales $= Y = 19.88 + 4.72X$

$r^2 = 0.7630 = 76.30\%$

## How is it used and applied?

Other applications of simple regression are:

- Total manufacturing costs is explained by only one activity variable (such as either production volume or machine hours), i.e., $TC = a + b\,Q$.

- A security's return is a function of the return on a market portfolio (such as Standard & Poor's 500), i.e., $r_j = a + \beta r_m$ where $\beta =$ beta, a measure of uncontrollable risk.

- Consumption is a function of disposable income, i.e., $C = a + b\,Yd$ where b = marginal propensity to consume.

- Demand is a function of price, i.e., $D = a - bP$.

- Average time to be taken is a function of cumulative production, i.e., $Y = a\,X^{-b}$ where b represents a learning rate in the learning curve phenomenon.

- Trend analysis that attempts to detect a growing or declining trend of time series data, i.e., $Y = a + bt$ where $t =$ time.

# 22. Trend Equation

## Introduction

Trends are the general upward or downward movements of the average over time. These movements may require many years of data to determine or describe them. The basic forces underlying trends include technological advances, productivity changes, inflation, and population change.

## How is it computed?

The trend equation is a common method for forecasting sales or earnings. It involves a regression whereby a trend line is fitted to a time series of data.

The linear trend line equation can be shown as

$$Y = a + bX$$

The formulas for the coefficients *a* and *b* essentially the same as for *simple regression*. They are estimated using the least-squares method, which was discussed in Sec. 19, Regression Analysis.

However, for regression purposes, a time period can be given a number so that $\sum X = 0$. When there is an odd number of periods, the period in the middle is assigned a value of 0. If there is an even number, then $-1$ and $+1$ are assigned the two periods in the middle, so that again $\sum X = 0$.

With $\sum X = 0$, the formula for $b$ and $a$ reduces to

$$b = \frac{n\sum tY}{n\sum t^2}$$

$$a = \frac{\sum Y}{n}$$

## Example 1

This example demonstrates the use of trend equations in cases which an even number and an odd number of periods occur.

Case 1 (odd number):

|       | 20x1 | 20x2 | 20x3 | 20x4 |
|-------|------|------|------|------|
| $t =$ | -2   | -1   | 0    | +1   |

Case 2 (even number):

|       | 20x1 | 20x2 | 20x3 | 20x4 | 20x5 | 20x6 |
|-------|------|------|------|------|------|------|
| $t =$ | -3   | -2   | -1   | +1   | +2   | +3   |

In each case, $\sum t = 0$.

## Example 2

| Year | Sales (in millions) |
|------|---------------------|
| 20x1 | $ 10                |
| 20x2 | 12                  |
| 20x3 | 13                  |
| 20x4 | 16                  |
| 20x5 | 17                  |

Since the company has five years of data, which is an odd number, the year in the middle is assigned a zero value.

| Year | t | Sales(in millions (Y) | tY | $t^2$ | $Y^2$ |
|------|-----|------|------|------|------|
| 20x1 | -2 | $ 10 | -20 | 4 | 100 |
| 20x2 | -1 | 12 | -12 | 1 | 144 |
| 20x3 | 0 | 13 | 0 | 0 | 169 |
| 20x4 | +1 | 16 | 16 | 1 | 256 |
| 20x5 | +2 | 17 | 34 | 4 | 289 |
| | 0 | 68 | 18 | 10 | 958 |

$$b = \frac{(5)(18)}{5(10)} = 90/50 = 1.8$$

$$a = \frac{68}{5} = 13.6$$

Therefore, the estimated trend equation is

$$Y' = \$13.6 + \$1.8\,t$$

To project 20x6 sales, we assign +3 to the t value for the year 20x6.

$$Y' = \$13.6 + \$1.8\,(3)$$
$$= \$19$$

## How is it used and applied?

Managers use the trend equation for forecasting purposes, such as to project future revenue costs. They should use the trend equation, however, only if the time series data reflect the gradual shifting or growth pattern over time.

See also Sec. 23, Decomposition of Time Series.

# 23. Decomposition of Time Series

## Introduction

When sales exhibit seasonal or cyclical fluctuation, we use a forecasting method called *classical decomposition* to deal with seasonal trend, and cyclical components together.

## How is it computed?

We assume that a time series $(Y_t)$ is combined into a model that consists of the four components--trend (T), cyclical, (C), seasonal (S), and random (R). This model is of a multiplicative type i.e.,

$$Y_t = T \times C \times S \times R$$

The classical decomposition method is illustrated step by step, by working with the quarterly sales data. The approach basically requires the following four steps:

1. Determine seasonal indexes, using a four-quarter moving average.

2. Deseasonalize the data.

3. Develop the linear least-squares equation in order to identify the trend component of the forecast.

4. Forecast the sales for each of the four quarters of the coming year.

## *Example*

We illustrate the classical decomposition approach by working with the  quarterly sales data presented in Table 23.1 and Figure 23.1 These data show sales of DVD (in thousands of units) for a particular maker over the past four years.

We begin our analysis by showing how to identify the seasonal component of the time series. Looking at Figure 23.1, we can easily see a seasonal pattern of DVD sales. Specifically, we observe that sales are lower in the second quarter of each year, followed by higher sales in quarters 3 and 4. The computational procedure used to eliminate the seasonal component is explained below, step by step.

*Step 1*. We use a moving average to measure the combined trend of cyclical (TC) components of the time series. This way we eliminate the seasonal and random components, S and R.

More specifically, Step 1 involves the following sequences of steps:

**Table 23.1: Quarterly Sales Data for DVDs over the Past 4 Years**

| Year | Quarter | Sales |
|------|---------|-------|
| 1 | 1 | 5.8 |
|  | 2 | 5.1 |
|  | 3 | 7.0 |
|  | 4 | 7.5 |
| 2 | 1 | 6.8 |
|  | 2 | 6.2 |
|  | 3 | 7.8 |
|  | 4 | 8.4 |
| 3 | 1 | 7.0 |
|  | 2 | 6.6 |
|  | 3 | 8.5 |
|  | 4 | 8.8 |
| 4 | 1 | 7.3 |
|  | 2 | 6.9 |
|  | 3 | 9.0 |
|  | 4 | 9.4 |

## Figure 23.1: Quarterly DVD sales time series

a) Calculate the 4-quarter moving average for the time series, which we discussed in the above. However, the moving average values computed do not correspond directly to the original quarters of the time series.

b) We resolve this difficulty by using the midpoints between successive moving-average values. For example, since 6.35 corresponds to the first half of quarter 3 and 6.6 corresponds to the last half of quarter 3, we use (6.35+6.6)/2 = 6.475 as the moving average value of quarter 3. Similarly, we associate (6.6+6.875)/2 = 6.7375 with quarter 4. A complete summary of the moving-average calculation is shown in Table 23.2.

## Table 23.2: Moving Average Calculations for the DVD Sales Time Series

| Year | Quarter | Sales | Four-Quarter Mov. Av. | Centered Mov. Ave. |
|------|---------|-------|-----------------------|--------------------|
| I | I | 5.8 | | |
| | 2 | 5.1 | | |
| | | | 6.35 | |

| Year | Quarter | Sales | Four-Quarter Mov. Av. | Centered Mov. Ave. |
|------|---------|-------|------------------------|--------------------|
|      | 3       | 7.0   |                        | 6.475              |
|      |         |       | 6.6                    |                    |
|      | 4       | 7.5   |                        | 6.7375             |
|      |         |       | 6.875                  |                    |
| 2    | I       | 6.8   |                        | 6.975              |
|      |         |       | 7.075                  |                    |
|      | 2       | 6.2   |                        | 7.1875             |
|      |         |       | 7.3                    |                    |
|      | 3       | 7.8   |                        | 7.325              |
|      |         |       | 7.35                   |                    |
|      | 4       | 8.4   |                        | 7.4                |
|      |         |       | 7.45                   |                    |
| 3    | I       | 7.0   |                        | 7.5375             |
|      |         |       | 7.625                  |                    |
|      | 2       | 6.6   |                        | 7.675              |
|      |         |       | 7.725                  |                    |
|      | 3       | 8.5   |                        | 7.7625             |
|      |         |       | 7.8                    |                    |
|      | 4       | 8.8   |                        | 7.8375             |
|      |         |       | 7.875                  |                    |
| 4    | I       | 7.3   |                        | 7.9375             |
|      |         |       | 8                      |                    |
|      | 2       | 6.9   |                        | 8.075              |
|      |         |       | 8.15                   |                    |
|      | 3       | 9.0   |                        |                    |
|      | 4       | 9.4   |                        |                    |

c)   Next, we calculate the ratio of the actual value to the moving average value for each quarter in the time series having a 4-quarter moving average entry. This ratio in effect represents the seasonal-random component, SR=Y/TC. The ratios calculated this way appear in Table 23.3.

## Table 23.3: Seasonal Random Factors for the Series

| Year | Quarter | Mov. Av | Four-Quarter Mov. Av | Centered Mov. Av TC. | Sea.-Rand. SR=Y/TC |
|------|---------|---------|----------------------|----------------------|--------------------|
|      |         | Sales   | .                    |                      |                    |
| 1    | 1       | 5.8     |                      |                      |                    |
|      | 2       | 5.1     |                      |                      |                    |
|      |         |         | 6.35                 |                      |                    |
|      | 3       | 7.0     |                      | 6.475                | 1.081              |
|      |         |         | 6.6                  |                      |                    |
|      | 4       | 7.5     |                      | 6.738                | 1.113              |
|      |         |         | 6.875                |                      |                    |
| 2    | 1       | 6.8     |                      | 6.975                | 0.975              |
|      |         |         | 7.075                |                      |                    |
|      | 2       | 6.2     |                      | 7.188                | 0.863              |
|      |         |         | 7.3                  |                      |                    |
|      | 3       | 7.8     |                      | 7.325                | 1.065              |
|      |         |         | 7.35                 |                      |                    |
|      | 4       | 8.4     |                      | 7.400                | 1.135              |
|      |         |         | 7.45                 |                      |                    |
| 3    | 1       | 7.0     |                      | 7.538                | 0.929              |
|      |         |         | 7.625                |                      |                    |
|      | 2       | 6.6     |                      | 7.675                | 0.860              |
|      |         |         | 7.725                |                      |                    |
|      | 3       | 8.5     |                      | 7.763                | 1.095              |
|      |         |         | 7.8                  |                      |                    |
|      | 4       | 8.8     |                      | 7.838                | 1.123              |
|      |         |         | 7.875                |                      |                    |
| 4    | 1       | 7.3     |                      | 7.938                | 0.920              |
|      |         |         | 8                    |                      |                    |
|      | 2       | 6.9     |                      | 8.075                | 0.854              |
|      |         |         | 8.15                 |                      |                    |
|      | 3       | 9.0     |                      |                      |                    |
|      | 4       | 9.4     |                      |                      |                    |

d) Arrange the ratios by quarter and then calculate the average ratio by quarter in order to eliminate the random influence.

For example, for quarter 1

$(0.975+0.929+0.920)/3=0.941$

e)   The final step, shown below, adjusts the average ratio slightly (for example, for quarter 1, 0.941 becomes 0.940), which will be the seasonal index, as shown in Table 23.4.

**Table 23.4: Seasonal Component Calculations**

| Quarter | Sea. Rand.<br>SR | Seasonal<br>Factor S | Adjusted<br>S |
|---------|------------------|----------------------|---------------|
| 1       | 0.975            |                      |               |
|         | 0.929            |                      |               |
|         | 0.920            | 0.941                | 0.940         |
| 2       | 0.863            |                      |               |
|         | 0.860            |                      |               |
|         | 0.854            | 0.859                | 0.858         |
| 3       | 1.081            |                      |               |
|         | 1.065            |                      |               |
|         | 1.095            | 1.080                | 1.079         |
| 4       | 1.113            |                      |               |
|         | 1.135            |                      |               |
|         | 1.123            | 1.124                | 1.123         |
|         |                  | 4.004                | 4.000         |

*Step 2*: After obtaining the seasonal index, we must first remove the effect of season from the original time series. This process is referred to as deseasonalizing the time series. For this, we must divide the original series by the seasonal index for that quarter. This is shown in Table 23.5 and graphed in Fig. 23.2.

*Step 3*: Looking at the graph in Figure 23.2, we see the time series seem to have an upward linear trend. To identify this trend, we develop the least squares trend equation. This procedure is also shown in Table 23.5.

**Figure 23.2: Quarterly DVD sales time series – original versus deseasonalized**

**Table 23.5: Deseasonalized Data**

| Year | Quarter | Sales | Seas. S | Des. Data | t | tY | t² |
|------|---------|-------|---------|-----------|---|-----|-----|
| 1 | 1 | 5.8 | 0.940 | 6.17 | 1 | 6.17 | 1 |
|   | 2 | 5.1 | 0.858 | 5.94 | 2 | 11.89 | 4 |
|   | 3 | 7.0 | 1.079 | 6.49 | 3 | 19.46 | 9 |
|   | 4 | 7.5 | 1.123 | 6.68 | 4 | 26.72 | 16 |
| 2 | 1 | 6.8 | 0.940 | 7.23 | 5 | 36.17 | 25 |
|   | 2 | 6.2 | 0.858 | 7.23 | 6 | 43.35 | 36 |
|   | 3 | 7.8 | 1.079 | 7.23 | 7 | 50.59 | 49 |
|   | 4 | 8.4 | 1.123 | 7.48 | 8 | 59.86 | 64 |
| 3 | 1 | 7.0 | 0.940 | 7.45 | 9 | 67.01 | 81 |
|   | 2 | 6.6 | 0.858 | 7.69 | 10 | 76.91 | 100 |
|   | 3 | 8.5 | 1.079 | 7.88 | 11 | 86.64 | 121 |
|   | 4 | 8.8 | 1.123 | 7.84 | 12 | 94.07 | 144 |
| 4 | 1 | 7.3 | 0.940 | 7.76 | 13 | 100.94 | 169 |
|   | 2 | 6.9 | 0.858 | 8.04 | 14 | 112.57 | 196 |
|   | 3 | 9.0 | 1.079 | 8.34 | 15 | 125.09 | 225 |
|   | 4 | 9.4 | 1.123 | 8.37 | 16 | 133.98 | 256 |
|   |   |   |   | 117.82 | 136 | 1051.43 | 1496 |

| | | | |
|---|---|---|---|
| t-bar= | 8.5 | y-bar= | 7.3638 |
| b = | 0.1469 | | |
| a = | 6.1147 | | |

which means y = 6.1147 + 0.1469 t for the forecast periods:

| t= | 17 |
|---|---|
| | 18 |
| | 19 |
| | 20 |

**Table 23.6: Quarter-To-Quarter Sales Forecasts for Year 5**

| Year | Quarter | Trend Forecast | | Seasonal Factor | Quarterly Forecast |
|---|---|---|---|---|---|
| 5 | 1 | 8.6128 | (a) | 0.940 | 8.0971 |
| | 2 | 8.7598 | | 0.858 | 7.5170 |
| | 3 | 8.9067 | | 1.079 | 9.6121 |
| | 4 | 9.0537 | | 1.123 | 10.1632 |

Note: (a) y = 6.1147 + 0.1469 t = 6.1147 + 0.1469 (17) = 8.6128

*Step 4*: Develop the forecast using the trend equation and adjust these forecasts to account for the effect of season. The quarterly forecast, as shown in Table 6.7, can be obtained by multiplying the forecast based on trend times the seasonal factor.

### How is it used and applied?

The classical decomposition model is time-series model used for forecasting. This means that the method can used only to fit the time-series data, whether it is monthly, quarterly, or annual. The types of time-series data the company deals with include earnings, cash flows, market share, and costs. As long as the time series displays the patterns of seasonality and cyclicality, the model constructed should be very effective in projecting the future variable.

## 24. Measuring Accuracy of Forecasts

### Introduction

The performance of a forecast should be checked against its own record or against that of other forecasts. There are various statistical measures that can be used to measure performance of the model.

## How is it computed?

The performance is measured in terms of forecasting error, where error is defined as the difference between a predicted value and the actual result. Error (e) = Actual (A) - Forecast (F)

There are three common measures for summarizing historical errors.

1.  *Mean absolute deviation* (MAD) is the mean or average of the sum of the errors for a given data set taken without regard to sign. The formula for calculating MAD is:

$$MAD = \frac{\Sigma |e|}{n}$$

2.  *Mean squared error* (MSE) is a measure of accuracy computed by squaring the individual errors for each item and then finding the average value of the sum of those squares. MSE gives greater weight to large errors than to small errors, since the errors are squared before being summed. The formula for calculating MSE is:

$$MSE = \frac{\Sigma e^2}{n - 1}$$

3.  *Mean absolute percentage error* (MAPE): Sometimes it is more useful to compute the forecasting errors in percentages rather than in amounts. The MAPE is calculated by finding the absolute error in each period, dividing this by the actual value of that period, and then averaging these absolute percentage errors, as shown below.

$$MAPE = \frac{\Sigma |e|/A}{n}$$

The following example illustrates the computation of MAD, MSE, and MAPE.

### Example 1

Sales data of a microwave oven manufacturer and calculation of relevant errors are given in Table 24.1.

## Table 24.1: Calculation of Errors

| Period | Actual(A) | Forecast(F) | e(A-F) | \|e\| | e² | Absolute Percent Error \|e\|/A |
|--------|-----------|-------------|--------|------|----|------------------------------|
| 1 | 217 | 215 | 2 | 2 | 4 | 0.0092 |
| 2 | 213 | 216 | -3 | 3 | 9 | 0.0014 |
| 3 | 216 | 215 | 1 | 1 | 1 | 0.0046 |
| 4 | 210 | 214 | -4 | 4 | 16 | 0.0190 |
| 5 | 213 | 211 | 2 | 2 | 4 | 0.0094 |
| 6 | 219 | 214 | 5 | 5 | 25 | 0.0023 |
| 7 | 216 | 217 | -1 | 1 | 1 | 0.0046 |
| 8 | 212 | 216 | -4 | 4 | 16 | 0.0019 |
| | | | -2 | 22 | 76 | 0.0524 |

Using the figures,

$$\text{MAD} = \Sigma \, |e| \, /n = 22/8 = 2.75$$
$$\text{MSE} = \Sigma \, e^2 \, / (n - 1) = 76/7 = 10.86$$
$$\text{MAPE} = \Sigma \, |e|/A / n = .0524/8 = .0066$$

One way these measures are used is to evaluate forecasting ability of alternative forecasting methods. For example, using either MAD or MSE, a forecaster could compare the results of exponential smoothing with □ (see Sec. 18) and select the one that performed best in terms of the lowest MAD or MSE for a given set of data. Also, it can help select the best initial forecast value for exponential smoothing.

## Figure 24.1: Monitoring forecast errors

## How is it used and applied?

It is important to monitor forecast errors to insure that the forecast is performing well. If the model is performing poorly based on some criteria, the forecaster might reconsider the use of the existing model or switch to another forecasting model or technique. Forecasting control can be accomplished by comparing forecasting errors to predetermined values, or limits. Errors that fall within the limits would be judged acceptable while errors outside of the limits would signal that corrective action is desirable (See Figure 24.1).

## Monitoring forecasts

Forecasts can be monitored using either tracking signals or control charts.

### *Tracking Signals*

A tracking signal is based on the ratio of cumulative forecast error to the corresponding value of MAD.

Tracking signal $= \Sigma(A - F) / MAD$

The resulting tracking signal values are compared to predetermined limits. These are based on experience and judgment and often range from plus or minus 3 to plus or minus 8. Values within the limits suggest that the forecast is performing adequately. By the same token, when the signal goes beyond this range, corrective action is appropriate.

### *Example 2*

Returning Example 1, the deviation and cumulative deviation have already been computed:

MAD $= \Sigma |A - F| / n = 22 / 8 = 2.75$

Tracking signal $= \Sigma (A - F) / MAD = -2 / 2.75 = -0.73$

A tracking signal is as low as - 0.73, which is substantially below the limit (-3 to -8). It would not suggest any action at this time.

*Note:* After an initial value of MAD has been computed, the estimate of the MAD can be continually updated using exponential smoothing.

$MAD_t = \alpha(A - F) + (1 - \alpha) MAD_{t-1}$

### *Control Charts*

The control chart approach involves setting upper and lower limits for individual forecasting errors instead of cumulative errors. The limits are multiples of the estimated standard deviation of forecast, $S_f$, which is the square root of MSE. Frequently, control limits are set at 2 or 3 standard deviations.

$$\pm 2(\text{or } 3) S_f$$

*Note:* Plot the errors and see if all errors are within the limits, so that the forecaster can visualize the process and determine if the method being used is in control.

## Example 3

For the sales data in Table 24.2, using the naive forecast, we will determine if the forecast is in control. For illustrative purposes, we will use 2 sigma control limits.

**Table 24.2: Error Calculations**

| Year | Sales | Forecasts | Error | Error$^2$ |
|------|-------|-----------|-------|-----------|
| I | 320 | | | |
| 2 | 326 | 320 | 6 | 36 |
| 3 | 310 | 326 | -16 | 256 |
| 4 | 317 | 310 | 7 | 49 |
| 5 | 315 | 317 | -2 | 4 |
| 6 | 318 | 315 | 3 | 9 |
| 7 | 310 | 318 | -8 | 64 |
| 8 | 316 | 310 | 6 | 36 |
| 9 | 314 | 316 | -2 | 4 |
| 10 | 317 | 314 | 3 | 9 |
| | | | -3 | 467 |

First, compute the standard deviation of forecast errors

$$S_f = \sqrt{e^2/(n-1)} = \sqrt{467/(9-1)} = \sqrt{58.375} = 7.64$$

Two sigma limits are then plus or minus 2(7.64) = -15.28 to +15.28

Note that the forecast error for year 3 is below the lower bound, so the forecast is not in control (See Figure 24.2). The use of other methods such as moving average, exponential smoothing, or regression might produce a better forecast.

*Note:* A system of monitoring forecasts needs to be developed. The computer may be programmed to print a report showing the past history when the tracking signal "trips" a limit. For example, when a type of exponential smoothing is used, the system may try a different value of $\alpha$ (so the forecast will be more responsive) and to continue forecasting.

**Figure 24.2: Control charts for forecasting errors**

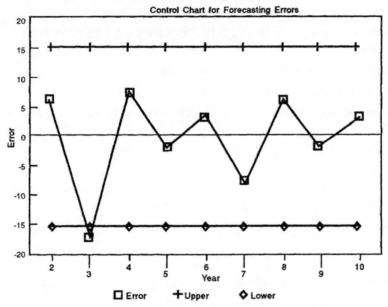

## 25. Cost of Prediction Errors

### Introduction

There is always a cost involved in a failure to predict a certain variable accurately. The cost of prediction errors associated with sales, expenses, and purchases can be significant.

### How is it computed?

The cost of the prediction error is basically the contribution or profit lost because of an inaccurate prediction. It can be measured in terms of lost sales, disgruntled customers, or idle machines.

### Example

Assume that a retail store has been selling a toy doll having a cost of $0.60 for $1.00 each. The fixed cost is $300. The store has no privilege to return any unsold dolls. It has predicted sales of 2,000 dolls. However, unforeseen competition has reduced sales to 1,500 dolls. The cost of its prediction error—that is, its failure to predict demand accurately, is calculated as follows:

1.  Initial predicted sales = 2,000 dollars

    Optimal decision: purchase 2,000 dollars

    Expected net income = $500 [(2,000 dollars x $0.40 contribution) – $300 fixed cost]

2.  Alternative parameter value = 1,500 dolls

    Optimal decision: purchase 1500 dollars

    Expected net income = $300 [(1,500 dollars x $0.40 contribution) – $300 fixed cost]

3.  Results of original decision under alternative parameter value

    Expected net income:

    Revenue (1,500 dolls x $1.00) – cost of dollars (2,000 dollars x $0.60) – $300 fixed cost = $1,500 – $1,200 – $300 = $0

4.  Cost of prediction error = (2) – (3) = $300

## How is it used and applied?

It is important to determine the cost of the prediction error in order to minimize the potential detrimental effect of future profitability. The cost of the prediction error can be substantial, depending on the circumstances. For example, failure to make an accurate projection of sales could result in poor production planning, too much or too little purchase of labor, and so on, thereby causing potentially huge financial losses.

Business people need to keep track of past prediction records to ensure that (1) future costs can be minimized and (2) better forecasting methods can be developed.

# 26. $\chi^2$ (Chi-Square Test)

## Introduction

The $\chi^2$ (chi-square) test is a statistical test of the significance of a difference between classifications or sub-classifications. The test is applied to sample data in testing whether or not two qualitative population variables are independent.

## How is the test performed?

The $\chi^2$ test involves three steps.

*Step 1*. Calculate the $\chi^2$ statistic, which is defined as:

$$\chi^2 = \frac{\Sigma(f_0 - f_e)^2}{f_e}$$

Where $f_0$ = individual observed frequencies of each class

$f_e$ = individual expected frequencies of each class

*Step 2.* Find the table value at a given level of significance (see Table 6 in the Appendix).

*Step 3.* If the calculated value is greater than the table value, we reject the full hypothesis, which means that the two variable are classifications are associated.

## Example

Consider the following survey regarding restaurants:

|  | With outdoor cafe | Without outdoor cafe | Total |
|---|---|---|---|
| With à la carte menu | 466 | 169 | 635 |
| With prix fixe menu | 180 | 29 | 209 |
| Total | 646 | 198 | 844 |

The null hypothesis is: The menu and the indoor/outdoor cafes are independent.

In order to calculate $\chi^2$, we need to construct an expected value table on the basis of the assumption that menu and indoor/outdoor cafes are independent of each other. If no association exists, it is to be expected that the proportion of à la carte and prix fixe restaurants with outdoor cafes or tables will be the same as that without outdoor cafes. First, we compute the expected frequencies based on the premise of independence:

$635/844 = 0.7524$ $\qquad$ $209/844 = 0.2476$

Now, we can compute the expected values from the proportions of totals as follows:

| 0.7524 | x | 646 | = | 486 |
|---|---|---|---|---|
| 0.2476 | x | 646 | = | 160 |
| 0.7524 | x | 198 | = | 149 |
| 0.2476 | x | 198 | = | 49 |

These expected values give the following table:

|  | With outdoor cafe | Without outdoor cafe | Total |
|---|---|---|---|
| With à la carte menu | 486 | 149 | 635 |
| With prix fixe menu | 160 | 49 | 209 |
| Total | 646 | 198 | 844 |

*Step 1.* Calculate $\chi^2$. We are interested in how far the observed table differs from the expected table.

$$\chi^2 = \frac{(466 - 486)^2}{486} + \frac{(180 - 160)^2}{160} + \frac{(169 - 149)^2}{149} + \frac{(29 - 49)^2}{49}$$

$$= 14.171$$

*Step 2.* $\chi^2$ value at the 0.05 level of significance with one degree of freedom (from Table 6 in the Appendix) is 3.841. The degree of freedom is calculated as (no. rows − 1) x (no. of columns − 1) = (2 − 1) x (2 − 1) = 1.

*Step 3.* As shown in Fig. 26.1, since the calculated value is greater than the table value (14.171 > 3.841), we reject the null hypothesis, which means that the menu is associated with the outdoor/indoor restaurant setup.

**Figure 26.1: Chi-square test and rejection area.**

## How is it used and applied?

The chi-square test has many applications in business. It is a statistical test of independence (or association), to determine if membership in categories of one variable is different as a function of membership in the categories of a second variable. It is important to note, however, that there are limitations to this test: (1) The sample must be big enough for the expected frequencies for each cell (rule of thumb: at least 5); and (2) the test does not tell anything about the direction of an association.

Managers need to know whether the differences they observe among several sample proportions are significant or due only to chance. For example, marketing managers are concerned that their brand's share may be unevenly distributed throughout the country. They conduct a survey in which the country is divided into specific number of geographic regions and see if consumer's decisions as to whether or not to purchase the company's brand has anything to do with the geographic location. As another example, a financial manager might be interested in the differences in capital structure within different firm sizes in a certain industry. To see if firm sizes have the same capital structure (or firm sizes have nothing to do with the capital structure), what he or she needs to do is to survey a group of firms with assets of different amounts and divide them into groups. Each firm can be classified according to predetermined debt/equity ratio groups.

# Part 4
# Managing Cash and Receivables

## 27. Cash Flow Statement

### Introduction

Current profitability is only one important factor in success. Also essential is cash flow. In fact, a business can be profitable and still have a cash crisis. An example is a small business with a high level of credit sales but with a very long collection period. The business shows a profit but does not have the cash from those sales.

It is essential to know your cash flow in order to plan adequately. Should you cut back on cash payments? Where are you obtaining cash flow? Where are you spending your money? What products are cash drains or cash surpluses? Is there adequate money to pay bills and purchase required equipment? Are you liquid?

A *statement of cash flows* is useful because it provides valuable data that are not available in the balance sheet and income statement. The statement presents the sources and uses of cash and is a basis for cash flow analysis.

### How is it Computed?

The statement of cash flows classifies cash receipts and cash payments from (1) operating, (2) investing, and (3) financing activities. Let's look at each of these major sections.

1.   *Operating activities* relate to the manufacturing and selling of or the rendering of services. Cash inflows that come from operating activities include (a) cash sales or collections on receivables and (b) cash receipts from interest income

and dividend income. Cash outflows include (a) cash paid for merchandise and (b) cash paid for expenses.

2.  *Investing activities* relate to the purchase and sale of fixed assets (such as equipment and machinery) and the purchase of stocks and bonds of other businesses. Cash inflows comprise (a) amounts received from selling fixed assets and (b) receipts from sales of stocks and bonds of other companies. Cash outflows include (a) payments to purchase fixed assets and (b) disbursements to buy stocks and bonds of other entities.

3.  *Financing activities* relate to borrowing and repayment and to issuing stock and reacquiring previously issued shares. Cash inflows comprise (a) funds obtained from loans and (b) funds received from the sale of stock. Cash outflows include (a) paying off debt, and (b) repurchase of stock.

## Example

Consider Mr. Paul, who owns a business that sells appliances. The statement of cash flows for this small business follows:

| | | |
|---|---:|---:|
| Cash flow from operating activities: | | |
| Net income | | $30,500 |
| Add (deduct) items not impacting cash: | | |
| Depreciation | $ 3,500 | |
| Decrease in accounts receivable | 2,500 | |
| Increase in prepaid insurance and rent | (1,000) | |
| Increase in accounts payable | 2,000 | 7,000 |
| Net cash flow from operating activities | | $37,500 |
| Cash flow from investing activities: | | |
| Purchase of land | $(17,500) | |
| Purchase of building | (15,000) | |
| Purchase of store furnishings | (9,000) | |
| | | (41,500) |
| Cash flow from financing activities: | | |
| Long-term loans | $ 15,000 | 15,000 |
| Net increase in cash | | $11,000 |

An evaluation of the statement shows that earnings and cash flow have improved. This indicates good earnings performance as well as the fact that earnings are backed up by cash. The decrease in accounts receivable may reveal better collection efforts. The increase in accounts payable is a sign that suppliers have confidence in the business and are willing to provide interest-free financing. The acquisition of land, a building, and furnishings indicates a growing business undertaking capital expansion. The long-term loan indicates that part of the financing of assets is through debt. Overall, there was an increase in cash of $11,000 along with a net income of $30,500. This is a favorable sign taking into account the significant capital expenditures made.

## How is it Used and Applied?

Cash flow analysis is a valuable tool. The cash flow statement provides information about the way your business generates and uses cash. An analysis of the statement is helpful in appraising past performance, showing why cash flow increased or decreased, as well as looking at future direction, forecasting liquidity trends, and evaluating the ability to pay debt at maturity.

An analysis of the operating section determines the adequacy of cash flow generated from sales to satisfy operating expenses. Are you obtaining positive future net cash flows from your daily activities?

In examining the investing section, an increase in fixed assets indicates expansion and future growth. A contraction in business occurring from the sale of fixed assets without adequate replacement is a negative sign.

An appraisal of the financing section reveals the type of financing used. A determination should be made of the risk and the cost of obtaining those funds.

The statement of cash flows is different from the income statement. The statement of cash flows presents the cash receipts and cash payments of the business by source. It reveals where the cash is coming from and where it is going. The statement emphasizes cash flows; its bottom line is the cash balance at the end of the period.

The income statement looks not at cash flows but at the *profitability* of the business. It reveals net income—revenue less expenses. Revenue, which is income earned from operations and may or may not involve cash receipts, is earned from sales of merchandise and the rendering of services. A credit sale is recorded as revenue, although it does not involve receiving money; expenses which are incurred to obtain revenue and may or may not involve cash payment, may result from either conducting operations (e.g., operating expenses) or financing the business (e.g., interest expense). Bills received for accrued expenses during the year (e.g., utilities) reduce profit but do not involve cash payments until such later time when these bills are actually paid. For example, a telephone bill covering the month of December 2007 is an expense for the year 2007. This expense reduces net income. However, the bill may not be paid until January 2008.

# 28. Using Float

## Introduction

*Float* is defined as the difference between the cash balance your records show and the cash balance the bank's records show. Float results from writing checks that have not yet cleared (disbursement float). Float makes it possible for your bank book balance to be negative while the bank shows your balance as being positive.

There are several types of delays in processing checks:

1.  Mail float—the time required for a check to move from someone to you.

2.  Processing float—the time needed for you to enter the payment in your records.

3.  Deposit collection float—the time for a check to clear.

    Figure 28.1 is a schematic float calendar for a business.

## Figure 28.1: Schematic float calendar

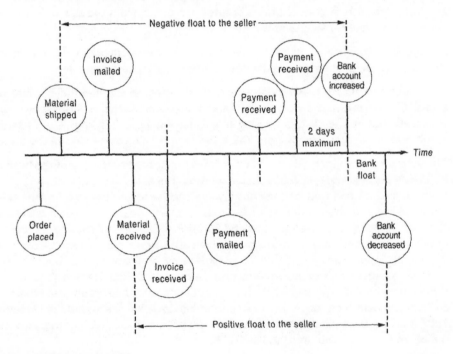

## How is it Computed?

The acceleration of cash inflow enables you to profit through reduced collection float. If deposits average $20,000 per day and the collection time can be reduced by 3 days, the business will have $60,000 in additional usable funds. Assuming a rate of return of 10 percent, the value of those funds is $6000 per year in savings.

If float is used effectively, you may get an "interest-free" loan from the bank. For example, assume you have a $5,000 balance in your checking account (non-interest-bearing) and $150,000 in your money market account. You write a check for $20,000, which you expect to clear in 5 days. On the fifth day, you transfer $15,000 from the savings account to the checking account to cover the check. You have successfully used 5 days of float to earn interest on the $15,000 for 5 days. The check will clear because your checking account balance is $20,000 ($15,000 + $5,000).

The amount of float depends on both (1) the time lag and (2) the dollars involved. Float may be determined in dollar-days, multiplying the lag in days by the dollar amount delayed. The cost of float is the interest lost because the money was not available for investment or the interest paid because money had to be borrowed during the lag period. The cost of float is computed by multiplying the average daily float by the cost of capital (opportunity cost) for the time period under consideration.

## Example

George Harris owns a mail-order business and is concerned about cash float. He examines the following information:

| Item | Dollar amount | | Number of days | | Dollar days |
|------|---------------|---|----------------|---|-------------|
| X | $35,000 | x | 2 | = | $ 70,000 |
| Y | 15,000 | x | 1 | = | 15,000 |
| Z | 40,000 | x | 5 | = | 200,000 |
| | $90,000 | | | | $285,000 |

Average daily float = $285,000/30 = $9,500

Average daily receipts = $90,000/30 = $3,000

Average daily days = $285,000/$90 000 = 3.1667 days

Average daily float = $3,000 x 3.1667 = $9,500

Average cost of float = $9,500 x 0.09 = $855

## How is it Used and Applied?

It is in your best interest to receive payments from your customers as quickly as possible and to make payments to your creditors as slowly as possible so that you can invest the funds and maximize your investment return. When you receive checks from customers, deposit them immediately. This allows you to have use of the funds as soon as the checks clear and minimizes the possibility that the check will be returned for insufficient funds. If you suspect the payor is in financial difficulty, it is best to make your claim against any available funds as quickly as possible. Similarly, it is smart to delay payments to creditors for as long as possible so that you can retain use of the money until the last minute.

Determine the causes for delays in depositing cash receipts and take corrective action. Ascertain how and where the cash receipts come, how cash is transferred to your bank account, the bank's policy regarding funds availability, and the length of time between when a check is received and when it is deposited. You want money available to you as soon as possible so you can earn interest.

See Sec. 29, Using a Lockbox to Get Money Sooner.

# 29. Using a Lockbox to Get Money Sooner

## Introduction

If your business receives many checks from customers, time and money are spent in processing these deposits. A lockbox arrangement may be appropriate.

A lockbox is a collection point (such as a post office box) placed near customers. Customer payments are mailed to strategic post office boxes in their local areas in order to shorten mailing and depositing time. Banks collect from these boxes several times a day and make deposits to your account.

## How is it Computed?

The following computation will help to determine whether a lockbox arrangement is feasible:

> Return on early collection of cash
> Less: Cost of lockbox
> Advantage or disadvantage

## *Example 1*

If it takes about 7 days to receive and deposit payments from customers, a lockbox arrangement for Beautiful Furniture may reduce the float time to 5 days. Assume that average daily collections are $50,000 and the return rate is 13 percent.

If a lockbox system is initiated, the decline in outstanding cash balances would be:

$$2 \text{ days} \times \$50,000 = \$100,000$$

The return that could be earned on these funds is:

$$\$100,000 \times 0.13 = \$13,000$$

The maximum monthly charge that should be paid for the lockbox system is:

$$\frac{\$13,000}{12} = \$1,083$$

## Example 2

A business owner is thinking of using a lockbox system costing $14,000 per year. Daily collections average $40,000. The lockbox arrangement will reduce the float period by 3 days. The rate of return is 12 percent.

The cost-benefit analysis is:

| | |
|---|---:|
| Return on early collection of cash | $14,400 |
| Less: Cost | 14,000 |
| Advantage of lockbox | $  400 |

## How is it Used and Applied?

To help determine whether you should use a lockbox, calculate the average dollar amount of checks received, the cost of clerical operations that would be eliminated, and the reduction in "mail float" days. Because per-item processing costs are typically significant, it is most beneficial to use a lockbox with low-volume, high-dollar collections. The system is becoming available to businesses with high-volume, low-dollar receipts as technological advances lower the per-item cost of lockboxes.

# 30. Bank Reconciliation

## Introduction

Preparation of a bank reconciliation is based on information included in the bank statement: deposits made, checks cleared, and charges or credits (deductions or additions) to the account. For example, a bank charge is a deduction from an account, whereas the amount collected on a customer's note is an addition. Canceled checks, debit memoranda for charges, and credit memoranda for credits are typically enclosed with the bank statement.

The ending balance on the bank statement rarely agrees with the ending balance in the cash accounts according to the books; thus, a bank reconciliation is needed to reflect the reconciling items. Once the reconciliation is completed, the adjusted bank balance must agree with the adjusted book balance. When this occurs, both records are correct.

## How is it Computed?

The cash balance per the books must be the same as the balance in the bank account at the end of the period. Reconciling differences relate to (1) items shown on the business' books but not on the bank statement and (2) items shown on the bank statement but not on the business' books. Examples and explanations of each follow.

## Reconciling Items for the Bank Statement

The bank balance is adjusted for several types of items that are reflected on the business' books but not on the bank statement.

### Outstanding checks.

Checks that have been issued by the business but have not yet cleared the bank. The total of the outstanding checks is deducted from the bank balance. An exception is an unclear certified check—a check for which the back immediately sets aside funds for payment. A certified check is not deemed outstanding, since both parties—the business and the bank—know about it.

### Deposits in transit.

Cash that has been received at the end of the period but is either not yet deposited or was deposited after the bank prepared its statement. Deposits in transit are added to the bank balance.

### Errors in recording checks.

Mistakes include transposition errors made in the recording of checks. An item should be added to the back balance, for instance, if it was previously overstated on the books.

### Bank errors in charging or crediting the business account.

If a business account is charged in error for another firm's cleared check, the business bank balance is understated, so the business should add the amount of this check to its own bank balance, However, if a deposit made by the business was incorrectly credited to the account of another business, the other business should make the adjustment and reduce its bank balance.

## Reconciling Items for the Books.

The books balance (cash account) is adjusted for items that are shown on the bank statement but are not reflected on the books. Such items include the following:

## Bank charges.

Bank service fees reduce the book balance, but these amounts are not known until the bank statement is received. Examples include monthly service charges, cost per check, check printing costs, and stop-payment fees.

## NSF (not sufficient funds) checks.

Checks that have "bounced" due to insufficient funds in the customer's checking account. In such a case, the business bank issues a debit memorandum for the dishonored amount and the book balance is reduced.

## Collections.

Notes and other items collected by the bank for a nominal fee. The proceeds received less the charge (in the form of credit memorandum) are credited to the business' account. The net amount is added to the book balance.

## Errors on the books.

Various kinds of mistakes may occur on the books. Two examples of mistakes and corrections follow (assume that the amount of the check is correct).

1.  A $100 check is written, which is more that the $90 amount entered as a cash disbursement. In this case, cash disbursements are understated by $10; thus, the balance per books should be reduced by this amount.

2.  A $50 check is written, which is less than the $60 amount shown as a cash disbursement. Here, cash disbursements are overstated, and the book balance should be increased by $10 to correct the error.

After the bank reconciliation has been prepared, journal entries are made for the reconciling items that affect the book balance. A journal entry is needed because the amounts on the books must be updated to reflect any items on the bank statement of which the business was unaware during the period. Reconciling items entered as adjustments to the bank balance are journalized, however, because they are already on the books. Such reconciling items will probably be shown on the next back statement.

## Example

A business provides the following date in connection with preparation of its bank reconciliation on Juan 30, 20x8;

| | |
|---|---:|
| Balance per bank | $4,889 |
| Balance per books | 440 |
| Outstanding checks: | |
| Check 410 | 500 |
| Check 423 | 200 |
| Deposit in transit | 300 |
| Collection on note: | |
| Principal | 200 |
| Interest | 16 |
| Collection fee on note | 12 |
| NSF check | 100 |
| Monthly service charge | 15 |

The following shows the proper form for the bank reconciliation:

## A BUSINESS
### Bank Reconciliation
### June 30, 20x8

| | | |
|---|---:|---:|
| Balance per bank | | $4,889 |
| Add: Deposits in transit | | <u>300</u> |
| | | $5,189 |
| | | |
| Less: Outstanding checks | | |
| 410 | $500 | |
| 423 | <u>200</u> | 700 |
| Adjusted bank balance | | <u>**$4,489**</u> |
| | | |
| Balance per books | | $440 |
| Add: Proceeds on note | | 216 |
| | | <u>$4,616</u> |
| | | |
| Less: | | |
| NSF check | $100 | |
| Collection fee | 12 | |
| Service charge | <u>15</u> | 127 |
| Adjusted book balance | | <u>**$4,489**</u> |

## How is it Used and Applied?

A bank's reconciliation is prepared and used by a business to assure that the balance per the depositor's records agrees with the balance per the bank's records after accounting for all reconciling items. If a discrepancy exists after the bank reconciliation has been prepared, an investigation should be make to uncover any errors or irregularities, such as fraud perpetrated by the bookkeeper.

# 31. Putting Excess Cash to Work

## Introduction

The business owner should invest excess cash for a return but still retain liquidity. Marketable securities are readily tradable securities with short-term debt maturities (i.e., 1 year or less). The management of marketable securities is a major part of cash management. Some businesses have a marketable security portfolio in excess of their cash balance. The objectives of investing in marketable securities are to ensure that cash is readily available, to ensure the safety of principal, and to minimize the risk of loss.

## How is it Computed?

Holding-period return (HPR) is the total return earned from holding an investment (such as stock) for a period of time. It is determined from current income (dividend income or interest income) and capital gain or loss. Holding-period return is computed as:

$$\text{HPR} = \frac{\text{current income} + \text{capital gain (or loss)}}{\text{purchase price}}$$

### *Example*

Consider the following investments in Stock X and Stock Y over a 1-year period of ownership:

|                                          | Stock X | Stock X |
|------------------------------------------|---------|---------|
| Purchase price (beginning of year)       | $100    | $100    |
| Cash dividend received (during the year) | 8       | 12      |
| Sales price (end of year)                | 110     | 95      |

Combining the capital gain (or loss with the current income, the total return on each investment is found as follows:

|  | Stock X | Stock Y |
|---|---|---|
| Cash dividends | $ 8 | $12 |
| Capital gain (loss) | 10 | (5) |
| Total return | $18 | $ 7 |

$$\text{HPR (Stock X)} = \frac{\$8 + 10}{\$100} = \frac{\$18}{\$100} = 18\%$$

$$\text{HPR (Stock Y)} = \frac{\$12 - \$5}{\$100} = \frac{\$7}{\$100} = 7\%$$

## How is it Used and Applied?

In selecting marketable securities, consider the type, marketability, maturity date, rate of return, transaction cost, default risk, maximum amount to be invested, maximum/minimum dollar amount to be traded, and trend in interest rates. The business owner must balance the return desired against the risk he or she is willing to assume. As a general rule, the return on marketable securities is low, but they are liquid and safe. Risk takes the form of a lack of marketability, possible loss of principal (the amount invested), and the susceptibility to changing interest rates (e.g., as interest rates rise, the price of fixed-income securities declines). The business owner should demand a higher return when default risk is greater and the maturity period is longer.

## 32. What Is the Equivalent Tax Yield?

### Introduction

The equivalent taxable yield is the rate of return on a nontaxable investment as it would be on a taxable basis. Today, all business owners are tax conscious.

Bonds issued by states, school districts, port authorities, counties, and fire districts are tax exempt. On the other hand, bonds issued by corporations yield taxable income. As a result, a municipal bond investment remains an attractive tax savings opportunity for all small business owners.

### How is it Computed?

$$\text{Equivalent taxable yield} = \frac{\text{Tax} - \text{free return}}{1 - \text{marginal tax rate}}$$

The business owner is usually faced with the decision of whether to purchase taxable or exempt bonds. The decision is easy if the risk of the investments is assumed to be equal. A business owner should invest in exempt bonds instead of taxable bonds if the interest on the exempt bonds is greater than the interest on the taxable bonds times 1 minus the taxpayer's marginal tax rate expressed as a decimal. This means that the business owner should invest in tax-exempt municipal bonds if

Return on the tax-exempt bonds > Return on the taxable bonds x
(1 - marginal tax bracket)

## Example 1

Jack Tryon operates as a sole proprietorship and is in the 28 percent tax bracket. He is offered a tax-exempt bond paying 9 percent interest, and a taxable corporate bond paying 12 percent. Jack should invest in the tax-exempt bond paying 9 percent because its yield will be greater than the 8.64 percent generated by the corporate taxable bond computed as follows:

$$12\% \times (1 - 0.28) = 8.64\%$$

## Example 2

Amanda Clinton is a 50 percent partner in a partnership that plans to purchase bonds. Both she and her partner are in the 31 percent tax bracket. The partnership is offered a tax-exempt bond paying 7 percent interest, and a taxable corporate bond paying 11 percent. The partnership should invest in the taxable bond paying 11 percent because its yield will be greater at 7.59 percent than the 7 percent yield generated by the tax-exempt municipal bond computed as follows:

$$11\% \times (1 - 0.31) = 7.59\%$$

## Example 3

The Payout Corporation is in the 25 percent tax bracket. The corporation is offered a tax-exempt bond paying 7 percent interest, and a taxable corporate bond paying 10 percent. The corporation should invest in the taxable bond paying 10 percent because its yield will be greater at 7.50 percent than the 7 percent yield generated by the tax-exempt municipal bond computed as follows:

$$10\% \times (1 - 0.25) = 7.50\%$$

## How is it Used and Applied?

Individuals use the equivalent taxable yield to determine what their tax-free rate of return would be on a taxable basis. This enables them to compare alternative tax-free and taxable investments.

The main factor in deciding whether to make an investment is the determination of equivalent taxable yield. If the income generated by the investment is fully taxable, then any earnings must be further reduced by the applicable tax rate to determine after-tax earnings. Other factors such as liquidity and marketability also influence the risk pertaining to the investment.

Many business owners consider the exclusion of interest on municipal bonds to be one of the few remaining tax shelters for them. This means that if the business owner operated as a corporation, it would avoid taxes of as much as 35 percent on bond interest. If the enterprise operated as either a sole proprietorship or a partnership, the tax savings would be as much as 39.6 percent.

# 33. Determining the Optimal Cash

## Introduction

There are two techniques for deciding how much cash to maintain at any given time, considering that both holding cash and investing have both advantages and disadvantages. The purpose of cash models is to satisfy cash requirements at the least cost.

## How is it Computed?

Two models are useful in determining the optimal level of cash.

### *The Baumol's Model.*

The Baumol's model attempts to determine the optimum amount of transaction cash under conditions of certainty. The objective is to minimize the sum of the fixed costs of transactions and the opportunity cost of holding cash balances. These costs are expressed as:

$$F \frac{(T)}{C} + i \frac{(C)}{2}$$

where F = fixed cost of a transaction

T = total cash needed for the time period

i = interest rate on marketable securities

C = cash balance

The optimal level of cash (C*) is:

$$C^* = \sqrt{\frac{2FT}{i}}$$

## Example I

You estimate a cash need for $4,000,000 in cash over a 1-month period. The cash account is expected to be disbursed at a constant rate. The opportunity interest rate is 6 percent per annum, or 0.5 percent for a 1-month period, and that the transaction cost each time borrowing or withdrawing occurs is $100.

The optimal transaction size (the optimal borrowing or withdrawal lot size) and the number of transactions that the company should make during the month is calculated as follows:

$$C^* = \sqrt{\frac{2FT}{i}} = \sqrt{\frac{2(100)(4,000,000)}{0.005}} = \$400,000$$

The optimal transaction size is $400,000. The average cash balance is:

$$\frac{C^*}{2} = \frac{\$400,000}{2} = \$200,000$$

The number of transactions required is:

$$\frac{\$4,000,000}{\$400,000} = 10 \text{ transactions during the month}$$

See Fig. 33.1 for a pictorial representation for this example.

**Figure 33.1: Optimal cash balance**

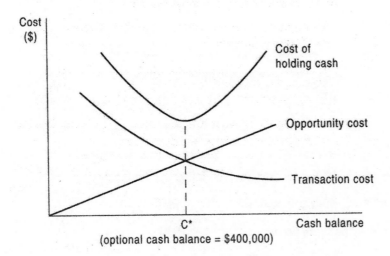

103

## The Miller-Orr Model.

You can use a stochastic model for cash management when *uncertainty* exists for cash payments—that is, there is irregularity of cash payments. The Miller Orr model sets upper and lower limits on cash balances. When the upper limit is reached, a transfer of cash to marketable securities is made. When the lower limit is reached, a transfer from securities to cash occurs. A transaction will not occur as long as the cash balance stays within the limits.

Factors taken into account in the Miller Orr model are the fixed costs of a securities transaction (F), assumed to be the same for buying as well as selling; the daily interest rate on marketable securities (i); and the variance of daily net cash flows ($\sigma^2$)--($\sigma$ is sigma). The objective is to meet cash requirements at the lowest possible cost. A major assumption of this model is the randomness of cash flows. The control limits in the Miller-Orr model are "*d*" dollars as an upper limit and 0 dollars at the lower limit. When the cash balance reaches the upper level, d less z dollars (optimal cash balance) of securities are bought, and the new balance becomes z dollars. When the cash balance equals zero, z dollars of securities are sold and the new balance again reaches z. Of course, in practice the minimum cash balance is established at an amount greater than zero because of delays in transfer; the higher minimum in effect acts as a safety buffer.

The optimal cash balance, z, is computed as

$$z = \sqrt[3]{\frac{3F\,\sigma^2}{4i}}$$

The optimal value for d is computed as 3z. The average cash balance approximates

$$\frac{(z+d)}{3}$$

LL = actual value for the lower limit LL is set by management.

The upper control limit, UL, can be computed as

$$UL = 3z - 2LL$$

## Example 2

You wish to use the Miller-Orr model. The following is supplied:

| | |
|---|---|
| Fixed cost of a securities transaction | $10 |
| Deviation in daily net cash flows | $50 |
| Daily interest rate on securities (10%/360) | 0.000277 |

The optimal cash balance, the upper limit of cash needed, and the average cash balance are determined as follows:

$$Z = \sqrt[3]{\frac{3(10)(50)}{4(0.000277)}} = \sqrt[3]{\frac{3(10)(50)}{0.001108}} = \sqrt[3]{\frac{1,500}{0.001108}} = \sqrt[3]{31,353,790}$$

$$= \$108$$

The optimal cash balance is $108; the upper limit is $324 (3 x $108); and the average cash balance is

$$\$144 = \left(\frac{\$108 + \$324}{3}\right)$$

When the upper limit of $324 is reached, $216 of securities ($324 - $108) will be purchased to bring the account to the optimal cash balance of $108. When the lower limit of zero dollars is reached, $108 of securities will be sold to again bring it to the optimal cash balance of $108.

**Figure 33.2: Optimal cash balance and limits**

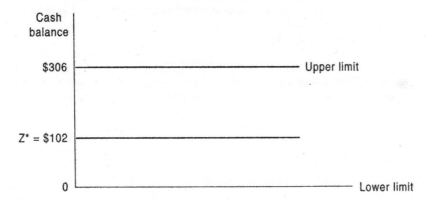

## How is it Used and Applied?

Cash management models can be used effectively to decide the right amount of cash to keep. You will not want to keep more money than necessary to cover day-to-day operating expenses. However, emergency cash funds are necessary. The models aid in finding the right balance between the cash balance and funds to be placed in short-term investment accounts. Financial managers can find the optimal amount of cash to have on hand based on needs, costs, rate of return, and other relevant factors. William Baumol's model is used to determine the optimum amount of transaction cash under known, certain business conditions. The objective is to minimize the sum of fixed costs associated with transactions and the opportunity cost of holding cash balances. The Miller-Orr model is a stochastic approach used when uncertainty exists regarding cash payments. This model embraces the following features:

◆ The model places upper and lower limits for cash balances.

◆ When the upper limit is reached, a transfer of cash is made to marketable securities.

◆ When the lower limit is reached, a transfer is made from marketable securities to cash.

◆ A transaction will not take place as long as the cash balance falls within the limits.

◆ The objective of the model is to meet cash requirements at the lowest possible cost.

# 34. Cash Ratios

## Definition

Cash utilization indicates how well your small business is using its money in running the business, keeping liquid to pay bills and earning a return. Cash availability measures how much money is free for your operating expenses and debt payments. Adequate cash flow is needed not only to stay afloat but also for expansion, purchase of new assets, and to pay vendors.

The need for cash and its utilization depends on the type of small business; a retail store selling high-priced appliances needs more cash to buy expensive inventory than a service-oriented business such as an accounting firm that has no inventory.

## How is it Computed?

Several cash ratios are commonly employed:

1. $\dfrac{\text{Cash flow}}{\text{Total debt}}$

2. $\dfrac{\text{CashFlow}}{\text{Long-term debt}}$

3. $\dfrac{\text{Cash + marketable securities}}{\text{Total current assets}}$

4. $\dfrac{\text{Cash + marketable securities}}{\text{Total current liabilities}}$

5. $\dfrac{\text{Cash + marketable securities + receivables}}{\text{Year's cash expenses}}$

6.  Cash flow-to-capital expenditures ratio:

$$\frac{\text{Cash flow from operations} - \text{dividends}}{\text{Expenditures for plant and equipment}}$$

7.  Cash flow adequacy ratio:

$$\frac{\text{Five-year sum of cash flow from operations}}{\text{Five-year sum of capital expenditure, inventory additions and cash dividends}}$$

## Example

Two cash flow ratios are calculated based on the following company information:

|                | 20x7        | 20x8        |
| -------------- | ----------- | ----------- |
| Cash flow      | $ 600,000   | $ 300,000   |
| Total debt     | 2,000,000   | 2,500,000   |
| Long-term debt | 1,000,000   | 1,300,000   |

The relevant ratios are:

|                             | 20x7 | 20x8 |
| --------------------------- | ---- | ---- |
| Cash flow to total debt     | 30%  | 12%  |
| Cash flow to long term debt | 60%  | 23%  |

From 20x7 to 20x8, the company has experienced a significant deterioration in liquidity. The company may be in a cash squeeze and unable to meet its obligations when they fall due.

## How is it Used and Applied?

The cash flow-to-total debt ratio indicates a business' ability to satisfy its debts. It is useful in predicting potential bankruptcy. Cash flow to long-term debt appraises the adequacy of available funds to meet concurrent obligations. Of course, not all the cash flow will be available to pay debt. Some of it will be needed for such things as buying new assets (e.g., property, plant, equipment, inventory).

The ratio of cash plus marketable securities to current liabilities indicates the amount of cash immediately available to satisfy short-term debt. This ratio is much more conservative than the acid test ratio (see Sec. 88, Quick (Acid Test) Ratio). The more your current debt is covered with cash and near-cash assets, the better will be your ability to meet supplier and creditor claims. Further, the ratio provides a "warning sign" of cash deficiencies and helps prevent a crisis situation in which current debt cannot be paid.

A high ratio of cash plus marketable securities to working capital makes it easier to obtain financing at reasonable rates because the liquidity of the small business appears better.

Concern is also directed to how many times a business' immediate liquid resources are sufficient to meet cash expenses. Cash can be improved through the better management of receivables and, inventory, encouraging cash sales rather than credit sales, delaying vendor payments, and borrowing money.

The cash flow-to-capital expenditures ratio indicates a business' ability to maintain plant and equipment from cash provided from operations, rather than by borrowing. You are better off obtaining funds internally from the business because there are no financing costs associated.

The purpose of the cash flow adequacy ratio is to determine the degree to which a business has generated sufficient cash flow from operations to cover capital expenditures and net investment in inventories. To remove cyclical and other unstable influences, a 5-year total is used in the computation. A ratio of 1 shows that the business has covered its needs based on attained growth levels without resorting to external financing. If the ratio goes below 1, internally generated cash may be insufficient to maintain current operating growth levels. This ratio may also reflect the effect of inflation on the funds needs of the business.

In evaluating cash, you should also note whether a portion is unavailable for use (restricted). For example, a compensating balance does not constitute "free" cash. (Interest income is not earned.) A compensating balance is a deposit a bank can use to offset an unpaid loan.

Cash held as a time deposit or in a temporary escrow account also is not available funds. An escrow account contains money you temporarily deposit with a neutral third party in conformity with a contract; you have no control over the escrow money until the terms of the agreement have been satisfied. When you sell store furniture and equipment, for example, the buyer might insist that you put escrow money on deposit for 2 months to reimburse the buyer for defects in the furniture and equipment needing repairs.

See Sec. 35, Cash Flow from Operations.

# 35. Cash Flow from Operations

## Introduction

Cash flow from operations represents the cash earnings of a small business. Utilization of cash flow ratios shows the degree to which net income is backed up by a liquid source of funds. Cash reinvestment into a business indicates the ability of the owner to position himself or herself for future growth.

## How is it Computed?

The process of analyzing a company's cash flow is as follows.

1.  Cash flow from operations is calculated as:

    | Net income |
    | --- |
    | Add: Noncash expenses (e.g., depreciation, amortization) |
    | Less: Noncash revenue (e.g., amortization of deferred revenue) |
    | Cash flow from operation |

2.  This calculation is followed by analyzing the operational cash flow over net income:

    $$\frac{\text{Cash flow from operations}}{\text{Net income}}$$

3.  A third calculation is derived by stating the cash flow generated from operations less cash payments required to pay debt principal, dividends, and capital expenditures.

4.  Cash reinvestment ratio is determined by identifying cash employed and cash obtained:

    Cash employed =

    Increases in gross plant and equipment + increase in net working capital

    Cash obtained = income after tax plus depreciation

5.  The cash reinvestment ratio is calculated as follows:

    $$\frac{\text{Cash employed}}{\text{Cash obtained}}$$

6.  Cash flow coverage ratio =

    $$\frac{\text{net operating income + lease expende + depreciation}}{\text{interest + lease expense + [preferred dividends/(1-taxrate)]-[principal payments/(1-tax rate)]}}$$

## *Example*

A condensed income statement for a company and the pertinent cash flow analysis follow:

| | | |
|---|---|---|
| Sales | | $1,000,000 |
| Less: Cost of sales | | 300,000 |
| Gross margin | | $ 700, 000 |
| Less: Operating expenses | $100,000 | |
| Salary | 200,000 | |
| Rent | 50,000 | |
| Telephone | 80,000 | |
| Depreciation | 60,000 | |
| Amortization expense | | |
| Total operating expenses | | 490,000 |
| Income before other items | | $ 210,000 |
| Other revenue and expense | | |
| Interest expense | $ 70,000 | |
| Amortization of deferred revenue | 40,000 | |
| Total revenue and expense | | 30,000 |
| Net income | | $180,000 |

The ratio of cash flow from operations to net income is 1.55, calculated as follows:
Cash flow from operations:

| | | |
|---|---|---|
| Net income | | $180,000 |
| Add: | | |
| Noncash expenses | $80,000 | |
| Depreciation | 60,000 | |
| Amortization expense | | |
| | 140,000 | |
| Less: Noncash revenue | | |
| Amortization of deferred revenue | | (40,000) |
| Cash flow from operations | | $280,000 |

$$\frac{\text{Cash flow from operations}}{\text{Net income}} = \frac{\$280,000}{\$180,000} = 1.55$$

## How is it Used and Applied?

Earnings are of higher quality if they are backed up by cash, since cash can be used to meet debt payments, buy fixed assets, and so forth.

A high cash reinvestment ratio indicates that more cash is being used in the business.

Further, a business with a high percentage of internally generated cash earnings has better liquidity.

See Sec;34, Cash Ratios.

# 36. Cash Forecasting

## Introduction

Accurate cash forecasting is important for the success of a small business. Cash forecasting is crucial in projecting financial needs, spotting areas of financial strength or weakness, formulating a realistic timetable in which to accomplish goals, and comparing expectations to actual results. Once you know your expected cash position, you can plan expenditures, such as asset acquisition, debt repayment, operating expenses, such as advertising, and wage settlements.

In deciding on the forecasting period to use, consider the nature of your operation. If you have stable sales, a quarterly forecast is suitable. On the other hand, if your sales are unstable, a monthly forecast will help you keep up to date.

The forecasting period also depends on your exposure to economic conditions and the business cycle; for example, if you are subject to 3 months seasonality, a quarterly forecasting period is logical.

## How is it Prepared?

There are two kinds of forecasts: short term and long term. A short-term forecast usually covers 1 year or less, while a long-term forecast covers more than 1 year. A long-term forecast is simply an extension of a short-term forecast.

A short-term forecast is more detailed and reliable than a long-term forecast because the short time span makes projections easier. A short-term forecast tells you whether you can carry on financial and operating activities over the next year and is crucial if you are experiencing cash problems or significant variability in cash. Will you need a short-term loan? When can you repay it? Do you have excess cash to invest? It is crucial for a small business to have a short-term forecast because of the need for tight control over cash.

The steps in constructing a short-term forecast are as follows:

1. Take into account temporary fluctuations in cash flow.
2. Select a representative period to depict cash flows, such as quarterly or monthly.
3. Plan for unusual cash receipts and cash payments.

A new small business should start off with a monthly forecast broken down by week, because control is essential in the early stages. Once the business matures, a quarterly forecast broken down by month is adequate.

The advantages to short-term forecasting are:

◆ Providing the basis for the long-term forecast

◆ Providing a schedule for loan repayments

◆ Timing of borrowing so as to lower interest costs

◆ Timing cash flow to take advantage of cash discounts for early payment to suppliers.

A long-term cash forecast shows major acquisitions of assets, major asset disposals, planned debt financing, and the introduction of new products and/or services. It also provides a basis for judging whether there is sufficient net cash inflows to support growth.

A forecast of cash collections and potential write-offs of customer balances is essential in cash budgeting. The critical step in making such a forecast is estimating the cash collection and bad debt percentages (based on an aging of customer balances) and applying them to sales or accounts receivable balances. Two examples follow.

## Example 1

Phil Blake owns a toy store. The accounts receivable balance on June 1 is $35,000, of which $20,000 applies to sales made in April and $15,000 applies to May sales. Past experience indicates that the pattern of collection is as follows: Month of sale, 45 percent; second month, 30 percent; third month, 24 percent; and uncollectible, 1 percent. Credit sales for June are $200,000. Cash collections for June are computed as follows:

| | |
|---|---|
| April sales ($20,000 x 24%/25%) | $ 19,200 |
| May sales ($15,000 x 30%/55%) | 8,182 |
| June sales ($200,000 x 45%) | 90,000 |
| Total | $117,382 |

## Example 2

The following information is provided for Milich's Clothing Store:

| | | | |
|---|---|---|---|
| Cash sales | $14,000 | $12,000 | $16,000 |
| Credit sales | $100,000 | $96,000 | $124,000 |

Previous experience based on aging of receivables shows that collections typically take place in the following pattern:

◆ No collections are made in the month of sale.

◆ Seventy percent of the sales of any month are collected in the following month.

◆ Twenty-five percent of sales are collected in the second following month.

◆ Five percent of sales are uncollectible.

November's cash receipts are:

Cash receipts:

| | |
|---|---|
| Cash sales | $ 16,000 |
| Cash collections | |
| September sales ($100,000 3 25%) | 25,000 |
| October sales ($96,000 3 70%) | 67,200 |
| Total cash receipts | $108,200 |

## How is it Used and Applied?

Your cash forecast should cover both the peak and ebb points of sales. For example, a cash forecast for a toy store or gift shop would be erroneous if it did not consider Christmas sales along with projected sales during the slowest part of the year. The seasonality of the business is crucial in making projections.

As a rule of thumb, avoid making large payments (e.g., operating expenses, debt repayment) at the low point in the cash cycle.

# 37. Accounts Receivable Ratios

## Definition

Five important accounts receivable ratios indicate how effectively a company is managing its investment in receivables

## How is it Computed?

The five most useful ratios are listed below.

$$\frac{\text{Annuals credit sales}}{\text{Average accounts receivable}}$$

1. Accounts receivable turnover:

   Accounts receivable turnover indicates how fast the company is collecting from customers.

   Average accounts receivable:

   $$\frac{\text{Beginning accounts receivable} + \text{ending accounts receivable}}{2}$$

   If sales vary greatly during the year, monthly or quarterly sales figures should be used to achieve proper averaging so that the ratio is not distorted. Further, sales should be adjusted for any extraordinary items (e.g., one-time sales that will not be repeated).

2. Average collection period:

   $$\frac{365 \text{ days}}{\text{Accounts receivable turnover}}$$

   The average collection period indicates how long it takes to collect a receivable.

3. Trend in accounts receivable =

   Accounts receivable (last year) – accounts receivable (this year)

4. Accounts receivable by total assets:

   $$\frac{\text{Accounts receivable}}{\text{Total assets}}$$

5. Accounts receivable by sales:

   $$\frac{\text{Acounts receivable}}{\text{sales}}$$

*Note:* To judge the appropriateness of a company's collection and credit policy, a company's ratios must be compared with industry norms or ratios of major competitors within the same industry.

## Example

A company reports the following data for the years ended December 31, 20x7, and December 31, 20x8.

|                      | 20x7       | 20x8       |
|----------------------|------------|------------|
| Sales                | $ 400,000  | $ 500,000  |
| Total assets         | 600,000    | 650,000    |
| Accounts receivable  | 50,000     | 90,000     |

On January 1, 20x7, accounts receivable was $45,000.

For this company, three ratios are used to analyze accounts receivables:

|  |  | 20x7 |  | 20x8 |  |
|---|---|---|---|---|---|
| a. | Accounts receivable turnover (sales/average accounts receivable) | $\dfrac{\$400,000}{\$47,500}$ | = 8.42 | $\dfrac{\$500,000}{\$70,000}$ | = 7.14 |
| b. | Collection period (365/ turnover) | $\dfrac{365}{8.42}$ | = 43.3 days | $\dfrac{365}{7.14}$ | = 51.1 days |
| c. | Accounts receivable to total assets | $\dfrac{\$50,000}{\$600,000}$ | = 8.3% | $\dfrac{\$90,000}{\$650,000}$ | = 13.8% |

In this example, the realization risk in accounts receivable is higher in 20x8. This is shown by a lower turnover rate, a longer collection period, and a higher ratio of accounts receivable to total assets in that year.

## How is it Used and Applied?

Accounts receivable ratios are determined to appraise the degree of risk in accounts receivable. In general, higher accounts receivable turnovers are good signs of successful small businesses since they show that these businesses collect faster from customers, and are therefore in a better position to invest funds. An excessively high ratio relative to industry averages, however, may signal that the owner's credit policy is too tight, and the business is not tapping its earnings potential through sales to higher-risk customers. Before modifying credit policy, an owner should weigh the profit potential against the risk inherent in selling to more risk-prone customers.

In terms of the collection period, the longer receivables are outstanding past the anticipated payment date compared to industry norms, the lower is the expectation of collection. In general, a "red flag" is raised when the customer's account is more than 30 days past due. In times of economic hardship, collection periods increase. Appraise separate collection periods by type of customer, product line, and market territory. An aging schedule is also available. In some cases, however, a longer collection period may be warranted, for example, in a business that has extended its credit terms to introduce a new product or to meet heightened competition.

A sharp increase in accounts receivable compared to the prior year may indicate higher realization risk. This could imply that the business is selling to more marginal-credit customers. The owner must examine the trends in accounts receivable to total assets and in accounts receivable to sales to identify unusual increases in receivables.

Accounts receivable ratios are also examined as an indication of a business' liquidity. A high turnover ratio and short collection period—indications that a business is able to collect quickly from customers—is considered favorable by creditors because it shows that the business is efficiently managing its cash flow.

To judge the appropriateness of an owner's collection and credit policy, a small business' ratios must be compared with industry averages or ratios of major competitors within the same industry. Trend analysis should be performed, looking at the ratio for' the business owner over the years. Are things getting better or worse?

# 38. Managing Accounts Receivable

## Introduction

In extending credit to retail customers, you should take into account both the amount and the terms, which will influence your sales and the resulting profitability, the collection period, and the number of delinquent or uncollectible accounts. If you set stringent credit terms, you will have lower sales and net income, less money tied up in customer balances, lower bad-debt losses, but adverse customer reaction. If your credit policy is too lax, you will experience higher sales, higher accounts receivable balances, and more bad debts.

Accounts receivable management assists small business owners in determining the opportunity cost associated with holding receivable balances. Key components of this type of analysis are a determination of a business' investment in accounts receivable, and relaxation of credit standards—both aspects of receivable management that have an impact on the owner's bottom line. Each is discussed below.

## Investment in Accounts Receivable

The amount invested in accounts receivable is the cost tied up in the account.

### How Is It Computed?

Investment in accounts receivable

$$= \frac{\text{days held}}{360} \times \text{annual credit sales}$$

Investment in accounts receivable

$$= \text{average accounts receivable} \times \text{cost}$$

## *Example 1*

Assume that a small business sells on terms of net 30 days, with accounts that are on average 20 days past due. Annual credit sales are $600,000. The investment in accounts receivable is:

$$\frac{50}{360} \times \$600,000 = \$83,333.28$$

## *Example 2*

Assume that the cost of a product is 30 percent of its selling price, and that the cost of capital is 10 percent of its selling price. Sales average $70,000 per month and accounts are paid 4 months after sale. The small business owner wants to determine his investment in receivables from this product.

| | |
|---|---:|
| Accounts receivable (4 months @$70,000) | $280,000 |
| Investment in accounts receivable [$280,000 x (0.30 + 0.10)] | 112,000 |

## Relaxation of Credit Standards

The small business owner will find it useful to evaluate whether to give credit to marginal customers.

## *How Is It Computed?*

Compare the earnings on additional sales obtained and the added cost of the receivables. In a situation where a small business has idle capacity, the additional earnings equal the contribution margin on the incremental sales, because fixed costs are constant. The additional cost on the additional receivables is derived from the greater number of uncollectible accounts and the opportunity cost associated with tying up funds in receivables for a longer time period.

$$\text{New average unit cost} = \frac{\text{total cost}}{\text{units}}$$

Additional profitability = additional units x contribution margin per unit

Additional bad debts = additional receivables x bad debt percentage

Opportunity cost in accounts receivable =

  additional investment in accounts receivable x minimum return

## Example 3

The following illustrates a company's analysis of whether he or she should relax credit standards.

| | |
|---|---|
| Sales price per unit | $120 |
| Variable cost per unit | $80 |
| Fixed cost per unit | $15 |
| Annual credit sales | $600,000 |
| Collection period | 1 month |
| Minimum return | 16% |

If the company liberalized the credit policy, the business projected that the following would occur:

◆ Sales would increase by 40 percent.

◆ The collection period on total accounts would be 2 months.

◆ Bad debts on the increased sales would be 5 percent.

Preliminary calculations:

| | |
|---|---|
| Current units ($600,000/$120) | 5,000 |
| Additional units (5,000 x 0.4) | 2,000 |

The new average unit cost was calculated as follows:

| | Units | x | Unit cost | = Total cost |
|---|---|---|---|---|
| Current units | 5,000 | x | $95 | $475,000 |
| Additional units | 2,000 | x | $80 | 160,000 |
| Total | 7,000 | | | $635,000 |

New average unit cost $= \dfrac{\text{total}}{\text{units}}$ = $635,000/7,000 = $90.71 (rounded)

Note that, at idle capacity, fixed cost remained constant. Thus, the incremental cost is just the variable cost of $80 per unit, which would cause the new average unit cost to drop.

Advantage of relaxing credit standards
   Additional profitability:

| | |
|---|---:|
|     Incremental sales volume | 2,000 units |
|     × contribution margin per unit | × $40 |
|     (selling price 2 variable cost): $120 2 $80 | |
|   Incremental profitability | $80,000 |

Disadvantage of relaxing credit standards
   Incremental bad debts:

| | |
|---|---:|
|     Incremental units × selling price: | $240,000 |
|     2,000 × $120 | |
|     Bad debt percentage | × .05 |
|     Additional bad debts | $12,000 |

**Opportunity cost of funds tied up in accounts receivable**

**Average investment in accounts receivable after change in policy:**

$$\frac{\text{Credit sales}}{\text{Accounts receivable turnover}} \times \frac{\text{unit cost}}{\text{selling price}} = \$105,828$$

$$\frac{\$840,000(a)}{6} \times \frac{\$90.91}{\$120}$$

   (a) 7,000 units × $120 5 $840,000
Current average investment in accounts receivable:

$$\frac{\$600,000}{12} \times \frac{\$95}{\$120} \qquad 39,583$$

| | | |
|---|---|---:|
| Additional investment in accounts receivable | | $66,245 |
|   × minimum return | | × 0.16 |
| Opportunity cost of funds tied up | | $10,599 |
| Net advantage of relaxation in credit standards | | |
|   Additional earnings | | $80,000 |
|   Less: Additional bad debts | $12,000 | |
|   Opportunity cost | 10,599 | 22,599 |
| Net savings | | $57,401 |

# How is it Used and Applied?

Small business owners need to monitor their investment in receivables and analyze whether offering a discount would hasten collections, resulting in improved earnings. If excessive funds are tied up in accounts receivable, owners risk draining their resources and lowering profitability. Owners must weigh the risks involved in extending credit to marginal customers against the rewards of increased sales. The analysis described above reveals whether these moves improve overall profitability despite the fact that receivable balances are outstanding longer.

Receivable terms should be liberalized when you want to dispose of excessive inventory or obsolete items. Longer receivable terms are suitable for retailers whose products are sold in advance of "demand" seasons (e.g., swimsuits). If products are perishable, short credit terms or even payment on delivery is recommended.

You may have to change your credit policy based on changing circumstances. When times are good, you may give additional credit. However, in bad times, such as in a recession, it is smart to tighten up on granting credit, because higher unemployment rates, salary freezes, and employee givebacks reduce customer's ability to pay their bills. The amount of credit you can safely extend also depends on competitive factors and the incomes of your customers.

Credit policy also varies with the type of business. A vegetable or fruit store will most likely sell only on a cash basis because of the perishability of the product. An appliance store will likely include sales on the installment-payment basis because of the long life of its product line. A service business may ask for advance payments (retainers) or may bill clients when services are rendered.

Your credit policy should be flexible and tied to the peculiar characteristics of the customer (e.g., age, occupation, income), merchandise or services offered, selling price, cost of the item, profit margin (profit divided by selling price), goals of the business, cash position, liquidity, degree of competition, and shipping arrangements.

# PART 5
# Controlling Inventory

## 39. Inventory Ratios

### Introduction

Inventory ratios reveal the turnover and age of inventory. Types of inventory include raw materials, work-in-process (partially completed goods), and finished goods (completed goods). Knowing whether excess inventory exists is critical, since corporate funds that are being tied up in inventory could be invested elsewhere. Excess inventory is also associated with a high carrying cost for storing goods as well as risk of obsolescence.

### How is it Computed?

1.  Inventory turnover $= \dfrac{\text{cost of goods sold}}{\text{average inventory}}$

    Where

    Average inventory $= \dfrac{\text{beginning inventory} + \text{ending inventory}}{2}$

If the inventory amount at year-end is not typical due to cyclicality, a quarterly or monthly average should be used.

2.  Number of days inventory held (age of inventory)

    $= \dfrac{365}{\text{inventory turnover}}$

3.  Sales to inventory:

$$\frac{\text{sales}}{\text{inventory}}$$

## Example 1

A company reports the following data on its finished goods inventory for a two-year period:

|  | 12/31/20x7 | 12/31/20x8 |
|---|---|---|
| Finished goods | $10,000 | $15,000 |
| Cost of sales | 70,000 | 80,000 |

Assume that as of January 1, 20x7, finished goods inventory is $9,000.

The inventory turnover and the number of days inventory is held are calculated below:

|  | 20x7 | 20x8 |
|---|---|---|
| Inventory turnover | ($70,000/$9,500*) = 7.4 | ($80,000/$12,500) = 6.4 |
| Age of inventory | (365/7.4) = 49 days | (365/6.4) = 57 days |

*average inventory = ($9,000 + $10,000)/2 = $95,000

## Example 2

A company provides the following data on two years of performance:

|  | 20x7 | 20x8 |
|---|---|---|
| Sales | $200,000 | $290,000 |
| Total inventories | 40,000 | 43,000 |

The percentage increase in sales is 45%, while the advance in total inventories is only 7.5%. This analysis indicates that the company has good inventory control.

## How is it Used and Applied?

Sound inventory management leads to maximum return at minimum risk. A buildup of inventory may indicate to the owner uncertain future sales. Inventory buildup is indicated when inventory increases at a rate that is much greater than the rate of increase in sales. A low ratio of sales to inventory relative to other businesses in the industry means less efficient utilization of inventory in generating revenue.

Further, a decrease in the ratio of sales to inventory means that purchasing of goods has increased faster than sales, or that sales have declined relative to inventory. In general, it is best when the ratio remains fairly constant, even for a growing business.

Inventory turnover is the cycle of using and replacing materials. It is a ratio: the number of "turns" to the investment in a year. If a business sells $100,000 worth of products a year and has an average inventory valued at $50,000, it has two turnovers a year. If the same company produced sales of $100,000 with an average inventory worth $25,000, it would have four turns a year. More turns reduces investment and saves carrying costs as well.

Some businesses use an inventory turnover ratio as an inventory control method. Managers insist on a certain number of turns a year. This control should not be carried very far, however. A high turnover rate means very low inventories, but very low inventories may mean being out of stock more often. High turnover and low inventories at the same time also force frequent and often uneconomical small reorders, which can result in higher unit costs.

Sales volume and reasonable inventory turnover ratios are also related. It is not difficult to obtain more turns when sales volume is high. However, if sales volume decreases to half and inventories are also cut in half in order to keep the turnover ratio constant, there will probably be more stock-outs. This could lead to costly, frequent, and small-quantity reorders, as well as idle production—although, of course, if sales fell this much, idle production might be justified.

The turnover rate should be determined for each major inventory category. A low turnover rate may indicate (1) overstocking, (2) obsolescence, or (3) deficiencies in the product or sales effort. Further, a business with a poor inventory turnover is viewed by suppliers and creditors as possessing greater liquidity risk. In some cases, however, a low rate of turnover is justified, such as when higher inventory levels occur in expectation of rapidly rising prices (e.g., for oil). A high turnover rate may indicate that the business does not keep adequate inventory levels, a situation that could result in lost business if inventory is not on hand. Further, the turnover rate may be unrepresentatively high if a business uses its "natural year-end" to calculate inventory, because the inventory balance at that time of year would be unusually low.

The business owner can take certain control measures to minimize inventory buildup and their consequent negative effects. These include setting minimum and maximum acceptable turnover rates, evaluating physical counts to spot goods that are not moving, and improving the purchasing process.

# 40. How Much to Order (Economic Order Quantity) and When to Order (Reorder Point)

## Introduction

One of the most common problems facing managers is inventory planning. This is understandable since inventory usually represents a sizable portion of a business' total assets and, more specifically, on the average, more than 30 percent of total current assets in U.S. industry. Too much money tied up in inventory is a drag on profitability. The purpose of inventory planning is to develop policies which will achieve an optimal investment in inventory. This objective is accomplished by determining the optimal level of inventory necessary to minimize inventory-related costs.

Inventory-related costs fall into three categories:

1. Ordering costs, which includes all costs associated with preparing a purchase order.

2. Carrying (holding) costs, which include storage costs for inventory items plus the cost of money tied up in inventory.

3. Shortage (stock-out) costs, which include costs incurred when an item is out of stock, such as the lost contribution margin on sales plus lost customer goodwill.

Many inventory planning models are available that try to answer the following two questions:

1. How much to order?

2. When to order?

The first question is answered through the economic order quantity (EOQ) model. The second question is answered by means of the reorder-point (ROP) formula.

## How is it Computed?

### Economic Order Quantity

The economic order quantity (EOQ) determines the order quantity that results in the lowest sum of carrying and ordering costs. The EOQ is computed as:

$$EOQ = \sqrt{\frac{2OD}{C}}$$

# Example 1

Assume that the Buena Park Store buys sets of steel at $40 per set from an outside vendor. It will sell 6400 sets evenly throughout the year. The store desires a 16 percent return on its inventory investment, which is the interest charge on borrowed money. In addition, rent, taxes, etc., for each set in inventory is $1.60 per year. The ordering cost is $100 per order. Thus the carrying cost per set is 16%($40) + $1.60 = $8.00 per year. Therefore,

$$EOQ = \sqrt{\frac{2(6,400)(\$100)}{\$8.00}} = \sqrt{160,000} = 400 \text{ sets}$$

Number of times per year to place an order =

$$\frac{D}{EOQ} = \frac{6,400}{400} = 16 \text{ orders}$$

Total inventory costs = Carrying cost + Ordering cost

$$\frac{EOQ}{2} \times C + \frac{D}{EOQ} \times O$$

$$= \frac{400}{2} (\$8) + \frac{6,400}{400} (\$100)$$

$$= \$1,600 + \$1,600 = \$3,200$$

Based on these calculations, the Buena Park Store should order 400 sets of steel each time it places an order, and it should place an order 16 times during the year. This policy will be most economical, costing the store $3200 per year.

# Reorder Point

Reorder point (ROP), which tells when to place a new order requires knowledge of the *lead time*, which is the time interval between placing an order and receiving delivery. The reorder point can be calculated as follows:

ROP = (average usage per unit of lead time x lead time) + safety stock

First, multiply average daily (or weekly) usage by the lead time in days (or weeks) to yield the lead time demand. Then add safety stock to this to provide for the variation in lead time demand to determine the reorder point. If average usage and lead time are both certain, no safety stock is necessary and can be dropped from the formula.

# Example 2

Assume that, for the store in Example 1, lead time is constant at 1 week, and that there are 50 working weeks in a year. Then the reorder point is 128 sets [(6400 sets/50 weeks) x 1 week]. Therefore, when the inventory level drops to 128 sets, a new order should be placed. Suppose, however, that the store is faced with variable usage for its steel and requires a safety stock of 150 additional sets. Then the reorder point is 128 sets plus 150 sets, or 278 sets.

Figure 40.1 shows this inventory system when the order quantity is 400 sets and the reorder point is 128 sets.

## Figure 40.1: Basic inventory system with EOQ and reorder point

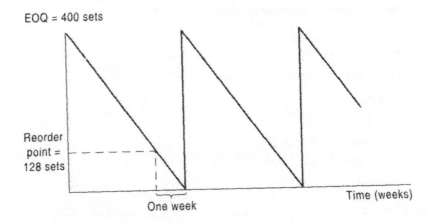

## How is it Used and Applied?

It is important to realize some strong assumptions underlying the EOQ model:

1. Demand is fixed and constant throughout the year.
2. Lead time is known with certainty.
3. No quantity discounts are taken.
4. No shortages are permitted.

These assumptions may be unrealistic, but the model is still useful in inventory planning for many businesses. In fact, in many situations the assumptions hold or nearly hold. For example, subcontractors who must supply parts on a regular basis to a primary contractor face a constant demand. Even when demand varies, the assumption of uniform usage is valid or nearly valid. Demand for automobiles, for example, varies from week to week over a season, but the weekly fluctuations tend to cancel each other so that seasonal demand can be assumed constant.

Purchasing managers need to know two things: (1) how much to order and (2) when to order. In the face of uncertain reality, managers must determine the safety stock in order to determine the reorder point. Otherwise, they will face the serious consequences of shortages and lost customers.

See also Sec. 43, Allowing for Safety Stock.

# 41. Calculating Quantity Discounts (EOQ with Quantity Discounts)

## Introduction

The economic order quantity (EOQ) model does not take into account quantity discounts, which is not realistic in many real-world cases. Usually, the more you order, the lower is the unit price you pay. *Quantity discounts* are price reductions for large orders offered to buyers to induce them to buy in large quantities.

## How is it Computed?

The buyer's goal is to select the order quantity that will minimize total costs, where total cost sum of carrying cost, ordering cost, and product cost is:

Total cost = carrying cost + ordering cost + product cost

$$= C\left(\frac{Q}{2}\right) + O\left(\frac{D}{Q}\right) + PD$$

where $C$ = carrying cost per unit

$O$ = ordering cost per order

$D$ = annual demand (requirements) in units

$Q$ = order quantity

A step-by-step approach in computing EOQ with quantity discounts is summarized below.

1.  Compute the economic order quantity (EOQ) when price discounts are ignored and the corresponding costs using the new cost formula given above. Recall that

$$EOQ = \sqrt{\frac{2OD}{C}}$$

2.  Compute the costs for those quantities greater than the EOQ at which price reductions occur.

3.  Select the value of $Q$ that will result in the lowest total cost.

## Example

As a continuation of Example I in the previous section (Sec. 40, How Much to Order (Economic Order Quantity) and When to Order (Reorder Point), assume further that Buena Park Store has been offered the following price discount schedule:

| Order quantity (Q) | Unit price (P) |
|---|---|
| 1-499 sets | $40.00 |
| 500-999 sets | 39.90 |
| 1000 or more sets | 39.80 |

First, recall from Sec. 40 that the EOQ with no discounts is 400 sets.

$$\text{Total cost} = \$8 \left(\frac{400}{2}\right) + \$100 \left(\frac{6,400}{400}\right) + \$40(6,400)$$

$$= \$1,600 + 1,600 + 256,000 = \$259,200$$

Exhibit 41.1 provides cost information for different order quantities.

We see that the value which minimizes the sum of the carrying cost and the ordering cost but not the purchase cost is EOQ = 400 sets. The farther we move from the point 400, the greater is the sum of the carrying and ordering costs. Thus, 400 is obviously the only candidate for the minimum total cost value within the first price range. Q = 500 is the only candidate within the $39.90 price range, and Q = 1000 is the only candidate within the $39.80 price bracket. These three quantities are evaluated in Table 41.1. We find that the EOQ with price discounts is 500 sets. Hence, Buena Park Store is justified in going to the first price break, but the extra carrying cost of going to the second price break more than outweighs the savings in ordering and in the cost of the product itself.

**Table 41.1: Annual costs with varying order quantities.**

| Order quantity | 400 | 500 | 1,000 |
|---|---|---|---|
| Ordering cost: $100 x (6,400/order quantity) | $1,600 | $1,280 | $640 |
| Carrying cost: $8 x (order quantity/2) | 1,600 | 2,000 | 4,000 |
| Product cost: unit price x 6,400 | 256,000 | 255,360 | 254,720 |
| Total cost | $259,200 | $258,640 | $259,360 |

## How is it Used and Applied?

There are favorable and some unfavorable features of buying in large quantities. The advantages are lower unit costs, lower ordering costs, fewer stock-outs, and lower transportation costs. On the other hand, there are disadvantages such as higher inventory carrying costs, larger capital requirements, and a higher probability of obsolescence and deterioration.

Whenever quantity (or price) discounts are offered, the purchasing manager must weigh the potential benefits of reduced purchase price and fewer orders that will result from buying in large quantities against the increase in carrying costs caused by higher average inventories. He or she should receive credit for overall savings resulting from quantity buying.

# 42. Determining production run size

## Introduction

*Production run size* is an optimum production run quantity which minimizes the sum of carrying and setup costs.

## How is it Computed?

Production run size is computed just as the economic order quantity is, except that the ordering cost in the EOQ formula is replaced by the setup cost. The setup cost is the cost incurred each time a batch is produced. It includes the engineering cost of setting up the production runs or machines, the paperwork cost of processing the work order, and the ordering cost to provide raw materials for the batch.

The economic production run size is computed from

$$Q = \sqrt{\frac{2SD}{C}}$$

where $C$ = carrying cost per unit, $S$ = setup cost per order, $D$ = annual demand (requirements) in units, and $Q$ = production run size (quantity).

## Example

ABC Manufacturers has an annual demand for 2,000 units of a product which it produces. The cost of setting up for production is $80, and the carrying cost is $2.00 per unit.

The economic production run size is computed as follows:

$$Q = \sqrt{\frac{2SD}{C}} = \sqrt{\frac{2(2,000)(\$80)}{\$2.00}} = \sqrt{160,000} = 400 \text{ sets}$$

Total production cost  = carrying cost + setup cost
= C (run size/2) + O (D/run size)
= $2 (400/2) + $80 (2000/400)
= $800

Total number of runs per year = D/run size = 2,000/400 = 5 times

## How is it Used and Applied?

Manufacturers need to know the run size that results in the lowest production costs in order to develop a budget for material purchases, labor hiring, and overhead spending. This model is predicated on a constant demand on inventory. When demand (or usage) is not constant, the business must carry extra units of inventory, called safety stock.

See Sec. 40, How Much to Order (Economic Order Quantity) and When to Order (Reorder Point), and Sec. 43, Allowing for Safety Stock.

# 43. Allowing for Safety Stock

## Introduction

When lead time and demand (or usage) are not certain (or variable), the firm must carry extra units of inventory, called *safety stock*, as protection against possible stock-outs. To determine the appropriate level of safety stock size, the service level or stock-out costs must be considered. Safety stock must be added to the reorder point (ROP), which tells when to place an order. Service level can be defined as the probability that demand will not exceed supply during the lead time. Thus, a service level of 90 percent implies a probability of 90 percent that usage will not exceed supply during lead time. Exhibit 43.1 shows a service level of 90 percent.

To determine the optimal level of safety stock size, it is desirable to measure the costs of not having enough inventory, or stock-out costs.

We will discuss three cases for computing the safety stock. The first two do not recognize stock-out costs; the third case does.

## How is it Computed?

In the case of uncertain usage and/or lead time, the reorder point (ROP) is computed as:
ROP     = expected usage during lead time + safety stock
        = lead time x average usage per unit of time + safety stock

### Case 1: Variable demand rate, constant lead time

ROP = Expected demand during lead time + safety stock

$$= \overline{d}LT + z\sqrt{LT}\,(\sigma_d)$$

where
$\overline{d}$ = average demand
LT = lead time
$\sigma_d$ = standard deviation of demand rate
z = standard normal variate (See Table 7 in the Appendix)

## Figure 43.1: Service Level of 90 Percent

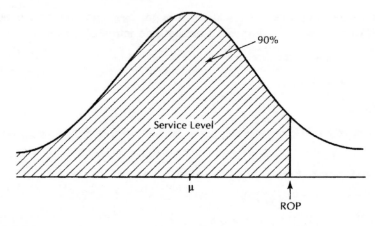

## *Example 1*

Norman's Pizza uses large cases of tomatoes at an average rate of 50 cans per day. The demand can be approximated by a normal distribution with a standard deviation of 5 cans per day. Lead time is 4 days. Thus,

$\bar{d}$ = 50 cans per day.

LT = 4 days

$\sigma_d$ = 5 cans

How much safety stock is necessary for a service level of 99%? And what is the ROP?

For a service level of 99%, z = 2.33 (from Table 7, Normal Distribution, in the Appendix). Thus,

Safety stock = $2.33 \sqrt{4}$ (5) = 23.3 cans

ROP = 50(4) + 23.3 = 223.3 cans

## Case 2: Constant demand, variable lead time

ROP = Expected demand during lead time + safety stock

= d $\overline{LT}$ + z d ($\sigma_{LT}$)

where

d = constant demand

$\overline{LT}$ = average lead time

$\sigma_{LT}$ = standard deviation of lead time

131

## Example 2

SVL's Hamburger Shop uses 10 gallons of cola per day. The lead time is normally distributed with a mean of 6 days and a standard deviation of 2 days. Thus,

$d$ = 10 gallons per day.

$\overline{LT}$ = 6 days

$\sigma_{LT}$ = 2 days

How much safety stock is necessary for a service level of 99%? And what is the ROP?

For a service level of 99%, z = 2.33. Thus,

Safety stock = 2.33 (10)(2) = 46.6 gallons

ROP = 10(6) + 46.6 = 106.6 gallons

**Figure 43.2: Service Level of 99 Percent**

## Case 3: Incorporation of Stock-Out Costs.

This case specifically recognizes the cost of stock-outs or shortages, which can be quite expensive. Lost sales and disgruntled customers are examples of external costs. Idle machines and disrupted production scheduling are examples of internal costs.

The probability approach is illustrated to show how the optimal safety stock can be determined in the presence of stock-out costs.

## Example 3

Assume that ABC store buys sets of steel at $40 per set from an outside vendor. ABC will sell 6400 sets evenly throughout the year. The carrying cost per set is $8. If the lead time and demand are certain, the reorder point is:

$$\text{Reorder point} = 1 \text{ week} \times \frac{6,400}{50 \text{ weeks}} = 1 \times 128 = 128 \text{ sets}$$

Assume that the total usage over a 1 week period is uncertain and expected to be:

| Total usage | Probability |
|---|---|
| 78 | .20 |
| 128 | .40 |
| 178 | .20 |
| 228 | .10 |
| 278 | .10 |
| | 1.00 |

The stock-out cost is estimated at $12 per set. Fifure 43.3 shows the computation of safety stock. The computation shows that the total costs are minimized at $1,200 when a safety stock of 150 sets is maintained. Therefore, the reorder point is:

128 sets + 150 sets = 278 sets

## Figure 43.3: Computation of safety stock

| Safety stock levels in units | Stockout and probability | Average stockout in units | Average stockout costs | No. of orders | Total annual stockout costs | Carrying costs | Total |
|---|---|---|---|---|---|---|---|
| 0 { | 50 with .2<br>100 with .1<br>150 with .1 | 35[*] | $420[**] | 16 | $6,720[***] | 0 | $7,140 |
| 50 { | 50 with .1<br>100 with .1 | 15 | 180 | 16 | 2,880 | 400[****] | 3,280 |
| 100 | 50 with .1 | 5 | 60 | 16 | 960 | 800 | 1,760 |
| 150 | 0 | 0 | 0 | 16 | 0 | 1,200 | 1,200 |

[*]50(.2) + 100(.1) + 150(.1) = 10 + 10 + 15 = 35 units.
[**]35 units × $12.00 = $420.
[***]$420 × 16 times = $6,720.
[****]50 units × $8.00 = $400.

## How is it Used and Applied?

In reality, managers face either uncertain lead time or uncertain demand, or both. If they have knowledge about the probability distribution and the stock-out costs; however, they will be able to determine the optimal safety stock and the resulting reorder point.

# 44. Calculating Inventory Dollar Burden

## Introduction

Inventory represents a sizable portion of the total assets of a business and, more specifically, on the average, more than 30 percent total current assets in U.S. industry. Excessive money tied up in inventory is a drag on profitability, which will bring down return on investment.

## How is it Computed?

There are three ways to compute and control the inventory dollar burden:

> By total carrying and ordering costs
>
> By dollar limits
>
> By time limits

### *Total Inventory Costs*

The inventory dollar consists primarily of the cost of carrying an item in inventory and the cost of ordering items. Opportunity and goodwill costs must also be considered.

$$\text{Carrying cost} = C\left(\frac{Q}{2}\right)$$

$$\text{Ordering cost} = O\left(\frac{D}{Q}\right)$$

where   $C$ = carrying cost per unit

   $O$ = ordering cost per order

   $D$ = annual demand (requirements) in units

   $Q$ = order quantity

Total inventory costs = carrying costs + ordering costs

There are also costs that may be harder to quantify, reflecting opportunities and customer goodwill lost due to not carrying enough stock. These should be optimized against the standard cost of carrying excessive inventory (safety stock).

## Example

Assume that a business sells around 100 bottles of glue a month ($D = 100$). The owner orders 500 bottles at a times ($Q = 500$). It costs $5 per month to keep the glue in inventory based on rent per unit per square foot, insurance, utilities, etc.; these are the unit carrying costs ($C = 5$). The manager also considers obsolete goods and spoilage by multiplying $C$ times the percentage of goods and adding it to the value of $C$. Therefore, the carrying costs, on average, are $C \times (Q/2) = 5 \times 500/2 = \$1,250$ per month. Paperwork and labor to place and receive an order costs $25 ($O = 25$). At sales of 100 bottles per month ($D = 100$), ordering costs are $O \times (D/Q) = 25 \times (100/50) = \$50$. The total inventory costs are $\$1,250 + \$50 = \$1,300$.

## Dollar Limits

Most businesses set dollar limits or budgets on the amount they will allow to be invested in each class of materials. Each class has an account in the accounting department showing its investments, and the inventory planning and control manager is responsible for seeing that the amounts stay within the allowed budgets.

This approach is usually applied only to broad classes of materials and not to individual items: It is just too costly to set dollar limits for each item separately. Dollar limits do not tell inventory managers when or how much to reorder; all it does is tell them not to exceed an upper investment limit. The managers have to determine how much of each individual item to provide, while keeping the investment for the item class within the limit.

## Time Limits

Time limits are a common way to put dollar limits into effect. To translate dollar limits into time limits, all that is necessary is to divide the dollar limit by the dollar usage per month. A $20,000 limit is a 2-month limit for an item used at a rate of $10,000 per month.

While dollar limits can best be used directly to control broad classes of items, time limits can easily be applied to every item. In fact, one single time limit can apply to any number of items at the same time.

Time limits do not determine directly when or how much to order. They merely say, for example, that you should not have more than 30 days supply on hand. This indirectly sets upper limits on how much should be ordered at one time. To hold the average investment for a class of items down to a month's usage, the inventory controller should never order more than a month's supply of any item on a single order.

For long-lead-time items, time limits control when reorders are released as well as how much is ordered. If it takes 3 months lead time to receive an item and inventories are limited to 1 month's supply at one time, it will be necessary to place a new order every month for 1 month's needs, but each order will always be for the third month ahead. Thus, there will always be several orders out at the same time. (Items on order do not count in the inventory so far as investment is concerned.)

The inventory "coverage" (the quantity on hand plus the amount on order) is the true available inventory. Assuming reliable lead times, the coverage, in our example, is adequate even though much of it is, for the moment, in the form of open orders rather than stock on hand. The short time limit permitted for stock on hand does not mean that we have to stock out of long-lead-time items.

Time limits are easy to set, easy to change, and easy to operate. And they can be different for different items. If an item's use changes, the time limit can remain unchanged because the reordering quantity can be changed to reflect the new requirements.

A disadvantage of time limits is that they are not often the very best for entire groups of products, although they are usually applied to entire groups. A 30-day limit is probably too much for some items in a group and too little for others. For this reason, both dollar limits and item limits, while commonly used, are not always appropriate.

## How is it Used and Applied?

The calculation of inventory dollar burden is a critical step toward controlling inventory investments.

Dollar limits should be used with discretion when prices or business levels change; otherwise they automatically tighten or loosen the amount allowed to be carried. If, for example, prices rise and the dollar limits are not changed, the inventory manager has to reduce the quantities carried. Similarly, if business improves, dollar limits, if unchanged, hold down the inventories when some increase is really needed to support the larger master production schedule.

## 45. Using the ABC System for Inventory Control

### Introduction

*ABC analysis* focuses on the most critical items: gross profitability, sensitive price or demand patterns, and supply excesses or shortages. The ABC method requires the classification of inventory into one of three groups—A, B, or C—according to the potential savings associated with a proper level of inventory control. Class A items, needing close control, are high-dollar-volume items. They may include 80 percent of total inventory cost but only 1 percent of total items stocked. Class B is an intermediate-dollar-volume group—perhaps 15 percent of dollars and 30 percent of items. Class C is the rest— 5 percent of dollars and 69 percent of items. Table 45.1 illustrates an ABC distribution.

**Table 45.1: ABC Inventory Distribution**

| Inventory classification | Population (%) | Dollar usage (%) |
|:---:|:---:|:---:|
| A | 1 | 80 |
| B | 30 | 15 |
| C | 69 | 5 |

## How is it Computed?

To institute the ABC method:

1. Compute annual dollar volume by inventory type anticipated (annual demand times unit cost).

2. Segregate merchandise into components based on annual dollar value.

3. Rank inventory in terms of annual dollar volume, ranging from high to low (e.g., A = top 80 percent, B = next 15 percent, C = last 5 percent).

   Tag inventory with the appropriate classification and record the classifications in the inventory records. The following example illustrates.

### *Example*

Garner Auto Supply Co. has arranged its 10 inventory items in order of annual dollar volume. Table 45.2 shows the ordered list, with dollar volume also expressed in percentages. The ordered list is examined in order to arrive at an ABC classification of the items.

Figure 45.1 shows the same 10 items grouped into classes A, B, and C. The two A items account for almost 86 percent—about eight times as much annual dollar volume as the three B items—while the three B items account for about three times as much as the five C items. It is clear that A items should receive major attention, B items moderate attention, and C items little attention.

**Table 45.2: Inventory items in annual-dollar-volume order**

| Stock number | Annual demand | Unit cost | Annual dollar volume | Percent |
|---|---|---|---|---|
| 510 | 35,000 | $ 30.50 | $1,067,500 | 53.2 |
| 310 | 1,000 | 650.00 | 650,000 | 32.4 |
| 001 | 2,000 | 55.00 | 110,000 | 5.5 |
| 378 | 20,000 | 5.00 | 100,000 | 5.0 |
| 423 | 4,200 | 10.00 | 42,000 | 2.1 |
| 188 | 500 | 36.00 | 18,000 | 0.9 |
| 320 | 35 | 275.00 | 9,625 | 0.5 |
| 115 | 100 | 44.00 | 4,400 | 0.2 |
| 275 | 400 | 5.00 | 2,000 | 0.1 |
| 323 | 800 | 1.75 | 1,400 | 0.1 |
| | | | $2,004,925 | 100.0 |

**Figure 45.1: ABC classification**

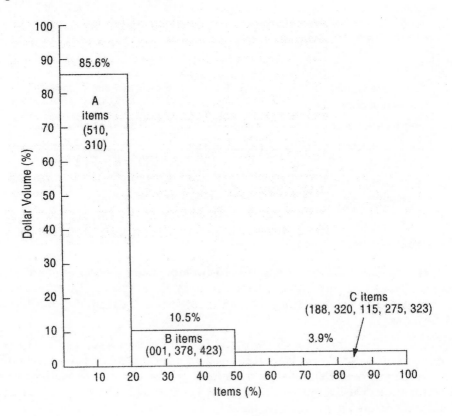

## How is it Used and Applied?

Perpetual inventory records should be maintained for class A items, which require accuracy and frequent, often daily, attention. Class B items are less expensive than A items but are still important and require intermediate control. Class C items include most of the inventory items. Since they are usually less expensive and less used, they require less attention. There is usually a high safety stock level for C items. Blanket purchase orders should exist for A items and only "spot buys" for B and C items.

Examples of inventory controls that may be based on ABC classification are:

### Purchasing

A purchase order for a class A item might be signed by the president, one for a class B item by the head of the purchasing department, and one for a class C item by any purchasing agent.

### Physical inventory check

Count A items monthly, B items twice a year, and C items annually.

### Forecasting

Forecast A items by several methods with resolution by a prediction committee, forecast B items by simple trend projection, and forecast C items by best guess of the responsible purchasing agent.

*Safety stock.* No safety stock for A items, 1 month supply for B items, and 3 months' supply for C items.

# Part 6

# Buying and Selling Products and Services

## 46. Sales Ratios

### Introduction

It is tempting to think that if sales numbers are going up, everything is fine. But sales figures must always be considered in the light of other, related factors. You need to know not only the actual amount of sales, but how you are doing in relative terms. Sales ratios are used to measure these relative values.

### How are They Computed?

$$\text{Quality of sales} = \frac{\text{cash sales}}{\text{total sales}}$$

Sales dollars differ in quality depending on whether the sale is a cash or a credit sale (credit sales are of less quality because the business does not yet have the use of the money and there is always the risk of non-collection), credit risk, profitability generated, recurring or one-time sale, and costs associated with the sale. Sales are affected by competition, economic environment, product leadership, market position, and so on.

$$\text{Sales growth} = \frac{\text{net sales (current year)} - \text{net sales (prior year)}}{\text{net sales (prior year)}}$$

A decline in sales growth is a negative sign.

Sales growth (adjusted for inflation)

= [(net sales (current year) X [CPI (prior year)/CPI (current year)]) - net sales (prior year)]/net sales (prior year)

where CPI is the Consumer Price Index.

For example, if the CPI at the end of 20x7 is 128 and it is 134 at the end of 20x8, the 20x8 deflator is 95.5 percent. If 20x8 net sales are $300,000, then deflated net sales are $286,500. If in this case 20x7 sales were $280,000, then sales increased in 20x8 by only $6500 in "real dollars"—not $20,000.

$$\text{Sales per customer} = \frac{\text{net sales}}{\text{average number of customers}}$$

where

Average number of customers =

$$\frac{\text{customers at beginning of year} + \text{customers at end of year}}{2}$$

To take into account the effects of inflation, real dollar sales growth may be computed. Sales growth adjusted for inflation is more meaningful than nominal sales growth because the changes in prices are considered.

$$\text{Growth in customers} = \frac{\text{customers at end of year} - \text{customers at beginning of year}}{\text{customers at beginning of year}}$$

$$\text{Backorders} = \frac{\text{net sales}}{\text{number of transactions}}$$

(Average dollar sales may be based on a quarterly or monthly average.)

Backorders represent future sales because orders have been received but the merchandise is not yet ready. In general, back-orders are favorable because they represent guaranteed future business and indicate that the company's products are in high demand. Backorders may increase when marketing efforts (e.g., advertising, sales promotion) are enhanced or when there are good economic times.

$$\text{Order size} = \frac{\text{net sales}}{\text{number of transactions}}$$

The cost and time of handling an order is about the same whether it is for a high or a low dollar amount. Therefore, higher-ticket items result in greater revenue while the cost of processing the orders (e.g., telephone, catalogs) remains constant.

Change in order size (adjusted for inflation) = (average order size x [CPI (prior year)/CPI (current year)]) - average order size (prior year)

For example, assume that the average order size in 20x7 and 20x8 was $2400 and $2,425, respectively. In unadjusted dollars, order size increased by $25. Assuming an inflation rate of 6 percent, the deflated order size is $2,280. In constant dollars, the average order size decreased by $120, a negative sign.

The change in order size may be adjusted for inflation to see if there has been a "real" increase or decrease. An increase (after inflation) is a favorable indicator.

Order growth =[number of transactions (current year) - number of transactions (prior year)]/number of transactions (prior year)

$$\text{Order response rate} = \frac{\text{average number of transactions (3 years)}}{\text{average number of solicitations (3 years)}}$$

A 3-year period gives a representative time period. Alternatively, a 5-year period may be used.

A higher response rate is favorable because it means that customers have been positively influenced by solicitations. Solicitations may be made by mail, telephone, or media advertisement (e.g., newspaper, television, radio).

The business owner is interested in knowing how much is bought by each customer and wants to prompt the customer to purchase more, perhaps by advertising, special promotion, changing the salesperson, or increasing the number of calls.

$$\text{Sales response rate} = \frac{\text{average dollar sales (3 years)}}{\text{average solicitations (3 years)}}$$

$$\text{Customer contact ratio} = \frac{\text{calls to customers}}{\text{total calls}}$$

These ratios indicate the degree to which the business directs its energies to current customers. There is a greater likelihood of making a sale to an existing customer than a new one. It is therefore advantageous to have a strong customer base. In mailing sales literature (promotions, letters, and catalogs), telephoning, and visiting, emphasis should be placed on existing customers. The response rate is better because current customers already have a high opinion of the company and are comfortable placing orders, whereas new customers may be unsure.

## *Example*

In 20x7, net sales were $4,000,000 and the number of customers was 1,000. In 20x8, net sales were $5,000,000 and the number of customers was 1,200.

The growth rate in sales from 20x7 to 20x8 was 25 percent ($1,000,000/$4,000,000), which is outstanding. The sales-per-customer ratio increased from $4,000 ($4,000,000/1000 to $4,167 ($5,000,000/1200) between 20x8 and 20x9. This is also favorable, because the revenue per account has improved, generating greater profitability to the business.

## How is it Used and Applied?

Sales ratios help the manager evaluate the performance of marketing in generating revenue. A business is growing when it experiences a healthy annual percentage increase in customers that is consistent with its annual percentage increase in sales. An increasing trend of sales per customer is favorable because it means that customers have more confidence in the business or are being influenced by marketing efforts to buy more.

Sales growth indicates that the business is expanding and marketing efforts have been successful. It is best when the growth is consistently upward—rising in a roughly straight line—because this means that stable growth is being maintained. It should be noted that growing too fast may present a problem in the long term if that growth is financed exclusively with overburdening debt. In real dollars, positive growth in sales is necessary after adjusting for changes in inflation.

Variability in sales may be unavoidable, depending on the nature of the business. In such a case, average sales over a 5- to 10-year period should be used in ratio computations to eliminate temporary distorting effects. If sales fluctuate greatly, uncertainty makes future predictions difficult.

The manager should try to implement policies to obtain cash at the time of sale, such as by offering a discount or by stipulating in order to take advantage of a special promotion.

If the costs of processing orders increase, selling price has to be increased proportionately to maintain profit levels. If average order size in inflation-adjusted dollars decreases, the business has a problem. The expected order size may influence the manager's decision on which existing products to advertise and which to deemphasize.

An increase in the backorder ratio may mean that additional workers should be hired in receiving, processing, manufacturing, or distribution. It could also mean that present employees are not working efficiently. An increasing ratio may be a sign of possible future customer dissatisfaction for not receiving their orders on time.

Backorders may result in higher costs associated with multiple deliveries, duplicate work, and hours spent keeping track of the backorders and their status.

# 47. How Good is the Merchandise?

## Introduction

*Sales returns* are merchandise given back to the seller because of defects. *Sales allowances* are reductions in selling price of goods because of a specific problem (e.g., breakage, defects).

The ratio of sales returns and allowances to sales indicates how much of sales were returned or discounted because of customer dissatisfaction.

## How is it Computed?

$$\frac{\text{Sales returns and allowances}}{\text{Sales}}$$

$$\frac{\text{Net sales}}{\text{Gross sales}}$$

Net sales = gross sales – sales returns and allowances

A decline in this ratio means a decrease in net sales due to returned merchandise.

## *Example*

A business reports the following information:

|                              | 20x7      | 20x8      |
|------------------------------|-----------|-----------|
| Sales return and allowances  | $  60,000 | $  90,000 |
| Sales                        | 1,000,000 | 1,200,000 |

The applicable ratios are:

20x7 sales returns and allowances to sales = .06

20x8 sales returns and allowances to sales = .075

The increased sales returns and allowance indicates possible problems with the merchandise. The reasons for the returns must be identified and corrective steps implemented. Are the returns due to defective merchandise, damaged goods, not consistent with advertisements, or not as ordered?

## How is it Used and Applied?

The amount of sales returns and allowances is a good indicator of the quality of the merchandise sold. If returns and allowances are high compared to sales, buyers are not pleased. This will have a negative impact on the reputation of the business' product line. Further, the business may have to incur freight charges for returning the goods.

# 48. Factoring in Trade Discounts

## Introduction

Manufacturers and wholesalers of certain types of merchandise frequently give large reductions from the list prices quoted in their catalogs. These reductions are called *trade discounts*. Rather than printing separate catalogs for all classes of potential purchasers (wholesalers, retailers, consumers), the seller gives intermediate or trade buyers (wholesalers, retailers) separate discount sheets that list the discounts. Thus the trade discount is not a true discount but an adjustment of price.

## How is it Computed?

The formula for computing a trade discount is

Discount = list price x discount rate

The *net cost* is the price the buyer pays for the item. The *net cost price* is the list price less any discount and may be computed as:

Net cost price = list price – discount

## *Example 1*

A television set with a list price of $450 is offered to wholesalers at a 20 percent trade discount. The cost to the wholesalers is computed as follows:

Net cost price = list price – discount

= $450 – ($450 x 0.20) = $450 - $90 = $360

The trade discount formula may also be stated as the list price multiplied by the complement of the discount rate. The *complement* of the discount rate is the difference between the discount rate and 100 percent. The formula is:

Net cost price = list price x complement of discount rate (100% - discount rate)

## *Example 2*

Using the data in Example 1, the price of the television to wholesalers is computed as

Net cost price = list price x complement of discount rate (100% - discount rate)

= $450 x (100% - 20%) = $450 x 0.80 = $360

Transportation costs, if applicable, are not subject to trade discounts and are added to the net cost price.

## How is it Used and Applied?

Trade discounts are an easy way to make changes in prices without printing new catalogs. As prices change, new schedules of discounts may be issued without requiring new catalogs.

# 49. Calculating Cash Discounts

## Introduction

Cash discounts are offered to encourage buyers to pay their bills quickly. Cash discounts are applied to bills paid within a specified period of time. Hence cash discounts tend to narrow the time gap between the sale of items and receipt of payment.

## How is it Computed?

Cash discounts are referred to as *terms* and may appear on a bill as, for example, 2/10, net 30, or 2/10, n/30, where

| | | |
|---|---|---|
| 2 | = | percentage of discount |
| 10 | = | number of days within which the buyer may pay in order to qualify for the discount |
| net 30 | = | number of days within which payment must be made at the full price |

The formula for the discount is:

Discount = list price x discount rate

The formula for the net price is:

Net price = list price – discount

## Example I

An invoice of $300 was received by Mr. Paul, the proprietor of a food store. The invoice was dated March 6, and carries terms of 2/10, n/30. If payment is made by March 16, the discount is $6, and the net cost is $294 computed as follows:

| Discount | = | List price x discount rate |
|---|---|---|
| | = | $300 x 0.02 = $6 |
| Net price | = | List price – discount |
| | = | $300 - $6 = $294 |

If payment is made on March 17, the full $300 must be paid.

Some companies offer various cash discounts, depending on when payment is made. For example, 2/10, 1/20, n/30 means that the company offers a 2 percent discount if the buyer pays within 10 days and a 1 percent discount if the buyer pays after 10 days but within 20 days; the full price amount is due within 30 days.

## Example 2

Albee Co. receives an invoice dated September 11 for $7250 with terms of 2/10, 1/20, n/30.

The due date for the 2/10 discount is September 21, and the net cost will be $7105, computed as follows:

Sept. 11   Invoice date

<u>+ 10</u>   Days in Discount period

Sept. 21

Net cost = list price – (list price x discount rate)

= $7250 – ($7,250 x  0.02) = $7,250 - $145 = $7,105

The due date for the 1/20 discount is October 1, and the net cost will be $7,177.50, computed as follows:

Sept. 11   Invoice date

<u>+ 20</u>   Days in Discount period

31

<u>- 30</u>   Number of days in Sept.

Oct. 1

Net cost = list price – (list price x discount rate)

= $7,250 – ($7,250 x  0.01) = $7,250 - $72.50 = $7,177.50

The due date for the n/30 discount is October 11, computed as follows:

Sept. 11   Invoice date

+ 30   Days in Discount period

41

- 30   Number of days in Sept.

Oct. 11

No discount is given for payments made after 20 days, so the full $7250 is due on October 11.

Although in most cases the cash discount period begins with the "invoice" or purchase date, the discount period may also begin either on the date of the receipt of goods (ROG) or on the first date after the end of the month (EOM).

The ROG discount period is used primarily where there is a significant gap between the date of sale and the delivery date. It eliminates the problem of asking a buyer to pay for goods not yet received in order to get a discount.

The EOM discount period is used primarily as a convenience by companies that use traditional end-of-month billing practices.

## Example 3

Rex Co. places an order on April 2 for parts which are delivered on April 15, with an invoice for $1,250 at terms of 5/20 ROG. To receive the discount, Rex Co. must pay by May 5, computed as follows:

Apr. 15   Date of receipt of goods

+ 20   Days in Discount period

35

+ 30   Number of days in Apr.

May 5

The net cost will be $1,187.50, computed as follows:

Net cost = list price − (list price x  discount rate)

= $1,250 − ($1,250 x  0.05) = $1,250 - $62.50 = $11,877.50

## Example 4

Jethro Co. receives an invoice for $900 dated May 8, with terms of 2/15 EOM.

The terms specify EOM, so payment is due June 15 days after the end of the month and Jethro must pay the bill by June 15.

The net cost will be $882, computed as follows:

$$\text{Discount} = \text{list price x discount rate}$$
$$= \$900 \times 0.02 = \$18$$
$$\text{Net cost} = \text{list price} - \text{discount}$$
$$= \$900 - \$18 = \$882$$

## Example 5

As is shown below, the last date on which a discount can be taken depends on whether the terms stipulate ROG, EOM or invoice date.

| Invoice date | Goods Received | Terms | Last day on which discount can be taken |
|---|---|---|---|
| Inv. $500 Oct. 3 | Oct. 8 | 2/10, n/30 ROG | Oct. 18 |
| Inv. $700 Oct. 3 | Oct. 8 | 2/10, n/30 EOM | Nov. 10 |
| Inv. $850 Oct. 3 | Oct. 8 | 2/10, n/30 | Oct. 13* |

*Calculated from invoice date

To determine whether the owner should offer a discount for the early payment of accounts receivable, he or she has to compare the return on freed cash from faster collection versus the cost of the discount, where:

Return on freed cash = reduction in average accounts receivable balance x rate of return

## Example 6

The following information applies to a business:

| | |
|---|---|
| Current annual credit sales | $2,000,000 |
| Collection period | 2 months |
| Terms | net 30 |
| Minimum rate of return | 12% |

The owner is thinking of offering a 3/10, net 30, discount. He expects 30 percent of the customers to take advantage of the discount. It is anticipated that the collection period will be reduced to 1 month.

The discount is advisable, as show below.

Advantage of a discount

Increased earnings

Average accounts receivable before a change in credit policy

$$\left( \frac{\text{credit sales}}{\text{accounts receivable turnover}} \right) = \frac{\$2,000,000}{6}$$

Average accounts receivable after a change in credit policy

$$\left(\frac{\$2,000,000}{12}\right)$$

|  |  |
|---|---:|
|  | $333,333 |
|  | $166,667 |
| Reduction in average accounts receivable balance | $166,666 |
| x rate of return | 0.12 |
| Return | $ 20,000 |
| Disadvantage of a discount: |  |
| Cost of the discount: 0.03 x 0.30 x $2,000,000 | $ 18,000 |
| Net advantage of discount | $ 2,000 |

## How is it Used and Applied?

A seller may offer a discount for the early payment of cash to improve the company's cash position. The sooner the seller is paid, the sooner she can put the money to work. It is also a good idea for the purchaser to take a discount when offered. The opportunity cost to the buyer of not taking a discount is substantial.

See also Sec. 6, Trade Credit.

# 50.  Single Equivalent Discount and Chain Discount

## Introduction

Rather than give various increasing single discounts to different classes of purchasers, some  businesses use chain discounts. Chain discounts are successive discounts on the same item. After initially discounting an item, the second discount is then applied to the discounted price to arrive at the net cost price. These steps have the advantage of appearing to be better than a single discount, as well as emphasizing to the buyer the fact that he or she is receiving more than one discount.

## How is it Computed?

Either of two methods may be used to compute the net cost price when chain discounts are involved.

### Method I

Determine the single equivalent discount and then compute the net cost price as shown in Example 2. To compute the equivalent discount, multiply the complements of the discount rate and subtract the result from 100%.

## Example 1

The single equivalent discount of a chain discount of 10 percent and 20 percent is computed as follows.

Step 1:     (100% - 10%) x (100% - 20%) = 90% x 80%

Step 2:     0.90 x 0.80 = 0.72 = 72%

Step 3:     Single equivalent discount = 100% - 72% = 28%

Note that the single equivalent discount permits the seller to compare different chain discounts.

## Example 2

A stereo is offered to wholesalers at a list price of $600, less discounts of 25 and 20 percent. The single equivalent discount is computed as follows:

Step 1:     (100% - 25%) x (100% - 20%) = 75% x 80%

Step 2:     0.75 x 0.80 = 0.60 = 60%

Step 3:     100% - 60% = 40%

Net cost price = list price – (list price x discount rate)

= $600 – ($600 x 0.40) = $600 - $240 = $360

An alternative method is as follows.

Step 1. $600 x 0.25 = $150     Price x first discount rate = first discount

Step 2. $600 - $150 = $450     Price – first discount = discounted price

Step 3. $450 x 0.20 = $90     Discounted price x second discount rate
= second discount

Step 4. $450 - $90 = $360     Discounted price – second discount
= net cost price

## Method 2

The net cost price can be computed directly by multiplying the list price by complement of each discount in the series. It does not make any difference in what order the discounts are arranged.

## Example 3

Assume the same information as in Example 2 and calculate the net cost price by using method 2.

The complements of the discount are

$$100\% - \$25\% = 75\% = 0.75$$

$$100\% - 20\% = 80\% = 0.80$$

Then

Net cost price = list price x complement of each discount

$$= 600 \times 0.75 \times 0.80 = \$600 \times 0.60 = \$360$$

## Example 4

Company A gives a 20 percent discount on all items purchased. Company B gives chain discounts of 15 and 10 percent. If Jane Snell, a business owner, buys $500 in supplies from Company B, she saves $17.50 by dealing with company B rather than with company A, computed as follows.

| Company A | Company B |
|---|---|
| Discount = list price x discount rate | Single equivalent discount: |
| = $500 x 0.20 = $100 | 1. (100% - 15%) |
| | x 100% - 10%) = 85% x 90% |
| | 2. 0.85 x 0.90 = 0.765 = 76.5% |
| | 3. 100% - 76.5% = 23.5% |
| | Discount = list price |
| | x single equivalent discount rate |
| | = $500 x 0.235 = $117.50 |
| | |
| Savings from dealing with company B | = $117.50 - $100 = $17.50 |

*Alternative solution:*

| | |
|---|---|
| Difference between the two discounts | 23.5% - 20% = 3.5% |
| Savings: | $500 x 0.035 = $17.50 |

## Example 5

Rick James orders four digital watches which list at $75 each, less discounts of 10 and 5 percent. A shipping charge of $6 is added to the invoice. The cost is $262.50, computed as follows:

Total list price = $75 x 4 = $300

Complements of discounts:

100% - 10% = 90% = 0.90
100% -  5% = 95% = 0.95

Net price = list price x complement of each discount
= $300 x 0.90 x 0.95 = $256.50
Total cost = net price + additional costs
= $256.50 + $6 shipping = $262.50

## How is it Used and Applied?

Single equivalent discount and chain discount techniques enable the seller to adjust prices for different classes of purchasers, generate new business, and keep old and established customers. These discount techniques also have the advantage of appearing to be larger than a single discount, as well as emphasizing to the buyer the fact that he or she is receiving more than one discount.

See Sec. 48, Factoring in Trade Discounts; and Sec. 49, Calculating Cash Discounts.

# 51. Markup Calculations

## Introduction

In order to make a profit, a business owner must sell his products for more than the product's cost. The difference between the product's cost and the selling price is called the *markup*. Business owners frequently face decisions on the pricing and relative profitability of their products. Pricing decisions are complex and difficult, and there is no single way of computing a product-cost figure that is universally relevant for all pricing decisions. Three major influences on pricing decisions include customers, competitors, and costs.

## How is it Computed?

Often a selling price is based directly on the cost of the item. A markup may be added to cost based on what is typically in the industry. The formula for a markup is:

Selling price = cost + markup

Markup is generally expressed in terms of percentage:

$\quad$ % markup = percentage base x 100

where

$\quad$ Percentage base $\quad$ = markup/selling price or cost

By substitution, we have

$$\text{\% markup} = \frac{\text{markup}}{\text{selling price or cost}} \times 100$$

If the business owner uses the selling price as the base, the formula is:

$$\text{\% markup} = \frac{\text{markup}}{\text{selling price}} \times 100$$

The business owner can also use the percent markup to compute either the cost or the selling price using the following formula:

$$\text{selling price or cost} = \frac{\text{markup}}{\text{\% markup}} \times 100$$

## Example 1

A washing machine selling for $300 costs the seller $200. The markup is $100, computed as follows:

$\quad$ Selling price – cost = markup

$\quad$ $300 - $200 = $100

## Example 2

A product costs $100 to manufacturer and is subject to a 50 percent markup. The selling price is $150, computed as follows:

| | |
|---|---|
| Cost | $100 |
| Markup (50% x $100) | 50 |
| Selling price | $150 |

## Example 3

A book selling for $8 costs the seller $6. The percent markup based on selling price is 25 percent, computed as follows:

155

Markup = selling price − cost

$2 =   $8 - $6

% markup = $\dfrac{\text{markup}}{\text{selling price}}$   x 100

= $\dfrac{\$2}{\$8}$   x 100 = 25%

## Example 4

A book has a markup of $2, which is 25 percent of the selling price. The selling price is $8, computed as follows:

% markup = $\dfrac{\text{markup}}{\text{selling price}}$   x 100

25% markup = $\dfrac{\$2}{\$8}$   x 100

0.25 x selling price = $2

$2/0.25 = $8

## How is it Used and Applied?

Cost information is a vital component of all pricing decisions. The estimated time period for sales is also important in determining the price of a product or service. For example, high setup costs for a special-order or short-run product or service must be absorbed by a limited number of sales if the owner is to make a profit. On the other hand, determination of the long-run cost and pricing of a product or service will enable the owner to decide whether or not to make a product and/or to enter a new market and compete with existing products.

The final selling price for a product or service depends on its cost and the desired markup. The markup used can reflect either the standard used in a particular industry or the amount the business owner determines is necessary to earn a reasonable rate of profit. The markup percentage may vary among products based on risk, product demand, perishability, volume, seasonality, competition, etc.

If a product is consistently priced below its cost, it will drain off sizable amounts of a business' capital and resources and may eventually lead to insolvency and bankruptcy.

See Sec. 52, Cost as a Basis.

# 52. Cost as a Basis

## Introduction

The cost of a manufactured product is the total of direct material, direct labor, and factory overhead. The cost of a product to a retailer is the price paid. On the other hand, the cost of a service is the total of the costs to render it, including salaries and materials.

## How is it Computed?

When cost is used as the basis for markup, it is sometimes referred to as markon. It has the advantage of expressing clearly the fact that the price increase is added directly to the basis (cost).

To calculate the cost from the percentage markup and the selling price, we solve the formula for cost as follows:

$$\% \text{ markup} = \frac{\text{markup}}{\text{cost}} \times 100$$

Since markup = selling price – cost, by substitution we have

$$\% \text{ markup} = \frac{\text{selling price} - \text{cost}}{\text{cost}} \times 100$$

$$\frac{\% \text{ markup}}{100} = \frac{\text{selling price}}{\text{cost}} - 1$$

$$\frac{\% \text{ markup}}{100} + 1 = \frac{\text{selling price}}{\text{cost}}$$

$$\text{Cost} = \frac{\text{selling price}}{(\% \text{ markup}/100) + 1}$$

Note that the denominator of this equation [(% markup/100) + 1] is simply 1 plus the percentage markup expressed as a decimal.

To calculate selling price from cost and percentage markup, we restate the formula as follows:

Selling price – cost = markup

Selling price = cost + markup

Since

$$\% \text{ markup} = \frac{\text{markup}}{\text{cost}} \times 100$$

then

$$\frac{\% \text{ markup}}{100} \times \text{cost} = \text{markup}$$

By substitution we have

$$\text{Selling price} = \text{cost} + \left(\frac{\% \text{ markup}}{2} \times \text{cost}\right)$$

Note that % markup/100 is simply the percentage expressed as a decimal.

## Example 1

A music CD that sells for $6 cost $4. The percentage markup based on cost is 50 percent, computed as follows:

Selling price – cost = markup

$6 - $4 = $2

$$\% \text{ markup} = \frac{\text{markup}}{\text{Cost}} \times 100$$

$$= \frac{\$2}{\$4} \times 100 = 50\%$$

## Example 2

An item is selling for $72 and has a 20 percent markup on cost. The cost of the item is $60, calculated as follows:

$$\text{Cost} = \frac{\text{selling price}}{(\% \text{ markup}/100) + 1}$$

$$= \frac{\$72}{(20\%/100) + 1}$$

$$= \frac{\$72}{0.20} + 1$$

$$= \frac{\$72}{1.20} = \$60$$

## Example 3

If a sweater which costs $10 has a markup of 30 percent on cost, its selling price is $13, computed as follows:

$$\text{Selling price} = \text{cost} + \frac{\% \text{ markup}}{100} \times \text{cost}$$

$$= \$10 + (.030)(\$10)$$
$$= \$10 + \$3$$
$$= \$13$$

*Alternative solution:*  If we let cost = 100%, then

Selling price = cost + markup

$$= 100\% + 30\% = 130 \% \text{ of cost}$$
$$= 130\% \times \text{cost}$$
$$= 1.3 \times \$10 = \$13$$

## How is it Used and Applied?

Markup formulas that are based on the cost of the product or service will result in a realistic selling price. If the cost to manufacture the product or provide the service increases, the retail price will also increase by a proportionate amount. This procedure ensures that the product or service will be sold at a price that will earn the business owner a reasonable rate of product.

See Sec. 51, Markup Calculations

# 53. Commission Computation

## Introduction

When business owners hire salespeople, they may use one of several compensation techniques. Some receive a salary, others a commission based on the sales they make, and some are paid through a combination of both salary and commission.

## How is it Computed?

A commission is a fee paid for a service rendered and is usually expressed as a percentage of the sales revenue received by the business. If the commission is based on a single percentage, it is called straight commission. In variable, or sliding-scale commission, two or more percentages are used. A draw, or advance against future commissions may also be used. By using this method, an employer allows a salesperson to draw a regular amount of money each week to help the employee get through "slow" sales period. The formula for computing the amount of commission earned is:

Commission rate x sales = commission earned

## Example 1

Suppose that an employee of Drake Stationary Store works on a 25 percent commission basis. The commission rate multiplied by the sales in dollar equals the amount of commission earned. Thus the commission on $800 of sales is 4200, computed as follows:

Commission rate x sales = commission earned

25% x $800 = $200

## Example 2

An employer pays 25 percent commission on sales up to $1000 and 10 percent on the amount of sales above $1000. The commission on $1400 of sales is $290, computed as follows:

Commission rate x sales = commission earned

0.25 x $1000 = $250

0.10 x $400* = __40__

Total earned = $290

*The amount above $1000 is $400 ($1400 - $1,000).

## Example 3

An employee of Olden Sales draws $200 at the beginning of a week and earns a commission of $240 by the end of the week. The employee collects a commission of $40 at the end of the week, computed as follows:

Commission rate - draw = difference paid to employee

$240 - $200 = $40

## Example 4

Belle Music pays its salespeople the following commission on all sales:

> 2 percent on the first $1000 in sales
>
> 5 percent on the next $1000 in sales
>
> 8 percent on any sales over $2000

Commissions are paid monthly. Determine to the nearest cent the commissions earned by the following employees:

| Employee | | Sales | | Commissions |
|----------|-------|------------|---|-------------|
| P. Latch | 2% x | $,1000 | = | $ 20.00 |
| | 5% x | 569.80 | = | 28.49 |
| | Total | $1,569.80 | = | $ 48.49 |
| | | | | |
| E. Marks | 2% x | $1,000 | = | $ 20.00 |
| | 5% x | 1,000 | = | 50.00 |
| | 8% x | 1,486 | = | 118.88 |
| | Total | $3,486 | | $188.88 |

## How is it Used and Applied?

Paying a salesperson a commission based on his or her results is an effective and equitable method of rewarding an employee's performance. Under this system, ambitious and successful salespeople are rewarded with high compensation for their efforts. At the same time, a practice of allowing employees a draw gives them a salary during periods of slow sales. The draw can also be used to monitor employee performance. Under this procedure, employees who fail to earn their draw for a stated period of time can be terminated for low productivity.

# 54. Cost-Volume-Profit Analysis

## Introduction

A company would not want to sell a product or render a service unless it is at least breaking even. To break even on your products or services, you must be able to calculate the sales volume needed to cover your costs, and how to use this information to your benefit. You must also be familiar with how your costs react to changes in volume, and how price change affects your profits. Further, you must know what effect expense reductions will have. Breakeven analysis aids in profit planning.

Breakeven formulas are useful to all businesses in determining the point at which a business can begin to turn a profit. The three most common breakeven formulas, described below, determine the breakeven point, the margin of safety, and the cash breakeven point.

# 1. Breakeven Point

## Introduction

The breakeven point is the sales volume at which total revenue equals total costs, resulting in zero profit – that is, the minimum sales necessary to avoid a loss.

By knowing the breakeven point, you know which products and/or services to emphasize and which to de-emphasize (perhaps even to drop). The knowledge allows you to improve operating results and facilities planning, because you know how much must sell of a new item even before you introduce it.

## How Is It Computed?

Breakeven is that point where total sales are exactly the same as total costs. That is:

$$S = VC + FC$$

$$S - VC = FC$$

where S = sales, VC = variable cost, (S – VC) = contribution margin, and FC = fixed cost.

*Note:* At the breakeven point, the contribution margin equals total fixed cost.

This approach allows you to solve for break-even sales or for other unknowns as well. An example is selling price. If you want a desired before-tax profit (P), solve for P in the following equation:

$$S = VC + FC + P$$

The guidelines for breaking even are:
- ◆ An increase in selling price lowers breakeven sales.
- ◆ An increase in variable cost increases breakeven sales.
- ◆ An increase in fixed costs increases breakeven sales.

## Example 1

A product has a fixed cost of $270,000 and a variable cost of 70% of sales. The point of break-even sales can be calculated as follows:

| | | | | |
|---|---|---|---|---|
| S | = | VC | + | FC |
| 1 S | = | .7S | + | $270,000 |
| 0.3S | = | | | $270,000 |
| S | = | | | $900,000 |

If the selling price per unit is $100, break-even units are 9,000 ($900,000/$100). If desired profit is $40,000, the sales needed to obtain that profit (P) can be calculated as follows:

| | | | | | | |
|---|---|---|---|---|---|---|
| S | = | VC | + | FC | + | P |
| 1S | = | 0.7S | + | $270,000 | + | $40,000 |
| 0.3S | = | | | $310,000 | | |
| S | = | | | $1,033,333 | | |

## Example 2

If the selling price per unit is $30, the variable cost per unit is $20, and the fixed cost is $400,000, the break-even units (U) can be calculated as follows:

| | | | | |
|---|---|---|---|---|
| S | = | FC | + | VC |
| $30U | = | $400,000 | + | $20U |
| $10U | = | $400,000 | | |
| U | = | 40,000 | | |

The break-even dollar amount is:

40,000 units x $30 = $1,200,000

## Example 3

You sell 800,000 units of an item. The variable cost is $2.50 per unit. Fixed cost totals $750,000. The selling price (SP) per unit should be $3.44 to break even:

| | | | | |
|---|---|---|---|---|
| S | = | VC | + | FC |
| $30U | = | $20U | + | $400,000 |
| $10U | = | | | $400,000 |
| U | = | | | 40,000 |

## Example 4

Assume your selling price is $40, your sales volume is 20,000 units, your variable cost is $15 per unit, your fixed cost is $120,000, your after-tax profit is $60,000, and your tax rate is 40%. To determine how much you have available to spend on research (R), consider this equation:

| S | | VC | + FC | + P | + R |
|---|---|---|---|---|---|
| ($40 x 20,000) | = | ($15 x 20,000) | + $120,000 | + $100,000* | + R |
| $280,000 | = | R | | | |

| | | |
|---|---|---|
| * After-tax profit: | | $ 60,000 = 0. 6 x before-tax profit |
| $\dfrac{\$\,60{,}000}{.6}$ | = | before-tax profit |
| $100,000 | = | before-tax profit |

## Example 5

Assume your selling price is $40, your variable cost is $24, your fixed cost is $150,000, your after-tax profit is $240,000, and your tax rate is 40%. To determine how many units you must sell to earn the after-tax profit, consider the following equation:

| S | | FC | + | VC | + | P |
|---|---|---|---|---|---|---|
| $40 U | = | $150,000 | + | $24 U | + | $400,000* |
| $16 U | = | $550,000 | | | | |
| U | = | 34,375 | | | | |

| | | |
|---|---|---|
| *0.6 X before-tax profit | = after-tax profit | |
| 0.6 x before-tax profit | = $240,000 | |
| Before-tax profit | $=\dfrac{\$240{,}000}{0.6}$ | = $400,000 |

## Example 6

Assume your selling price is $50 per unit, your variable cost is $30 per unit, your sales volume is 60,000 units, your fixed cost is $150,000, and your tax rate 30%. To determine the after-tax profit, use the following equation:

| S | | VC | + FC | + | P |
|---|---|---|---|---|---|
| ($50 x 60,000) | = | ($30 x 60,000) | + 150,000 | + | P |
| 1,050,000 | = | P | | | |
| After-tax profit | = | $1,050,000 | x 0.70 | = | $735,000 |

## Example 7

You are considering making a product presently purchased outside for $0.12 per unit. The fixed cost is $10,000, and the variable cost per unit is $0.08. Use the following equation to determine the number of units you must sell so that the annual cost of your machine equals the outside purchase cost.

| S | = | VC | + | FC |
|---|---|----|---|-----|
| $0.12 U | = | $0.08 U | + | $10,000 |
| $0.04 U | = | | | $ 10,000 |
| U | = | | | 250,000 |

## Sales Mix

Break-even analysis requires some additional considerations when your company produces and sells more than one product. Different selling prices and different variable costs result in different unit contribution margins. As a result, break-even points vary with the relative proportions of the products sold, called the *sales mix*. In break-even analysis, it is necessary to predetermine the sales mix and then compute a weighted average contribution margin (CM). It is also necessary to assume that the sales mix does not change for a specified period.

### How It Is Computed?

The break-even formula for the company as a whole is:

$$\text{Break-even sales in units (or in dollars)} = \frac{\text{Fixed Costs}}{\text{Weighted Average Unit CM (or CM Ratio)}}$$

## Example 8

Your company has fixed costs of $76,000 and two products with the following contribution margin data:

| | Product A | Product B |
|---|---|---|
| Selling price | $15 | $10 |
| Less: Variable cost | 12 | 5 |
| Unit CM | $ 3 | $ 5 |
| | | |
| Sales mix | 60% | 40% |

The weighted average unit contribution margin is:

$3(.6)    +    $5(.4)   =    $3.80

Your company's break-even point in units is:

$76,000/$3.80 per unit = 20,000 units

which is divided as follows:

Product A:    20,000 units    x    60%    =    12,000 units

Product B:    20,000 units    x    40%    =    8,000 units

## 2. Margin of Safety

### Introduction

The *margin of safety* is a risk indicator that stipulates the amount by which sales may decline before losses are experienced.

### How Is It Computed?

$$\text{Margin of safety} = \frac{\text{Expected sales - Breakeven sales}}{\text{Expected sales}}$$

The lower the ratio, the greater the risk of reaching the break-even point.

### Example 9

If expected sales are $40,000 and breakeven sales are $34,000, the expected margin of safety is:

$$\text{Margin of safety} = \frac{\$40,000 - \$34,000}{\$40,000} = 15\%$$

## 3.   Cash Breakeven Point

### Introduction

The cash breakeven point is the sales volume that will cover all cash expenses during a period. Note that not all fixed operating costs involve cash payment (e.g., depreciation expenses).

## How Is It Computed?

The cash break-even point equation is as follows:

$$S = VC + FC \text{ (after deducting depreciation)}$$

The cash breakeven point is lower than the usual breakeven point because noncash charges are subtracted from fixed costs.

## Example 10

If the selling price is $25 per unit, the variable cost is $15 per unit, and total fixed cost is $50,000, which includes depreciation of $2,000, the cash break-even point is:

$$\$25U = \$15U + \$48,000$$
$$\$10U = \$48,000$$
$$U = 4,800$$

## How is it Used and Applied?

Cost-volume-profit analysis relates to the way in which profit and costs change with a change in volume. A relatively small percentage reduction in sales can cause a major decline in earnings. It is therefore important for the owner to keep sales at or exceeding planned levels, and above the breakeven point. Cost-volume-profit analysis examines the impact on earnings of changes in such factors as variable cost, fixed cost, selling price, volume, and product mix. It thus aids in the planning process. A breakeven analysis is used to determine whether or not the breakeven point can be achieved.

Breakeven analysis is used for many purposes, including to determine:

- The sales volume required to break even
- The sales volume necessary to earn a desired profit
- The improvement in revenue required to "get out of the red"
- The effect that changes in selling price, variable cost, fixed cost, and output have on profit
- The selling price that should be charged
- The desired variable cost per unit or fixed costs

The applications of breakeven analysis are many, including introducing a new product or service, modernizing facilities, starting a new business, and evaluating production and administrative activities.

Breakeven analysis is used to organize thinking on important broad aspects of any business – for example, determining the breakeven occupancy rate for an inexpensive motel or the breakeven passenger load rate for a small chartered bus service.

The margin of safety is a measure of operating risk. The larger the ration, the safer is the situation is due to the reduction in risk in reaching the breakeven point.

The cash breakeven point is used when a business has a minimum cash available, or when the opportunity cost of holding excess cash is high.

Breakeven analysis is important when beginning a new activity, such as starting a new line of business, or introducing a new product or service.

Sales mix analysis is vital to the overall success of the business. It is needed at all managerial levels. Top managers may have to make important strategic decisions involving mergers, buyouts, acquisitions, and divestitures as part of diversification. Business owners may have to decide on which segments (e.g., product lines, services, divisions, sales, territories, departments, salespersons, etc.) to keep, drop, or add.

The managers of retail stores such as Thrifty and Save-On must constantly check their product mix. For example, the retailer may have to decide which products to replace with high-margin vacation products before the summer begins.

Examples of questions that are commonly answered by breakeven formulas include the following:

- ◆ What is the financial feasibility of a proposed investment?
- ◆ Have the business' breakeven possibilities been improving or deteriorating?
- ◆ Will advertising generate sufficient sales to justify the cost of a campaign?
- ◆ Would introduction of a new product add or detract from profitability?
- ◆ What will be the impact of labor negotiations?
- ◆ Would modernization of production facilities pay for itself?
- ◆ What bid price should be offered on a contract?
- ◆ Should the contract with a vendor or customer be renegotiated?

See Sec. 124, Averages (Means): Simple and Weighted.

# 55. Contribution Margin Analysis

## Introduction

Contribution margin analysis is used to evaluate the performance of the manager and activity. Contribution margin equals sales less variable cost.

## How is it Computed?

The contribution margin income statement looks at cost behavior. It shows the relationship between variable cost and fixed cost, irrespective of the functions a given cost item is associated with.

Illustrative Contribution Margin Income Statement

Sales
<u>Less variable cost of sales</u>
Manufacturing contribution margin
<u>Less variable selling and administrative expenses</u>
Contribution margin
<u>Less fixed cost</u>
<u>Net income</u>

Further analysis is provided by determining the *contribution margin ratio*:

$$\text{Contribution margin ratio} = \frac{\text{contribution margin}}{\text{sales}}$$

## Accepting or Rejecting a Special Order

You may receive a special order for your products at a lower price than usual. Normally, you may refuse such an order since it will not yield a satisfactory profit. However, if sales are slumping, such an order should be accepted if the incremental revenue obtained from it exceeds the incremental costs involved. The company should accept this price since it is better to receive some revenue than to receive nothing at all. A price that is lower than the regular price is called a *contribution price*. This contribution approach to pricing is most appropriate when: (1) there is a distressing operating situation where demand has fallen off, (2) there is idle capacity, or (3) there is sharp competition or a competitive bidding situation.

### *Example 1*

Your company has a 100,000-unit capacity. You are producing and selling only 90,000 units of a product each year at a regular price of $2. If the variable cost per unit is $1 and the annual fixed cost is $45,000, the income statement follows:

|  | Total | Per Unit |
|---|---|---|
| Sales (90,000 units) | $180,000 | $2.00 |
| Less: Variable costs (90,000 units) | 90,000 | 1.00 |
| Contribution margin | $90,000 | $1.00 |
| Less: Fixed cost | 45,000 | 0.50 |
| Net income | $45,000 | $0.50 |

The company received an order calling for 10,000 units at $1.20 per unit, for a total of $12,000. The buyer will pay the shipping expenses. Although the acceptance of this order will not affect regular sales, you are reluctant to accept it because the $1.20 price is below the $1.50 factory unit cost ($1.50 = $1.00 + $0.50). You must consider, however, that you can add to total profits by accepting this special order even though the price offered is below the unit factory cost. At a price of $1.20, the order will contribute $0.20 per unit (contribution margin per unit = $1.20 - $1.00 = $0.20) toward fixed cost, and profit will increase by $2,000 (10,000 units x $0.20). Using the contribution approach to pricing, the variable cost of $1 will be a better guide than the full unit cost of $1.50. Note that the fixed costs will not increase.

| | Per Unit | Without Special Order (90,000 Units) | With Special Order (100,000 Units) | Difference |
|---|---|---|---|---|
| Sales | $2.00 | $180,000 | $192,000 | $12,000 |
| Less: Variable costs | 1.00 | 90,000 | 100,000 | 10,000 |
| Contribution margin | $1.00 | $ 90,000 | $ 92,000 | $ 2,000 |
| Less-. Fixed cost | 0.50 | 45,000 | 45,000 | |
| Net income | $0.50 | $45,000 | $47,000 | $2,000 |

## Analyzing the Make-or-Buy Decision

Deciding whether to produce a component part internally or to buy it from a supplier is called a *make-or-buy decision*. This decision involves both qualitative factors (e.g.. product quality and long-term business relationships with subcontractors) and quantitative factors (e.g., cost). The quantitative effects of the make-or-buy decision are best seen through incremental analysis.

## *Example 2*

You have prepared the following cost estimates for manufacture of a subassembly component based on an annual product of 8,000 units:

| | Per Unit | Total |
|---|---|---|
| Direct material | $ 5 | $40,000 |
| Direct labor | 4 | 32,000 |
| Variable factory overhead applied | 4 | 32,000 |
| Fixed factory overhead applied | | |
| (150% of direct labor cost) | 6 | $48,000 |
| Total Cost | $19 | $152,000 |

A supplier offers the subassembly at a price of $16 each. Two-thirds of fixed factory overhead, (which represent executive salaries, rent, depreciation, and taxes,) continues regardless of the decision. To determine whether to make or buy the product, you must evaluate the relevant costs that change between the alternatives. Assuming productive capacity will be idle if not used to produce the subassembly, the analysis is as follows:

| | Per Unit | | Total of 8,000 Units | |
|---|---|---|---|---|
| | Make | Buy | Make | Buy |
| Purchase price | | 16 | | 128,000 |
| Direct material | $ 5 | | $40,000 | |
| Direct Labor | 4 | | 32,000 | |
| Variable overhead | 4 | | 32,000 | |
| Fixed overhead that can | | | | |
| be avoided by not making | 2 | | 16,000 | |
| Total relevant costs | $15 | $16 | $120,000 | $128,000 |
| Difference in favor of making | $ 1 | | $ 8,000 | |

The make-or-buy decision must be evaluated in the broader perspective of considering how best to utilize available facilities. The alternatives include:

1. Leaving facilities idle
2. Renting out idle facilities
3. Using idle facilities for other products

## Determining Whether to Sell or Process Further

When two or more products are produced simultaneously from the same input by a joint process, these products are called *joint products*. The term *joint costs* is used to describe all the manufacturing costs incurred prior to the point at which the joint products are identified as individual products that is, the *split-off point*. At the split-off point some of the joint products are in final form and can be sold to the consumer, whereas others require additional processing. In many cases, however, you might have an option: you can sell the goods at the split-off point or process them further in the hope of obtaining additional revenue. Joint costs are considered irrelevant to this sell-or-process-further decision, since the joint costs have already been incurred at the time of the decision and, therefore, represent sunk costs. The decision will rely exclusively on additional revenue compared to the additional costs incurred due to further processing.

## Example 3

Your company produces products A, B, and C from a joint process. Joint production costs for the year are $120,000. Product A may be sold at the split-off point or processed further. The additional processing requires no special facilities, and all additional processing costs are variable. The sales value at the split-off point of 3,000 units is $60,000. The sales value for 3,000 units after further processing is $90,000 and the additional processing cost is $25,000.

| | |
|---|---:|
| Incremental sales revenue | $30,000 |
| Incremental costs of additional processing | 25,000 |
| Incremental gain or CM of additional processing | $ 5,000 |

It is profitable for product A to be processed further. Keep in mind that the joint production cost of $120,000 is not included in the analysis. Since it is a sunk cost, it is irrelevant to the decision.

## Adding or Dropping a Product Line

Deciding whether to drop an old product line or add a new one requires an evaluation of both qualitative and quantitative factors. However, any final decision should be based primarily on the impact on contribution margin or net income.

## Example 4

Your company has three major product lines: A, B, and C. You are considering dropping product line B because it is being sold at a loss. The income statement for these product lines follows:

| | Product A | Product B | Product C | Total |
|---|---:|---:|---:|---:|
| Sales | $10,000 | $15,000 | $25,000 | $50,000 |
| Less: Variable costs | 6,000 | 8,000 | 12,000 | 26,000 |
| Contribution margin | $ 4,000 | $ 7,000 | $13,000 | $24,000 |
| Less: Fixed costs | | | | |
| Direct | $ 2,000 | $ 6,500 | $ 4,000 | $12,500 |
| Allocated | 1,000 | 1,500 | 2,500 | 5,000 |
| Total | $ 3,000 | $ 8,000 | $ 6,500 | $17,500 |
| Net Income | $ 1,000 | $(1,000) | $ 6,500 | $ 6,500 |

Direct fixed costs are identified directly with each of the product lines, whereas allocated fixed costs are common fixed costs allocated to the product lines using some base (e.g., space occupied). Common fixed costs typically continue regardless of the decision and thus cannot be saved by dropping the product line to which they are distributed.

The following calculations show the effects on your company with and without product line B.

|  | Keep Product B | Drop Product B | Difference |
|---|---|---|---|
| Sales | $50,000 | $35,000 | $(15,000) |
| Less: Variable cost | 26,000 | 18,000 | (8,000) |
| Contribution margin | 24,000 | 17,000 | (7,000) |
| Less: Fixed costs |  |  |  |
| Direct | $12,500 | $ 6,000 | $ (6,500) |
| Allocated | 5,000 | 5,000 | --------- |
| Total | $17,500 | $11,000 | $ (6,500) |
| Net Income | $ 6,500 | $ 6,000 | $ 500 |

The analysis demonstrates that by dropping product line B your company will lose an additional $500. Therefore, product line B should be kept. One of the great dangers in allocating common fixed costs is that such allocations can make a product line look less profitable than it really is. Because of such an allocation, product line B showed a loss of $1,000 but it actually contributes $500 ($7,000 - $6,500) to the recovery of common fixed costs.

## Utilizing Scarce Resources

In general, the emphasis on products with higher contribution margins maximizes your company's net income. This is not true, however, when there are constraining factors or scarce resources. A *constraining factor* is the factor that restricts or limits the production or sale of a given product. It may be machine hours, labor hours, or cubic feet of warehouse space. In the presence of these constraining factors, maximizing profit depends on getting the highest contribution margin per unit of the factor (rather than the highest contribution margin per unit of *product output*).

## Example 5

Your company produces products A and B with the following contribution margins per unit and an annual fixed cost of $42,000.

|  | Product A | Product B |
|---|---|---|
| Sales | $8 | $24 |
| Less: Variable costs | 6 | 20 |
| Contribution margin | $2 | $ 4 |

As is indicated by the contribution margin, product B is more profitable than product A since it contributes more to your company's profits ($4 versus $2). But assume that your company has a limited capacity of 10,000 labor hours. Further, assume that product A requires 2 labor hours to produce and product B requires 5 labor hours. One way to express this limited capacity is to determine the contribution margin per labor hour.

|  | Product A | Product B |
|---|---|---|
| Contribution margin per unit | $2.00 | $4.00 |
| Labor hours required per unit | 2 | 5 |
| Contribution margin per labor hour | $1.00 | $0.80 |

Since product A returns the higher contribution margin per labor hour, it should be produced and product B should be dropped.

Another way to look at the problem is to calculate the total contribution margin for each product.

|  | Product A | Product B |
|---|---|---|
| Maximum possible production | 5,000 units* | 2,000 units** |
| Contribution margin per unit | x $2 | x $4 |
| Total contribution margin | $10,000 | $8,000 |

*(10,000 hours/2 hours)

**(10,000 hours/5 hours)

Again, product A should be produced since it contributes more than product B ($10,000 versus $8,000)

## How is it Used and Applied?

Contribution margin analysis is valuable in a manager's decision making with respect to pricing strategy and which products to push. When performing manufacturing and selling functions, the manager is faced with the problem of choosing among alternative courses of action. Typical questions to be answered include: Which products are profitable? Where should I sell the products? What prices should I charge for products and services? How should I make the products? Contribution margin helps to evaluate alternatives arising from production, special advertising, and so on.

Often business is sought during the slack season, when it may be financially beneficial to bid on extra business at a competitive price that covers all variable costs and makes some contributions to fixed costs plus profits. A knowledge of your variable fixed costs is necessary to make an accurate bid price determination.

The applications of contribution margin include analysis of performance and whether to:

◆ Accept or reject a special order in cases when idle capacity exists
◆ Keep, drop, or add a product line
◆ Make or buy a certain part

A short–term special order for a product at a lower price than customary may be received. Normally, such an order may be rejected because it will not generate a reasonable profit. However, in poor economic times, the order may be accepted if the additional revenue obtained exceeds the additional costs. The order should be accepted as long as there is a contribution margin.

If contribution margin analysis is used to determine the best utilization of capacity, the alternative with the highest contribution margin per unit is selected, assuming that interchangeable capacity exists. The emphasis on products with higher contribution margins maximizes the business' total net income, even though total sales may decrease. This is not true, however, where there are constraining factors and scarce resources. A constraining factor is one that restricts or limits the production or sale of a given product. The constraining factor may be machine hours, labor hours, or cubic feet of warehouse space. In the presence of constraining factors, maximizing total profits depends on obtaining the highest contribution margin per unit of the factor (rather than the highest contribution margin per unit of product output).

This analysis can also be used to appraise proposals and programs. Contribution margin analysis can be used to determine the price on a contract or order for a product or service based on the desired profit.

Contribution margin analysis is valuable in evaluating the performance of a business. A high contribution margin ratio is preferred, since it shows a greater contribution to profits for each sales dollar generated.

### Disadvantages of Contribution Margin Income Statement

◆ Not accepted for financial reporting or tax purposes
◆ Ignores fixed overhead as a product cost
◆ Difficult to segregate fixed cost and variable cost

## 56. How Does Product Demand React to a Price Change?

### Introduction

One of the most important concepts in gauging demand is the determination of elasticity, which tells how sensitive quantity demand is to a change in a factor in the demand function. The principal factors in demand elasticity are:

1. The price of the good (in the case of price elasticity)
2. Income (in the case of income elasticity)
3. The price of a substitute product (in the case of cross-elasticity)
4. Advertising (in the case of promotional elasticity)

Only price elasticity is discussed explicitly here, since other elasticity concepts are similar with respect to their calculations and implications.

## How is it Computed?

Price elasticity, denoted by $e_p$, is the ratio of a percentage change in quantity demanded (Q) to a percentage change in price (p):

$$ep = \left(\frac{\Delta Q}{\Delta p}\right)\left(\frac{P}{Q}\right)$$

where $\Delta$ represents a change. The price elasticity of demand is classified into three categories:

If $e_p > 1$, demand is elastic.

If $e_p = 1$, demand is unitary.

If $e_p < 1$, demand is inelastic.

## *Example*

If the selling price of a product is increased, to $22 from $20, it is estimated that sales volume will decrease by 900 units (from 20,000 units to 19,100 units). The product 's price elasticity of demand is calculated as:

$$ep = \left(\frac{(\Delta Q)}{\Delta p}\right)\left(\frac{(P)}{Q}\right) = \left(\frac{900}{2}\right)\left(\frac{20}{20000}\right) = 0.45$$

which means that a 1 percent change in price will bring about a 0.45 percent change in demand. The product under study is considered to be price inelastic, since the $e_p$ is less than 1 in absolute value.

## How is it Used and Applied?

Economists have established the following relationships between price elasticity ($e_p$) and total revenue (TR), which can aid a firm in setting its price:

| Price | $e_p > 1$ | $e_p = 1$ | $e_p < 1$ |
|-------|-----------|-----------|-----------|
| Price rises | TR falls | No change | TR rises |
| Price falls | TR rises | No change | TR falls |

Firms need to be aware of the elasticity of their own demand curves when they set product prices. For example, a profit-maximizing firm would never choose to lower its price in the inelastic range of its demand curve such a price decrease would only decrease total revenue (see the above table) and at the same time increase costs, since output would rise. The result would be a drastic decrease in profits. In fact, when costs are rising and the demand is inelastic, the firm would have no difficulty passing on the increases by raising the price to the customer.

When there are many substitutes and demand is elastic, increasing prices may lead to a reduction in total revenue rather than an increase. The result may be lower profits rather than higher ones.

Similarly, managers are sometimes surprised by the lack of success of price reductions, though this merely reflects the fact that demand is relatively inelastic. In such a case, they may have to rely on other marketing efforts such as advertising and sales promotion in order to increase market share.

Business owners and marketing managers must ascertain how competitive their products are in the marketplace in order to determine the products' market share. The concept of elasticity aids managers in setting prices. Various elasticity measures allow marketing managers to see how effective each of the demand determinants (i.e., advertising, price change, and external factors) is going to be. In this way marketing resources may be utilized more profitably and efficiently.

# Part 7
# Putting Money to Work

## 57. Figuring the Risk-Return Trade-off

### Introduction

Integral to many business decisions, is the concept of a risk-return trade-off. All financial decisions involve some sort of risk-return trade-off. The greater the risk associated with any financial decision, the greater the return expected from it and vice versa. For example, in managing working capital, the less inventory you keep, the higher the expected return (since less of your current assets is tied up), but also the greater the risk of running out of stock and thus losing potential revenue.

There also exists a trade-off between liquidity and return. Greater liquidity results in more safety, but lower return.

### How is it Computed?

### *Example*

Companies A and B are identical in every respect but one: Company B has invested $20,000 in T-bills, which has been financed with equity. Assume a 50% tax rate. The balance sheets and earnings of the two companies are shown below.

|  | Company A | Company B |
|---|---|---|
| Cash | $2,000 | $2,000 |
| Marketable Securities |  | 20,000 |
| Other Current Assets | 50,000 | 50,000 |
| Fixed Assets | 100,000 | 100,000 |
| Total | $ 152,000 | $ 172,000 |
|  |  |  |
| Current Liabilities | $30,000 | $30,000 |
| Long-Term Debt | 50,000 | 50,000 |
| Owner's Equity | 72,000 | 92,000 |
| Total | $ 152,000 | $ 172,000 |
|  |  |  |
| Net Income | $20,000 | $20,800 (a) |

Current ratio

$$\frac{\$52,000}{\$30,000} = 1.73 \qquad \frac{\$72,000}{\$30,000} = 2.4$$

Return on total assets (ROA)

$$\frac{\$20,000}{\$152,000} = 13.16\% \qquad \frac{\$20,800}{\$172,000} = 12.09\%$$

(a)  During the year Company B held $20,000 in T-bills, which earned a 8 percent return or $1,600 for the year or $800 after taxes.

Note that Company A has a current ratio of 1.73 and earns 13.16 percent return on its total assets. Company B, on the other hand, has a higher liquidity as expressed by a current ratio of 2.4, but earns only 12.09%.

As a means of increasing its liquidity, the business may choose to invest additional monies in cash or/and marketable securities such as T-bills and commercial papers. Such action involves a trade-off, since such assets are likely to earn little return.

## How is it Used and Applied?

Proper assessment and balance of the various risk-return trade-offs available is part of creating a sound financial and investment plan. Obviously, given two equally risky projects, we would choose the one with a greater expected return. The key in many business decisions is that you are faced with a tradeoff -- risk vs. return. Decision makers, therefore, must ask, "Are the extra return worth the risk?"

# 58. Opportunity Cost

## Introduction

Opportunity cost is the revenue forfeited by rejecting an alternative use of time or facilities to favor another alternative.

## How is it Computed?

Opportunity cost = annual return rate foregone x fraction of year x capital invested

## Example

A company has money tied up in accounts receivable because of a collection problem. The funds tied up for a 3-month period were $400,000. The company earns 10 percent per annum. The opportunity cost is:

$$\$400,000 \times 10\% \times \frac{3}{12} = \$10,000$$

## How is it Used and Applied?

Management uses opportunity-cost analysis when choosing among alternatives in making decisions. The opportunity cost is a consideration in whether to, for example, increase production, liberalize credit policy, or manufacture a different product. Its significance in decision making is that the best outcome can be sought, since this analysis considers what it would cost if the best available alternative is not taken. The opportunity-cost approach is used to solve short-term, nonroutine decision problems.

# 59. How Many Years Does It Take to Get Your Money Back (Payback Period)?

## Introduction

The payback period is the number of years it takes to recover an initial investment. Analyzing the payback period of an investment assists in evaluating a project's risk and liquidity.

## How is it Computed?

1. **Payback period.**

$$\text{Payback period} = \frac{\text{initial investment}}{\text{annual cash inflow}}$$

2. **Discounted payback period**. This computation takes into account the time value of money. It is calculated by adding the present value of each year's cash inflows until they equal the initial investment. The payback period will be longer using the discounted method, because money is worth less over time.

3. **Payback reciprocal.** This is the reciprocal of the payback time.

$$\text{Payback reciprocal} = \frac{1}{\text{payback period}}$$

The payback reciprocal gives a quick but accurate estimate of the *internal rate of return (IRR)* on an investment when the project life is more than twice the payback period and the cash inflows are uniform during every period.

## Example 1

A company is considering offering a new product, which will initially cost the company $250,000. Expected cash inflows are $80,000 for the next 5 years. The company wants its money back in 4 years. The payback analysis is as follows:

$$\text{Payback period} = \frac{\text{initial investment}}{\text{annual cash inflow}} = \frac{\$250,000}{\$80,000 \text{ per year}} = 3.125 \text{ years}$$

Because the payback period (3.125) is less than the cutoff payback period (4), the company should offer the new product.

## Example 2

A company invests $40,000 and receives the following cash inflows:

|  |  |
|---|---|
| Year 1 | $15,000 |
| Year 2 | $20,000 |
| Year 3 | $28,000 |

$$\$35,000 + \frac{\$5,00}{\$28,000}$$

2 years + 0.18 = 2.18 years

Payback period = 2.18 years

To determine the payback period when there are unequal cash inflows each year, add up the annual cash inflows to determine the amount of the cash outlay. The answer is the length it takes to recover the initial investment.

## Example 3

Assume the same facts as in Example 2 and a cost of capital of 10 percent. Then

$$\text{Discounted payback} = \frac{\text{initial cash outlay}}{\text{discounted annual cash inflows}}$$

| Year 1 | | Year 2 | | Year 3 |
|--------|---|--------|---|--------|
| $15,000 | + | $20,000 | + | $28,000 |
| x 0.9091 | | x 0.8264 | | x 0.7513 |
| $13,637 | + | $16,528 | + | $21,036 |

$$\$30,165 + \frac{\$9,835}{\$21,036}$$

2 years + 0.47 = 2.47 years

## Example 4

A business is considering three projects, each involving an initial investment of $6,000. Each project is anticipated to result in annual cash inflows of $1,500.

$$\text{Payback period} = \frac{\$6,000}{\$1,500} = 4 \text{ years}$$

$$\text{Payback reciprocal} = \frac{1}{4} = 25\%$$

The company is earning roughly 25 percent on its money.

## How is it Used and Applied?

The payback period is one of the methods management uses to select among alternative proposals. A shorter payback period is desirable because it indicates less risk, improved liquidity, and faster rate of return. A benefit of payback is that it permits companies that have a cash problem to evaluate the turnover of scarce resources in order to recover those funds invested more quickly.

Some believe that payback should not be used in unstable, uncertain industries subject to rapid technological change because the future is so unpredictable that there is no point in guessing what cash flows will be more than 2 years from the present.

Advantages of payback are that it is easy to use and understand, handles investment risk effectively, and can be used as a supplement to other, more sophisticated techniques since it does indicate risk.

Deficiencies of payback analysis are that it ignores the time value of money, does not consider cash flows received after the payback period, and does not measure profitability.

# 60. How Do You Calculate Future Values? How Money Grows?

## Introduction

A dollar now is worth more than a dollar to be received later. This statement sums up an important principle: money has a time value. The truth of this principle is not that inflation might make the dollar received at a later time worth less in buying power. The reason is that you could invest the dollar now and have more than a dollar at the specified later date.

Future value (also called "compounding") is the value of an investment at a future date based on a rate of interest being paid at stated time intervals. Future value includes not only the earned rate of interest, but also the compounding effect of earning interest on the interest already accrued. Interest may be compounded at different intervals, such as daily. The more often the compounding, the higher , the future value is.

## How is it Computed?

Financial calculators marketed by several manufacturers, (e.g., Hewlett-Packard, Sharp, and Texas Instruments) have a "future (compound) value" function. Future value is also incorporated as a built-in function in spreadsheet programs such as Excel.

For the discussion of the concepts of compounding and time value, let us define:

$F_n$    = future value = the amount of money at the end of year n

P    = principal

i    = annual interest rate

n    = number of years

Then,

$F_1$    = the amount of money at the end of year 1

     = principal and interest = $P + iP = P(1+i)$

$F_2$    = the amount of money at the end of year 2

     = $F_1(1+i) = P(1+i)(1+i) = P(1+i)^2$

The future value of an investment compounded annually at rate i for n years is

$$F_n = P(1+i)^n = P \times T_1(i,n)$$

where $T_1(i,n)$ is the compound amount of $1 and can be found in Table I in the Appendix.

## Example 1

You place $1,000 in a savings account earning 8 percent interest compounded annually. How much money will you have in the account at the end of 4 years?

$$F_n = P(1+i)^n$$

$$F_4 = \$1,000 (1 + 0.08)^4 = \$1,000 \, T_1(8\%,4 \text{ years})$$

From Table I, the $T_1$ for 4 years at 8 percent is 1.361. Therefore,

$$F_4 = \$1,000 (1.361) = \$1,361.$$

## Example 2

You invested a large sum of money in the stock of TLC Corporation. The company paid a $3 dividend per share. The dividend is expected to increase by 20 percent per year for the next 3 years. You wish to project the dividends for years 1 through 3.

$$F_n = P(1+i)^n$$

$$F_1 = \$3(1+0.2)^1 = \$3 \, T_1(20\%,1) = \$3 \, (1.200) = \$3.60$$

$$F_2 = \$3(1+0.2)^2 = \$3 \, T_1(20\%,2) = \$3 \, (1.440) = \$4.32$$

$$F_3 = \$3(1+0.2)^3 = \$3 \, T_1(20\%,3) = \$3 \, (1.728) = \$5.18$$

## Intra-year Compounding

Interest is often compounded more frequently than once a year. Banks, for example, compound interest quarterly, daily and even continuously. If interest is compounded m times a year, then the general formula for solving the future value becomes:

$$F_n = P \left(1 + \frac{i}{m}\right)^{nxm} = P \times T_1(i/m, nxm)$$

The formula reflects more frequent compounding (nxm) at a smaller interest rate per period (i/m). For example, in the case of semi-annual compounding (m = 2), the above formula becomes

$$F_n = P(1+i/2)^{nx2} = P \times T_1(i/2, nx2)$$

185

## Example 3

You deposit $10,000 in an account offering an annual interest rate of 20 percent. You will keep the money on deposit for five years. The interest rate is compounded quarterly. The accumulated amount at the end of the fifth year is calculated as follows:

$$F_n = P(1 + \frac{i}{m})^{nxm} = P \times T_1(i/m, nxm)$$

where    $P = \$10,000$

$$i/m = 20\%/4 = 5\%$$

$$nxm = 5 \times 4 = 20$$

Therefore,

$$F_5 = \$10,000(1 + .05)^{20} = \$10,000\ T_1(5\%, 20) = \$10,000\ (2.653) = \$26,530$$

## Example 4

Assume that $P = \$1,000$, $i = 8\%$ and $n = 2$ years.  Then for

Annual compounding (m=1):

$$F_2 = \$1,000(1 + 0.08)^2 = \$1,000\ T_1(8\%, 2) = \$1,000(1.166) = \$1,166.00$$

Semiannual compounding (m=2):

$$F_2 = \$1,000(1 + \frac{0.08}{2})^{2x2}$$

$$= \$1,000(1 + .04)^4 = \$1,000\ T_1(4\%, 4)$$

$$= \$1,000(1.170)$$

$$= \$1,170.00$$

Quarterly compounding (m=4):

$$F_2 = \$1,000\ (1 + \frac{0.08}{4})^{2x4}$$

$$= \$1,000(1 + .02)^8 = \$1,000\ T_1(2\%, 8)$$

$$= \$1,000(1.172)$$

$$= \$1,172.00$$

As the example shows, the more frequently interest is compounded, the greater the amount accumulated. This is true for any interest for any period of time.

## Future Value of an Annuity

Two types of annuities are discussed below: the ordinary annuity with the payment at the end of the year, and the annuity due when the payment is made at the beginning of the year. In addition, the discussion examines the future difference in value between these two annuities.

## Ordinary Annuity

An ordinary annuity is defined as a series of payments (or receipts) of a fixed amount for a specified number of periods. Each payment is assumed to occur at the end of the period. The future value of an annuity is a compound annuity which involves depositing or investing an equal sum of money at the end of each year for a certain number of years and allowing it to grow.

Let $S_n$　　= the future value on an n-year annuity

　　$A$　　= the amount of an annuity

Then we can write

$$S_n = A(1+i)^{n-1} + A(1+i)^{n-2} + ... + A(1+i)^0$$
$$= A[(1+i)^{n-1} + (1+i)^{n-2} + ... + (1+i)^0]$$
$$= A \times S = A\left[\frac{(1+i)^n - 1}{i}\right] = A \times T_2(i,n)$$

where $T_2(i,n)$ represents the future value of an annuity of $1 for n years compounded at *i* percent and can be found in Table 6-2 in the Appendix.

## Example 5

You wish to determine the sum of money you will have in a savings account at the end of 6 years by depositing $1,000 at the end of each year for the next 6 years. The annual interest rate is 8 percent. The $T_2(8\%, 6$ years) is given in Table 6-2 as 7.336. Therefore,

$$S_6 = \$1,000\ T_2(8\%,6) = \$1,000\ (7.336) = \$7,336$$

## Example 6

You deposit $30,000 semiannually into a fund for ten years. The annual interest rate is 8 percent. The amount accumulated at the end of the tenth year is calculated as follows:

$$S_n = A \times T_2(i,\ n)$$
where A　　= $30,000

　　$i$　　= 8%/2 = 4%

　　$n$　　= 10 × 2 = 20

Therefore,

$$S_n = \$30,000\ T_2(4\%, 20)$$
$$= \$30,000\ (29.778) = \$893,340$$

## Example 7

Michael receives an annual annuity of $2,000 that is invested at 10 percent immediately upon receipt of the annual payment. At the end of the 5-year annuity, Michael will have accumulated the following sums.

$$S_n = A \times T_2(i, n) = \$2,000\ T_2(10\%, 5)$$
$$= \$2,000\ (6.105) = \$12,210.20$$

Michael will have $12,210.20 at the end of the annual annuity if it is invested at 10 percent.

## Annuity Due

The formula for computing the future value of an annuity due must take into consideration one additional year of compounding, since the payment comes at the beginning of the year. Therefore, the future-value formula must be modified to take this into consideration by compounding it for one more year:

$$S_n = A \times T_2(i,n) \times (1 + i)$$

## Example 8

Using the same investment as Example 7, the future-value computations for the annuity due would be as follows:

$$S_n = A \times T_2(i,n) \times (1 + i)$$
$$= \$2,000(10\%, 5)\ (1 + 0.1)$$
$$= \$2,000\ (6.1051)\ (1.01) = \$13,431.22$$

## Future-Value Difference between Ordinary Annuity and Annuity Due.

The future-value difference between the ordinary annuity and an annuity due in our examples is $13,431.22 - $12,210.20 = $1,221.02. Generally speaking, an annuity due is preferable over an ordinary annuity, since an amount equivalent to an additional year of compounding is received.

# Can a computer help?

Financial calculators marketed by several manufacturers (e.g., Hewlett-Packard, Sharp, Texas Instruments) have a "future (compound) value" function. Future value is also incorporated as a built-in function in spreadsheet programs such as Lotus 1-2-3. For example, Excel has a routine **FV(rate,nper,pmt,pv,type)**, which calculates the future value of an investment based on periodic, constant payments and a constant interest rate.. To calculate the future value of an annuity due, use the formula FV x (1 + interest).

# How is it Used and Applied?

The time value of money is a critical consideration in financial and investment decisions. For example, compound interest calculations are needed to determine future sums of money resulting from an investment. Future-value calculations are widely used to determine what a sum of money invested at interest rate $i$ will be worth in $n$ years. Future-value computation can also be used to determine a growth rate, how many years it will take to reach a financial goal, and what interest rate is being charged on a loan.

Future-value computations are used to help decide where to invest a certain sum of money. This calculation is used every time a decision must be made about a long-term investment, whether the investment is in government bonds, a savings account, or any other interest-bearing financial instrument.

Future-value computation is used when deciding on an optimum investment vehicle. For example, a bank versus a mutual fund versus buying a stock versus buying a bond. Future-value determination based on periodic equal payments will give the accumulated amount in a fund such as a retirement account, sinking fund, or a bank account. The computation enables a distinction between the accumulated principal and interest, and a determination of the equal annual cash payment, interest rate, or number of periods.

The future annuity computation reveals what equal annual payments will be worth at a future date. For example, an individual might want to calculate how much income is generated after 30 years of depositing $2,000 a year into an IRA account, or the annual deposit necessary to generate $1 million after 20 years. Future-value computations are also extremely important when determining how much will be accumulated in a pension fund within a certain period of time at a certain interest rate at specified compounding intervals.

# 61. Determining Annual Deposits (Sinking Funds)

## Introduction

Sinking fund computation is a calculation that can be used to find the annual deposit (or payment) necessary to accumulate a future sum. A sinking fund is a sum of money dedicated to fund a particular purpose, such as a retiring portion of a bond issue at the time it is due, or having sufficient funds for capital expansion.

## How is it Computed?

The formula for computing a sinking fund problem is:

$$S_n = A \times T_2(i,n)$$

Where $S_n$ = compound sum of an n-period ordinary annuity

$A$ = annual amount of money to be deposited to create sinking fund in n years

$i$ = interest rate the sinking-fund account earns

$n$ = number of years the sinking fund will exist

$T_2$ = compound sum of annuity interest factor

Solving for A, we obtain:

$$\text{Sinking fund amount} = A = \frac{S_n}{T_2(i,n)}$$

## Example

A company needs to create a $15 million sinking fund at the end of 8 years at 10 percent interest to retire $15 million in outstanding bonds. The amount that should be deposited in the account at the end of each year is:

$S_8 = \$15$ million

$T_2(10\%, 8 \text{ years}) = 11.436$

$$A = \frac{\$15,000,000}{11.436} = \$1,311,647.42$$

Thus, if the company deposits $1,311,647.42 at the end of each year for the next 8 years in an account earning 10 percent interest, it will accumulate the $15 million needed to retire the bonds.

## How is it Used and Applied?

Business people may need to make sinking fund computations in order to accumulate a desired sum at a future date so as to pay off debt or buy capital assets. A sinking fund provision may also be incorporated into a loan agreement to protect the creditors.

# 62. Determining the Number of Periods Required

## Introduction

You might want to know how long it will take for your money to double or how long it will take to reach your monetary goal.

## How is it Computed?

### Case I: Single-Deposit Investment

The number of years it will take to reach a certain future sum can be computed as follows:

$$F_n = P \times T_1(i,n)$$

Solving for $T_1$, we obtain:

$$T_1(i,n) = \frac{F_n}{P}$$

where $F_n$ = future value in period n, and $P$ = a present sum of money or base-period value.

### Example I

At an interest rate of 12 percent, you want to know how long it will take for your money to double. The value is computed as follows:

$$F_n = \$2.00 \text{ and } P = \$1.00$$

Therefore,

$$T_1(12,n) = \$2.00/\$1.00 = 2$$

From Table I in the Appendix, a $T_1$ of 2 at 12 percent is at n = almost 6 years. It will take almost 6 years.

## Example 2

You want to have $250,000. You have $30,000 to invest. The interest rate is 12 percent. The number of years it will take to reach your goal is computed below:

$$\text{Factor} = \frac{\$250,000}{\$30,000} = 8.333$$

From Table 1, n is approximately 18.5 years.

## Case 2: Equal Periodic Deposits

The number of years it will take for equal periodic deposits to reach a certain future sum can be computed as follows:

$$= P \times T_2(i,n)$$

Solving for $T_2$, we obtain:

$$T_2(i,n) = \frac{F_n}{P}$$

where $F_n$ = future value in period *n*, and P = a present sum of money or base-period value.

## Example 3

You want $500,000 in the future. The interest rate is 10 percent. You can deposit $80,000 each year. The number of years it will take to accomplish this objective is computed below:

$$\text{Factor} = \frac{\$500,000}{\$80,000} = 6.25$$

From Table 2, we see that n is approximately 5 years.

## Can a Computer Help?

More exact answers can be obtained using computer software. For example, Lotus 1-2-3 has a routine @CTERM (*payment, interest, future-value*), which calculates the number of compounding periods for a single-deposit investment. It also has @TERM (*payments, interest, future-value*), which calculates how long it will take for equal periodic payments to reach a specific amount at a given interest rate. Furthermore, many financial calculators contain preprogrammed formulas and perform many present-value and future-value applications. They include Radio Shack, Hewlett-Packard, Sharp, and Texas Instruments.

## How is it Used and Applied?

When you have an investment goal, such as for capacity expansion, a retirement fund, or a sinking fund, you can determine how long it will take for you to reach your monetary goal.

# 63. Rules of 69 and 72

## Introduction

The *rule of 72* is a rule-of-thumb method used to determine how many years it takes to double investment money. The *rule of 69*, which is very similar to the rule similar to the rule of 72, also states how long it takes an amount of money invested at *r* percent per period to double.

## How is it Computed?

Using the rule of 72, dividing the number 72 by the fixed rate of return gives the number of years it takes for annual earnings from the investment to double. That is,

$$\frac{72}{r} \text{ (in percent)}$$

Using the rule of 69,

$$\frac{69}{r} \text{ (in percent)} + 0.35 \text{ period}$$

## *Example*

Richard bought a piece of property yielding an annual return of 25 percent. This investment will double in less than three years, because

$$\frac{72}{25} = 2.88 \text{ years}$$

Alternatively, using the rule of 69,

$$\frac{69}{25} + 0.35 = 2.76 + 0.35 = 3.11 \text{ years}$$

## How is it Used and Applied?

These are simply handy rules of thumb to determine how long it takes to double money in an investment. Both methods may be used in conjunction. Without looking up the present value and future value in tables or using a financial calculator, it is easy to see the number of years it will take for an investment to double.

# 64. Computing Interest Rate

## Introduction

You might want to know about the interest rate you are charged on a loan or the interest rate you must earn on your annual deposits to reach your investment goal.

## How is it Computed?

### Case 1: Single-Deposit Loan

The interest rate you are charged on a loan can be computed as follows:

$$F_n = P \times T_I(i,n)$$

Solving for $T_I$, we obtain

$$T_I(i,n) = \frac{F_n}{P}$$

where $F_n$ = future value in period n, and P = a present sum of money or base-period value.

### Example I

You agree to pay back $3,000 in 6 years on a $2,000 loan made today. You are being charged an interest rate of 7 percent, calculated as follows:

$$T_I(i,6) = \frac{\$3,000}{\$2,000} = 1.5$$

From Table I in the Appendix, a $T_I$ of 1.5 at 6 years is at 7 percent.

### Case 2: Equal Periodic Deposits

The interest rate you must earn on your annual deposits to reach your investment goal can be computed as follows:

$$F_n = P \times T_2(i,n)$$

Solving for $T_2(i,n)$, we obtain

$$T_2(i,n) = \frac{F_n}{P}$$

where $F_n$ = future value in period n, and P = a present sum of money or base-period value.

## Example 2

You want to have $500,000 accumulated in a pension plan after 9 years. You deposit $30,000 per year. The interest rate you must earn is computed below.

Factor = $500,000/$30,000 = 16.667

From Table 2, the interest rate is approximately 15 percent.

## Can a computer help?

More exact answers can be obtained using computer software. For example, Lotus 1-2-3 has a routine @RATE *(future-value, present-value, term)*, which calculates the interest rate you are charged on a loan. Furthermore, many financial calculators include programmed formulas and perform many present-value and future-value applications. They include Radio Shack, Hewlett-Packard, Sharp, and Texas Instrument models.

## How is it Used and Applied?

The information is useful when you need to calculate the compound rate of an investment or the interest rate you are being charged on a loan. The businessperson can compare the interest rate he comes up with to the interest rate the financial institution is quoting to see if the two agree.

# 65. How to Calculate After-Tax Cash Flows

## Introduction

Income taxes make a difference in many capital budgeting decisions. The project which is attractive on a before-tax basis may have to be rejected on an after-tax basis and vice versa. Income taxes typically affect both the amount and the timing of cash flows. Since net income, not cash inflows, is subject to tax, after-tax cash inflows are not usually the same as after-tax net income.

# How is it Computed?

Let us define:

S = Sales

E = Cash operating expenses

d = Depreciation

t = Tax rate

*Note:* Before-tax cash inflows (or cash savings) = **(S – E)** and

Net income = **(S - E – d)**

By definition,

After-tax cash inflows = Before-tax cash inflows - Taxes

= (S - E) - (S - E - d) (t)

Rearranging gives the short-cut formula:

After-tax cash inflows = (S – E) (1 – t) + (d) (t)

= After-tax cash inflows from operations + Tax shield

Or

= After-tax net income + depreciation

= (S – E – d) (1 – t) + d

As can be seen, the deductibility of depreciation from sales in arriving at taxable net income reduces income tax payments and thus serves as a *tax shield*.

Tax shield = Tax savings on depreciation = (d)(t)

## Example 1

Assume that:

S = $12,000

E = $10,000

d = $500 per year using the straight line method

t = 30%

Then,

After-tax cash inflow = ($12,000 - $10,000) (1 - .3) + ($500)(.3)

= ($2,000)(.7) + ($500)(.3)

= $1,400 + $150 = $1,550

Note that a tax shield    = tax savings on depreciation = (d)(t)

$$= (\$500)(.3) = \$150$$

Since the tax shield is *dt,* the higher the depreciation deduction, the higher the tax savings on depreciation. Therefore, an accelerated depreciation method (such as double-declining balance) produces higher tax savings than the straight-line method. Accelerated methods produce higher present values for the tax savings which may make a given investment more attractive.

## How is it Used and Applied?

In making a capital investment decision, after-tax cash flow data must be used before net-present-value analysis can be implemented.

See Sec. 66, What Is Present Value? How Much Is Money Worth Now?

## *Example 2*

The Navistar Company estimates that it can save $2,500 a year in cash operating costs for the next ten years if it buys a special-purpose machine at a cost of $10,000. No residual value is expected. Depreciation method used is straight-line. Assume that the income tax rate is 30%, and the after-tax cost of capital (minimum required rate of return) is 10%. Should the company buy the machine? Use the NPV method.

*Step 1:*   Calculate after-tax cash savings:

Note that depreciation by straight-line is $10,000/10 = \$1,000$ per year. Thus,

After-tax cash savings    = (S - E) (1 - t) + (d)(t)

$$= \$2,500(1 - .3) + \$1,000(.3)$$

$$= \$1,750 + \$300 = \$2,050$$

*Step 2:*   To see if this machine should be purchased, the net present value can be calculated.

$$PV = \$2,050 \times T_4(10\%, 10 \text{ years}) = \$2,050 (6.145) = \$12,597.25$$

Thus, $NPV = PV - I = \$12,597.25 - \$10,000 = \$2,597.25$

Since NPV is positive, the machine should be bought.

# 66. What Is Present Value? How Much Is Money Worth Now?

## Introduction

Present value is the method for determining the current value money based on a future yield; it is also called discounting. The concept of present value assumes that money received or paid out in the future is not worth as much as money today. Investing a discrete value of money necessarily implies an opportunity cost. Thus, given some future value, what is the equivalent value money today or its present value?

## How is it Computed?

Financial calculators offered by several manufacturers calculate present value. In addition, it is incorporated as a built-in function in spreadsheet programs such as Excel.

Recall from Sec. 60, How Do You Calculate Future Values? How Money Grows?, that

$$F_n = P(1+i)^n$$

Therefore,

$$P = \frac{F_n}{(1 + i)^n} = F^n \times \left( \frac{1}{(1 + i)^n} \right) = F_n \times T_3(i, n)$$

Where $T_3$ (i, n) represents the present value of $1 and is given in Table 3 in the Appendix.

## Example 1

You have been given an opportunity to receive $20,000 6 years from now. If you can earn 10 percent on your investments, what is the most you should pay for this opportunity?  To answer this question, you must compute the present value of $20,000 to be received 6 years from now at a 10 percent rate of discount. $F_6$ is $20,000, I is 10 percent, and n is 6 years. $T_3$ (10%, 6) from Table 3 is 0.565.

$$P = \$20,000 \left( \frac{1}{(1 + 0.1)^6} \right) = \$20,000 \, T_3 \, (10\%, 6) = \$20,000(0.564) = \$11,280$$

This means that you can earn 10 percent on your investment, and you would be indifferent to receiving $11,280 now or $20,000 6 years from today since the amounts are time equivalent. In other words, you could invest $11,300 today at 10 percent and have $20,000 in 6 years.

## Present Value of Mixed Streams of Cash Flows

The present value of a series of mixed payments (or receipts) is the sum of the present value of each individual payment. We know that the present value of each individual payment is the payment times the appropriate $T_3$ value.

## Example 2

You are thinking of starting a new product line that initially costs $32,000. Your annual projected cash inflows are:

| | |
|---|---|
| 1 | $10,000 |
| 2 | $20,000 |
| 3 | $5,000 |

If you must earn a minimum of 10 percent on your investment, should you undertake this new product line?

The present value of this series of mixed streams of cash inflows is calculated as follows:

| Year | Cash inflows | x $T_3(10\%, n)$ | Present Value |
|---|---|---|---|
| 1 | $10,000 | 0.909 | $9,090 |
| 2 | $20,000 | 0.826 | $16,520 |
| 3 | $5,000 | 0.751 | $3,755 |
| | | | $29,365 |

Since the present value of your projected cash inflows is less than the initial investment, you should not undertake this project.

## Present Value of an Annuity

Interest received from bonds, pension funds, and insurance obligations all involve annuities. To compare these financial instruments, we need to know the present value of each. The present value of an annuity is a method of discounting an annuity to determine its worth in present-day dollars. It shows the amount of the lump-sum payment that would have to be received today to equal the annuity.

This analysis accommodates two types of annuities – ordinary annuities in which the equal payment comes at the end of the year, and annuities due in which the equal payment is made at the beginning of the year.

## Ordinary Annuity

The present value of an ordinary annuity ($P_n$) can be found by using the following equation:

$$P_n = A \times \frac{1}{(1+i)^1} + A \times \frac{1}{(1+i)^2} + \ldots + A \times \frac{1}{(1+i)^n}$$

$$= A \times \frac{1}{(1+i)^1} + \frac{1}{(1+i)^2} + \ldots + \frac{1}{(1+i)^n}$$

$$P_n = A \times \sum_{t=0}^{n} \frac{1}{(1+i)^t} = A \times \left[ \frac{1}{i} \left( 1 - \frac{1}{(1+i)} \right) \right] = A \times T_4(i,n)$$

where $T_4(i,n)$ represents the present value of an annuity of $1 discounted at $i$ percent for $n$ years and is found in Table 4 in the Appendix.

## Example 3

Assume that the cash inflows in Example 2 form an annuity of $10,000 for 3 years. Then the present value is

$$P_n = A \cdot T_4(i,n)$$

$$P_3 = \$10,000 \, T_4(10\%, 3 \text{ years}) = \$10,000 \, (2.487) = \$24,870$$

## Example 4

Judy has been offered a 5-year annuity of $2,000 a year or a lump sum payment today. Since Judy wants to invest the money in a security paying 10 percent interest, she decides to take the lump-sum payment today. How large should the lump-sum payment be to equal the 5-year, $2,000 annual annuity at 10 percent interest?

Using the present-value interest factor for an ordinary annuity (PVIFA) of 5 years paying 10 percent interest provides an easy solution:

$$P_n = A \times T_4 \, (i,n) = \$2,000 \, T_4(10\%, 5\text{years})$$

$$= \$2,000 \times 3.79908$$

$$= \$7,598.16$$

The lump-sum payment today for Judy should be $7,598.16 to equal the 5-year, $2000 annual annuity at 10 percent interest.

## Annuity Due

The formula for the computation of the present value of an annuity due must take into consideration one additional year of compounding since the payment occurs at the beginning of the year. Therefore, the future formula must be modified as follows:

$$P_n = A \times T_4(i,n)(1 + i)$$

using the present-value interest factor for an annuity $T_4$.

## Example 5

Using the same information as in Example 4 and the present-value interest factor for an annuity $T_4$ of 5 years paying 10 percent interest modified for an annuity due:

$$
\begin{aligned}
P_n &= A \cdot T_4(i,n)(1 + i)(1 + i) = \$2{,}000 \times T_4(10\%, 5 \text{ years}) (1 + 0.1) \\
&= \$2{,}000 \times 3.79908 \times 1.10 \\
&= \$8{,}357.97
\end{aligned}
$$

## Present-Value Difference between Ordinary Annuity and Annuity Due

The present-value difference between an ordinary annuity and an annuity due is substantial. In the above examples, the difference is $8,357.97 - $7,598.16 = $759.81. Generally, an annuity due is preferable over an ordinary annuity, since an additional year of compounding is essentially received.

## Can a computer help?

Computer software can be extremely helpful in making present-value calculations. For example, PV(rate,nper,pmt,fv,type) of Excel determines the present value of an investment, based on a series of equal payments, discounted at a periodic interest rate over the number of periods, To calculate the present value of an annuity due, use the following formula: PV x (1 + interest). Financial calculators can do this too.

## How is it Used and Applied?

The determination of the present value of money is crucial in evaluating the choice of a future investment. It is also used in the discounting process to determine the rate of interest actually being charged on a loan or other financing arrangement. The number of periods involved in a financing situation may also be computed.

Present-value analysis is used to assess the financial attractiveness of investments. This important technique is used in making capital budgeting decisions to select the optimum alternative long-term investment opportunity. It helps to identify where money should be placed, whether leasing or buying is the best option, whether a business should be kept or sold, and whether a new product introduced or equipment replaced with new equipment. Time-value-of-money analysis compares proposals on the same basis, converting everything into present value is identified. Present-value tables are used to make financial decisions when there are competing choices such as which job to take or whether to seek graduate education.

Present value of an annuity is used to compute what an annuity is worth in today's money at a particular rate of interest for a designated time period. Present value of an annuity is also used to determine the equal annual payment, interest rate, and the length of time.

Present-value- of annuity computations enable selection of the best mutually exclusive proposal or project, revealing which alternative is most financially advantageous. It can be applied to situations involving loans, leases equity or debt investments, capital expansion, product-line selection, and so forth.

Annuities and their current worth are important to look at when analyzing pension plans, insurance policies, and investments. Present value enables determination of the price to pay for an investment, such as a bond that pays semiannual interest. Discounting applications also reveal the interest rate that is being charged on a loan, and the number of years necessary to pay of that loan and the number of years necessary to pay off that loan.

# 67. Calculating Loan Payments

## Introduction

A loan may be paid off in periodic equal installments and include varying portions of principal and interest during its term. Examples include auto loans, mortgage loans, and most commercial loans. The longer the loan period, the higher is the interest cost.

## How is it Computed?

There are two ways to find the periodic amortized amount:

1.  Divide the principal loan amount (A) by $T_4$, which a Table 4 factor (Present Value of an Annuity of $1); that is,

    $$\text{Amount of loan} = A = \frac{P}{T_4}$$

2.  Use a handy table such as Table 5 (a table of monthly installment loan payments in the Appendix). The table provides the monthly payment required to retire a $1,000 installment loan for a selected interest rate and term. The monthly payment covers both principal and interest, since the table has the interest charges built into it.

## Example 1

Assume that a business borrows $2,000 to be repaid in three equal installments at the end of each of the next 3 years. The bank charges 12 percent interest. The amount of each payment is

$$P = \$2,000$$

$$T_4(12\%, 3 \text{ years}) = 2.402$$

Therefore, $A = \dfrac{\$2,000}{2.402} = \$832.64$

## Example 2

A retailer wants to take out a $15,000, 12%, 48-month loan. The following shows how to calculate:

◆ the monthly installment loan payment
◆ the total loan payment
◆ the total finance charge

Using Table 5, she needs to follow these three steps:

Step 1: Divide the loan amount by $1,000.

$15,000/$1,000 = 15

Step 2: Find the payment factor from Table 5 for a specific interest rate and loan maturity.

The Table 5 payment factor for 12% and 48 months is $26.34

Step 3: Multiply the factor obtained in Step 2 by the amount from Step 1.

$26.34 x 15 = $395.10

(a)  Monthly installment loan payment = $395.10.

(b)  Total loan payments = $18,964.80 ($395.10 x 48 months)

(c)  The difference between $18,964.80 and the principal ($15,000) represents the finance charge on the loan---that is, $3,964.80.

## Can a Computer Help?

Spreadsheet programs can be used in making loan calculations. For example, Excel has a function PMT(rate,nper,pv,fv,type), which calculates the payment on a loan at a given interest rate for a specified number of payments. Many financial calculators have similar features. *Note:* PMT assumes that payments occur at the end of each payment period (an ordinary annuity). If you make payments at the beginning of each period (an annuity due), you must use the formula PMT/(1 + *interest*).

Once we compute the periodic loan amount, we can develop a *loan amortization schedule*. Each loan payment consists partly of interest and partly of principal. The interest component of the payment is greatest in the first period (because the principal balance is the highest) and subsequently declines, whereas the principal portion is the smallest in the first period (because of the high interest) and increases thereafter, as showing in the following example.

## Example 3

Using the same data as in Example 1, we set up the following amortization schedule:

| Year | Payment | Interest | | Repayment of Principal | | Remaining Balance |
|------|---------|----------|---|------------------------|---|-------------------|
| 0 | | | | | | $2,000.00 |
| 1 | $832.64 | $240.00 | (a) | $592.64 | (b) | $1,407.36 |
| 2 | $832.64 | $168.88 | | $663.76 | | $743.60 |
| 3 | $832.64 | $89.23 | | $743.41 | (c) | |

(a) Interest is computed by multiplying the loan balance at the beginning of the year by the interest rate. Therefore, interest in year 1 is $2,000(0.12) = $240; in year 2 interest is $1,407.36(0.12) = $168.88; and in year 3 interest is $743.60(0.12) = $89.23. All figures are rounded.

(b) The reduction in principal equals the payment less the interest portion ($832.64 - $240.00 = $592.64)

(c) Not exact because of accumulated rounding errors.

Borrowers want to know not only the amount of the periodic payment, but also and perhaps more important, how much they can save in total interest if they prepay the loan.

## How is it Used and Applied?

Business owners and managers must be able to calculate the periodic payment amount and break it down into principal-reduction and interest portions. They have to check the accuracy of bank calculations.

# 68. Ranking Proposals and Projects

## Introduction

The *ranking* (profitability) index is used to differentiate the net present values of competing proposals. It compares the initial cash investment to the discounted value of future net cash inflows. The index is used to rank projects in order of their attractiveness.

## How is it Computed?

$$\text{Profitability index} = \frac{\text{present value of cash inflows}}{\text{present value of cash outflows}}$$

*Rule of Thumb:* Accept a proposal with a profitability index equal to or greater than one. If the index is less than one, the company is losing money on the proposal.

*Warning:* A higher profitability index does not always coincide with the higher net present value.

## Example 1

Assume that the following information is provided about two proposals:

|  | Proposal A | Proposal B |
| --- | --- | --- |
| Initial investment | $100,000 | $10,000 |
| Present value of cash inflows | 500,000 | 90,000 |

The net present value of Proposal A is $400,000 and that of Proposal B is $80,000. Based on net present value, Proposal A appears better than Proposal B; however, this would be an incorrect conclusion, because a budget constraint exists. The profitability index should be used in evaluating proposals when budget constraints exist. In this case, Proposal B's profitability index of nine surpasses Proposal A's index of five. The net result is that Proposal B should be selected over Proposal A.

## Example 2

A *contingent proposal* is one that requires acceptance of another, related proposal. Hence, the proposals must be looked at together, and a profitability index should be computed for the group, as indicated below:

| Project | Investment | Present value | Profitability | Index ranking |
|---------|-----------|---------------|---------------|---------------|
| A | $70,000 | $112,000 | 1.6 | 1 |
| B | 100,000 | 145,000 | 1.45 | 2 |
| C | 110,000 | 126,500 | 1.15 | 5 |
| D | 60,000 | 79,000 | 1.32 | 3 |
| E | 40,000 | 38,000 | 0.95 | 6 |
| F | 80,000 | 95,000 | 1.19 | 4 |

The budget constraint is $250,000. Projects A, B, and D should be selected, as indicated by the following calculations.

| Project | Investment | Present value |
|---------|-----------|---------------|
| A | $ 70,000 | $112,000 |
| B | 100,000 | 145,000 |
| D | 60,000 | 79,000 |
| | $230,000 | $336,000 |

where net present value = $336,000 - $230,000 = $106,000

## Example 3

Consider the following proposals:

| Proposal | Present value of cash outflow | Present value of cash inflow |
|----------|-------------------------------|------------------------------|
| A | $160,000 | $210,000 |
| B | 60,000 | 40,000 |
| Total | $220,000 | $250,000 |

The combined profitability index is:

$$\text{Profitability index} = \frac{\$250,000}{\$220,000} = 1.14$$

## How is it Used and Applied?

In capital budgeting, the profitability index is used to rank competing proposals to determine a priority order given a budget constraint. Proposals of different dollar magnitude are ranked on comparative basis.

Capital rationing takes place when a business is not able to invest in projects that have a net present value greater than or equal to zero. Typically, the firm establishes an upper limit to its capital budget based on budgetary constraints. *Special notes:* With capital rationing, the project with the highest ranking index rather than the highest net present value should be selected for investment.

# 69. Determining Internal Rate of Return (Time-Adjusted Rate of Return)

## Introduction

The *internal rate of return* (IRR) is the return earned on a business proposal---that is, the. discount rate equating the present value of cash inflows to the initial investment. The internal rate of return assumes that cash inflows are reinvested at the internal rate. It is used to determine whether to make capital expenditures.

## Internal Rate of Return Where Unequal Cash Inflows Exist

### How Is It Computed?

This computation uses the trial-and-error method while working through the present-value tables (see the Appendix). Step-by-step, the IRR is computed as follows:

1. Compute net present value at the cost of capital, denoted as $r_1$.
2. See if net present value is positive or negative.
3a. If net present value is positive, use a higher rate ($r_2$) than $r_1$.
3b. If net present value is negative, use a lower rate ($r_2$) than $r_1$.
3c. The exact internal rate of return at which net present value equals zero is sometimes between the two rates.
4. Compute net present value using $r_2$.
5. Perform interpolation for the exact rate.

### Example I

A project costing $100,000 is expected to generate the following cash inflows:

| Year | Cash inflow |
|------|-------------|
| 1 | $50,000 |
| 2 | 30,000 |
| 3 | 20,000 |
| 4 | 40,000 |

Using trial and error, the interest rate is calculated as follows:

| Year | At 16% | Present Value | At 18% | Present Value |
|---|---|---|---|---|
| 1 | 0.862 | $  43,100 | 0.847 | $  42,350 |
| 2 | 0.743 | 22,290 | 0.718 | 21,540 |
| 3 | 0.641 | 12,820 | 0.609 | 12,180 |
| 4 | 0.552 | 22,080 | 0.516 | 20,640 |
| | | $ 100,290 | | $  96,710 |
| Investment | | -100,000 | | -100,000 |
| Net present Value | | $      290  - | | $      3,290 |

The internal rate of return on this project is a little more than 16 percent, because at that rate the net present value of the investment is approximately zero.

## Internal Rate of Return Where Equal Cash Inflows Exist

### How Is It Computed?

The internal rate of return is computed first by determining a factor (which happens to be the same as the *payback period*) and then looking up the rate of return in a table of the present value of an annuity of $1 (see Table 4 in the Appendix).

## Example 2

Assume that $100,000 is invested in a proposal that will produce annual cash inflows of $15,000 for the next 20 years. Then

$$\frac{\$100,000}{\$15,000} = 6.6667$$

Consult the present value of an annuity of $1 table (see Table 4 in the Appendix). Looking across 20 years, find the factor closest to 6.6667-i.e., 6.6231, in the 14 percent column.

## Example 3

Assume the following investment:

| | |
|---|---|
| Initial investment | $12,950 |
| Estimated life | 10 years |
| Annual cash inflows | $ 3,000 |
| Cost of capital | 12% |

The calculation of internal rate of return (IRR), including the interpolation to achieve the exact rate, is:

$$\text{Present value of annuity factor} = \frac{\$12,950}{\$3,000} = 4.317$$

The value 4.317 is somewhere between 18 and 20 percent in the 10-year line of the present value of an annuity of $1 table. Using interpolation,

| Present value of annuity factor | | |
| --- | --- | --- |
| 18% | 4.494 | 4.494 |
| IRR | | 4.317 |
| 20% | 4.192 | ____ |
| | 0.302 | 0.177 |

Therefore,

$$\text{IRR} = 18\% + \frac{0.177}{0.302}\ (20\% - 18\%)$$

$$= 18\% + 0.586\ (2\%) = 18\% + 1.17\% = 19.17\%$$

Because the internal rate of return (19.17%) exceeds the cost of capital (12%), this analysis concludes that the project should be accepted.

## Can a computer help?

Spreadsheet programs can be used in making IRR calculations. For example, *Excel* has a function IRR(values, guess). Excel considers negative numbers as cash outflows such as the initial investment, and positive numbers as cash inflows. Many financial calculators have similar features. As in Example 3, suppose you want to calculate the IRR of a $12,950 investment (the value -12950 entered in year 0 that is followed by 10 monthly cash inflows of $3,000). Using a guess of 12% (the value of 0.12), which is in effect the cost of capital, your formula would be @IRR(values, 0.12) and Excel would return 19.15%, as shown below.

| Year 0 | 1 | 2 | 3 | 4 | 5 | 6 | 7 | 8 | 9 | 10 |
| --- | --- | --- | --- | --- | --- | --- | --- | --- | --- | --- |
| -12950 | 3000 | 3000 | 3000 | 3000 | 3000 | 3000 | 3000 | 3000 | 3000 | 3000 |
| IRR = | 19.15% | | | | | | | | | |
| NPV = | $4,000.67 | | | | | | | | | |

*Note:* The *Excel* formula for NPV is NPV (discount rate, cash inflow values) + I, where I is given as a negative number.

## How is it Used and Applied?

If the IRR is greater than the cost of capital, the project should be accepted. The advantages of using the IRR method are that it does not consider the time value of money and, therefore, is more exact and realistic than the accounting rate of return method. The shortcomings of this method are that (1) it is time-consuming to compute, especially when cash inflows are not even (although most business calculators have a program for calculating IRR), and (2) it fails to recognize the varying sizes of investment in competing projects and their respective dollar profitabilities.

# 70. Capitalization Rate

## Introduction

*Capitalization rate*, also called *cap rate* or *income yield*, is a widely used method of determining the rate of return on a real estate investment.

## How is it Computed?

The capitalization rate is found by dividing the net operating income (NOI) for the first year by the total investment.

## *Example*

Assume that net operating income equals $18,618 and purchase price equals $219,000. Then the cap rate is

$18,618/$219,000 = 8.5%

If the market rate is 10 percent, the fair market value of similar property is $18,618/10% = $186,180. The property may be overpriced.

## How is it Used and Applied?

The capitalization rate, when applied to the earnings of an investment, determines its appraisal or market value. The higher the cap rate, the lower the perceived risk to the investor and the lower the asking price paid. Whether a piece of property is over-priced or not depends on the rate of similar property derived from the marketplace.

There are two limitations to use of the cap rate: (1) It is based on only the first year's NOI; and (2) it ignores return through appreciation in property value.

The cap rate assists real estate investors who are interested in buying income-producing property in ascertaining the value of that property. A business owner may use the cap rate to determine the appraised value of a property to see if it qualifies for the loan under consideration.

# 71.   Gross Income Multiplier

## Introduction

The *gross income multiplier* is one method of determining the price of income-producing property. Other methods are the net income multiplier (NIM) (see Sec. 72) and the capitalization rate (see Sec. 70). This rule-of-thumb valuation, or pricing formula, is also used for acquiring companies.

## How is it Computed?

The gross income multiplier is obtained by dividing the asking price (or market value) of the property by the current gross rental income.

## *Example*

Assume that current gross rental income is $23,600 and the asking price is $219,000. Then the gross income multiplier is

$$\frac{\$219,000}{\$23,600} = 9.28$$

A property in a similar neighborhood may be valued at "eight times annual gross." Thus, if its annual gross rental income amounts to $23,600, the value is taken as 8 x $23,600 = $188,800, which means that the property may be overvalued.

## How is it Used and Applied?

The gross income multiplier is used to determine the value of a property. Applications of this approach in other industry sectors include the following:

1.   In the publishing industry, new, fast-growing magazines are worth 5 to 10 times before-tax annual earnings.
2.   Radio stations sell for 7.5 times earnings or cash flows.
3.   Insurance agencies sell for 150 percent of annual commissions.
4.   Automobile repair garages sell for 3 times average monthly receipts.

The real estate industry uses this approach to determine an approximate market value of a property. This approach should be used with caution, however, since different properties have different operating expenses that must be taken into account in determining value.

This rule-of-thumb pricing formula can be used for purchasing companies; however, reliance on this technique alone can result in gross oversimplification of the market value of a property.

See Sec. 142, Determining How Much Your Business is Worth.

# 72. Net Income Multiplier

## Introduction

The *net income multiplier* (NIM) is a method of determining the price of income-producing property. The other methods are the gross income multiplier (see Sec. 71) and the capitalization rate (see Sec. 70).

## How is it Computed?

$$\text{NIM} = \frac{\text{purchase price}}{\text{net operating income (NOI)}}$$

where NOI is the gross income less allowances for vacancies and operating expenses, except depreciation and debt payments.

## Example

Assume that NOI is $18,618 and the asking price is $219,000. The net income multiplier is calculated as follows:

$$\frac{\$219,000}{\$13,618} = 11.76$$

## How is it Used and Applied?

A property in a similar neighborhood may be valued at "10 times annual net." Thus, if its annual gross rental income amounts to $18,618, the value is taken as 10 x $18,618 = $186,180, which means that the property may be overvalued.

Real estate professionals can use this approach to determine an approximate market value for a property. This approach is better than the GIM approach since it takes into account vacancies and operating expenses.

# Part 8

# Scheduling, Planning, and Efficiency Measures

## 73. How Are Your Assets Operating?

### Introduction

The *operating assets ratio* analyzes the percentage of a company's assets used to generate revenue.

### How is it Computed?

$$\text{Operating assets ratio} = \frac{\text{operating assets}}{\text{total assets}}$$

### *Example*

A company reports the following information for 20x7 and 20x8:

|                                   | 20x7      | 20x8      |
| --------------------------------- | --------- | --------- |
| Operating assets                  | $100,000  | $200,000  |
| Total assets                      | 500,000   | 600,000   |
| Operating assets to total assets  | 20%       | 33.3%     |

Analysis shows that there has been an increase in the productive assets over the year, which should result in improved operations, and greater productive capacity, and therefore greater revenue.

## How is it Used and Applied?

The operating assets ratio isolates those assets that are actively employed in current operations. Such assets exclude both past-oriented and future-oriented assets. Past-oriented assets arise from prior errors, inefficiencies, or losses because of competitive factors or changes in business plans. Past-oriented assets, such as obsolete goods, idle plants, receivables under litigation, delinquent receivables, and nonperforming loans (no interest being recognized), have not yet been formerly recognized in the accounts. Future-oriented assets, such as land held for speculation and factories under construction, are acquired for corporate growth or for generating future sales. Nonoperating assets reduce profits and return on investment, because there is no benefit to current operations - that is, they neither generate sales nor reduce costs. Nonoperating assets are a "drain" on the company and may require financing.

# 74.   Repairs and Maintenance Ratios

## Introduction

Repairs and maintenance need to be conducted to ensure that fixed assets are in proper working condition. Repair and maintenance ratios demonstrate the level of investment that a company makes in these types of activities.

## How is it Computed?

There are two common repair and maintenance ratios by which a company's commitment can be measured:

1.     Repairs and maintenance to fixed assets :

$$\frac{\text{Repairs and maintenance}}{\text{Fixed assets}}$$

2.     Repairs and maintenance to sales:

$$\frac{\text{Repairs and maintenance}}{\text{Sales}}$$

## *Example*

A company provides two years of data relative to its fixed asset:

|  | 20x7 | 20x8 |
|---|---|---|
| Fixed assets | $200,000 | $ 175,000 |
| Repairs and maintenance | 7,800 | 4,100 |
| Replacement cost | 400,000 | 430,000 |

Replacement cost is the cost to replace the existing fixed asset with a new one.

There is now less maintenance of facilities, as indicated by the lower ratio of repairs to fixed assets—from 3.9 percent ($7,800/$200,000) in 20x7 to 2.3 percent ($4,100/$175,000) in 20x8, the substantially higher replacement cost relative to historical cost of the fixed assets, and the reduction in property, plant, and equipment from 20x7 to 20x8.

## How is it Used and Applied?

Failure to perform adequate maintenance for productive assets and failure to replace obsolete fixed assets with new and more efficient equipment will result in manufacturing and operating problems. By understanding the implications of these repair and maintenance ratios, users will be able to investigate possible problems, thus minimizing a risk that these failures would have a long-term negative effect on the company.

# 75. Maintenance and Repair Index

## Introduction

The *maintenance and repair index* reveals how much maintenance and repair time was needed for each direct hour of labor. The ratio is best used to compare groups of similar machinery.

## How is it Computed?

Maintenance and repair index

$$= \quad \frac{\text{Maintenance and repair hours}}{\text{Total direct labor hours}}$$

## *Example*

Harry Cohen is evaluating the condition of machinery in his manufacturing business. He wants to evaluate the following information:

|  | 20x7 | 20x8 |
|---|---|---|
| Maintenance and repair hours | 500 | 1,500 |
| Total direct labor hours | 30,000 | 28,000 |
| Maintenance and repair hour to total direct labor | 1.7% | 5.4% |

The analysis shows that the increase in the ratio from 20x7 to 20x8 is unfavorable. It indicates that more maintenance and repairs are being required, which indicates that the business is sustaining more problems with its machinery.

## How is it Used and Applied?

The extent of repairs necessary compared to direct labor input may reflect the quality of manufacturing equipment. An increasing trend in the percentage may reveal that the business has had to cope with an increasing number of machinery malfunctions.

# 76. Utilization of Space

## Introduction

A business should use its space fully, not waste it. Floor space should generate sufficient revenue to justify the cost. If this is not the case, the space is not profitable and perhaps the location should be abandoned or the company moved elsewhere. Business activity is compared to space as a measure of effective utilization and efficiency.

There should be sound planning to assure that employees have just enough space in which to do their jobs effectively and safely, and which is healthy (e.g., enough air) and psychologically pleasing (e.g., sufficient lighting).

Parking lot space should be sufficient to accommodate customers and employees. However, the space should not be excessive because of the high cost associated with land.

Because real estate costs are significant for owned property, it is important to generate adequate earnings to cover the cost.

For rented property, rental charges are typically significant. Rents may be tied to a price index and/or vary with sales. Rents are typically higher in newer locations than in older ones because of the higher cost of construction. Further, rents in urban areas are higher than in rural areas because urban land is more expensive. The ratio of rent expense to sales indicates how well space is being used in the manufacturing process.

## How is it Computed?

There are several ways to calculate the efficiency of space use, using sales, production, profitability, customer base, staff level, and rentals.

$$\text{Revenue per square foot} = \frac{\text{net sales}}{\text{square feet of space}}$$

$$\text{Production per square foot} = \frac{\text{total units produced}}{\text{square feet of space}}$$

$$\text{Profit per square foot} = \frac{\text{net income}}{\text{square feet of space}}$$

$$\text{Customer space} = \frac{\text{number of customers}}{\text{square feet of space}}$$

$$\text{Employee space} = \frac{\text{square feet of space}}{\text{number of employees}}$$

$$\text{Parking lot space} = \frac{\text{square feet of parking lot space}}{\text{number of employees}}$$

$$\text{Rent per square foot} = \frac{\text{rent expense}}{\text{square feet of space}}$$

$$\text{Rent expense ratio} = \frac{\text{rent expense}}{\text{net sales}}$$

$$\text{Expenses per square foot for owned property} = \frac{\text{expense of owning property}}{\text{square feet of space}}$$

Where expenses of owning property include insurance, real estate taxes, depreciation, maintenance, and utilities.

## Example

A business owner uses the following information to appraise how well space in his business is being used:

|  | 20x7 | 20x8 |
|---|---|---|
| Sales | $3,000,000 | $4,000,000 |
| Net income | 2,000,000 | 1,500,000 |
| Units produced | 200,000 | 250,000 |
| Square feet | 100,000 | 100,000 |

The relevant ratios are:

|  | 20x7 | 20x7 |
|---|---|---|
| Revenue per square foot | $30 | $40 |
| Profit per square foot | 10 | 15 |
| Production per square foot | 2.0 | 2.5 |

The ratio show better utilization of space in generating revenue, profit, and production volume in 20x8. The business has experienced an improved level of efficiency over the period 20x7 – 20x8.

## How is it Used and Applied?

A decline in the ratios of (1) net sales to space and (2) number of customers to space are negative indicators, because they show improper space planning and usage. Perhaps the business is losing accounts or the space is just too large. These ratios will differ significantly among various types of businesses. For example, a business with a few small accounts that require a large showroom will have a low ratio. However, a mail-order business with many customers and high-priced merchandise operating out of a small office will have a high ratio.

Space ratios can be used to determine whether square footage should be expanded or contracted. Further, if rental charges for space occupied are excessive, the lease should be modified at its expiration or the company should be moved to a new location.

The profit return on space is also important to consider when deciding whether to expand or relocate. In indicates whether the space used historically generated acceptable profit levels.

A determination should be made as to whether plant space is being utilized effectively in production. An attempt should be made to keep rental costs down without sacrificing units produced.

The sales-to-space ratio should be examined to determine whether the space used is providing an adequate return in the form of revenue generation. This is particularly true when leasing is very expensive. An example is a retail store in a fashionable neighborhood. High-rent locations may be suitable for high-priced items, but not low-priced ones. In the latter case, the revenue obtained may be inadequate to cover the significant rental payments.

The rent-to-space ratio of a business may be compared to other competitors to determine the management of space. In evaluating the space of a new location, consideration should be given to geographic location to meet customer needs, security, public transportation, and zoning requirements.

If the ratio of rent expense to sales is decreasing, this may indicate business growth. There is efficient utilization of physical facilities.

The business should establish space standards by job description. For example, executives may have private rooms, whereas factory workers may have small workstations.

# 77.  Efficiency Measurements

## Introduction

It is important to gauge the efficiency and effectiveness of your business so as to maximize profitability. Are your capital assets and operations efficient in carrying on the daily activities of the business? Have sales and earnings grown consistently over the years?

## How is it Computed?

Three common measures of efficiency involve profit margin, return on total assets, and return on physical plant:

$$\text{Profit margin} = \frac{\text{net income}}{\text{sales}}$$

$$\text{Return on total assets} = \frac{\text{net income}}{\text{total assets}}$$

$$\text{Return on property, plant, and equipment} = \frac{\text{net income}}{\text{productive assets}}$$

## *Example*

A business experienced the following for the period 20x7 to 20x8:

|  | 20x7 | 20x8 |
|---|---|---|
| Sales | $600,000 | $900,000 |
| Total assets | 300,000 | 310,000 |
| Net income | 60,000 | 200,00 |

An analysis of the data reveals the following:

$$\text{Increase in sales} = \frac{\$300,000}{\$600,000} = 50\%$$

$$\text{Increase in profit} = \frac{\$140,000}{\$60,000} = 23\%$$

|  | 20x7 | | 20x8 | |
|---|---|---|---|---|
| Profit margin | $\dfrac{\$60,000}{\$600,000}$ | $= 10\%$ | $\dfrac{\$200,000}{\$900,000}$ | $= 22\%$ |
| Return on assets | $\dfrac{\$60,000}{\$300,000}$ | $= 20\%$ | $\dfrac{\$200,000}{\$310,000}$ | $= 64.5\%$ |

Worker efficiency has improved sharply, since sales generated per employee increased from $1,200 per employee ($60,000/50) to $3,333 per employee ($200,000/60). These are all very positive efficiency and productive trends.

## How is it Used and Applied?

Compare profitability to sales and assets to ascertain the success of the business. Cost controls and/or better manufacturing procedures may be needed to bolster profits.

There are other ways to determine how efficient your business is; which of the measures you use depends a great deal on your industry. You may wish to look at several.

◆ Input/output relationship—What was put in the product or service in terms of time and cost, and what was received in terms of quantity, quality, and revenue. Was the effort expended worth the results attained?

◆ New products.

◆ New customer accounts.

◆ Manufacturing costs to units produced.

◆ Production volume to labor hours.

◆ Reduced equipment downtime.

◆ Trends in sales and profit.

◆ The number of years of profitable operations.

◆ Trends in production volume.

◆ Trends in market share.

See Sec. 137, Employee Efficiency.

# 78.   Direct Costs-to-Sales Ratios

## Introduction

Direct costs include direct materials, direct labor, direct factory overhead, and other costs such as direct travel and computer usage.  Direct costs relate *directly* to the product or service. Direct cost ratios are commonly employed in analyzing operational cost activity. Indirect costs, on the other hand, are difficult to trace to specific revenue.

# How is it Computed?

There are several ratios to relate costs to sales, such as looking at direct material, direct labor, overhead and travel.

$$\text{Direct material to sales} = \frac{\text{direct material}}{\text{sales}}$$

$$\text{Direct labor to sales} = \frac{\text{direct labor}}{\text{sales}}$$

$$\text{Direct factory overhead to sales} = \frac{\text{direct factory overhead}}{\text{Sales}}$$

Other indirect costs to sales include:

$$\text{Direct travel to sales} = \frac{\text{direct travel}}{\text{sales}}$$

$$\text{Computer usage to sales} = \frac{\text{computer usage}}{\text{sales}}$$

and so on.

## *Example*

The following information if provided for a business:

|                          | 20x7        | 20x8        |
|--------------------------|-------------|-------------|
| Direct labor             | $1,100,000  | $1,200,000  |
| Direct factory overhead  | 1,150,000   | 1,340,000   |
| Sales                    | 1,000,000   | 1,200,000   |

The relevant ratios are:

|                          | 20x7 | 20x8  |
|--------------------------|------|-------|
| Direct labor to sales    | 10%  | 16.7% |
| Factory overhead to sales| 15   | 28.3  |

The increase in production costs compared to sales over the year indicates less efficiency and productivity in the manufacturing process than in the past. Cost excesses have taken place, which might indicate inadequate supervision and planning.

## How is it Used and Applied?

The production manager should analyze the ratios of production cost elements to sales. The reasons for changes in the ratios should be identified as a basin on which to estimate and plan production. If production costs increase significantly as a percentage of sales, it is a negative indication with regard to the business' manufacturing operations. In this case, the owner should ask: is cost control lacking, and if so, who was at fault. The owner must identify whether the problem is internal (e.g., poor supervision) or external (e.g., general economic problems) and take corrective steps.

If, for example, analysis reveals that delivery charges have skyrocketed compared to sales, investigation should determine whether the reason is poor traffic routing and planning or increased fuel costs.

# Part 9
# Preparing Financial Statements and Charts

## 79.  Balance Sheet Basics

### Introduction

The *balance sheet* presents the assets, liabilities, and owner's capital of a small business and enables the owner to evaluate its financial condition. The balance sheet is cumulative and thereby differs from the income statement, which shows the profit earned for a given time interval only.

The balance sheet lists the type and amount of each asset, liability, and capital account (of partners) as of the last day of the reporting period. This listing is necessary so that the proprietor knows the specific items that he or she owns (i.e., cash, inventory, equipment), what is owed (accounts payable, loans payable), and the amount of ending equity in the business (capital). The equity at the end of the period consists of the capital investments made plus the profits earned less any withdrawals.

The balance sheet is classified into major groups of assets and liabilities in order to facilitate analysis of the financial health of the business.

Assets may be broken down into the following categories:

*Current assets* are those assets which are expected to be converted into cash within I year. Examples are cash, accounts receivable, and inventory.

*Fixed assets* are assets employed in the production of goods or services and having a life greater than I year. They have tangible physical substance and include land, building, machinery, and automobiles. Unlike inventory, these assets are not being held for sale in the normal course of business.

*Intangible assets* are assets with a long-term life that lack physical substance, such as a right granted by the government (patent) or by another company (franchise or license).

An example is the right acquired by paying a fee to open a fast-food franchise.

High-risk assets may involve future write-offs. An example of a high-risk asset is obsolete inventory, receivables from financially troubled customers, rental equipment not actually being leased, and undesirable real estate.

Liabilities may be classed as either current or noncurrent. One year is the demarcation line.

## How is it Computed?

Assets - liabilities = capital (owner's equity)

### A BUSINESS
### Balanced Sheet – December 31, 20XX

| | |
|---|---|
| Current Assets | Current Liabilities |
| Cash | Accrued Expenses Payable |
| Receivables | Accounts Payable |
| Inventory | Short-term Loans Payable |
| Office Supplies | Noncurrent Liabilities |
| Fixed Assets | Mortgage Payable |
| Automobiles | Long-term Loans Payable |
| Less: Accumulated Depreciation | |
| Equipment | Total Liabilities |
| Less: Accumulated Depreciation | |
| Intangible Assets | Owner's Equity |
| Franchise Fees | Mr. A, Capital |
| Total Assets | Total Liabilities and Capital |

$$\text{Realization risk in assets} = \frac{\text{high risk assets}}{\text{total assets}}$$

## Example 1

### CHARLENE DRAKE
### Balanced Sheet – October 31, 20XX

| | | | |
|---|---|---|---|
| Assets | | | |
| Cash | | | $10,000 |
| Accounts Receivable | | | 20,500 |
| Office Supplies | | | 10,500 |
| Office Equipment | | | 30,000 |
| Total Assets | | | $71,000 |
| Liabilities and Capital | | | |
| Liabilities | | | |
| Accounts Payable | | | $30,000 |
| Capital | | | |
| Balance, Oct. 1, | | $35,600 | |
| Net Income for Oct. | $5,800 | | |
| Less: Withdrawals | 400 | | |
| Increase in Capital | | 5,400 | |
| Total Capital | | | 41,000 |
| Total Liabilities and Capital | | | $71,000 |

# Example 2

## JOHN WESTON
## Classified Balanced Sheet – December 31, 20XX

Assets
  Current Assets

| | | |
|---|---:|---:|
| Cash | $ 3,000 | |
| Accounts Receivable | 6,000 | |
| Inventory | 5,000 | |
| Office Supplies | 1,000 | |
|   Total Current Assets | | $15,000 |
| Long-Term Investments | | |
|   Investment in X Company Stock | | 2,000 |
| Property, Plant, and Equipment | | |
|   Land | $20,000 | |
|   Building | 30,000 | |
|   Machinery | 7,000 | |
|   Delivery Truck | 5,000 | |
|   Total Property, Plant, and Equipment | | 62,000 |
| Intangible Assets | | |
|   Patents | | $ 3,000 |
| Deferred Charges | | |
|   Deferred Moving Costs | | 1,000 |
| Total Assets | | $83,000 |
| Liabilities and Capital | | |
|   Current Liabilities | | |
|     Accounts Payable | $8,000 | |
|     Notes Payable (9 months) | 4,000 | |
|     Accrued Liabilities | 2,000 | |
|     Total Current Liabilities | | $14,000 |
|   Noncurrent Liabilities | | |
|     Mortgage Payable | | 30,000 |
|     Total Liabilities | | $44,000 |
| Capital, Dec. 31 | | 39,000 |
| Total Liabilities and Capital | | $83,000 |

## How is it Used and Applied?

The balance sheet is useful to the owner of a small business for evaluation and control purposes, because it indicates what resources the business has and what it owes. For example, an analysis of the balance sheet can help the owner to determine whether there are sufficient resources to pay debt.

The balance sheet position will tell the owner whether it will be easy or difficult to obtain credit based on the business' financial position.

The owner is interested in the quality of the assets in terms of the amount and timing of the realization into cash. Asset quality is affected by economic conditions and the nature of business operations.

# 80. Profit and Loss Statement

## Introduction

The income statement reports the revenue less the expenses of a business. If total revenue exceeds total expenses, there is a profit. The profit will increase the owner's equity in the business. In the opposite case, there is a loss.

*Revenue* is the increase in capital arising from the sale of merchandise (as by a retail business) or the performance of services (as by an engineer).

*Expenses* decrease capital and result from performing those functions necessary to generate revenue. The amount of an expense is equal to the cost of the inventory sold, the value of the services rendered (e.g., salaries expense), or the expenditures necessary for conducting business operations (e.g., rent expense) during the period. *Selling expenses* are those incurred to obtain the sale (e.g., advertising, salesperson salaries) and in distributing the merchandise to the customer (e.g., freight paid on a shipment). *General and administrative expenses* apply to the costs of running the business as a whole and do not relate to the selling function. Examples are office salaries and depreciation on office furniture.

Other revenue (expense) relates to incidental sources of revenue and expense of a *nonoperating* nature. These revenue or expense sources do not apply to the major activities of the business. They are typically of a financial nature. Examples are interest income and interest expense.

## How is it Computed?

### A SERVICE BUSINESS

### Income Statement

### For the Year Ended December 31, 20XX

Revenue (professional fees earned, commission income)

Less: Expenses

Net Income

A business that has inventory (retail store, manufacturer, wholesaler) shows the following income statement:

## A RETAIL STORE

### Income Statement

### For the Month Ended October 31, 20XX

Sales
Less: Cost of Goods (Merchandise) Sold
  Beginning Inventory + Purchases (or Cost of Goods Manufactured) =
  Cost of Goods Available − Ending Inventory
Cost of Goods Sold
Gross Profit
Less: Operating Expenses
  Selling Expenses
  General and Administrative Expenses
Net Income

## Example 1

Charlene Drake is a self-employed engineer. For the month of October 20XX, she earned income of $10,000 from services rendered. Her business expenses were: telephone, $1,000; electricity, $500; rent, $2,000; secretarial salary, $300; and office supplies used, $400. Her income statement for the period is as follows:

### CHARLENE DRAKE

### Income Statement

### For the Month Ended October 31, 20XX

| | | |
|---|---:|---:|
| Revenue from Professional Services | | $10,000 |
| Less: Operating Expenses | | |
| Telephone | $1,000 | |
| Electricity | 500 | |
| Rent | 2,000 | |
| Secretarial Salary | 300 | |
| Office Supplies | 400 | |
| Total Operating Expenses | | 4,200 |
| Net Income | | $ 5,800 |

## Example 2

### JOHN WESTON

### Classified Income Statement

### For the Month Ended December, 20XX

| | | | |
|---|---|---|---|
| Revenue | | | |
| Gross Sales | | $40,000 | |
| Less: Sales Returns and Allowances | $1,000 | | |
| Sales Discounts | 500 | 1,500 | |
| Net Sales | | | $38,500 |
| Cost of Goods Sold | | | |
| Inventory, Jan. 1 | | $ 1,000 | |
| Add: Purchases | | 15,000 | |
| Cost of Goods Available for Sale | | $16,000 | |
| Less: Inventory, Dec. 31 | | 5,000 | |
| Cost of Goods Sold | | | 11,000 |
| Gross Profit | | | $27,500 |
| | | | |
| Operating Expenses | | | |
| Selling Expenses | | | |
| Advertising | $3,000 | | |
| Salespeople's Salaries | 2,000 | | |
| Travel and Entertainment | 1,000 | | |
| Depreciation on Delivery Truck | 500 | $ 6,500 | |
| General and Administrative Expenses | | | |
| Officers' Salaries | $5,000 | | |
| Rent | 2,000 | | |
| Insurance | 1,000 | 8,000 | |
| Total Operating Expenses | | | $14,500 |
| Operating Income | | | $13,000 |
| Other Expenses (net) | | | |
| Interest Expense | | $ 2,000 | |
| Less: Interest Income | $ 500 | | |
| Dividend Income | 1,000 | 1,500 | |
| Other Expenses (net) | | | 500 |
| Net Income | | | $12,500 |

## How is it Used and Applied?

The income statement provides a detailed listing of the sources and amounts of revenues and expenses. This breakdown allows the owner to determine trends in revenue and expense items. For example, if revenue is decreasing, the owner will want to know why and how sales can be improved. The owner will want to know if a given expense item (e.g., telephone) is disproportionately large so that he or she can determine the reasons why and possibly control that expense item.

An analysis of the income statement indicates the current and future earning power of the business. The owner is interested in the effect of decisions on profitability.

The income statement shows whether the small business is making money for the period. It indicates whether revenue is sufficient to meet expenses. It reveals whether costs are excessive and need to be reduced. It also reveals the productivity of the business.

Income statements covering different time periods are easily compared; the comparison over time of revenue sources, expense items, and the relationship between them might reveal areas requiring attention and corrective action. For example, if service revenue or sales have declined sharply over the past several months, action is needed to reverse this trend.

If profit relative to sales is down, it may indicate the failure to control costs.

The owner should compare labor growth to sales: Labor costs may be disproportionate to operational activity.

The owner uses the income statement to evaluate past performance, which, to some extent, is indicative of success in the future.

# 81. Ratios, Proportions, and Percentages

## Introduction

As a business owner, you have to make sense out of the numbers in the financial statements prepared for your business. Therefore, the numbers must be put in a meaningful context.

A *ratio* compares two or more numbers (quantities, costs). Further, a cost can be allocated according to a ratio.

A *proportion* occurs when two ratios are equal, such as $2:1 = 4:2$.

The term *percent* (%) means per 100. Therefore, 60 percent is the same as 60/100 (or 0.60 or 6/10 or 3/5).

## How is it Computed?

A ratio may be expressed as:

$$\frac{a}{b}$$

A percentage of an item to the total may be computed as follows:

$$\frac{\text{item amount}}{\text{total}}$$

A proportion expresses the equality of two ratios:

$$\frac{a}{b} = \frac{c}{d}$$

In a *direct proportion*, as one ratio increases (decreases), so does the other. In an inverse proportion, as one ratio increases, the other decreases, and vice versa.

A *percentage* is obtained by multiplying a number (called the base) by a percent (called the rate):

Percentage = rate x base

  Or

Rate = $\dfrac{\text{percentage}}{\text{base}}$

Or

Base = $\dfrac{\text{percentage}}{\text{rate}}$

## Example 1

If profit is $60,000, and sales are $1,200,000, the profit margin is 5 percent.

## Example 2

To allocate $200,000 of profit to three partners in the ratio of 5:4:1,

5/10 x $200,000 = $100,000

4/10 x $200,000 =   80,000

1/10 x $200,000 =   20,000

                    $200,000

When one term in a proportion is missing, cross-multiplication will find it.

## Example 3

A new owner of a small business wants to determine how much profit should be earned relative to the amount invested. To do so, he/she will compare it against an existing competitor. The competitor reports a profit of $100,000 on a total investment of $200,000. The new owner invests $40,000. The expected profit is $20,000, as computed below:

$$x:40 = 100:200$$
$$x/40 = 100/200$$
$$200x = 400$$
$$x = 20$$

## Example 4

For the first 3 months of the year, advertising costs were $5000, while sales volume was $100,000. The owner of the business wants to know the relationship between advertising and sales.

$$\$5,000:\$100,000 = 5:100 = 1:20$$

## Example 5

A construction job requires 8 workers for 6 days. The owner wants to know how many workers will be needed to complete the job in 2 fewer days.

$$x/8 = 6/4$$
$$4x = 48$$
$$x = 12 \text{ workers}$$

## Example 6

Phil invests $60,000 and Bill invests $20,000 in their partnership. It is agreed that profits will be shared in the same proportion as the capital investment. If Phil's share of the profit is $15,000, then Bill receives

$$\$60,000/\$20,000 = \$15,000/x$$
$$3/1 = \$15,000/x$$
$$3x = \$15,000$$
$$x = \$5,000$$

## Example 7

A business owner wants to know what her income was last year if she was in the 40 percent tax bracket and paid $25,000 in taxes.

$$\text{Base} = \frac{\text{percentage}}{\text{rate}} = \$25,000/0.40 = \$62,500$$

Another useful calculation is:

New quantity = original quantity + increase (or - decrease)

## Example 8

A business had inventory on 1/1/20x8 of 650 units. In the first quarter of the year, the inventory increased by 10 percent. The inventory on 3/31/20x8 was:

New quantity = original quantity + increase

= 650 + 65 = 715

## Example 9

The price of a product, including an 8 percent sales tax, was $25. The price of the product itself is determined as follows:

New quantity = original quantity + increase

$$\$25 = x + 8\%x$$
$$\$25 = 1.08x$$
$$\$25/1.98 = x$$
$$\$23.15 = x$$

## Example 10

After a 20 percent discount, the selling price of a product is $80. The regular price is found as:

New quantity = original quantity - decrease

$$\$80 = x - 0.20x$$
$$\$80 = 0.80x$$
$$\$80/0.80 = x$$
$$\$100 = x$$

The discount is:

$$\$100 - \$80 = \$20$$

To obtain the equivalent before-tax rate of return on a tax-free investment, we use the following formula:

$$\frac{\text{Tax-free rate of return}}{1 - \text{tax rate}}$$

## Example 11

The equivalent before-tax rate of return of earning 4 percent on a tax-free bond assuming a 30 percent tax bracket is:

$$0.04/(1 - t) = 0.04/(1 - 0.3) = 0.04/0.7 = 5.7\%$$

## How is it Used and Applied?

A comparison of numbers in the form of a ratio is more enlightening than either of the numbers individually. For example, the profit of a business can be compared to the total assets in the business and to sales to obtain rates of return. Ratios can be compared to those of similar businesses to determine relative position. Percentages make it easier to determine the importance of each item (e.g., costs, product revenue) in relation to the total (e.g., total costs, total product revenue) and to each other. Percentages are also useful in determining the percentage change in an item over time. For example, a 60 percent increase in sales over a 1 year period is a very favorable sign.

The business owner may use proportions in connection with producing products. In other words, a mix of products may be manufactured to result in a combination generating the highest overall profit for the business.

# 82. Charts and Graphs

## Introduction

A business manager can use charts and graphs to visually show important information in an interesting way. Charts may be used to indicate sales dollars or units, costs, profits, or number of employees.

There are three types of charts. A *line* chart shows change over time. A *bar* chart compares related information and may present relative importance. A *pie* chart presents a unit's contribution to the whole. The chart should be accompanied by an explanation. For example, a comment may be made about the trend and the reasons for changes in direction.

## How is it Prepared?

The chart or graph should be at the proper place within a report or presentation. There should be a balance between visual presentation and narrative discussion.

To condense the information on a graph so it is clear, legends and footnotes may be used below the graph. The title should appear above the graph. If the graph needs an explanation of a part(s), it should be annotated with small notes on the side of it.

A line chart is shown in Fig. 82.1, a bar chart in Fig. 82.2, and a pie (circle) chart in Fig. 82.3.

### Figure 82.1: A line chart

### Figure 82.2: A bar chart

**Figure 82.3: A pie chart**

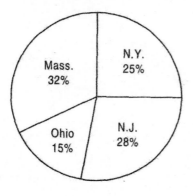

Total Sales by Geographic Area

## Example

A chart may appear as follows:

**Summary of Employees**

| Category | 20x8 | 20x7 |
|----------|------|------|
| Increases | | |
| Clerical | 23 | 20 |
| Operations | 18 | 16 |
| Total | 41 | 36 |
| Sales | $600,000 | $400,000 |

The chart indicates that there was a 13.9 percent (5/46) increase in staff due to increased work load. The higher labor cost was well worth it, because of the significant increase in sales revenue (50 percent) generated from new business.

## How is it Used and Applied?

Charts and graphs may be used by the small business manager to show financial and nonfinancial information in an understandable manner, especially to those who are not familiar with the business. Further, presenting a group of complex numbers and calculations may bore and confuse readers. Visual presentations may be able to communicate mathematical information in digestible form. Visual discussions may be helpful in staff meetings, presentations to lenders and investors, and when courting potential customers.

235

Analysis of sales, production, and advertising are types of trend data that work well in graphic form. They can be shown as both budgeted and actual figures, and may be given by month and year.

# Part 10

# How Healthy is the Business?

## 83. Comparing Accounts over the Years (Horizontal Analysis)

### Introduction

*Horizontal analysis* is a time series analysis of financial statements covering more than one accounting period. Horizontal analysis looks at the percentage change in an account over time. It shows direction. Vertical analysis is covered in the next section.

### How is it Computed?

$$\text{Percentage change} = \frac{\text{dollar change}}{\text{base year amount}} = \frac{\text{year 2} - \text{year I}}{\text{year I}}$$

### Example

Horizontal analysis across two years yields the following outcome: If sales in 20x7 and 20x8 were $100,000 and $300,000, respectively, the increase is $200,000/$100,000 = 200 percent.

### How is it Used and Applied?

By examining the magnitude and direction of a financial statement item, an owner can evaluate the reasonableness of the trend. A five-year period of analysis is recommended.

Trend analysis identifies areas of wide divergence, and alerts owners to the need for further evaluation. For example, a large increase in sales returns and allowances coupled with a decrease in sales would be a cause for concern. An owner might compare these results with those of competitors to investigate whether the problem is industrywide, or particular to the business.

The trend may be distorted for a one-time unusual item, and therefore the financial figures should be adjusted to exclude the extraordinary item. Examples are a one-time substantial gain from the sale of land held for 50 years, and a one-time government contract.

See Sec. 84, Comparing Accounts within the Current Year.

# 84. Comparing Accounts within the Current Year

## Introduction

In *common size (vertical)* analysis of financial statements, an item is used as a base value and all other accounts in the financial statement are compared to this base value.

## How is it Computed?

On the balance sheet, total assets equal 100 percent. In vertical analysis, each asset is stated as a percentage of total assets. Similarly, total liabilities and stockholders' equity are assigned 100 percent, with a given liability or equity account stated as a percentage of total liabilities and stockholders' equity.

On the income statement, 100 percent is assigned to net sales, with all revenue and expense accounts then related to it.

The following examples illustrate vertical analysis of financial statement data for Tie City.

### Example 1

| | | |
|---|---|---|
| Net sales | $300,000 | 100% |
| Less: Cost of sales | 60,000 | 20 |
| Gross profit | $240,000 | 80% |
| Less: Operating expenses | 150,000 | 50 |
| Net income | $ 90,000 | 30% |

## Example 2

| | | |
|---|---|---|
| Current assets | $200,000 | 25% |
| Noncurrent assets | 600,000 | 75 |
| Total assets | $800,000 | 100% |

## How is it Used and Applied?

Common size percentages can be compared from one period to another to identify areas that require improvements in performance.

Vertical analysis tends to exhibit the internal structure of the business, indicating the relation of each income statement account to revenue. It shows clearly the mix of assets that produces the income and the mix of sources of capital, regardless of whether they are provided by current or long-term liabilities or by owners' capital.

The vertical percentages of a particular business should be compared to those of competing business or to industry percentages so that relative position may be ascertained.

As in horizontal analysis, vertical analysis is not an end in itself. The owner must be prepared to probe deeper into the areas that the analysis indicates may have possible problems.

See Sec. 83, Comparing Accounts over the Years (Horizontal Analysis).

# 85. How to Use Index Numbers

## Introduction

An *index number* is a percentage by which an amount in a given year is expressed as a ratio to a base-year figure. Index numbers can be used for quantity, price, and value. Index numbers can be used to make clearer relationships among financial figures. In an *index-number trend series*, an index is assigned to a base year and values for other years are computed by reference to the base year.

## How is it Computed?

A base year that is most representative (typical, normal) of the business' operations is selected and assigned an index of 100. All index numbers are computed with regard to the base year. When there is a very long time period under examination (e.g., 10 years), the base year may be based on an average of a few years (e.g., 3 years).

$$\text{Index} = \frac{\text{current year amount}}{\text{base year amount}}$$

*Caution:* As with the computation of year-to-year percentage changes, certain fluctuations in a series, such as changes from negative to positive amounts, cannot be expressed by means of index numbers.

An index number for production cost might be based on price per unit in a typical year. For example, if the price per unit was $20 in the first year (selected as the base year), the owner would just multiply the units produced in each year by the base price per unit to derive a constant-dollar amount of production.

There are several types of indexes and several ways to compute them. They include single, composite, value, Laspeyres, Paasche, and link indices.

A *single index number* is used to compare individual products, while an *aggregate* (*composite*) *index number* applies to a group of products.

$$\text{Single index} = \frac{p_n \text{ or } q_n}{p_o \text{ or } q_o}$$

where $p_n$ = price of the product in a given year

$p_0$ = price of the product in the base year

$q_n$ = quantity of the product in a given year

$q_0$ = quantity of the product in the base year

*Note:* Quantity may be expressed in terms of either units produced or units sold.

A *value index* is the price of the product multiplied by the units sold (or produced).

$$\text{Value index} = \frac{p_n \times q_n}{p_o \times q_o}$$

To be useful, a composite index should be *weighted* based on the quantities of the product involved. For example, a price index of 120 for product x in a given year means that it was 20 percent higher in price than that in the base year – a single index. A price index of 140 percent for products A-Z is a composite index because it applies to a *basket* (more than one) of products.

*Laspeyres' composite index* weights the prices by the quantities at the *base year.* It is expressed as:

$$I(L) = \frac{\sum p_n q_n}{\sum p_o q_o}$$

Where $\sum$ = sum

*Paasche's index*, unlike the Laspeyre's index, uses the *current year's* quantities as the weights. It is expressed as:

$$I(P) = \frac{\Sigma P_n q_n}{\Sigma P_o q_o}$$

A *link relative index* always uses as the base the immediately preceding year. The index number is a percentage comparison to the prior year, which is beneficial when making year-to-year comparisons. However, this index formulation is *not* useful in deriving long-run comparisons.

If the owner wants to change the base to a more recent year to make it more up to date, then the original index should be divided by the index of the newly prescribed base year:

$$\text{Index (shifted)} = \frac{\text{original index}}{\text{old index of new year base}}$$

## Example 1

The base year is 20x6 and sales for that year are $600,000. An index number of 100 is assigned to 20x6. Sales for 20x7 and 20x8 are $660,000 and $500,000, respectively. The appropriate index numbers are:

20x7: $\dfrac{\$660,000}{\$660,000} = 110$

20x8: $\dfrac{\$500,000}{\$600,000} = 83$

An owner who sees this type of sharp decline in sales in 20x8 should study the causes and identify responsible parties.

## Example 2

The price of a product in the base year was $25; today the price is $30. The price index is:

$$\frac{P_n}{P_o} = \frac{\$30}{\$25} = 120\%$$

## Example 3

The quantity for a product sold in 20x8 was 60,000, while in 20x0 (the base year), the selling price was $7 and 25,000 units were sold.

$$\frac{q_n}{q_o} = \frac{60,000}{40,000} = 150\%$$

## Example 4

In 20x8, product x had a selling price of $10 and 30,000 units were sold; in 20x2 (the base year), the selling price was $7 and 25,000 units were sold.

$$\text{Simple value index} \quad \frac{P_n q_n}{P_n q_n} = \frac{\$10 \times 30,000}{\$7 \times 25,000} = \frac{\$300,000}{\$175,000} = 171\%$$

## Example 5

A business presents the following information for its products:

| Product | Average price 20x2 | Average price 20x8 | Quantities 20x2 | Quantities 20x8 |
|---------|-----------|-----------|-----------|-----------|
| A | $1.00 | $1.10 | 8,000 | 9,000 |
| B | 1.20 | 1.40 | 5,000 | 7,000 |
| C | 0.80 | 0.90 | 5,600 | 5,400 |

The Laspeyres' composite index for 20x8 for the three products using 20x2 as the base year is:

$$I(L) = \frac{\Sigma P_n q_0}{\Sigma P_n q_0} = \frac{\$20,840}{\$18,480} = 112.8\%$$

| Product | $P_n q_0$ | $P_0 q_0$ |
|---------|-----------|-----------|
| A | $ 8,800 | $ 8,000 |
| B | 7,000 | 6,000 |
| C | 5,040 | 4,480 |
| Total | $20,840 | $18,480 |

## Example 6

Assume the same information as in Example 5 except that we now compute Paasche's composite index as follows:

$$I(P) = \frac{\Sigma P_n q_n}{\Sigma P_0 q_n} = \frac{\$24,560}{\$21,720} = 113.1\%$$

| Product | $P_n q_n$ | $P_0 q_n$ |
|---------|-----------|-----------|
| A | $ 9,900 | $ 9,000 |
| B | 9,800 | 8,400 |
| C | 4,860 | 4,320 |
| Total | $24,560 | $21,720 |

## Example 7

A value index is to be shifted from 20x0 to 20x8. The 20x0 index was 100. The old index of 20x8 was 134. The new value index for 20x0 is:

$$\frac{100}{134} = 74.6\%$$

## How is it Used and Applied?

Index numbers are useful in measuring and clarifying important financial data. Sales, production, and costs may be expressed in index numbers. When comparing accounts covering more than 3 years, the year-to-year method of comparison may become too cumbersome. Often the best way to examine a long-term trend is through the use of index numbers. The owner can identify any financial statement accounts or items that seem to be out of line. This includes production volume, sales volume, prices, and costs. If the trend is illogical or signals a problem, the item should be investigated. Where possible, corrective action should be taken.

# 86. Growth Rate

## Introduction

*Growth rate* is the percentage change in earnings, sales, or total assets, compared to a base-year amount. It is also the compounded annual rate of growth in earnings.

## How is it Computed?

The compound annual rate of growth can be computed as

$$F_n = P \times T_1(i,n)$$

Solving this for $T_1$, we obtain

$$T_1(i,n) = \frac{F_n}{P}$$

The growth rate can be calculated using financial calculators and/or spreadsheet software.

## Example

Assume that your company has earnings per share of $2.50 in 20x1, and 10 years later the earnings per share has increased to $3.70. The compound annual rate of growth in earnings per share is computed as follows:

$$F_{10} = \$3.70 \text{ and } P = \$2.50$$

Therefore,

$$T_1(i, 10) = \frac{\$3.70}{\$2.50} = 1.48$$

From Table 1 an $T_1$ of 1.48 at 10 years is at $i = 4\%$. The compound annual rate of growth is therefore 4 percent.

## How is it Used and Applied?

The growth rate is used in many ways. Owners need to know the rate of growth in earnings in order to determine how they are doing financially. Performance is best measured over a 5-year period.

# 87. Current Ratio

## Introduction

Current assets have a life of 1 year or less and include such items as cash, accounts receivable, and inventory. The *current ratio*, which is subject to seasonal variability, is used to measure the ability of a business to pay its short-term bills out of current assets. Because it shows the margin of safety to cover any possible shrinkage in the value of current assets, it is an indicator of liquidity. The current ratio conveys the extent to which current assets are available to cover every $1 of short-term debt.

## How is it Computed?

$$\text{Current ratio} = \frac{\text{current assets}}{\text{current liabilities}}$$

In general, the current ratio for a business should be at least 2:1. The adequacy of the current ratio depends on the particular industry under examination. For a full understanding of the implications, a comparison must be made to competing business.

## Example

A business reports the following balance sheet information for 20x7 and 20x8:

|  | 20x7 | 20x8 |
|---|---|---|
| Current assets | $110,000 | $120,000 |
| Current liabilities | 70,000 | 55,400 |
| Current ratio | 1.57 | 2.17 |

The trend in the ratio has improved during the year, indicating better liquidity in 20x8 than in 20x7. For example, in 20x8, for each $1 owed to short-term creditors, there is $2.17 in current assets to cover it.

## How is it Used and Applied?

The current ratio measures the reserve of liquid funds in excess of current obligations that is available as a safety margin against uncertainty and against the random contingencies to which the flow of funds within a business is subject. Random shocks such as strikes, extraordinary losses, and other uncertainties, can temporarily and unexpectedly stop or reduce the inflow of funds.

If the current ratio increases significantly, but the quick ratio (see Sec. 88) remains constant, there may be an inventory buildup. A very high current ratio could mean that the owner is not aggressive in putting current assets to work in generating high returns. For example, cash could be invested in plant assets.

A high current ratio is needed when a business has difficulty borrowing on short notice.

A sharp decline in the current ratio indicates a deterioration in a business' liquidity, which may mean that the business will be unable to pay current debt when due. Liquidity means the readiness and speed with which current assets can be converted to cash.

A lower current ratio may mean that the owner will have greater difficulty borrowing short-term funds.

# 88. Quick (Acid Test) Ratio

## Introduction

The *quick ratio* is a stringent test of liquidity that compares the most liquid current (quick) assets to current debt.

## How is it Computed?

$$\text{Quick ratio} = \frac{\text{cash} + \text{marketable securities} + \text{accounts receivable}}{\text{current liabilities}}$$

Inventory is not included in the quick ratio because it takes a while for inventory to be converted into cash, and there is the possibility of obsolescence. Further, prepaid expenses are not included in this analysis because they cannot be converted into cash and hence are not capable of paying current liabilities.

The acid test ratio should generally be at least 1:1, but determining what is an acceptable ratio depends on the nature of the specific industry in which the business operates. Comparisons to competing businesses and trends over time should also be made.

## *Example*

Following is balance sheet information for a business for 20x7 and 20x8:

|                     | 20x7       | 20x8       |
|---------------------|------------|------------|
| Quick assets        | $160,000   | $150,000   |
| Current liabilities | 140,000    | 155,000    |

The acid test ratios are 1.14 for 20x7 and 0.97 for 20x8. The reduction in the ratio means less liquidity. For example, in 20x8, for each $1 in current debt, only $0.97 in quick assets are available to cover it.

## How is it Used and Applied?

A lower quick ratio may mean that the business will have greater difficulty borrowing short-term funds. A very low ratio may signal that the owner will be unable to make his or her short-term debt payments.

# 89. Operating Cycle

## Introduction

The *operating cycle* is the number of days taken to translate cash to inventory to accounts receivable and back to cash.

Cash  →  Inventory  →  Accounts receivable  →  Cash

## How is it Computed?

Operating cycle = age of inventory + collection period on accounts reveivable

## *Example*

Assume that inventory is held for 85 days, while it takes 45 days to collect from accounts receivable. The operating cycle is:

Operating cycle = 85 days + 45 days = 130 days

## How is it Used and Applied?

The business operator is interested in the operating cycle because it tells how long cash is tied up in inventory and receivables. A shorter operating cycle is preferred, since the freed cash can be invested for a return or used to pay bills. A shorter period also means less risk of inventory obsolescence and customer uncollectibility.

See Sec. 37, Account Receivable Ratios, and Sec. 39, Inventory Ratios.

# 90. Are Your Defensive Assets Sufficient?

## Introduction

The *defensive interval* ratio is a liquidity measure that shows the business" ability to meet its current obligations.

## How is it Computed?

$$\text{Defensive interval ratio} = \frac{\text{defensive assets}}{\text{projected daily operational expenditure} - \text{noncash charges}}$$

where

Projected daily operational expenditures =

(cost of sales + operating expenses + other ordinary cash expenses)/360

## *Example*

A business has cash of $30,000 marketable securities of $38,000, receivables of $46,000, projected daily expenditures of $450,000, and noncash charges of $20,000.

247

The defensive interval ratio is:

$$\frac{\$114,000}{(\$450,000 - \$20,000)/360} = \frac{\$114,000}{\$1,194.44} = 95 \text{ days (rounded)}$$

This analysis shows that defensive assets can cover projected daily expenditures by 95 days.

## How is it Used and Applied?

The defensive interval ratio indicates the time period during which the business can operate on its liquid assets without needing revenues from the next period's sources. It shows near-term liquidity as a basis for paying expenses.

# 91. Working Capital

## Introduction

*Working capital* compares current assets to current liabilities and indicates the liquid reserve available to meet contingencies and uncertainties. A high working capital balance is needed if the business is unable to borrow on short notice. Working capital must be compared to other financial statement elements, such as sales and total assets. A business owner can change the level of working capital to enhance profitability.

## How is it Computed?

Several types of calculations are commonly used to evaluate working capital. They compare working capital to a balance sheet or income statement item as an indicator of liquidity.

1.  Working capital     = current assets– current liabilities

2.  $\dfrac{\text{Working capital}}{\text{Sales}}$

3.  $\dfrac{\text{Working capital}}{\text{Total assets}}$

4.  Working capital provided from operations:

    Net Income

    Plus: Nonworking capital expenses (e.g., depreciation)

    Minus: Nonworking capital revenue (e.g., amortization of deferred revenue)

    Equals: Working capital provided from operations

5.	$\dfrac{\text{Working capital provided from operations}}{\text{Net income}}$

6.	$\dfrac{\text{Working capital provided from operations}}{\text{Total liabilities}}$

7.	$\dfrac{\text{Net income}}{\text{Working capital (beginning of year)}}$

8.	$\dfrac{\text{Cash}}{\text{Working capital}}$

## Example

A business reports the following information:

| | |
|---|---:|
| Working capital provided from operations | $100,000 |
| Net income | 300,000 |
| Current assets | 900,000 |
| Current liabilities | 500,000 |
| Noncurrent liabilities | 600,000 |

The industry averages of other businesses are:

| | |
|---|---:|
| Working capital | $1,100,000 |
| Working capital provided from operations to total liabilities | 30.5% |
| Working capital provided from operations to net income | 50.0% |

The applicable ratios for the business are:

| | |
|---|---:|
| Working capital | $400,000 |
| Working capital provided from operations to total liabilities | 9.1% |
| Working capital provided from operations to net income | 33.3% |

The analysis reveals that working capital generated from operations is inadequate to pay total debt – an outcome that indicates poor liquidity. Additionally, the business has less profits backed up by liquid funds than other businesses in the industry. Overall, the business' working capital is deficient relative to the industry averages.

## How is it Used and Applied?

The owner should watch the level of working capital closely, because loan agreements often include stipulations regarding the maintenance of minimum working capital levels.

To identify changes in the composition of working capital, the owner should determine the trend in the percentage of each current asset to total current assets. A shift from cash to inventory, for example, indicates less liquidity.

The working capital-to-sales ratio tells whether the business is using its liquid balance optimally, and how frequently working capital is turned over during the year. Is the business controlling working capital to produce sales? A low ratio indicates the business' ability to generate revenue from liquid funds. When sales increase, inventories also increase to meet sales demand. Accounts receivable and accounts payable also increase. The ratio indicates the relationship between purchasing and selling. A high ratio indicates cash availability for operations, but this may tie up cash and provide little return. A low ratio may make the business owner susceptible to adverse economic conditions. A problem situation occurs when sales volume increases significantly but account receivable are deteriorating in quality.

A high ratio of working capital provided by operations to net income is favorable, since a liquidity rating is higher when profits are backed up by liquid funds.

The ratio of working capital provided from operations to total liabilities indicates the extent to which internally generated working capital flow is available to pay obligations.

However, keep in mind that working capital is still *not* cash. You should not rely too much on working capital in an emergency. Cash is needed to pay liabilities and expenses. A high ratio of cash to working capital is desirable.

# 92. Liquidity Index

## Introduction

The *liquidity index* is the number of days that current assets are removed from cash.

## How is it Computed?

$$\text{Current asset} \times \text{days removed from cash} = \text{total}$$

$$\text{Index} = \frac{\text{total}}{\text{amount}} = \text{number of days}$$

## Example

The liquidity index for a typical business may be computed as:

| Current asset | Amount | × | Days removed from cash | = | Total |
|---|---|---|---|---|---|
| Cash | $ 20,000 | × | 0 | = | $0 |
| Account receivable | 50,000 | × | 30 | = | 1,500,000 |
| Inventory | 80,000 | × | 50 | = | 4,000,000 |
| Total | $150,000 | | | | $ 5,500,000 |

$$\text{Index} = \frac{\$5,500,00}{\$150,000} = 36.7$$

## How is it Used and Applied?

The liquidity index is used by the owner to determine a business' liquidity. The index reveals how many days it would take to convert the current assets to cash. A business with poor liquidity is viewed negatively by lenders, since it may not be able to meet its debt payments when due. The owner should be concerned with deficient liquidity, since the business may fail to operate because of insufficient funds. When liquidity difficulties exist, the owner must take corrective action.

# 93. Assessing Asset Utilization (Turnover)

## Introduction

*Asset utilization*, or *turnover*, indicates how well business assets are utilized to generate revenue. It is a measure of efficiency and performance. A declining trend in asset utilization means that assets are not contributing adequately to production.

## How is it Computed?

Several types of calculations are commonly used to analyze asset utilization. Each involves an examination of the ratio of sales to some other aspect of a business' assets.

1.  Total asset turnover

$$\frac{\text{Sales}}{\text{Total assets}}$$

2.    Sales to specific assets

Sales to cash:    $\dfrac{\text{Sales}}{\text{Cash}}$

Accounts receivable ratio:    $\dfrac{\text{Sales}}{\text{Accounts receivable}}$

Inventory ratio:    $\dfrac{\text{Sales}}{\text{Inventory}}$

Sales to working capital:    $\dfrac{\text{Sales}}{\text{Working capital}}$

Fixed asset turnover:    $\dfrac{\text{Sales}}{\text{Fixed assets}}$

Operating revenue to operating property:    $\dfrac{\text{Total operating revenue}}{\text{Operating property}}$

Sales to other assets:    $\dfrac{\text{Sales}}{\text{Other assets}}$

Higher ratios reflect favorably on the business' ability to employ assets effectively.

## Example

Implications of the use of the total asset turnover ratio are illustrated by comparing the performance of two businesses:

|                    | Business A     | Business B      |
|--------------------|----------------|-----------------|
| Sales              | $  1,000,000   | $ 20,000,000    |
| Total assets       | 10,000,000     | 10,000,000      |
| Turnover of assets | 0.1 times      | 2 times         |

This analysis shows that for Business A, each dollar invested in assets supports only $0.10 in sales, whereas Business B obtains $2 of sales for each dollar invested in assets. The appropriate question that should be prompted by this analysis is to ask why Business A's turnover is so low. Are there excess assets that generate little or no return? Are there idle assets that Business A should dispose of? Are the assets inefficiently or uneconomically utilized?

The conclusion of this analysis is that Business A can achieve more immediate and significant improvements by concentrating on improving turnover – by increasing sales, reducing its investment, or both.

# How is it Used and Applied?

Owners understand that assets should not be held by a business unless they contribute to sales or profitability; thus, utilization of many of these turnover ratios is critical to understanding the productivity of assets. Higher ratios of asset utilization are better because they indicate that assets are more productive in producing a return. A high ratio also implies the sales are being generated at low cost. A high ratio for one industry, however, may be considered a low ratio for another. On the other hand, a low fixed asset turnover may mean that the investment in plant and equipment is excessive relative to the value of output produced. In such a case, the owner might consider consolidating operations, perhaps by selling some assets and investing the proceeds for a higher return or using the fixed assets to expand into a more financially lucrative area. A low ratio may also indicate inadequate sales.

In certain special situations, such as developmental businesses, the meaning of asset turnover may have to be modified because most assets are committed to the development of future potential. Similarly, if abnormal supply situations exist or if strikes occur, these factors affect capital utilization and require separate evaluation and interpretation.

The following provides some guidance to interpreting high and low ratios:

◆ A high ratio of sales to cash may be caused by a cash shortage that could eventually result in a liquidity crisis if the owner has no other ready sources of funds. A low turnover may also indicate the holding of idle cash balances, resulting in less return being earned. Cash accumulated for specific purposes or contingencies may result in a temporary drop in the turnover ratio.

◆ A low ratio of sales to receivables may indicate overextension of credit, and collection problems. A high ratio may point to an overly stringent credit policy.

◆ A low ratio of sales to inventory may indicate overstocking, slow-moving goods, overestimation of sales, or a lack of balance in inventory. A temporary problem, such as a strike at a major customer, may also be responsible. A high turnover may represent underinvestment in inventory, which can cause deficient customer service and lost sales.

◆ A low ratio of sales to fixed assets may signal inefficient or obsolete equipment, excess capacity, or interruptions in the supply of raw materials.

◆ A low ratio of operating revenue to operating property means that the business is less productive in utilizing operating property.

# 94. Fixed-Asset Ratios

## Introduction

*Fixed-asset ratios* compare fixed assets to debt and capital. Fixed assets are assets that posses physical substance and a life in excess of 1 year. Fixed assets are bought for use in the operation of the business, such as building, machinery, and equipment. The ratio is favorable when the proceeds from and return on fixed assets substantially exceeds debt, because sufficient money will be available from the fixed assets to pay off that debt.

## How is it Computed?

Several different kinds of fixed asset ratios are used to measure different aspects of the business. Fixed assets may be compared to total assets, debt, and owners' equity.

1. Fixed assets to short-term debt:

$$\frac{\text{Fixed assets}}{\text{Short-term debt}}$$

2. Fixed asset mix:

$$\frac{\text{Fixed assets}}{\text{Total assets}}$$

3. Fixed assets to owners' equity:

$$\frac{\text{Fixed assets}}{\text{Owner's equity}}$$

4. Funded capital ratio:

$$\frac{\text{Long-term debt} + \text{owner's equity}}{\text{Fixed assets}}$$

## Example

The following information applies to a business:

|  | 20x7 | 20x8 |
|---|---|---|
| Fixed assets | $ 700,000 | $1,000,000 |
| Short-term debt | 300,000 | 400,000 |

The relevant ratios are:

|  | 20x7 | 20x8 |
|---|---|---|
| Fixed assets to short-term debt | 2.33 | 2.5 |

There are more fixed assets compared to short-term debt in 20x8, which is a good sign.

## How is it Used and Applied?

A business with high short-term debt may be unable to pay current obligations if most of its money is tied up in long-term assets. Financing fixed assets with current debt is a precarious financing strategy; rather, assets should be financed with liabilities of similar maturity.

A high ratio of fixed assets to total assets means a lot of money tied up in noncurrent, illiquid property, plant, and equipment. This means less flexibility in adjusting to changes in sales and market position. A possible way to lower this ratio and improve flexibility is to sell ineffective fixed assets and either subcontract the work or rent the property, plant, and equipment. However, the difference in cost between owning the fixed assets and renting them (or subcontracting) must also be considered.

A higher ratio of fixed assets to owners' equity may indicate a buildup in inactive fixed assets, resulting in excessive costs – such as for insurance, taxes, maintenance, and storage – which will raise the breakeven point.

The *funded capital ratio* shows the degree to which fixed assets are financed by long-term commitments of creditors.

A high ratio of sales to floor space for machinery indicates the efficient utilization of space.

See Sec. 93, Assessing Asset Utilization (Turnover)

# 95. Noncurrent Assets to Noncurrent Liabilities

## Introduction

A noncurrent asset or liability has a life of 1 year or more. Examples of noncurrent assets are building, equipment, furniture, and auto. Examples of noncurrent liabilities are mortgages payable and bonds payable. The ratio of noncurrent assets to noncurrent liabilities looks primarily at the relationship between property, plant, and equipment and long-term debt.

## How is it Computed?

$$\frac{\text{noncurrent assets}}{\text{noncurrent liabilities}}$$

## Example

A business has the following balance sheet information for 20x7 and 20x8:

| | 20x7 | 20x8 |
|---|---|---|
| Property, plant, and equipment | $ 800,000 | $700,000 |
| Long-term liabilities | 400,000 | 500,000 |

The ratio of noncurrent assets to noncurrent liabilities is 2 for 20x7 and 1.4 for 20x8. The trend in the ratio has dropped from 20x7 to 20x8, pointing to a possible solvency problem.

## How is it Used and Applied?

A decline in the coverage of long-term debt by noncurrent assets may trigger an alarm, because fewer long-term assets are available to cover debt when it is due.

Long-term debt will eventually be paid out of long-term assets; hence, a high ratio indicates protection.

A lower ratio of noncurrent assets to noncurrent liabilities means that it may be more difficult to borrow funds and, even if you can, you will probably be charged a higher interest rate.

# 96. Accounts Payable Ratios

## Introduction

*Accounts payable ratios* tell how long it takes a business to pay its suppliers. Accounts payable ratios indicate whether the business is in a good position to obtain short-term, unsecured (no collateral) credit in the form of cost-free funds (no interest is charged by the supplier).

Although accounts payable is considered current debt, it is typically renewed automatically as long as payments are being made. Credit terms are usually good because the supplier is anxious for the customer's business.

## How is it Computed?

Three accounts payable ratios are commonly used by businesses.

1. Sales to accounts payable:

$$\frac{\text{Sales}}{\text{Accounts payable}}$$

2. Accounts payable to average daily purchases (also called "day purchases in accounts payable"):

   Accounts payable
   Purchase/360 days

3. Accounts payable to total assets:

   Accounts payable
   Total assets

If accounts payable fluctuate widely, an average rather than the year-end balance should be used.

## Example

Assume the following information for two time periods:

|  | Year I | Year 2 |
|---|---|---|
| Accounts payable | $  50,000 | $  40,000 |
| Purchases | 800,000 | 750,000 |
| Sales | 2,000,000 | 1,300,000 |

The relevant ratios for each of the years are:

|  | Year I |  | Year 2 |  |
|---|---|---|---|---|
| Sales to account payable | $\dfrac{\$2,000,000}{\$50,000}$ | = 40 | $\dfrac{\$1,300,000}{\$40,000}$ | 32.5 |
| Days purchase in accounts payable | $\dfrac{\$50,000}{\$800,000/360}$ | = 22.5 | $\dfrac{\$40,000}{\$750,000/360}$ | = 19.2 |

The lower of the two sales-to-accounts payable ratios indicates the business' improved ability in year 2 to obtain short-term credit in the form of cost-free funds.

The decrease in the days purchases in accounts payable is a favorable sign because it shows that the owner is able to repay creditors more quickly in year 2 than in year 1.

## How is it Used and Applied?

The accounts payable ratios involve a trade-off between retaining operating cash and the credit rating of the business.

Owners use accounts payable ratios as indicators of a business' financial strength. For example, if trade credit declines, as indicated by an increase in the ratio of sales to accounts payable, creditors may have less faith in the business' financial health.

The days in accounts payable determines the average number of days that it takes for the owner to pay short-term creditors. The ratio is used to measure the degree to which accounts payable represents current rather than overdue obligations. The owner should make a comparison to the terms of purchase. If vendor terms are 60 days and the payment period is 50 days, the owner is paying bills too early. The payment should be delayed so interest can be earned.

A decline in the payment period may indicate that the business is taking advantage of prompt payment discounts or is using shorter purchase terms as leverage in negotiating with suppliers for lower prices. An increase in the payment period may indicate that the business is having financial difficulties, requiring it to stretch out its payable; on the other hand, this situation could also indicate that the business is managing its payables well, taking greater advantage of interest-free financing by delaying payments to creditors.

*Remember:* Stretching payables may work in the short term, but will have long-term negative effects on credit reputation. If payments must be slowed, explain why to suppliers and try to make partial payments.

# 97. Current Liability Ratios

## Introduction

Current liabilities are those due within 1 year, such as accounts payable, taxes payable, accrued expenses payable, and short-term notes payable.

Current liability ratios show the extent to which current debt payments will be required within the year. Understanding a business' liability position is critical, because if it is unable to pay current debt, it is illiquid.

## How is it Computed?

1.  Current liabilities to noncurrent liabilities:

$$\frac{\text{Current liabilities}}{\text{Noncurrent liabilities}}$$

2.  Current liabilities to total liabilities:

$$\frac{\text{Current liabilities}}{\text{Total liabilities}}$$

These ratios can be compared to industry averages.

## Example

Assume the following financial data for a  business:

| | |
|---|---|
| Current liabilities | $   500,000 |
| Noncurrent liabilities | 600,000 |
| Total liabilities | 1,100,000 |

The relevant ratios are:

| | |
|---|---|
| Current liabilities to noncurrent liabilities | 83.3% |
| Current liabilities to total liabilities | 45.5 |

These are compared to industry norms:

| | |
|---|---|
| Current liabilities to noncurrent liabilities | 45.0% |
| Current liabilities to total liabilities | 24.0 |

The business' liquidity is unfavorable relative to the industry norm, as indicated by the business' high level of current debt.

## How is it Used and Applied?

A high ratio of current liabilities to total liabilities indicates low business liquidity, because the portion of current debt is greater.  If the ratio is high, the owner should take steps to reduce the business' excessive short-term debt ---  steps such as financing on a long-term basis, or selling assets to obtain funds.

# 98.  How Much Debt Do You Have, and Can You Pay It?

## Introduction

*Leverage ratios* indicate the degree of debt within a  business' capital structure and its ability to pay the debt.  Financial leverage results from the owner's use of debt financing and leasing.

## How is it Computed?

Ten leverage ratios are used in analyzing a  business' financial position.

1.     Debt/equity ratio $= \dfrac{\text{total liabilities}}{\text{total capital}}$

2. $\dfrac{\text{Long-term debt}}{\text{Total capital}}$

3. Debt ratio = $\dfrac{\text{total liabilities}}{\text{total assets}}$

4. Capital structure ratio = $\dfrac{\text{average long-term debt}}{\text{long-term debt plus owner's equity}}$

5. $\dfrac{\text{Owner's equity}}{\text{Borrowed capital}}$

6. $\dfrac{\text{Interest}}{\text{Total capital}}$

7. $\dfrac{\text{Average working capital}}{\text{Average funded debt}}$

8. $\dfrac{\text{Average current liabilities}}{\text{Owner's equity}}$

9. Financial leverage index = $\dfrac{\text{return on owner's equity}}{\text{return on total assets}}$

10. Financial leverage ratio = $\dfrac{\text{total assets}}{\text{owner's equity}}$

*Note:* Total capital and owners' equity are interchangeable terms.

## Example

Leverage ratio information is derived from a business' balance sheet:

| | |
|---|---|
| Long-term liabilities | $500,000 |
| Total liabilities | 700,000 |
| Owners' equity | 300,000 |
| Cash flow provided from operation | 100,000 |

The business' ratios are:

| | |
|---|---|
| Long-term debt to owners' equity | 1.67 |
| Cash flow to long-term liabilities | 0.20 |
| Total liabilities to owners' equity | 2.33 |

These are compared to average norms taken from competitors:

| | |
|---|---|
| Long-term debt to owners' equity | 0.8 |
| Cash flow to long-term liabilities | 0.3 |
| Total liabilities to owners' equity | 1.5 |

After comparing the business' ratios with the industry norms, it is clear that the owners' solvency is worse than that of competing business. The business has significantly more total debt and long-term liabilities in its capital structure, and has lower cash flow to cover its debt.

## How is it Used and Applied?

In evaluating a business' performance, a high ratio of total liabilities to total owners' equity (financial leverage) indicates much risk because it may be a problem for the owner to pay interest and principal payments and also obtain reasonable future financing. A high debt/equity ratio is a particularly acute problem for businesses with cash problems, especially during recessionary periods. Carrying excessive amounts of debt will result in less financial flexibility for the business, because it is more difficult to obtain money in a tight money market. Further, having to pay high fixed interest charges will result in negative effects on earnings.

A favorable leverage situation exists when the return on borrowed funds exceeds the interest charge, provided that the owner is not in debt over his or her head. A desirable debt/equity ratio depends on many factors, including the rates of other businesses in the industry, access to further debt financing, and earnings stability.

A ratio greater than 1 for long-term debt to owners' equity indicates a higher long-term debt participation relative to equity capital.

The debt ratio (total liabilities to total assets) reveals the percentage of total funds obtained from creditors. The ratio indicates how much debt may be comfortably assumed, given the owners' financial status. Creditors would obviously rather see a low debt ratio.

Potential creditors are reluctant to provide financing to a business with a high debt posture; however, the size of debt taken on may be satisfactory, depending on the nature of the business.

If analysis reveals that interest on borrowed funds has increased, it is essential to know why. Is it because lenders demand a higher interest rate because of increase risk? Is it because overall market interest rates have risen?

The ratio of current debt to owners' equity is used to measure if short-term creditors are providing excessive capital resources to support operations relative to materials, supplies, and services. The adequacy of the ratio depends on such variables as the turnover rate of inventory and receivables, liquidity status, and so on.

Where there is considerable debt, a sharp drop in sales or in receivables turnover may mean that the owner will be unable to pay debt obligations. Interest on borrowed funds may even be greater than earnings, resulting in a loss. Even though debt might be high, however, the business may still be able to meet its obligations – for example, there may be a quick turnover in current assets, allowing timely debt payments; some current liabilities may be stretched or due dates extended; long-term debt may be restructured for later payment; or a substantial boost in cast earnings may take place.

If borrowed capital exceeds invested capital, proprietary risk is shared with the creditors. In general, invested capital should exceed borrowed capital. Analyzing the trend in the ratio of owners' capital shows a business' financial policy and objectives. This provides insight into the owners' financing preferences, such as whether the owner is inclined toward taking excessive risk.

The impact of leverage on operating results is positive when the return on equity capital exceeds the return on total assets. Leverage is favorable when the return on assets is higher than the cost of debt.

The financial leverage ratio measures the relationship between total assets and the owners' equity capital that finances them. In a business that uses leverage profitably, a higher financial leverage ratio will enhance the return on equity; at the same time, the risk inherent in a change in profitability is also greater.

The ratio of working capital to funded debt is employed to determine whether a business could liquidate its long-term debt obligations from working capital. Even if a business shows adequate profitability, it may not have sufficient liquid funds to pay long-term debt obligations.

# 99. What Obligations Are Pressing?

## Introduction

The ratio of "pressing" current to "patient" current liabilities describes the degree of flexibility of a business with regard to paying debt. "Pressing" liabilities are those that must be paid without excuse, such as taxes and loans payable. "Patient" liabilities are those that provide flexibility when financial difficulties exist (e.g., accounts payable). For example, in troubled times, a supplier may postpone or even downwardly adjust the amount of the debt.

## How is it Computed?

$$\frac{\text{Pressing current liabilities}}{\text{Patient current liabilities}}$$

## *Example*

Assume that a business' current liabilities consist of the following:

|  | 20x7 | 20x8 |
|---|---|---|
| Accounts payable (patient) | $ 400,000 | $ 350,000 |
| Taxes payable (pressing) | 50,000 | 60,000 |
| Bank loans payable (pressing) | 250,000 | 280,000 |

The ratios of pressing debt to patient debt are:

|  | 20x7 | | 20x8 | |
|---|---|---|---|---|
| Pressing debt to patient debt | $\dfrac{\$300,000}{\$400,000}$ | $= 0.75$ | $\dfrac{\$340,000}{\$350,000}$ | $= 0.97$ |

The higher ratio of pressing to patient short-term debt indicates that the business has greater liquidity risk in the second year than in the first.

## How is it Used and Applied?

If more pressing current liabilities exist, a potential problem could occur during recessionary times, because short-term creditors would demand to be paid. Loan agreements, for example, may provide that the principal of the loan be paid even if an interest payment is not. On the other hand, having more patient current liabilities will be to the owner's advantage. It may also be easier to renegotiate payment terms with "patient" creditors.

# 100. Ratios of Off-Balance-Sheet Assets and Liabilities

## Introduction

Unrecorded (off-balance-sheet) assets either represent resources of the business or are anticipated to have future benefit but are not shown on the balance sheet. This makes the business more valuable. Off-balance-sheet assets include tax-loss carryforward benefits, expected rebates, and purchase commitments where the business has a contract to purchase an item at a price below the going rate. Unrecorded (off-balance-sheet) liabilities are those that are not reported on the balance sheet but may require future payments or services. These make the business less valuable. Examples are lawsuits and cosigned loans.

## How is it Computed?

1. $\dfrac{\text{Off-balance sheet assets}}{\text{Total assets}}$

2. $\dfrac{\text{Off-balance sheet liabilities}}{\text{Total liabilities}}$

## Example

A business reports the following information:

|                             | 20x7      | 20x8      |
|-----------------------------|-----------|-----------|
| Off-balance-sheet liabilities | $ 20,000 | $ 50,000 |
| Total liabilities           | 100,000   | 130,000   |

The relevant ratios are:

|                                                  | 20x7  | 20x8  |
|--------------------------------------------------|-------|-------|
| Off-balance-sheet liabilities to total liabilities | 0.20  | 0.38  |

The increase in unrecorded liabilities may cause concern to the owner because of possible future payment. For example, there may be possible renegotiations of claims under city or county contracts.

## How is it Used and Applied?

Off-balance-sheet assets are positive aspects of financial position even though they are not shown on the balance sheet. Obviously, a going concern is assumed, since unrecorded assets would typically not be realized in a distress situation. Off-balance-sheet liabilities are negative signs of financial position, because they may require the use of business resources.

# 101. Earning Growth

## Introduction

*Earnings growth* shows whether the business is able to generate increasing profit as sales grow. *Deflated earnings growth* is the growth in profitability after adjusting for inflation.

## How is it Computed?

Earnings growth

$$= \frac{\text{net income (current year)} - \text{net income (prior year)}}{\text{net income (prior year)}}$$

Deflated earnings growth

$$= \frac{(\text{net income} \times [\text{CPI (prior year)/CPI (current year)}]) - \text{net income (prior year)}}{\text{net income (prior year)}}$$

where CPI = Consumer Price Index.

## Example

A business reported net income last year of $800,000 and this year it is $600,000. This is an unfavorable trend because there has been a percentage decline in profit of 25 percent, computed as follows:

$$\frac{\$600,000 - \$800,000}{\$800,000} = \frac{\$200,000}{\$800,000} = -25\%$$

## How is it Used and Applied?

There is a problem if sales rise but profits do not. If earnings are not consistent with revenue growth, possible reasons might be inadequate gross profit due to lower selling prices or increasing cost of goods sold, and/or the inability to keep expenses in check. Expenditures must positively benefit revenue to a greater extent.

Profit growth after adjusting for inflation is the key to assuring that the business is growing in real dollars.

A better measure is to compute average earnings growth over a 5-year period to show a reasonable trend.

# 102. Profit Margin

## Introduction

The profit margin shows the earnings generated from sales. There are three ways of evaluating profitability: comprising of net income, operating profit, and gross profit.

Gross profit must exist to cover operating expenses and earn a profit. It is easiest for the owner to improve gross profit because of the flexibility associated with buying and selling merchandise as well as cost containment.

## How is it Computed?

1.   Net profit margin $= \dfrac{\text{net income}}{\text{net sales}}$

2.   Operating profit margin $= \dfrac{\text{income before taxes and interest}}{\text{net sales}}$

3.   Gross profit margin $= \dfrac{\text{gross profit}}{\text{net sales}}$

   Gross profit $=$ sales $-$ cost of sales

Profit margin may vary widely within an industry, because it is subject to sales, pricing, and cost controls.

## Example

Analysis of a business' profit margin is based on the following data:

|  | 20x7 | 20x8 |
|---|---|---|
| Gross profit | $15,000 | $20,000 |
| Net income | 8,000 | 9,600 |
| Sales | 65,000 | 80,000 |

Relevant ratios are:

|  | 20x7 | 20x8 |
|---|---|---|
| Net profit margin | 0.12 | 0.12 |
| Gross profit margin | 0.23 | 0.25 |

The net profit margin is constant, indicating that the earning power of the business has remained static. The improvement in gross profit is probably a result of increased sales and/or better control of cost of sales. A lack of control in operating expenses is most likely the reason that gross profit margin increased but net profit margin remained constant, even though sales have increased.

## How is it Used and Applied?

Profit may be enhanced by obtaining additional revenue or by reducing costs. The profit of a business should be compared to that of competitors.

Profit margins vary among industries and among companies within the industry. Profit margin often depends on the type of product line; for example, profit margins are higher for fur coats but lower for groceries.

The profit margin shows the success of the owner in obtaining profit from operations. The higher the profit on each sales dollar generated, the better the business is doing financially. Profit may also be increased by controlling expenses. A high profit margin is advantageous because it indicates that the business is earning an attractive return on its cost of merchandise sold and operating expenses. A low profit margin may be due to a low gross profit arising from underpricing or lack of control over the cost of the merchandise. A low profit margin may also arise during expansion because adequate control may not be exercised over spending. High returns are prevalent in companies that have strong customer demand because of product quality or pricing and/or lack of competition.

By evaluating a business' profit margin relative to previous years and to industry norms, the owner can evaluate the business' operating efficiency and pricing strategy as well as its competitive position within the industry. The ratio of income to sales reveals the financial success of the business. The "bottom line" is what counts! Profit margin reveals the business' ability to generate earnings at a particular sales level.

A low gross profit margin may mean that the owner is overpaying for merchandise and/or that selling prices are too low. Another reason might be a change in sales mix from high-margin goods to low-margin ones. The gross profit margin may be maintained by the owner by pricing at a fixed multiple of cost of goods sold. For example, the markup might be consistently two times cost. Profit margins might be improved by charging the public at large on a direct order, considerably more than that charged to the retailer. However, this approach works only if customers are loyal and competition is virtually nonexistent. The gross profit margin is useful in comparing entities in different lines of business. However, one-time adjustments may distort the gross profit margin when comparisons are made.

# 103. Sales to Current Assets

## Introduction

Current assets are assets that have a life of 1 year or less, such as cash, inventory, and accounts receivable. The ratio of sales to current assets

## How is it Computed?

$$\frac{\text{Sales}}{\text{Current assets}}$$

## Example

A business reports the following information:

|  | 20x7 | 20x8 |
|---|---|---|
| Sales | $250,000 | $400,000 |
| Current assets | 100,000 | 120,000 |

The relevant ratios are:

|  | 20x7 | 20x8 |
|---|---|---|
| Sales to current assets | 2.5 | 3.33 |

A high ratio may mean that current assets are low, indicating deficient working capital. Perhaps current liabilities will become due before inventory and receivables turn to cash.

## How is it Used and Applied?

The amount of sales relative to current assets indicates adequacy of current assets. A low ratio implies excessive current assets or inadequate sales. Excessive current assets may mean a buildup in inventory that is tying up funds, or a buildup in customer balances. Ways to reduce the buildup are needed, such as offering cash discounts. If sales are insufficient, ways to boost sales should be devised, such as promotion plans.

# 104. Sales to Current Debt

## Introduction

Current debt is debt due within 1 year, such as accounts payable, short-term notes payable, and accrued expenses payable.

The ratio of sales to current debt looks at the extent to which short-term liabilities finances sales growth.

## How is it Computed?

$$\frac{\text{Sales}}{\text{Short-term debt}}$$

### Example

A business reports the following:

|  | 20x7 | 20x8 |
|---|---|---|
| Sales | $100,000 | $130,000 |
| Short-term debt | 40,000 | 40,000 |

The results of the computation are:

|  | 20x7 | 20x8 |
|---|---|---|
| Sales to short-term debt | 2.5 | 3.25 |

The analysis shows that in 20x8 the business is making better use of current debt in supporting its sales base.

## How is it Used and Applied?

The amount of short-term credit a business is able to obtain from suppliers depends on its level of sales of goods or services. This ratio enables the owner to analyze the relationship between these factors. The advantage of a larger amount of short-term credit is that it is relatively low cost and, in turn, reduces the investment in working capital.

# 105. Analysis of Expenses

## Introduction

Marketing involves getting, servicing, and keeping customers. Sellers expenses are incurred to obtain sales (advertising, sales promotion, salesperson salaries and commission) or to distribute merchandise (e.g., shipping).

Expenses are often related to sales to determine if proper cost controls exist and whether the expenditures are resulting in improved revenue and/or profitability.

Efficiency occurs when the business owner generates revenue (product and/or service) at the least practical expense.

If sales grow faster than total expenses, profit will increase. This is a positive indicator, particularly for a growing business.

## How is it Computed?

$$\text{Aggregate operating expense ratio} = \frac{\text{total operating expenses}}{\text{net sales}}$$

where operating expenses included general and administrative, and selling. Excluded are financial expenses (e.g., interest expense) and cost of goods sold.

For any specific expense that it is useful to compare to sales,

$$\text{Specific expense to net sales} = \frac{\text{specific expense}}{\text{net sales}}$$

$$\text{Selling expense ratio} = \frac{\text{selling expenses}}{\text{net sales}}$$

$$\text{Utilities ratio} = \frac{\text{utilities expense}}{\text{net sales}}$$

where utilities expense includes telephone, electricity, gas, and water provided by public utilities.

Percentage change in selling expenses

$$= \frac{\text{selling expenses (current year)} - \text{selling expenses (prior year)}}{\text{selling expense (prior year)}}$$

Percentage change in total expenses

$$= \frac{\text{total expenses (current year)} - \text{total expenses (prior year)}}{\text{total expenses (prior year)}}$$

Percentage change in profit =
    percentage change in sales - percentage change in total expenses

## Example

The following information is provided for a business:

|  | 20x7 | 20x8 |
|---|---|---|
| Operating expenses | $ 500,000 | $ 600,000 |
| Utilities expense | 30,000 | 40,000 |
| Selling expense | 200,000 | 250,000 |
| Telephone expense | 40,000 | 60,000 |
| Sales | 1,000,000 | 1,050,000 |

Relevant ratios are:

|  | 20x7 | 20x8 |
|---|---|---|
| Operating expenses to sells | 50.0% | 57.1% |
| Utilities expense to sells | 3.0 | 3.8 |
| Selling expense to sells | 20.0 | 23.8 |
| Telephone expense to sells | 4.0 | 5.7 |

The trend in the expenses relative to sales is unfavorable. Each of the expense ratios has increased relative to sales, meaning that there will be pass profitability. There is a need for a cost-reduction program.

## How is it Used and Applied?

If actual sales are expected to be below budgeted sales, expenses must be trimmed to maintain profit margins. A lower total expense-to-sales ratio indicates that the owner is controlling business expenses.

If sales increase, expenses will probably do likewise. However, the latter should increase at a slower rate if earnings growth is to occur. However, a rapidly growing business may have expenses (primarily marketing and research) that increase at a faster rate than revenue because of the attempt to achieve higher sales levels in *future years.*

A specific expense-to-sales ratio can be analyzed to ascertain whether that expense item is being controlled.  The item may be promotion and entertainment, fringe benefits, travel, training, supplies, automobiles, and so on.

The ratio of selling expenses to net sales shows the cost of making a sale of merchandise or rendering a service.  A low ratio is favorable because it indicates the efficient use of selling efforts. A high ratio is unfavorable because it shows an inability to obtain sales efficiently.  Further, a high ratio may mean that sales are increasing but earnings may not be because of high marketing costs.  It should be noted that if sales decline significantly, the expense-to-sales ratios will increase but not due to cost excesses.

When marketing expenses increase more than sales on a percentage basis, it means in aggressive marketing strategy.  The opposite is a contraction in marketing efforts.  A multi-year period should be used in evaluating the success of marketing sales, because a marketing program may not "bear fruit" until a later year.

Utilities expenses are generally uncontrollable by the owner because rates are usually set by regulatory agencies.  Further, a *minimum* use of utilities is necessary to keep plant facilities operational.  However, telephone and energy bills are to some extent controllable by the owner and may be included in a cost-containment program.

# 106.  Can You Cover Interest Payments?

## Introduction

Interest coverage ratios show the number of times interest expense is covered by earnings or cash flow.  The ratios show the degree of the decline in earnings that a business can absorb and still be able to pay interest.

## How is it Computed?

The two ways of figuring interest coverages are

$$\frac{\text{Income before taxes and interest}}{\text{Interest}}$$

and

$$\frac{\text{Cash flow from operations and interest}}{\text{Interest}}$$

Interest expense may also be compared to sales to determine if the business is relying too much on borrowed funds to finance sales growth and operating activities.

## Example

Interest coverages are evaluated for a business based on the following information from 2 years of operation:

|  | 20x7 | 20x8 |
|---|---|---|
| Income before tax | $ 100,000 | $ 105,000 |
| Cash flow from operations | 80,000 | 82,000 |
| Interest expense | 20,000 | 28,000 |

Relevant ratios are:

|  | 20x7 | 20x8 |
|---|---|---|
| Interest coverage based on earnings | 6 | 4.8 |
| Interest coverage based on cash flow from operations | 5 | 3.9 |

The decline in interest coverage from 20x7 to 20x8 is a negative sign, since less earnings and cash flow from operations are available to pay interest charges. This decline in the second year is a matter for concern.

In 20x8, there was $4.80 in income before taxes and interest for every $1.00 spent on interest. Further, $3.90 in cash earnings was the amount available to cover each $1.00 in interest expenses.

## How is it Used and Applied?

A business that is unable to pay interest is in a dangerous financial position. The trend in the coverage ratios reveals how much interest-bearing debt burden the business can handle.

It is better to use cash flow from operations than income before taxes as a basis on which to compare interest expense, since cash flow indicates the amount of actual cash that can be used to pay interest.

An owner prefers high ratios for his or her business, because high ratios indicate that the business is able to meet interest obligations with room to spare.

# 107. Operating Leverage

## Introduction

*Operating leverage* refers to the existence of fixed costs in the cost structure of a business, and represents operating risk. Fixed costs are expenses that remain constant regardless of changes in volume. Examples are rent, insurance, and property taxes.

## How is it Calculated?

The following ratios may be used to measure operating leverage:

1. $\dfrac{\text{Fixed cost}}{\text{Total cost}}$

2. $\dfrac{\text{Percentage change in operating income}}{\text{Percentage change in sales volume}}$

or

$\dfrac{\text{Change in profit/profit}}{\text{Change in quantity/quantity}}$

3. $\dfrac{\text{Net income}}{\text{Fixed charges}}$

An increase in ratios 1 and 2 or a decrease in ratio 3 indicates higher fixed charges for a business. This situation indicates greater operating risk for the business, because it will have to meet its fixed cost commitments, which cannot be cut to meet declining sales volume in the short term.

Higher fixed charges also result in greater earnings instability, because high leverage magnifies changes in earnings that result from small changes in sales.

## Example 1

Operating leverage is calculated based on data from the following comparative income statements for a business:

|  | 20x7 | 20x8 |
|---|---|---|
| Net income | $ 100,000 | $ 102,000 |
| Fixed cost | 40,000 | 55,000 |
| Variable cost | 25,000 | 27,000 |
| Total cost | 65,000 | 82,000 |

The business' operating leverage in 20x8 relative 20x7 was higher, as evidenced by the increase in the ratio of fixed costs to total cost and the decrease in the ratio of the net income to fixed costs.

|  | 20x7 | 20x8 |
| --- | --- | --- |
| Fixed cost to total cost | 61.5% | 67.1% |
| Net income to fixed cost | 2.5 | 1.85 |

## Example 2

An owner is evaluating the operating leverage of his business based on the following data:

- ◆ Selling price is $2 per unit
- ◆ Fixed cost is $50,000
- ◆ Variable cost is $1.10 per unit

The first case assumes a sales volume of 100,000 units; the second assumes a sales volume of 130,000 units.

| Sales Volume (in dollars) | - | Fixed Cost | - | Variable Cost | = | Net Income |
| --- | --- | --- | --- | --- | --- | --- |
| (100,000 x $2) | - | $50,000 | - | $110,000 | = | $40,000 |
| (130,000 x $2) | - | $50,000 | - | $143,000 | = | $67,000 |

The ratio of the percentage change in net income to the percentage change in sales volume is as follows:

$$\frac{\text{Change in net income}}{\text{Net Income}} = \frac{\$67{,}000 - \$40{,}000}{\$40{,}000} = \frac{\$27{,}000}{\$40{,}000} = 67.5\%$$

$$\frac{\text{Change in quantity}}{\text{Quantity}} = \frac{130{,}000 - 100{,}000}{100{,}000} = \frac{30{,}000}{100{,}000} = 30.0\%$$

$$67.5\%/30.0\% = 2.25$$

If fixed cost remains the same, the 2.25 figure tells you that for every 1% increase in sales above the 100,000-unit volume there will be a 2.25% increase in net income. Thus, a 10% jump in sales will boost net income 22.5%. The same proportionate operating leverage develops regardless of the size of the sales increase above the 100,000 unit level.

## How is it Used and Applied?

Manager and owners are interested in knowing the degree of operating leverage of their business. A high operating leverage means greater fixed cost commitments that have to be met even when sales volume declines. Owners must be aware that high degrees of operating leverage in combination with highly elastic product demand will result in high levels of variability in earnings, although such a condition may be inherent in the industry.

Businesses should note that the effects of operating leverage diminish as revenue increases above the breakeven point (the point where sales equal total costs), since the bases to which increases in earnings are compared become progressively larger. Hence, owners should examine the relationship between sales and the breakeven point.

Owners should note that a business with a high breakeven point is quite vulnerable to economic declines. A high ratio of variable cost to total cost indicates greater earnings stability, because variable cost can be adjusted more easily than fixed cost to meet a decline in product demand.

# 108. Fixed-Charge Coverage

## Introduction

The fixed-charge coverage ratio indicates whether a business is able to pay its able to pay its fixed commitments (e.g., rent, interest) from profits and cash earnings.

## How is it Computed?

Fixed-charge coverage involves two ratios:

1.  $\dfrac{\text{Income before taxes and fixed charges}}{\text{Fixed charges}}$

2.  $\dfrac{\text{Cash flow provided from operations and fixed charges}}{\text{Fixed charges}}$

### Example

The following information is given for a business:

|  | 20x7 | 20x8 |
|---|---|---|
| Income before taxes | $ 360,000 | $ 590,000 |
| Cash flow provided from operation | 300,000 | 500,000 |
| Fixed charges | 100,000 | 120,000 |

Relevant ratios are:

|  | 20x7 | 20x8 |
|---|---|---|
| Fixed-charge coverage based on income before tax | 4.6 | 5.9 |
| Fixed-charge coverage based on cash flow from operation | 4.0 | 5.2 |

The analysis reveals that the business is better able to meet its fixed charges based on earnings and out of cash flow from operations in 20x8 than in 20x7. For example, in 20x8, for each $1 in fixed charges there was $5.90 of earnings and $5.20 in cash flow from operations.

## How is it Used and Applied?

The fixed-charge coverage ratio is useful in gauging a business' ability to pay fixed costs. A low ratio indicates increased risk, because when business activity falls, the owner may be unable to meet fixed charges. In analyzing fixed charges, it is better for the owner to consider cash flow from operations than that from net income, since cash is used to meet fixed payments. A high fixed-charge ratio reflects favorably on the business' ability to refinance obligations as they mature.

In analyzing these ratios for a given business, it should be ascertained if the entity has stability in both operations and funs flow. Such stability provides more confidence in the business' ability to meet its fixed commitments.

The coverage ratios are influenced by the level of earnings and by the level of fixed charges, which depend significantly on the debt-to-equity relationship within capital structure.

# 109. Is Your Funds Flow Adequate?

## Introduction

The funds flow adequacy ratio show the degree to which a business can obtain adequate funds from operations to pay budgeted capital expenditures and increased inventories.

## How is it Computed?

$$\frac{\text{5-year sum of sources of funds from operations}}{\text{5-year sum of capital expenditures and inventory additions}}$$

A 5-year total is usually employed to eliminate cyclical and other distortions.

## Example

The following figures from a 5-year period are used to evaluate funds flow adequacy for a business:

| | |
|---|---|
| Capital expenditure | $ 800,000 |
| Additions to inventory | 500,000 |
| Funds from operations | 1,500,000 |

The funds flow adequacy ratio is:

$$\frac{\$1,500,000}{\$1,300,000} = 1.15$$

## How is it Used and Applied?

The owner uses this ratio to determine whether internally generated funds are adequate to assure growth. A ratio of 1 means that the owner has covered his or her needs based on attained growth levels without resorting to external financing. A ratio below 1 indicates that there may be insufficient internally generated funds to maintain current growth.

# 110. Discretionary Cost Ratios

## Introduction

*Discretionary cost ratios* are employed to evaluate costs that can easily be altered. Discretionary costs may be cut when the business is having problems and wants to stabilize its earnings. Discretionary costs include advertising, repairs and maintenance, and research and development.

## How is it Computed?

1.  Discretionary costs/sales:

    $$\frac{\text{Discretionary costs}}{\text{Sales}}$$

2.  Discretionary cost/related asset:

    $$\frac{\text{Discretionary costs}}{\text{Related assets}}$$

## Example 1

A business' discretionary costs for 2 years are:

|  | 20x6 | 20x7 |
|---|---|---|
| Repairs and maintenance | $ 10,000 | $ 6,000 |
| Sales | 100,000 | 110,000 |
| Fixed assets | 200,000 | 230,000 |

The ratios are:

|  | 20x6 | 20x7 |
|---|---|---|
| Repairs and maintenance/sales | 10% | 5.5% |
| Repairs and maintenance/fixed assets | 5% | 2.6% |

The declining trend in the ratio of repairs and maintenance to both sales and fixed assets indicates that there is insufficient maintenance of fixed assets, leading to possible future breakdowns. Although there are short-term profit benefits from cost reduction, the situation suggests that its continuance might have a detrimental impact in future years.

## Example 2

The owner of a business looked at the following relationship between advertising and sales:

|  | 20x6 | 20x7 | 20x8 |
|---|---|---|---|
| Sales | $ 120,000 | $ 150,000 | $ 100,000 |
| Advertising | 11,000 | 16,000 | 8,000 |

20x6 is the most typical year. Increasing competition is expected in 20x9.

Advertising to sales is 9.2 percent in 20x6, 10.7 percent in 20x7, and 8.0 percent in 20x8. In terms of base dollars, 20x6 is assigned 100. In 20x7, the index number is $16,000/$11,000 = 145.5; and in 20x8 it is $8,000/$11,000 = 72.7. These are negative indicators regarding 20x8. Advertising is at a lower level than in previous years. In fact, advertising should have risen due to the expected increased competition.

## How is it Used and Applied?

The business owner should recognize that cost-reduction programs may sometimes eliminate costs that are necessary to compete and prosper effectively. However, a reduction in discretionary costs may be necessary when the prior business strategy was deficient or ill-conceived. Further, a reduction in discretionary costs (e.g., advertising) may be suitable when a major competitor has gone out of business.

The owner should determine if the current level of discretionary costs conforms with the business' prior trends and with present and future requirements. Index numbers may be used in comparing current discretionary expenditures with base-year expenditures. A substantial increase in discretionary costs may have a positive effect on the business' earning power and future growth.

# 111. "Z-Score" Model: Forecasting Business Failure

## Introduction

The Z-score model is a quantitative model developed in an effort to predict bankruptcy (financial distress) of a business, using a blend of the traditional financial ratios and statistical method known as multiple discriminant analysis (MDA).

The Z score is known to be about 90 percent accurate in forecasting business failure 1 year into the future and about 80 percent accurate in forecasting it 2 years into the future.

## How is it Computed?

$$Z = 1.2 \times X_1 + 1.4 \times X_2 + 3.3 \times X_3 + 0.6 \times X_4 + 0.999 \times X_5$$

where

$$X_1 = \frac{\text{working capital}}{\text{total assets}}$$

$$X_2 = \frac{\text{retained earnings}}{\text{total assets}}$$

$$X_3 = \frac{\text{earnings before interest and taxes (EBIT)}}{\text{total assets}}$$

$$X_4 = \frac{\text{market value of equity (or net worth for private firms)}}{\text{book value of debt}}$$

$$X_5 = \frac{\text{sales}}{\text{total assets}}$$

The following guideline have been for classifying firms:

| Z score | Probability of Short-Term Illiquidity |
|---------|---------------------------------------|
| 1.8 or less | Very high |
| 1.81 - 2.99 | Not sure |
| 3.0 or higher | Unlikely |

## Example

A manufacturer has the following financial data selected from its financial statements:

Total assets = $2,000

EBIT = $266

Retained earnings = $750

Sales = $3,000

Market value of common and preferred stock (net worth for private firms) = $1,425

Book value of debt = $1,100

The calculation of the company's Z score is shown below:

| | | | | | | | |
|---|---|---|---|---|---|---|---|
| $X_1$ | = | $400/$2,000 | × | 1.2 | = | 0.240 |
| $X_2$ | = | $750/$2,000 | × | 1.4 | = | 0.525 |
| $X_3$ | = | $266/$2,000 | × | 3.3 | = | 0.439 |
| $X_4$ | = | $1,425/$1,100 | × | 0.6 | = | 0.777 |
| $X_5$ | = | $3,000/$2,000 | × | 0.999 | = | 1.499 |
| | | | | Z | = | 3.480 |

Since the company's Z score of 3.480 us well into the "unlikely" zone, there is virtually no chance that it will go bankrupt within the next 2 years.

## How is it Used and Applied?

The MDA may be used for a business or a group of businesses. The recent recessionary environment has witnessed an increasing trend in bankruptcies. Will your business go bankrupt? Is the business you are working for on the verge of bankruptcy? Who will go bankrupt? Your major customer? Your important supplier? Your borrower? If you can predict with reasonable accuracy that the business you are interested in is developing financial distress, you can better protect yourself and recommend means for corrective action. Some steps might be to curtail capital expansion, cut back on dividends, or engage in refinancing.

# Part 11
# Measuring Business Performance

## 112. Choosing Profitability Goals

### Introduction

Profit measures success. Making a profit is only the first step; making a profit large enough to survive and grow is the real challenge of a business. The ability to measure performance is essential in developing incentives and controlling operations towards the achievement of organizational goals.

### How is it Computed?

Three widely used measures of success of a business are:

1.   Earnings growth
2.   Rate of return on investments (ROI)
3.   Return on equity (ROE)

### 1. Earnings Growth

The earnings growth rate is used in many ways.  One application is the growth rate in earnings or dividends (g) required for the *Gordon's dividend growth model*:

$$P_0 = \frac{D_1}{r - g}$$

where $P_0$ = current price of a security, $D_1$ = expected dividend at the end of the first year, and $r$ = investor's required rate of return.

## 2. Return on Investment (ROI)

ROI relates net income to invested capital (total assets). It provides a standard for evaluating how efficiently management employs the average dollar invested in a business' assets, and whether that dollar came from owners or creditors. Furthermore, a better ROI can also translate directly into a higher return on the owners' equity.

ROI is calculated as:

$$\text{ROI} = \frac{\text{Net profit after taxes}}{\text{Total assets}}$$

## Example I

Consider the following financial data:

| | |
|---|---|
| Total assets | $100,000 |
| Net profit after taxes | 18,000 |

Then

$$\text{ROI} = \frac{\text{Net profit after taxed}}{\text{Total assets}} = \frac{\$18,000}{\$100,000} = 18\%$$

The problem with the ROI formula is that it tells you only how a business did and how well it fared within the industry. Other than that, it has very little value from the standpoint of profit planning.

## 3. Return on Equity (ROE)

Generally, a better management performance measure (i.e., a high or above-average ROI) produces a higher return to equity holders. However, even a poorly managed business that suffers from below-average performance can generate an above-average return on stockholders' equity, simply called the return on equity (ROE). This is because borrowed funds can magnify the returns a business' profits represent to stockholders.

The following formula ties together the ROI and the degree of financial leverage (use of borrowed funds). The financial leverage is measured by the equity multiplier, which is the ratio of a company's total asset base to its equity investment, or, stated another way, the ratio of how many dollars of assets held per dollar of stockholders' equity. It is calculated by dividing total assets by stockholders' equity. This measurement gives an indication of how much of a business' assets are financed by stockholders' equity and how much with borrowed funds.

The return on equity (ROE) is calculated as:

$$ROE = \frac{\text{Net profit after taxes}}{\text{Stakeholders' equity}} = \frac{\text{Net profit after taxes}}{\text{Total assets}} \times \frac{\text{Total assets}}{\text{Stockbrokers' equity}}$$

$$= ROI \times \text{Equity multiplier}$$

ROE measures the returns earned on the owners' (both preferred and common stockholders') investment. The use of the equity multiplier to convert ROI to ROE reflects the impact of leverage (use of debt) on stockholders' return.

The equity multiplier is

$$\text{The equity multiplier} = \frac{\text{Total assets}}{\text{Stockholders' equity}}$$

$$= \frac{\text{Total assets}}{\text{Total assets} - \text{Total liabilities}}$$

$$= \frac{1}{1 - \dfrac{\text{Total liabilities}}{\text{Total assets}}}$$

$$= \frac{1}{(1 - \text{debt ratio})}$$

## Example 2

For the company in Example 1, assume stockholders' equity of $45,000. Then

$$\text{Then, equity multiplier} = \frac{\text{Total assets}}{\text{Stakeholders' equity}} = \frac{\$100,000}{\$45,000} = 2.22$$

$$= \frac{1}{(1 - \text{debt ratio})} = \frac{1}{(1 - 0.55)} = \frac{1}{0.45} = 2.22$$

$$ROE = \frac{\text{Net profit after taxes}}{\text{Stockholders' equity}} = \frac{\$18,000}{\$45,000} = 40\%$$

$$ROE = ROI \times \text{equity multiplier} = 18\% \times 2.22 = 40\%$$

If the company used only equity, the 18% ROI would equal ROE. However, 55% of the firm's capital is supplied by creditors ($45,000/$100,000 = 45% is the equity-to-asset ratio; $55,000/$100,000 = 55% is the debt ratio). Since the 18% ROI all goes to stockholders, who put up only 45% of the capital, the ROE is higher than 18%. This example indicates the company was using leverage (debt) favorably.

## How is it Used and Applied?

Once you have calculated your ratios, compare them to your predetermined goals. Are your goals too high or too low? Have you compared your profits to similar firms in your industry?

ROE provides an important view of the positive contribution that debt can make to a business, but within a certain limit. Too much debt can increase the firms financial risk and thus the cost of financing.

If the assets in which the funds are invested are able to earn a return grater than the fixed rate of return requires by the creditors, the leverage is positive and the common stockholders' benefit. The advantage of this formula is that it enables the company to break its ROE into a profit margin portion (net profit margin), an efficiency-of-asset utilization portion (net profit margin), an efficiency-of-asset utilization portion (total asset turnover), and a use-of-leverage portion (equity multiplier). It shows that the company can raise shareholder return by employer leverage---taking on larger amounts of debts to help finance growth.

Since financial leverage affects net profit margin through the added interest costs, the manager must look at the various pieces of this ROE equation, within the context of the whole, to earn the highest return for stockholders. Financial managers have the task of determining just what combination of asset return and leverage will work best in the competitive environment. Most companies try to keep at least a level equal to what is considered "normal" within the industry.

# 113. Simple (Accounting) Rate of Return

## Introduction

The *simple rate of return* relates the returns generated by a project, as measured by average accounting income after taxes, to the average dollar size of the investment.

## How is it Computed?

$$\text{Simple rate of return} = \frac{\text{expected future annual income}}{\text{average investment}}$$

## *Example*

A proposal requires an initial investment of $6,500, has an expected life of 20 years, and will generate expected annual net income of $675. The owner wants to calculate the simple rate of return.

$$\frac{\$675}{\$6,500/2} = \frac{\$675}{\$3,250} = 20.8\%$$

($6,500 is divided by 2 to obtain an average.)

## How is it Used and Applied?

The simple rate of return is one method used by the business owner to compare the profitability among alternative investment opportunities and proposals; however, drawbacks of the method include its failure to (1) consider cash flows, (2) incorporate the time value of money, and (3) consider the payback period

See Sec. 59, How Many Years Does It Take to Get Your Money Back (Payback Period)?

# 114. Return On Total Assets

## Introduction

*Return on total assets* (ROA) equals net income after taxes divided by total tangible assets and measures the effectiveness of a business' assets to create profits.

## How is it Computed?

$$ROA = \frac{\text{net income after taxes}}{\text{average total assets}}$$

where

Average total assets = (beginning total assets + ending total assets)/2

Intangibles (e.g., goodwill) are usually not included in total assets because they are hard to measure and do not contribute to operating profits. However, an exception might be trademarks that do contribute profits.

## *Example*

The following data show a manufacturer's performance in two different years:

| Net income after taxes | $ 259,358 | $ 384,346 |
|---|---|---|
| Average total assets | | |
|     Beginning of year | 1,548,234 | 1,575982 |
|     End of year | 1,575,982 | 1,614,932 |
|     Average | $1,562,108 | $1,595,457 |
| Return on total assets (ROA) | 16.62% | 24.09% |

The analysis shows that there has been growth in the return on assets during the year, indicating greater productivity of assets in generating earnings.

## How is it Used and Applied?

ROA is probably the single most widely used measure of an entity's success. It indicates the productive utilization of business resources. If ROA is acceptable to the owner or manager, the proper investment decision is to maintain and improve facilities. For managerial use, ROA should be viewed as the product of two factors, net profit margin and total asset turnover.

High-technology businesses with a proprietary product line (the company is the only provider of important and high-demand goods to consumers) have the potential to earn high return rates on assets.

# 115. Residual Income

## Introduction

*Residual income* is the operating income that an investment center in a business is able to earn above some minimum return on its assets.

## How is it Computed?

Residual income = net operating income -
    (minimum rate of return on investment x total operating assets)

The minimum rate of return is often based on the cost of financing to the business.

## Example

Assume that a business has operating assets of $100,000,000 and net operating income of $18,000,000. The minimum return on assets is 13 percent. Residual income is:

| | |
|---|---|
| Net operating income | $18,000,000 |
| Less: Minimum return x total operating assets (13%x $100,000,000) | 13,000,000 |
| | $ 5,000,000 |

## How is it Used and Applied?

Residual income is an absolute amount of income rather than a rate of return, and it is used to evaluate departmental performance. An evaluation based on residual income encourages business owners to accept investment opportunities that have rates of return greater than the charge for invested capital. A manager being evaluated using return on investment (ROI) may be reluctant to accept new investments that lower his or her current ROI, even though the investment would be desirable for the entire business.

The advantages of using residual income in evaluating performance include the following: (1) it is an economic income that takes into account the minimum return that must be earned on assets; (2) the minimum rate of return can vary depending on the riskiness of the division; (3) different assets can be required to earn different returns depending on their risk; (4) the same asset may be required to earn the same return regardless of the department it is in; and (5) the effect of maximizing dollars rather than a percentage leads to goal congruence.

A major disadvantage of residual income is that it cannot be used to compare departments of different sizes; residual income tends to favor larger departments due to the larger amount of dollars involved.

The business owner should look favorably upon a higher residual income since it means that the business is not only earning a net income but it is also covering the opportunity cost of having assets tied up in the business.

The higher the ratio of residual income to net income, the better is the earnings quality. Residual income is viewed by many owners as a better measure of true earnings than net income.

# 116. Flexible-Budget Variance

## Introduction

*flexible budget* shows budgeted cost figures at various capacity levels (e.g., expected, optimistic, and pessimistic), and requires the operation of fixed and variable costs. A flexible budget enables the comparison of actual and budgeted results at virtually any level of activity, and is useful for evaluating the efficiency of both manufacturing and non-manufacturing activities.

## How is it Computed?

Flexible budget variance

= budget versus actual at a particular capacity level

If idle capacity exists, total variable costs will increase with increased production but ,total fixed costs will remain the same.

## Example

The following shows how a business would prepare a flexible budget to reflect a range of performance expectations.

|  | Pessimistic | Expected | Optimistic | Full Capacity |
|---|---|---|---|---|
| Units | 8,000 | 10,000 | 11,000 | 15,000 |
| Capacity level relative to expected | 80% | 100% | 110% | |
| Variable costs | $48,000 | $60,000 | $66,000 | |
| Fixed costs | $90,000 | $90,000 | $90,000 | |

Assuming that 8000 units were actually produced, with actual costs of $50,000 in variable costs and $91,000 in fixed costs, the flexible budget variance would be:

|  | Actual | Flexible budget | Flexible budget variance | |
|---|---|---|---|---|
| Variable | $50,000 | $48,000 | $2,000 | Unfavorable |
| Fixed | $91,000 | 90,000 | 2,000 | Unfavorable |

## How is it Used and Applied?

The flexible budget allows the owner to plan more efficiently by assessing costs at different capacity levels. The owner can foresee which operating strategies may be most suitable and what costs may be expected.

# 117. Variance between Actual Sales and Budgeted Sales

## Introduction

Sales variances analyze the deviation between expected and actual selling price and volume. Reasons for deviation are examined to improve the marketing of the business' products and services.

If actual revenue is below expectations, this is a negative situation for the business owner. Actual revenue may be less than budgeted revenue because of reduced selling price, decline in sales volume and market share, increase in sales returns because of poor quality, or advertising ineffectiveness.

## How is it Computed?

Total sales variance = expected sales revenue - actual sales revenue

The total sales variance should be separated into price and volume. Each should then be analyzed for the reasons behind the variance.

Sales price variance = (actual selling price − budgeted selling price) x actual units sold

Sales volume variance = (actual quantity − budgeted quantity) x budgeted selling price

### *Example*

Marchler Retail's budgeted sales for 20x7 were:

| | |
|---|---|
| Product A: 10,000 units at $6 per unit | $60,000 |
| Product B: 30,000 units at $8 per unit | 240,000 |
| Expected sales revenue | $300,000 |
| Actual sales for the year were: | |
| Product A: 8,000 units at $6.20 per unit | $49,600 |
| Product B: 33,000 units at $7.70 per unit | 254,100 |
| Actual sales revenue | $303,700 |

There is a favorable sales variance of $3,700, consisting of the sales price variance and the sales volume variance.

The sales price variances are:

| | | |
|---|---|---|
| Product A: ($6.20 versus $6.00) x 8,000 | $1,600 | Favorable |
| Product B: ($7.70 versus $8.00) x 33,000 | 9,900 | Unfavorable |
| Sales price variance | $8,300 | Unfavorable |
| The sales volume variances are: | | |
| Product A: (8,000 versus 10,000) x $6.00 | $12,000 | Unfavorable |
| Product B: (33,000 versus 30,000) x $8.00 | 24,000 | Favorable |
| Sales volume variance | $12,000 | Favorable |

## How is it Used and Applied?

The sales variances (price and volume) are prepared for product sales reports to gauge the performance of the marketing function. The sales manager is responsible for sales variances and must explain deviations to the owner. The sales price variance indicates whether the product is being sold at a discount or a premium. Sales price variances may be due to uncontrollable market conditions or to owner decisions.

The analysis of sales volume includes consideration of budgets, sales plans, industry and competitive comparisons, and manufacturing costs. Note that high sales volume does not automatically mean high profits, since there may be high costs associated with the products.

An unfavorable sales volume variance may arise from poor marketing or price cuts by competitors. If the unfavorable volume variance is coupled with a favorable price variance, the business may have lost sales by raising its prices.

The sales volume variance reflects the effect on the total budgeted contribution margin that is caused by changes in the total number of units sold. The variance may be caused by unpredictable product demand, lack of product demand, or poor sales forecasting.

An unfavorable total sales variance may signal a problem with the sales manager, who controls sales, advertising, and often pricing. Another possible cause of an unfavorable sales variance may be a lack of quality control, substitution of poorer quality components due to deficient purchasing, or deficient product design emanating from poor engineering.

Corrective action is needed to improve lagging sales. Such action may take the following forms:

◆ Improves sales planning.

◆ Improve product quality, design, packaging, or sales mix.

◆ Dispose of outdated styles and slow-moving stock.

◆ To stimulate sales, offer sales promotions, provide rebates, offer discounts, and give zero percent financing.

◆ Pay higher commission rates to salespeople to promote high-profit-margin items and slow-moving ones.

◆ Identify who is responsible for sales variances and take corrective action.

See Sec. 118, Variance between Actual Costs and Budgeted Costs.


# 118. Variance between Actual Costs and Budgeted Costs

## Introduction

If actual costs significantly exceed budgeted costs in a business, the owner should be alarmed as to the cause. While it may only be a tight budget estimate that the owner cannot realistically meet, it may be a serious problem indicating a lack of costs controls, misspending, and deficient planning. The business may be inefficient, requiring better cost management. Perhaps there is waste, and duplication of effort and facilities.

If only the budgetary process is at fault, budgets based on historical experience should incorporate the current operating environment. If a static (fixed) budget geared for only one level of activity is being used, a flexible (variable) budget should be implemented instead. In other words, if variances are due to poor estimation, improve the budgeting process.

## How is it Computed?

Variance = actual cost versus budgeted cost

If actual cost exceeds budgeted cost, the variance is unfavorable. It is favorable in the opposite case.

A variance should be computed for each major element within the business, including costs by product, customer, territory, salesperson, and so on.

Flexible budgeting distinguishes between fixed and variable charges. It adjusts costs based on the actual volume achieved. Price and quantity variances may be determined. The flexible budget compares actual costs for a specified output level. Budgeted figures may easily be developed based on various activity levels. Flexible budgets aid in measuring performance.

## *Example 1*

A business owner compared her budgeted costs to the actual costs for the year as follows:

|  | Budget | Actual | Variance | | Variance in percent# |
|---|---|---|---|---|---|
| Manufacturing costs | $150,000 | $200,000 | $50,000 | U* | 33.3 |
| Selling expenses | 30,000 | 42,000 | 12,000 | U | 40.0 |
| General and Administrative expense | 60,000 | 95,000 | 35,000 | U | 58.3 |
| Total | $240,000 | $337,000 | $97,000 | U | 40.4 |

*U = unfavorable variance.

#Variance in percent = variance amount/budgeted amount.

This business is in trouble: Actual costs are excessive compared to expectations. The reasons for the significant variance must be found immediately and corrective action implemented. If this situation continues, the continued existence of the business may become questionable.

## Example 2

To illustrate the difference between the static budget and flexible budget, assume that a business is budgeted to produce 6,000 units during the year. The budget for direct labor and variable overhead costs is set as shown below:

| | |
|---|---|
| Budgeted production | 6,000 units |
| Actual production | 5,800 units |
| Direct labor | $39,000 |

Variable overhead costs:

| | |
|---|---|
| Indirect labor | 6,000 |
| Supplies | 900 |
| Repairs | 300 |
| | $46,200 |

*Note:* Variable overhead costs are those that change with the volume of units produced.

Assume further that the business was able to produce only 5,800 units. If a static budget approach is used, the performance report will appear as follows:

| | Budget | Actual | Variance, * U or F† |
|---|---|---|---|
| Production in units | 6,000 | 5,800 | 200 (U) |
| Direct labor | $39,000 | $38,500 | $500 (F) |
| Variable overhead costs: | | | |
| Indirect labor | 6,000 | 5,950 | 50 (F) |
| Supplies | 900 | 870 | 30 (F) |
| Repairs | 300 | 295 | 5 (F) |
| Total conversion costs | $46,200 | $45,615 | $585 (F) |

\* A variance represents the deviation of actual cost from the standard or budgeted cost.

†U = unfavorable variance; F = favorable variance.

Apparently, these cost variances are useless, since they have been derived by comparing the actual costs incurred at a 5,800-unit level of activity to the budgeted costs at a different level of activity (6,000 units). From a control standpoint, it makes no sense to try to compare costs at one activity level with costs at a different activity level. It is like comparing oranges to apples, instead of comparing oranges that grow in Florida to oranges that grow in California. Such comparisons would make a production manager look good as long as the actual production is less than the budgeted production. Using the cost-volume formula and generating the budget based on the 5,800 actual units gives the following performance report:

Budgeted production    6,000 units

Actual production    5,800 units

| | Cost-volume Formula | Flexible Budget 5,800 units | Actual 5,800 units | Variance (U or F) |
|---|---|---|---|---|
| Direct labor | $6.50 per unit | $37,700 | $38,500 | $800U |
| Variable overhead: | | | | |
| Indirect labor | 1.00 | 5,800 | 5,950 | 150U |
| Supplies | 0.15 | 870 | 870 | 0 |
| Repairs | 0.05 | 290 | 295 | 5U |
| | $7.70 | $44,660 | $45,615 | $955U |

\*    assumed

\*\*   $6.50 per unit x 5,800 units = $37,700

Notice that all cost variances are unfavorable (U), as compared to the favorable cost variances on the performance report based on the static budget approach.

## How is it Used and Applied?

The reason and/or party responsible for the deviation between actual costs and budgeted costs should be determined, and corrective steps taken to correct unfavorable situations. However, a favorable variance (actual cost less than budgeted cost) should be learned from and taken advantage of.

When actual costs are out of line, the owner may consider doing the following:

◆ Implement a cost-reduction program to trim excessive expenditures. Use a flexible budget, which is extremely useful in cost control.

◆ Make volume purchases when discounts are attractive.

◆ Substitute cheaper materials.

◆ Restructure and reorganize to reduce "fat" in the business and make it leaner and more efficient.

◆ Eliminate duplicate activities and facilities.

◆ Merge operations to generate cost efficiencies.

◆ Combine facilities and equipment to achieve a more efficient productivity level and improve operations.

◆ Place "caps" on expense categories (such as travel and entertainment), requiring special permission to exceed maximum amounts.

◆ Change a production method or specification.

◆ Inspect at key points in the manufacturing cycle.

◆ Upgrade employee training.

◆ Improve supervision and scheduling.

◆ Computerize variance reporting for immediate feedback and analysis.

See Sec. 117, Variance between Actual Sales and Budgeted Sales.

# 119. Price Variance

## Introduction

The *price variance* compares the difference between the standard price and actual price for materials issued to production, labor hours incurred, or overhead.

## How is it Computed?

Price variance = (actual price versus standard price) x actual quantity

*Note:* Standard price means what the price should be.

### Example

Assume the following company standards:

|  |  |
|---|---|
| Direct material: 5 pounds @ $4 per pound | $20 per unit |
| Direct labor: 3 hours @ $12 per hour | $36 per unit |

Actual volumes and costs are:

|  |  |
|---|---|
| Production | 9,800 units |
| Purchase: 50,000 pounds @ $3 | $150,000 |
| Direct labor: 22,000 hours @ $10 | $220,000 |

The material price variance is:

($3 versus $4) x 50,000  Favorable

The labor price variance is:

($10 versus $12) 22,000 = $44,000  Favorable

## How is it Used and Applied?

Management uses the material price variance to evaluate the activity of its purchasing department and to understand the impact of raw material cast changes on company profitability. To correct for an unfavorable material cost price variance, management can increase selling price, substitute cheaper materials, change a production method or specification, or engage in a cost-reduction program. Management cannot material price variances when higher prices are the result of inflation or market shortages.

Where salary rates are set by union contract, the labor price variance will usually be minimal, since the standard labor rate is based on the contracted hourly wage rate. Possible reasons for a labor price variance include the following:

| Reason | Party responsible |
|---|---|
| Use of overpaid or excessive number of workers | Production manager or union contract |
| Poor job descriptions | Personnel |
| Production planning | Overtime |

If there is a shortage of skilled workers it may be impossible to avoid an unfavorable labor price variance.

# 120.  Quantity Variance

## Introduction

The *quantity variance* reveals excess or deficient usage of material or labor in production, and links this usage to cost consequence.

## How is it Computed?

Quantity variance = (actual quantity versus standard quantity) x standard price

The quantity variance is computed for both material and labor.

If the actual cost or quantity exceeds the standard cost or quantity, the usage to cost consequence.

## Example

Assume the following standards from a particular company:

Direct material: 5 pounds @ $4 per pound   $20 per unit

Direct labor: 3 hours @ $12 per hour    $36 per unit

Production volumes: 9800 units

Direct material used: 44,000 pounds

Direct labor: 22,000 @ $10 = $220,000

Then the material quantity variance is:

(Actual quantity versus standard quantity) x standard price

= (44,000 versus 49,000) x $4 = $20,000

The labor quantity variance is:

(Actual quantity versus standard quantity) x standard price

= (22,000 versus 29,400) x $12 = $88,800

In both cases in this analysis, the quantity variances are favorable.


## How is it Used and Applied?

Material and labor efficiency standards are typically estimated by engineers based on an analysis of the production process. The material quantity variance is typically the responsibility of the production department, but the purchasing department is responsible for acquiring inferior goods to economize on cost.

The reasons and responsible parties for unfavorable material quantity variances are:

| Reason | Party responsible |
|---|---|
| Improper specifications, insufficient quantities, failure to buy regularly | Purchasing |
| Poor mix of materials, poorly trained workers, improperly adjusted machines, poor production scheduling or design, lack of proper tools or machines, unexpected volume changes | Production manager |
| Failure to detect defective goods | Receiving |
| Inefficient labor, poor supervision, waste on the production line | Foreman |

To control against an unfavorable labor efficiency variance due to inadequate materials or sales orders, a daily direct labor report should be prepared. The causes and responsible parties for unfavorable labor efficiency variances are:

| Cause | Party responsible |
| --- | --- |
| Poor workers, poor training | Personnel or training |
| Inefficient flow of materials, wrong mixture of | |
| labor for a given job, inferior tools, idle time | |
| from production delays | Foreman |
| Employee unrest | Personnel or foreman |
| Improper functioning of equipment | Maintenance |
| Insufficient material supply or poor quality | Purchasing |

An unfavorable labor efficiency variance may indicate that better machinery is needed, plant layout should be revised, improved operating methods are needed, and/or better employee training and development are necessary.

# 121. Salesperson Variances

## Introduction

*Salesperson variances* are used to determine the effectiveness of the sales force by looking at cost and time spent by these employees.

## How is it Computed?

Several computations are utilized to gain insight into salesperson variances:

1. Total cost variance = actual cost versus standard cost
2. Variance in salesperson days = (actual days versus standard days) x standard rate per day
3. Variance in salesperson costs = (actual rate versus standard rate) x actual days
4. Total variance in calls = actual calls versus actual sales

   Total variance in calls = standard calls versus standard sale
5. Variance in calls = (actual calls versus standard calls) x standard sale
6. Variance in sales = (actual calls versus standard sale) x standard calls
7. Joint variance = (actual calls versus standard calls) x (actual sale versus standard sales)

## Example I

Assume the following sales data for a company:

| | |
|---|---|
| Standard cost | $240,000 |
| Standard salesperson days | 2,000 |
| Standard rate per salesperson day | $120 |
| Actual cost | $238,000 |
| Actual salesperson days | 1,700 |
| Actual rate per salesperson day | $2.30 |

The total cost variance is:

| | | |
|---|---|---|
| Actual cost | $238,000 | |
| Standard cost | 240,000 | |
| | $ 2,000 | F |

This analysis demonstrates a favorable variance.

The control variance is broken down into salesperson days and salesperson costs.

Variance in salesperson days =  (actual days versus standard days)

x standard rate per day = (1,700 versus 2,000) x $120 = $36,000  F

The variance is favorable because the territory was handled in few days than expected.

Variance in salesperson costs = (actual rate versus standard rate) x actual days

= ($140 versus $120) x 1,700 = $34,000  U

An unfavorable variance results because the actual rate per day is greater than the expected rate per day.

## Example 2

Assume that a salesperson called on 55 customers and sold to each an average of $2,800 worth of merchandise.  The standard number of calls is 50, and the standard sale is $2,400.  Variance analysis of calls and sales follows:

| | | |
|---|---|---|
| Total variance: | | |
| Actual calls x actual sale: 55 x $2,800 | $154,000 | |
| Standard calls x standard sale: 50 x $2,400 | 120,000 | |
| Variance | $ 34,000 | F |

Variance in calls:
(actual calls versus standard calls)
x standard sale: (55 versus 50) x $2,400          $12,000  F

Variance in sales:
(actual sale versus standard sale)
x standard calls: ($2,800 versus $2,400) x 50          $20,000  F

Joint variance:
(actual calls versus standard calls)
x (actual sale versus standard sale): (55 versus
50) x ($2,800 versus $2,400)          $2,000  F

## How is it Used and Applied?

Sales managers use sales person variances to appraise the sales force within a territory, including time spent and expenses incurred. Sales managers can keep track of salesperson costs and compare them to budget figures to determine whether salespersons are using their time and calls effectively in generating profitable sales.

Cost variances for the selling function may be analyzed by geographic region, product, or type of personnel.

# 122. Warehouse Cost Variance

## Introduction

*Warehouse cost variances* compare actual costs and standard costs to reveal the efficiency with which warehousing is being performed.

## How is it Computed?

Variances in warehousing costs can be calculated by looking at the cost per unit to store the merchandise and the number of orders anticipated. Calculations include:

1.  Total warehousing cost variance = total actual cost versus total standard cost.
2.  Variance in orders = (actual orders versus standard orders) x standard unit cost
3.  Variance in cost = (actual cost per unit versus standard cost per unit) x actual orders

## Example

Assume that a company supplies the following information regarding a product and warehouse costs:

| | |
|---|---|
| Standard cost | $12,100 |
| Standard orders | 5,500 |
| Standard unit cost | $2.20 |
| Actual cost | $14,030 |
| Actual orders | 6,100 |
| Actual unit cost | $2.30 |

Total warehousing cost variance is

| | |
|---|---|
| Actual cost | $14,030 |
| Standard cost | 12,100 |
| | $ 1,930  U |

For the analysis, the total variance is segregated into the variance in orders and the variance in cost:

| | |
|---|---|
| Variance in orders = (actual orders versus standard orders) × standard unit cost: (6,100 versus 5,500) × $2.20 | $1320  U |
| Variance in cost = (actual cost per unit versus standard cost per unit) × actual orders: ($2.30 versus $2.20) × 6,100 | $610  U |

## How is it Used and Applied?

Variances in warehousing costs are used by warehouse management to determine whether the warehousing functions being performed properly.   Analysis of warehousing costs are made to identify possible problems and take necessary cost-saving measures.

# 123. Incremental Cost and Incremental Revenue

## Introduction

Extra (marginal) cost is the change in total cost associated with a unit change in quantity. Extra (marginal) revenue is the rate of change in total revenue with respect to quantity sold.

# How is it Computed?

The calculation of MR indicates to a firm how total sales will change if there is a change in the quantity sold of a firm's product. In economics, marginal revenue must equal marginal cost in order for profit to be maximized, or MR = MC.

In a discrete range of activity---the activity in which firms operate in actual business---MR is equivalent to incremental (or differential) revenue (IR). MC is also viewed as being equivalent to incremental (or differential) cost (IC), which is the increment in cost between the two alternatives or two discrete volumes of output. Therefore, in reality, decisions affecting this type of activity should be made only when IR > IC. The marginal cost of the five-hundredth unit of output can be calculated by finding the difference between total cost at 499 units of output and total cost at 500 units of output. Thus, MC is the additional cost of one more unit of output, calculated as:

$$MC = \frac{\text{change in total cost}}{\text{change in quantity}}$$

MC is also the change in total variable cost associated with a unit change in output, because total cost changes even though total fixed cost remains unchanged. MC may also be considered the rate of change in total cost as the quantity (Q) of output changes; it is simply the first derivative of the total cost (TC) function. Thus,

$$MC \quad \frac{dTC}{dQ}$$

Similarly, the marginal revenue of the five-hundredth unit of output can be calculated by finding the difference between total revenue at 499 units of output and total revenue at 500 units of output. MR is thus the additional revenue derived from one more unit of output. It is calculated as:

$$MR = \frac{\text{change in total revenue}}{\text{change in quantity}}$$

MR may also be thought of as the rate of change in total revenue as the quantity (Q) of output changes and is simply the first derivative of the total revenue (TR) function. Thus,

$$MR = \frac{dTR}{dQ}$$

For profit to be maximized, MR must equal MC.

## Example

Consider the following TR and TC functions:

$$TR = \$1,000Q - \$5Q^2 \quad \text{and} \quad TC = \$20,000 + 200Q$$

MR and MC are:

$$MR = \frac{dTR}{dQ} = \$1,000 - \$10Q \quad \text{and} \quad MC = \frac{dTC}{dQ} = \$200$$

At the profit-maximizing output level, MR = MC; thus

$$MR = \$1,000 - \$10Q = \$200 = MC$$

Solving for Q gives

$$Q = 980 \text{ units}$$

which is the profit-maximizing quantity of output.


## How is it Used and Applied?

Marginal analysis utilizing the concepts of marginal revenue and marginal cost is a key principle in decision making that can be applied to financial and investment decisions. The analysis suggests that financial and investment decisions should be made and actions taken only when marginal revenues equals marginal costs. If this condition exists, a given decision should maximize the firm's profits.

Managers making any type of decision---such as marketing, operational, production, purchasing, financing, investment, and personnel decisions--must always weigh the marginal cost to be incurred against the marginal revenue to be derived from that decision. In practice, since decision makers typically work with incremental data (rather than marginal data), they have to weigh the incremental cost associated with the decision against the incremental revenue to be gained.

# Part 12

# Averages, Expectations, and Variability in Business Activities

## 124. Averages (Means): Simple and Weighted

### Introduction

Averages are frequently used in business as a uniform method of stating values—for example, the average inventory, average cost, average income, average sales per salesperson, average units produced per worker, average sick days per employee, average overhead per department, etc. An average is more meaningful if it is compared to something else. An average should be compared over time. For example, the trend in the average revenue per salesperson will reveal the success of changes in sales policies such as pricing, advertising and promotion, and reassignment of territories.

### How is it Computed?

A simple average (mean) is computed by adding all the numerical figures in a list and dividing by the number of figures in the list. The formula for a simple average is:

$$\text{Simple average} = \frac{S}{n}$$

Where $S$ = sum of the figures in the list and $n$ = number of figures in the list. *Note:* Excel has a function key, AVERAGE(list), for the calculation of a simple average.

A *weighted average* (mean) is an average of observations having different degrees of importance or frequency. The formula for a weighted average is:

Weighted average $= \sum w_i x_i$

where $x_i =$ the data values and $w_i =$ relative weight assigned to each observation, expressed as percentage or relative frequency.

## Example 1

A monthly sales report shows the following:

| | |
|---|---|
| Department A | $520,000 |
| Department B | 430,000 |
| Department C | 460,000 |
| Department D | 480,000 |

The simple average of sales is: ($520,000 + $430,000 + $460,000 + $480,000)/4 = $472,500

## Example 2

Total monthly sales are $1,200,000, and the number of salespeople is 20. The average salesperson generates sales of:

$1,200,000/20 = $60,000

## Example 3

A manufacturer uses three grades of labor to produce a finished product as follows:

| Grade of labor | Labor hours per unit of labor | Hourly wages (X) |
|---|---|---|
| Skilled | 6 | $10.00 |
| Semiskilled | 3 | 8.00 |
| Unskilled | 1 | 6.00 |

The arithmetic average (mean) labor cost per hour for this product can be computed as:

Simple average $=$ ($10.00 + $8.00 + $6.00)/3 $=$ $8.00 per hour

However, this computation implies that each grade of labor was used in equal amounts, and this is not the case. To calculate the average cost of labor per hour correctly, the weighted average should be computed as:

Weighted average = $10.00 (6/10) + $8.00 (3/10) + $6.00 (1/10)
= $9.00 per hour

where the weights used equal the proportion of the total labor required to manufacture the product.

## Example 4

A prospective acquirer wants to determine the price to offer for a targeted business. It is decided that the business valuation should be based on two times the weighted-average earnings over the last 3 years. The most current year is always given the greatest weight.

| Year | Net income | Weight | Weighted net income |
|------|-----------|--------|---------------------|
| 20x1 | $300,000 | 1 | $ 300,000 |
| 20x2 | 260,000 | 2 | 520,000 |
| 20x3 | 3650,000 | 3 | 1,050,000 |
| | | 6 | $1,870,000 |

Weighted-average earnings = $1,870,000/6 = $311,667
Business valuation = $311,667 x 2 = $623,334

## Example 5

Your small business has two loans outstanding. Loan 1 is for $300,000 with a 10 percent interest rate. Loan 2 is for $400,000 with an 8 percent interest rate. You want to determine the average interest rate.

A weighted-average interest rate is needed because the loans are for different amounts. The weighted-average interest rate equals 8.9 percent, computed as follows:

10%($300,000/$700,000) + 8%($400,000/$700,000) = 4.3% + 4.6% = 8.9%

## Example 6

You invest in securities. The amount invested, the months held, and the profit earned are as follows:

| Type | Investment | Months held | Profit |
|------|-----------|-------------|--------|
| A | $ 80,000 | 6 | $ 5,000 |
| B | 90,000 | 20 | 10,000 |
| C | 50,000 | 9 | 2,000 |
| Total | $220,000 | | $17,000 |

You need to calculate a weighted-average rate of return because the amounts invested and the time period held vary with each investment.

*Step 1.* Compute the rate of return per investment.

Profit/Investment
A: $5,000/$80,000 = 6.25%
B: $10,000/$90,000 = 11.11%
C: $2,000/$50,000 = 4.00%

*Step 2.* Annualize the rates of return so they are expressed on a common basis.

Annualized rate of return = (total return/number of months) × 12
A: (6.25%/6) × 12 = 12.50%
B: (11.11%/20) × 12 = 6.67%
C: (4.00%/9) × 12 = 5.30%

*Step 3.* Determine the weighted-average rate of return. Weighted-average rate of return

Weighted-average rate of return =

annualized rate of return total amount invested x amount invested in each security

12.50% ($80,000/$220,000) + 6.67%($90,000/$220,000) + 5.50% ($50,000/$220,000) = 4.5%
+ 2.7%                         + 1.2% = 8.4%

To compute a return rate for less than 1 year, use:

Return rate (less than 1 year) = (rate of return/12) x number of months held

## Example 7

If the annual rate of return is 15 percent, the rate of return to be earned in 3 months is:

(15%/12) × 3 = 3.75%

## How is it Used and Applied?

Whenever each value has a different degree of importance or frequency, the weighted-average formula may be used. An arithmetic average is used only when the values are equally weighted. Expected value is basically a weighted average, the weights being the probabilities of occurrence.

Managers of all functional areas of business must have an understanding of the difference between the arithmetic mean and the weighted mean in order to calculate the correct average.

For multiproduct lines, it is necessary to predetermine the sales mix and then compute a weighted-average contribution margin (CM) in order to perform breakeven and cost-volume-profit (CVP) analysis. The weights used here are sales mix ratios. See Sec. 54, Cost-Volume-Profit Analysis.

Financial managers need to know the minimum rate of return, which is in effect the weighted average cost of capital, in order to decide whether or not to accept a project. See Sec. 8, Estimating the Cost of Debt and Equity Financing.

An average is more meaningful if it is compared over time or expressed relative to another average. Examples are reporting the change in average departmental sales per month, comparing the average sales figure to average marketing expenses needed to obtain that revenue, average telephone expense per person, and average orders processed per clerk. An average can identify abuses, such as when employees are using business facilities such as copiers for personal use.

An average may identify a problem in operations, such as when average sales increase but profits are declining, or when units produced are increasing but the number of defects are skyrocketing, causing the unit cost actually to increase.

# 125. Median and Mode

## Introduction

The *median* is the middle value of a list of numbers when the numbers in the data set are arranged by order of importance---that is, it is the midpoint in a range of values. The *mode* is the most commonly occurring value in a data set. It is a meaningful statistic only when a particular value clearly occurs more frequently than any of the others.

## How is it Computed?

### Median

The formula for the position occupied by the median item is:

$$\frac{n + 1}{2}$$

where n is the number of items.

## Example

An employer has nine employees, all of whom earn different hourly wages. The employer wants to determine the median wage of his employees, whose wages are listed below:

<table>
<tr><th colspan="2">Unsorted Hourly Wages of Employees</th></tr>
<tr><th>Employee</th><th>Hourly wage rate</th></tr>
<tr><td>1</td><td>$3.75</td></tr>
<tr><td>2</td><td>5.25</td></tr>
<tr><td>3</td><td>4.25</td></tr>
<tr><td>4</td><td>6.25</td></tr>
<tr><td>5</td><td>6.50</td></tr>
<tr><td>6</td><td>4.00</td></tr>
<tr><td>7</td><td>4.50</td></tr>
<tr><td>8</td><td>5.75</td></tr>
<tr><td>9</td><td>8.00</td></tr>
</table>

The steps to calculate the median are as follows:

1. Sort the data by wage rate.

<table>
<tr><th colspan="2">Sorted Hourly Wages for Employees</th></tr>
<tr><th>Employee</th><th>Hourly wage rate</th></tr>
<tr><td>1</td><td>3.75</td></tr>
<tr><td>2</td><td>4.00</td></tr>
<tr><td>3</td><td>4.25</td></tr>
<tr><td>4</td><td>4.50</td></tr>
<tr><td>5</td><td>5.25</td></tr>
<tr><td>6</td><td>5.75</td></tr>
<tr><td>7</td><td>6.25</td></tr>
<tr><td>8</td><td>6.50</td></tr>
<tr><td>9</td><td>8.00</td></tr>
</table>

2. Locate the median item position:
   Median item position

   $$= \frac{n + 1}{2}$$

   $$\frac{n + 1}{2} = \frac{9 + 1}{2} = \frac{10}{2} = \text{fifth position}$$

3. Ascertain the value of the component occupying the median position. By a simple process of observation, we determine that employee 2 is in the median position, receiving $5.25 per hour.

## Mode

The mode is determined by observation, usually from a graphic. On such a graph, the modal value is the value at the point of highest density of activity.

The simple mode is shown in Exhibit 125.1.Sometimes a distribution can be bimodal. For example, if a retailer wishes to find the modal values of the distribution of weekly sales volume, a graph may be drawn as shown in Exhibit 125.2.

**Figure 125.1: Simple mode**

**Figure 125.2: Bimodal distribution**

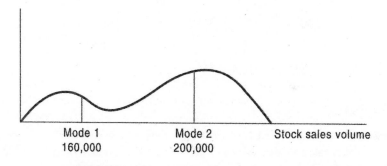

| Mode 1 | Mode 2 | Stock sales volume |
| 160,000 | 200,000 | |

## How is it Used and Applied?

The median is an essential measure of central tendency used in financial analysis when it is necessary to eliminate large deviations. For example, in a seasonal industry such as the manufacturer and sale of snow skis, it may be essential to identify the midpoint sales month. Use of the median may be misrepresentative, however, if the values of the observed items do not cluster at the center of the data set. In this case, modal analysis may be more appropriate.

There area wide variety of financial applications for modal analysis; including the evaluation of a product's peak selling periods when there are two clear distinctions. Modal analysis is useful with any financial or other data graph to display the most commonly occurring value. Modal analysis is useful with sales, income, utilization rates, population, and other data where there is a clearly occurring value. Use of a mode graph can be extremely effective in making presentations.

# 126. Expected Value and Standard Deviation

## Introduction

*Expected value* is a weighted average using the probabilities as weights. For decisions involving uncertainty, the concept of expected value provides a rational means for selecting the best course of action. Whenever we talk about the expected value, one statistic that goes with it standard deviation *Standard deviation* is a statistic that measures the tendency of data to be spread out. Intuitively, it is a margin of error associated with a given expected value.

## How is it Computed?

### Expected Value

The expected value $(\bar{r})$ is found by multiplying the probability of each outcome by its payoff:

$$\bar{r} = \sum r_i p_i$$

where $r_i$ is the outcome for the $i^{th}$ possible event and $p_i$ is the probability of occurrence of that outcome.

### Example 1

Consider the possible rates of return, depending on the states of the economy (i.e., recession, normal, and prosperity) that could be earned next year on a $50,000 investment in stock A or on a $50,000 investment in stock B.

| State of economy | Return $(r_i)$ | Probability $(p_i)$ |
|---|---|---|
| | Proposal A | |
| Recession | 5% | 0.2 |
| Normal | 20% | 0.6 |
| Prosperity | 40% | 0.2 |
| | Proposal B | |
| Recession | 10% | 0.2 |
| Normal | 15% | 0.6 |
| Prosperity | 20% | 0.2 |

The expected rates of returns are as follows.

Proposal A: $\bar{r}$ = (5%)(.2) + (20%)(.6) + (40%)(.2) = 19%

Proposal B: $\bar{r}$ = (10%)(.2) + (15%)(.6) + (20%)(.2) = 15%

## Standard Deviation

As a measure of risk, the standard deviation, denoted by (sigma), is defined as

$$\sigma = \sqrt{\frac{(r - \bar{r})_2}{n - 1}}$$

where is the mean or expected value. In this case the $i$'s are equally likely and therefore equally weighted. Note that we divide by $(n - 1)$.

## Example 2

One and one-half years of quarterly returns are listed below *for* Amko Motors stock:

| Time period | r(%) | $(r - \bar{r})$ | $(r - \bar{r})^2$ |
|:---:|:---:|:---:|:---:|
| 1 | 10 | 0 | 0 |
| 2 | 15 | 5 | 25 |
| 3 | 20 | 10 | 100 |
| 4 | 5 | -5 | 25 |
| 5 | -10 | -20 | 400 |
| 6 | 20 | 10 | 100 |
| | 60 | | 650 |

From this table, note that

$$\bar{r} = 60/6 = 10\%$$

$$\sigma = \sqrt{\frac{(r - \bar{r})^2}{n - 1}} = \sqrt{\frac{650}{6 - 1}} = \sqrt{130} = 11.40\%$$

On average, Amko Motors stock has returned 10 percent over the last six quarters, and the variability about its average return is 11.40 percent. The high standard deviation (11.40 percent) relative to the average return of 10 percent indicates that the stock is very risky.

Standard deviation is also a measure of the dispersion of a probability distribution. In this case, the smaller the deviation, the tighter is the distribution, and thus the lower is the riskiness of the investment. Standard deviation in this use is the square root of the mean of the squared deviations from the expected value (r):

$$\sigma = \sqrt{\sum (r - \bar{r})^2 \, p_i}$$

where $\bar{r} = \sum r p_i$

To calculate, proceed as follows:

Step 1. Compute the expected rate of return ($\bar{r}$).

Step 2. Subtract each possible return from r to obtain a set of deviations ($r - \bar{r}$).

Step 3. Square each deviation, multiply the squared deviation by the probability of occurrence for its respective return, and sum these products to obtain the variance

$$\sigma^2 = \sum(r_i - \bar{r})^2 p_i$$

Step 4. Finally, take the square root of the variance to obtain the standard deviation ($\sigma$).

## Example 3

In this example, standard deviations are computed for the data of Example 1.

To complete the step-by-step procedure, it is convenient to set up a table, as follows:

| Return ($r_i$) | Probability ($p_i$) | $r_i \cdot p_i$ (step 1) | ($r_i - r$) (step 2) | ($r_i - r$)$^2$ (step 3) | ($r_i - r$)$^2 p_i$ |
|---|---|---|---|---|---|
| | | Proposal A | | | |
| -5% | 0.2 | -1% | -24% | 576 | 115.2 |
| 20% | 0.6 | 12% | 1% | 1 | 0.6 |
| 40% | 0.2 | 8% | 21% | 441 | 88.2 |
| | | | | | 204 |
| | | | | (step 4) | $\sigma^2 = 204$ |
| | | | | | $\sigma = \sqrt{204}$ |
| | | | | | $\sigma = \underline{14.28\%}$ |
| | | Proposal B | | | |
| 10% | 0.2 | 2% | -5% | 25 | 5 |
| 15% | 0.6 | 9% | 0% | 0 | 0 |
| 20% | 0.2 | 4% | 5% | 25 | 5 |
| | | | | | 10 |
| | | | | | $\sigma^2 = 10$ |
| | | | | (step 4) | $\sigma = \sqrt{10}$ |
| | | | | | $\sigma = \underline{3.16\%}$ |

## Can a Computer Help?

Spreadsheet programs and financial calculators calculate standard deviation. For example, Excel has a function, STDEV that performs the calculation.

## How is it Used and Applied?

Standard deviation is used as an indicator of the risk involved in an investment, since it measures the variability of returns around the expected return from an investment. Financial managers can also use expected value and standard deviation to make important inferences from past data. Other applications of standard deviation include determining the variability in sales and earnings. Unstable or erratic sales and earnings mean uncertainty and therefore greater risk.

See Sec. 127, Coefficient of Variation.

# 127. Coefficient of Variation

## Introduction

The *coefficient of variation* is a measure of relative dispersion, or relative risk. It represents the degree of risk per unit of return.

## How is it Computed?

The coefficient of variation is computed by dividing the standard deviation $\sigma$ by the expected value $E(x)$, where

$$E(x) = \sum x_i p_i$$

where $x_i$ is the outcome for the ith possible event and $p_i$ is the probability of occurrence of that outcome, and

$$\sigma = \sqrt{\sum [x_i - E(x)]^2 p_i}$$

## Example

Consider two business proposals, A and B, with the following probability distribution of cash flows in each of the next five years:

| | Cash inflows | | | |
|---|---|---|---|---|
| Probability | .2 | .3 | .4 | .1 |
| A | $ 50 | $200 | $300 | $400 |
| B | 100 | 150 | 250 | 850 |

The expected value of the cash inflow for proposal A is:

$$\$50(.2) + \$200(.3) + \$300(.4) + \$400(.1) = \$230$$

The expected value of the cash inflow for proposal B is:

$$\$100(.2) + \$150(.3) + \$250(.4) + \$850(.1) = \$250$$

The standard deviations of proposals A and B are computed as follows:

For A:  $\sigma =$

$$\sqrt{(\$50 - 230)(.2) + (200 - 230)(.3) + (300 - 230)(.4) + (400 - 230)(.1)}$$
$$= \$107.70$$

For B:  $\sigma = \sqrt{(\$100 - 250)(.2) + (150 - 250)(.3) + (250 - 250)(.4) + (850 - 250)(.1)}$$

$$= \$208.57$$

Proposal B is more risky than proposal A, since its standard deviation is greater.

Note the following:

| Proposal | Expected value [E(x)] | Standard deviation ($\sigma$) |
|----------|-----------------------|-------------------------------|
| A | $107.7 | $230 |
| B | 208.57 | 250 |

The coefficient of variation for each proposal is:

For A:  $\dfrac{\$107.7}{\$230} = .47$

For B:  $\dfrac{\$208.57}{\$250} = .83$

Therefore, because the coefficient is a relative measure of risk, B is considered more risky than A.

## How is it Used and Applied?

The standard deviation is used as an indicator of the risk involved in an investment, since it measures the variability of returns around the expected return from an investment. Business managers can also use expected value and standard deviation to make important inferences from past data. The problem with the standard deviation is that it is a measure of absolute risk. It can only be used to compare investments with the same expected returns. Therefore, businesspeople use the coefficient of variation to compare projects with *differing* expected returns.

# 128. Normal Distribution

## Introduction

The normal distribution is the most popular probability distribution used for statistical decision making in business. A normal distribution has the following important characteristics:

1. The curve has a single peak.
2. The curve is bell-shaped.
3. The mean (average) lies at the center of the distribution, and the distribution is symmetrical around the mean.
4. The two tails of the distribution extend indefinitely and never touch the horizontal axis.
5. The shape of the distribution is determined by its mean ($\mu$) and standard deviation ($\sigma$).

## How is it Computed?

As with any continuous probability function, the area under the curve must equal to 1, and the area between two values of X (say, a and b) represents the probability that X lies between and b as illustrated on Figure 128.1.

**Figure 128.1: Normal distribution**

Further, since the normal distribution is symmetric, it has the valuable advantage that a known percentage of all possible values of x lie within a certain number of standard deviations of the mean, as shown in Figure 128.2.

**Figure 128.2: Normal distribution**

| Percent | 99.73% | 99% | 95.45% | 95% | 90% | 68.27 |
|---|---|---|---|---|---|---|
| Number of $\pm$ s | 3.00 | 2.58 | 2.00 | 1.96 | 1.645 | 1.00 |

That is, 68.27 percent of the values of any normally distributed variable lie within the plus or minus one of . The probability of the normal distribution as given above is difficult to work with in determining areas under the curve; each set of x values generates another curve (as long as the means and standard deviations are different). To facilitate computations, every set of x values is translated to a new axis-a Z set--with the translation defined as

$$Z = \frac{X - \mu}{\sigma}$$

The resulting values, called Z values, are the values of a new variable called the *standard normal variate*, Z. The translation process is shown in Exhibit 128.3

**Figure 128.3: Standard normal variate**

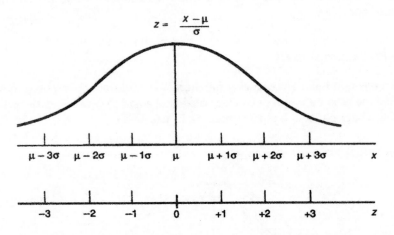

The new variable Z is normally distributed with a mean of zero and a standard deviation of 1. Tables of areas (see Table 6 in the Appendix) under this standard normal distribution have been compiled and widely published, so that areas under any normal distribution can be found by translating the X values to Z values and then using the tables for the standardized normal.

## Example

Assume that the total book value of an inventory is normally distributed with = $5,000 and = $,1000. Management may want to know the percentage of the population that lies between $3,000 and $7,000. To answer, two X values must be translated to Z values using the z formula:

$$Z_1 = \frac{\$3,000 - \$5,000}{\$1,000} = -2$$

$$Z_2 = \frac{\$10,000 - \$8,000}{\$1,000} = +2$$

Referring to the table of percentages (Figure 128.2), we see that 95.45 percent of the population lies between these two values (+2, -2). This means that total book value will lie between $6,000 and $10,000 with a probability of 0.9545.

## How is it Used and Applied?

Normal distribution is perhaps the most widely assumed distribution in statistical applications to business. This widespread use is because many business data follow this familiar bell-shaped pattern. Applications are numerous, including:

1. Evaluating capital expenditure projects whose cash flows are uncertain
2. Determining the chance of meeting the delivery date for a project
3. Determining safety stock (see Sec. 43, Allowing for Safety Stock)
4. Finding the chance of a business not losing money (or at least breaking even)

# Part 13
# Adequacy and Cost of Insurance Coverage

## 129. Determining How Much Insurance Is Needed

### Introduction

Commercial insurance falls into two major classes-individual insurance and group insurance. Individual insurance differs from group insurance in that the contract covers a person or family as opposed to a group of persons. Each contract sold covers an individual or family and is sold separately.

Key-person insurance is insurance purchased by a business seeking to protect itself against financial losses caused by the death or disability of a key employee. This type of insurance seeks to protect a business from the death or disability of an individual possessing a high degree of skill and knowledge, which might lead to serious loss to the firm in terms of reduced sales, increased costs, or restricted credit.

Disability income contracts are designed primarily to provide income coverage during the period of disability, but may, in some cases, also provide medical insurance protection.

### How is it Computed?

Ordinary insurance is generally sold in amounts of at least $1000. The premiums are calculated on an annual basis but may also be paid on a semiannual, quarterly, or monthly basis. The typical rule of thumb is that a worker with a spouse and two children should carry enough insurance to cover five times his or her annual income.

Another year of income should be added for each additional dependent. Thus, the formula for determining life insurance coverage for a family of four is:

Required life insurance protection = annual salary x 5

Key insurance coverage is based on the present value of lost revenue over a predetermined number of years.

For disability insurance, coverage must be at least 60 percent of salary, unless the business owner has sufficient personal resources to cover disability income needs. Thus, the formula for disability coverage is:

Salary x 60% = disability coverage

## Example 1

John Hamilton, a business owner, is married with two children. His annual salary from his business is $60,000. His life insurance protection should be $300,000, calculated as follows:

$60,000 x 5 = $300,000

## Example 2

Marilyn Johnson, a business owner, is married with three children. Her annual salary from her business is $75,000. Her life insurance protection should be $450,000, calculated as follows:

$75,000 x 5 = $375,000 + $75,000 = $450,000

## Example 3

It is estimated that the death of a key employee would reduce a firm's earnings by $50,000 annually for a period of at least 5 years. Key-person insurance for at least $210,600 should be purchased by the business owner, assuming a 6 percent rate of interest, calculated as follows:

$50,000 x 4.212 (present value of 6% for 5 years; see Appendix Table 4) = $210,600

## Example 4

Selena Combs, who earns a salary of $100,000 from a business, seeks disability insurance. She should obtain coverage of $60,000, calculated as follows:

$100,000 x 60% = $60,000

## How is it Used and Applied?

Life insurance should emphasize protection as opposed to investment. A contract with some investment element may also be proper if the business wants to meet protection and investment objectives with one contract. The business owner may also want protection against a loss of profits due to the death of a key employee by obtaining a life insurance contract that contains an investment element. This technique would protect the business during the employee's period of employment, and also provide him or her with retirement income out of the investment value of the policy should the employee live and eventually retire.

# 130. Factoring in Coinsurance and Copayment

## Introduction

The coinsurance principle has two basic purposes: (1) it prevents fire policyholders from underinsuring their property; and (2) it makes the insured bear a specified amount of the loss.

## How is it Computed?

A coinsurance clause provides that if the business owner will insure his property up to a given percentage of its value (usually 80 percent), the owner will be given the benefit of a lower premium. If the owner insures for less than a fixed percentage, he must bear a portion of the loss. The coinsurance formula is:

$$\frac{\text{Amount of insurance carried}}{\text{Amount of insurance required}} \times \text{loss} = \text{insurer's liability}$$

The coinsurance clause becomes inoperative if the loss is equal to or exceeds the stipulated percentage of value. Thus, assume that the insurance required (80 percent) is $80,000, the insurance obtained is $20,000, and the loss is $80,000. The insurance company will pay $20,000 or ($20,000/$80,000), the full value of the policy.

Insurance reimbursement is based on the lowest amount of either the face of the policy, the fair market value of the loss, or possible reimbursement.

Where property is insured with more than one company and the total concurrent insurance exceeds the actual loss, a standard pro rata clause applies; that is, the insured can collect from each company only its proportionate or pro rata share of the total amount of insurance.

## Example 1

The Nevilo Company had inventory worth $10,000, on which the firm has a fire insurance policy of $6,000 with an 80 percent coinsurance clause. Fire destroyed $4,000 worth of inventory. The firm will recover $3,000, calculated as follows:

$$\frac{\$6,000}{80\% \times \$10,000} \times \$4,000 = \$3,000$$

## Example 2

Theo, Kramer, and Arlo are partners in a business. The partnership obtained a $600,000 fire insurance policy on a building owned by the partnership. The policy contained an 80 percent coinsurance clause. Subsequently, the building was damaged by fire to the extent of $300,000. The building was worth $1,000,000 at the time the policy was issued and $800,000 at the time of the fire loss. The partnership will recover $281,250, calculated as follows:

$$\frac{\$600,000}{80\% \times \$800,000} \times \$300,000 = \$281,250$$

Because the partnership carried only $600,000 worth of insurance, it became a coinsurer with the insurance company for the difference of $40,000 ($640,000 - $600,000).

## Example 3

The following demonstrates insurance recovery under three different calculations:

| Case | Face of policy | Fair market value of property | Fair market value of loss |
|------|------|------|------|
| A | $ 4,000 | $10,000 | $ 6,000 |
| B | 6,000 | 10,000 | 10,000 |
| C | 10,000 | 10,000 | 4,000 |

Case A: $\dfrac{\$4,000}{80\% \times \$10,000} \times \$6,000 = \$3,000$ insurance reimbursement

Case B: $\dfrac{\$6,000}{80\% \times \$10,000} \times \$10,000 = \$7,500$ insurance reimbursement

Case C: $\dfrac{\$10,000}{80\% \times \$10,000} \times \$4,000 = \$5,000$ insurance reimbursement

Insurance reimbursement is based on the lowest of the face of the policy, the fair market value of the loss, or possible reimbursement. Therefore, in case B, the insured can recover only $6000, the amount of the policy. In case C, the insured can recover only $4000 (not $5000), the fair market value of the loss.

## Example 4

A business owner of a building worth $500,000, believing that her loss by fire will not exceed $200,000, obtains two standard fire policies with 80 percent coinsurance clauses, one from Company A for $120,000, and the other from Company B for $80,000. The firm subsequently sustains a fire loss of $200,000. Under the 80 percent coinsurance clause, the owner should have insured for 80 percent, or $400,000. She actually insured for $200,000, or half. She will therefore recover only half the loss, or $100,000. Under the pro rata clause, the recovery from each company will be as follows:

|  |  | Ratio | Loss |  | Amount recovered from each company |
|---|---|---|---|---|---|
| Company A | $120,000 | 12/20 | x $100,000 |  | $ 60,000 |
| Company B | 80,000 | 8/20 | x | 100,000 | 40,000 |
| Total | $200,000 |  |  |  | $100,000 |

## How is it Used and Applied?

The amount of insurance to be purchased is determined by the insured. In determining the proper amount, the business owner must give careful consideration to the value of the property and to any changes in the value, so that the insurance coverage can be adjusted periodically if required. The coinsurance clause does not mean that the insurance company will pay only 80 percent of any loss, or that the insured is prohibited from obtaining any insurance beyond 80 percent of the value. The owner is free to insure the property to 100 percent of the value if he or she believes it necessary, so that any loss will be paid in full. However, if the insured is careful and obtains coverage amounting to 80 percent or more of the value of the property, any losses sustained will be covered in full, as if the policy contained no coinsurance clause. The owner of destroyed property can use the insurance reimbursement formula to compute the insurance proceeds due because of a casualty loss.

# 131. Evaluating Insurance Risk

## Introduction

Every business owner or manager who is faced with the protection of a firm's assets must assess the various types of losses confronting his or her organization.

The owner must then measure these potential losses with respect to such matters as their likelihood of occurrence and their effect on the profitability and operation of the firm.

## How is it Computed?

To identify all potential losses, the business owner must first prepare a checklist of all possible losses that could occur. The basic list should include (1) direct property exposures, and (2) liability losses. In measuring these losses, the two methods most commonly used to measure loss severity are the maximum possible loss to one unit per occurrence and the maximum probable loss for one unit per occurrence. The maximum possible loss is the worst loss that could possibly happen; the maximum probable loss is the worst loss that is likely to happen. The maximum probable loss is usually less than the maximum possible loss.

### Example 1

Freeze Office Manufacturers owns a building with a fair market value of $400,000, excluding the land. The contents of the building, consisting of inventory, office equipment, and machinery, is worth $200,000. In case of complete destruction by fire or storm, the owner will lose $600,000, the maximum possible loss. However, assuming a maximum probable loss of less than $600,000 because the owner does not anticipate complete destruction of the premises, insurance coverage can be purchased for an amount less than $600,000.

### Example 2

Fenwick Producers occupies a new warehouse and pay rent of $50,000 annually on a 5-year lease. The owner feels that if the building is destroyed by fire, similar property will cost $100,000 per year to rent. Thus, the proprietor wishes to purchase insurance t cover this possible contingency. She feels that there is an equal chance that the property could be destroyed during any one of the five year that the business occupies the warehouse. Therefore, the owner seeks to insure the *average cost* of the total increase in rental costs if the warehouse should burn down. Using the present value of a $1 at 8 percent, the present value of the rental cost for the 5-year period at $50,000, representing the increased annual rental cost, Fenwick should obtain a policy for approximately $100,000, computed as follows:

| Year | Rental cost | Present value of $1 at 8%* | Amount |
|------|-------------|---------------------------|--------|
| 1 | $50,000 | 0.926 | $46,300 |
| 2 | 50,000 | 0.857 | 42,850 |
| 3 | 50,000 | 0.794 | 39,700 |
| 4 | 50,000 | 0.735 | 36,750 |
| 5 | 50,000 | 0.681 | 34,050 |
| | | | $199,650/2 = $99,825 |

*See Appendix Table 3.

This amount would protect Fenwick against any increased costs due to a required move to more expensive quarters in case the property is destroyed by fire or some other catastrophe.

This policy would be in addition to any possible business interruption insurance that the owner might wish to obtain to insure against loss of profits during the period that the business cannot produce or sell goods due to destruction of the rented premises.

## Example 3

Lux Realty rents a building for 3 years, receiving $10,000 per year in rental income. If the building is destroyed by a fire, the rental income will be lost. Using the present value of $1 at 8 percent, the present value of income for the 3-year period is $25,770, computed as follows:

| Year | Rental income | Present value of $1 at 8%* | Amount |
|------|---------------|---------------------------|--------|
| 1 | $10,000 | 0.926 | $ 9,260 |
| 2 | 10,000 | 0.857 | 8,570 |
| 3 | 10,000 | 0.794 | 7,940 |
| | | | $25,770 |

*See Appendix Table 3.

## Example 4

The Calx Company makes small personal computers. In the 10 years that the business has been assembling and selling computers, only one has caught fire. The fire caused extensive damage to the customer's office, so, in a gesture of goodwill, Calx paid for all fire damages and replaced the computer. The total cost to Calx was $50,000. Calx feels that, with improvements in computer technology, the probability of a computer fire is small and might occur only once a year and cause a maximum probable loss not exceeding $500,000.

Thus, Calx purchases a policy protecting against product liability with a limit of $500,000 per occurrence.

## How is it Used and Applied?

The business owner must first identify the continuous property and liability risk exposure of his or her business. The owner must also assess the frequency of product liability claims due to the "claims consciousness" of the public. Each potential loss must be assessed and evaluated in terms of current operating conditions and the prevailing economic environment. In determining the severity of a possible loss, the business owner must include a broad spectrum of losses that might result from a given event as well as the ultimate impact upon the firm.

# 132. Estimating the Value of a Claim

## Introduction

When the risk insured against causes a loss, it is essential for the business owner to receive fair payment from the insurer. Settlement should be neither excessive nor inadequate. To obtain equitable compensation, the business owner must have the ability to assess the actual loss sustained.

## How is it Computed?

Determining the value of a claim can be a difficult task. The following procedures provide formulas for measuring the actual loss sustained.

To estimate a fire insurance loss, the insured should use one of two valuation bases: (1) replacement cost or (2) actual cash value (which is replacement cost less physical depreciation). The formula for replacement cost is:

Accumulated depreciation x 2 + original cost = estimated replacement cost

(the factor 2 is used to reflect the effect of inflation on the original cost of the property).

To estimate the actual cash value, the following steps should be taken:

1.   Determine the estimated replacement cost.
2.   Estimate the physical, not tax, life of the property.
3.   Deduct the estimated expended life of the property to arrive at the actual cash value.

To estimate the value of inventory lost through theft or fire, the gross margin method (gross margin/net sales revenue) should be used. The formula is:

Beginning inventory

+ Net purchases
_____

Cost of goods available for sale

- Cost of goods sold
_____

Ending inventory

Another method for estimating the value of lost inventory is the retail inventory method. The formula is:

$\dfrac{\text{Cost}}{\text{Retail}}$ x (goods available for sale at retail - net sales revenue at retail)

= ending inventory at cost

## Example 1

Pylar Lumber owned equipment with an original cost of $100,000 and accumulated depreciation of $40,000. The business suffered a fire and used the replacement cost method to estimate the insurance proceeds. The replacement cost was determined to be $180,000, calculated as follows:

| | |
|---|---:|
| Accumulated depreciation ($40,000 x 2) | $ 80,000 |
| + Original cost ($100,000) | 100,000 |
| Estimated replacement cost | 180,000 |

## Example 2

The Green Pipe Company owned equipment with an original cost of $200,000 and accumulated depreciation of $60,000. The machinery had an estimated useful life of 10 years and had been in use for 4 years. The business suffered a fire and used the actual cash value method to estimate the expected insurance proceeds. The actual cash value of the loss was determined to be $192,000, calculated as follows:

| | |
|---|---:|
| Accumulated depreciation ($60,000 x 2) | $120,000 |
| + Original cost ($200,000) | 200,000 |
| Estimated replacement cost | $320,000 |
| - Depreciated life (4/10 years = 40% x $320,000) | 128,000 |
| Actual cash value | $192,000 |

## Example 3

Dupont Paint used the gross margin method to determine its fire loss. The firm's beginning inventory was $10,000, net purchases for the period were $70,000, net sales were $100,000, and the estimated gross margin was 40 percent. The estimated ending inventory lost was $20,000, calculated as follows:

| | |
|---|---|
| Beginning inventory | $10,000 |
| + Net purchases | 70,000 |
| = Cost of goods available for sale | $80,000 |
| - Cost of goods sold ($100,000 x 60%)* | 60,000 |
| = Ending inventory | $20,000 |

*(Retail 100% - gross margin 40%)

## Example 4

Echo Parts used the retail sales method to determine its fire loss. The cost-to-retail ratio was 60 percent, and the goods available for sale at retail were $300,000. The net sales at retail for the period were $270,000. The ending inventory, at cost, lost in the fire was $18,000, calculated as follows:

60% x ($300,000 - $270,000) = $18,000

## How is it Used and Applied?

Property and liability insurance policies usually require that the insured give prompt notice of any loss to the insurance company. Within a stated period of time, usually 60 days, the insured must also provide a "proof of loss." The proof provides details of the theft or loss, detailed replacement or repair estimates, and a list of inventories lost or damaged. The insured is also expected to cooperate with the insurance company in processing the claim and supplying any receipts, accounting records, and legal documents requested.

# Part 14
# Hiring and Compensating Employees

## 133. Permutations and Combinations

### Introduction

Permutations enable business managers to determine the number of ways something can be arranged. Combinations determine the number of ways things can be combined when the arrangement or order is not important. Permutations and combinations can be used to assign personnel to jobs.

### How is it Computed?

Permutations are computed by the following formula:

$$P = \frac{n!}{(n-r)!}$$

P means the number of ways to arrange n things taken r at a time. The "!" stands for factorial, and means that whatever the number is, multiply it times the series of whole numbers preceding it. Thus $5! = 5 \times 4 \times 3 \times 2 \times 1 = 120$. As a special case, $0! = 1$.

### *Example 1*

Suppose that only three management internship positions are available for five qualified applicants. In how many different ways can three individuals from among the five be assigned to the three different management positions?

$$P = \frac{n!}{(n-r)!} = \frac{5!}{(5-3)!} = \frac{5 \times 4 \times 3 \times 2 \times 1}{2 \times 1} = 60$$

Combinations are computed by the following formula:

$$C = \frac{n!}{r!(n-r)!}$$

Note that only the "r!" was added in the denominator of the permutation formula. C is the number of combinations of n things taken r at a time.

## Example 2

Referring to the situation described in Example 1, suppose that the three available positions can all be considered comparable, and not really different for practical purposes. In how many different ways can the three applicants be chosen from among the five qualified people to fill the three management positions?

$$C = \frac{n!}{r!(n-r)!} = \frac{5!}{3!(5-3)!} = \frac{5 \times 4 \times 3 \times 2 \times 1}{(3 \times 2 \times 1)(2 \times 1)} = 10$$

## How is it Used and Applied?

Permutations can be used to determine how many possible variations there are. For instance, a business owner may advertise two job openings, one for a copywriter and one for an artist. If 10 people who are qualified for either position apply, in how many ways can the openings be filled? Since the jobs are different, the order of selecting people matters: X as copywriter and Y as artist is different from Y as copywriter and X as artist. The solution is found by counting permutations:

$$P = \frac{10!}{(10-2)!} = \frac{10!}{8!} = 10 \times 9 = 90$$

Therefore there are 90 different ways to fill the openings.

Unlike permutations, where the order in which the objects are arranged is important, combinations are concerned with the number of possible different groupings of objects without regard to the order. For example, a business owner advertises two job openings for computer programmers, both with the same salary and job description. In how many ways can the openings be filled if 10 people apply? Since the two jobs are identical, the order of selecting the applicants is not important. Choosing X and Y for the positions is the same as choosing Y and X. Thus, the answer is a number of combinations that is half as large as the number of permutations in the previous example:

$$C = \frac{n!}{r!(n-r)!} = \frac{10!}{2!(10-2)!} = \frac{90}{2} = 45$$

There are many uses for combinations. Suppose that a business owner wants to analyze all possible failures of a system. There are a dozen different components of the system that can fail (n = 12), but the owner needs to evaluate only those cases where two fail at the same time (r = 2). At first glance the numbers may not look so bad, but

$$C = \frac{12!}{(2!(12-2))} = \frac{12 \times 11}{2} = \frac{132}{2} = 66 \text{ combinations}$$

Therefore, the owner may have to analyze all 66 situations.

# 134.  Sizing up Human Resource Needs

## Introduction

The determination of the human resources needs of a business must complement the operating structure of the organization. Human resource management requires a knowledge of the organization's needs and objectives. Part of this process is determination of the number of personnel with a specific expertise that must be provided if a business' sales and production goals are to be achieved.

## How is it Computed?

Time studies can be utilized to establish work standards. For example, if management sets a given number of units to be produced in a given period, and the number of employee hours necessary to produce the unit is determined, the total number of hours needed to produce the product is calculated and divided by the average number of hours in an employee's workweek. The result can be used to determine the number of employees needed to meet sales and production goals. This is shown mathematically as:

$$\frac{\text{Units to be produced} \times \text{Number of employee hours necessary to produce unit}}{\text{Average number of hours in employee's workweek}}$$

= number of employees needed to meet sales goals

Absentee workers are workers who do not come to work. The most common measure for determining the number of employees that must be hired to compensate for absenteeism is to divide the number of employee days lost times 100 by the average number of employees times the number of workdays. This is shown mathematically as:

$$\frac{\text{Number of days lost} \times 100}{\text{Average number of employees}} \times \text{workdays}$$

= required number of employees that must be hired to replace absentee workers

Turnover may be due to retirement, death, resignation, or some other factor forcing separation from the business. Turnover statistics are calculated by taking the total number of people at the beginning and end of a period, averaging the numbers, and dividing the average into the total number of people who worked in the business for the period minus the average. The result multiplied by 100 is the turnover rate. This is shown mathematically as:

$$\text{Turnover} = \frac{\text{total number of employees working for business for period}}{\text{total number of employees at beginning and end of period/2}}$$
$$- \text{average number of employees} \times 100 \times 100$$

## Example 1

Pinetree Furniture Stores project that during the year it will produce 10,000 school desks for sale to schools. Prior experience indicates that each desk takes 20 hours to manufacture, and that all employees work 18,000 hours a year. Pinetree must employ 11 persons, computed as follows:

10,000 desks x 20 hours = 200,000 hours.

$$\frac{200,000 \text{ hours}}{18,000 \text{ hours}} = 11 \text{ employees (approximate)}$$

## Example 2

Quality Appliances is concerned about the high rate of absenteeism in its workforce. The owner wishes to hire enough persons to meet production goals and to cover any "unauthorized vacations." Prior experience shows that 18 workdays are lost each month, that the average number of employees hired by the business over the last 6-month period was 783, and that there are an average of 23 workdays in a month. There are currently 1000 employees. Quality Appliances will have to hire an additional 100 persons for the month of July, computed as follows:

$$\frac{\text{Number of employee days lost} \times 100}{\text{Average number of employees} \times \text{number of workdays}} =$$

$$\frac{18 \text{ employees days lost} \times 100}{783 \text{ employees} \times 23 \text{ workdays}}$$

$$= \frac{1,800}{18,009} = 10\%$$

10% x 1,000 employees = 100 additional employees

## Example 3

The Shoe Box had 200 people employed at both the beginning and end of the year. It issued 300 W-2's, for people who were formerly employed during the year and for those still employed at year-end. The turnover ratio is 50 percent, calculated as follows:

$$\frac{200 + 200}{2} = 200$$

$$\frac{300 - 200}{200} = 0.50 \times 100 = 50$$

Thus, the manager must expect to hire 50 employees to compensate for employee turnover.

## How is it Used and Applied?

When determining human resource needs, the inventory of current employees must be matched against the economic goals of the business. Although the business may have made long-range forecasts based on strategic business planning, more specific human resource planning must be made to meet immediate sales and production objectives. This strategy involves prediction of the number of sales units, or units to be produced, for the coming period, and translating this number into the number of persons necessary to meet these sales or production goals. Analysis of absenteeism and turnover rates must also be made to compensate for any shortfall in the work force. These procedures will provide the needed lead time necessary for effective recruitment.

# 135. Calculating the Cost of a Fringe Benefits Program

## Introduction

Employee benefits are the current and deferred nonmonetary rewards that employees receive as a condition of their employment. The owner must define the firm's objectives, design a program to meet those objectives, implement the program, and administer it. Most employee benefits programs receive favorable tax treatment because they are a deductible expense, while the employer's cost is either nontaxable or deferred income to the employee. From a tax viewpoint, the benefits are particularly attractive because their nontaxability gives benefits a greater after-tax value as compared to a salary increase. "Cafeteria"-style fringe benefit programs have become extremely popular, because employees can periodically choose what particular benefits they desire within an overall cost limit.

## How is it Computed?

The following fringe benefits are excludable from taxable income:

- ◆ No-additional-cost services such as free standby flights offered to airline employees.
- ◆ Qualified employee discounts if (1) they are available to employees on a nondiscriminatory basis, and (2) the discounts relate to qualified property or services offered for sale to customers in the same line of business in which the employee works.
- ◆ Working-condition fringe benefits such as the use of a company car for business purposes, bodyguard services, or on-the-job training.
- ◆ *De minimis* fringe benefits, such as the typing of personal letters by a secretary, the occasional personal use of a photocopying machine, and coffee and donuts furnished to employees.
- ◆ Employer-provided group term life insurance premiums paid by an employer for employee coverage up to $50,000 per person. If the employer-provided group term life insurance is for coverage in excess of $50,000, the cost of the excess coverage is taxable to the employee.
- ◆ Group accident and health insurance plan premiums paid by an employer on group accident and health insurance policies, as well as benefits collected.
- ◆ Certain dependent-care assistance plans, with a limit of $5000 on the tax exclusion.
- ◆ Employer-provided transportation between the employee's residence and place of work, provided that the van (1) has a seating capacity of eight adults plus a driver and (2) is used at least 80 percent of the time for transporting employees.
- ◆ Employer-provided meals and lodging furnished to the employee provided that (1) the meals have been furnished for the convenience of the employer and (2) the meals have been furnished on the employer's business premises.
- ◆ Incidental or indirect benefits provided by an employer, such as the payment of an employment agency fee by an employer for a new employee.

To qualify for tax-favored treatment, fringe benefits must be offered on a nondiscriminatory basis to essentially all employees.

### Example 1

Barclay Equipment contemplates paying $2,100 for group term life insurance and group health insurance in lieu of $2,100 in additional salary.

Since the employer receives a $2,100 tax deduction whether the expenditure is for salary or insurance, the employer is indifferent between the two alternatives.

Assume that the employee is in a 30 percent tax bracket. While $2100 in salary gives rise to $1470 [$2,100 x 70% (100% - 30%)] = cash after tax, the fringe benefits are nontaxable, so the employee keeps $2,100 in benefits after tax. If, on the other hand, the employee were to purchase the fringe benefits directly and could not take a tax deduction for their cost, approximately $2,100 of salary would be required to buy the same benefits, or $2,100 (1 - 0.3) = $1470. The employees would most likely favor this arrangement, since they wind up with more on an after-tax basis. Happier employees will be more productive.

## *Example 2*

Jane Raymond, an employee of Star Furniture, incurs expenses of $5,000 for business meals and entertainment during the year. If Jane is reimbursed for these expenses, the reimbursement is nontaxable to her. If, on the other hand, Star Furniture provides a salary supplement, the payment is taxable but Jane can deduct 50 percent of the expenses under the Internal Revenue Code. If Star Furniture reimburses Jane, she reports no income or deductions, but Star can deduct only 50 percent of the $5,000 reimbursement, or $2,500. If Star is subject to a 25 percent corporate tax rate, then the reimbursement will cost the business $4,375 in after-tax dollars, computed as follows:

| | |
|---|---|
| Total reimbursement | $5,000 |
| Amount deductible (50%) | $,2500 |
| Corporate tax rate | 25% |
| Tax benefit (deduction) | - $625 |
| Cost to Star Corporation in after-tax dollars ($5000 - $625) | $4,375 |

## How is it Used and Applied?

Unlike cash salary, fringe benefits such as life and health insurance plans or child-care assistance cannot be traded for other services. To some employees with no interest in life insurance, free group insurance, or child-care assistance, the benefits would be worthless. There are, however, other solutions. For such employees, a "cafeteria plan," wherein employees can pick and choose among several fringe benefits, may help mitigate this problem. Salary might also prove to be more satisfying compensation. Thus fringe benefits are really equivalent to the payment of ordinary cash compensation, producing a definite tax liability reduction based on the business' maximum tax rate.

There are also nontax factors that must be considered. These include the incentive effects as well as the administrative costs of reimbursement plans. Reimbursement plans may encourage overspending, although the absence of such benefits may lead to inefficiency in production, low employee morale, high employee turnover, and the inability of the business owner to attract qualified personnel.

Although a large portion of employee benefits are not required by law, employers incur these costs because they accomplish organizational objectives.

# 136. Determining Profit-Sharing Bonus

## Introduction

Studies have shown that employees can be motivated to be more productive by the use of individual incentive plans. A number of profit-sharing plans exist that are designed to effect large-group cooperation and promote efficiency and productivity while reducing waste. In essence, these plans constitute an attempt to share in productivity gains. They include the following: (1) the Scanlon plan, a bonus arrangement; (2) a percentage of profits after a target amount has been reached; (3) a fixed amount; (4) a formula that involves calculating the bonus both before and after deducting the bonus and/or income taxes; and (5) graduated or scaled amounts.

The *Scanlon* plan uses the compensation for normal labor cost per unit of product produced. If, through more cooperation and greater efficiency, labor costs are reduced, the entire amount saved (or some fraction) is distributed among the workers in the form of a bonus. For example, it is determined from past records that labor costs constitute 40 percent of sales. If, through cooperative efforts, these costs can be reduced to 35 percent, then 5 percent of sales is divided among employees on the basis of seniority and/or salary levels. The Scanlon plan, a group incentive plan, has become widely accepted in compensation circles for its motivational value and innovative usefulness within the business. The Scanlon plan employs both monetary compensation and a type of union-management relationship. The plan stresses labor-management cooperation and a system of processing suggestions. Under the Scanlon plan, production supervisors and union representatives meet to discuss individual suggestions and develop general production plans. Employees benefit through the production-savings bonus.

While an incentive bonus may be given to a key executive, the efforts of rank-and-file employees should also be recognized. A fixed bonus arrangement can be utilized for certain sales personnel having equal access to all the customers in a market. For example, paying a $1,000 bonus to a car salesperson who sells the most cars in a 3-month period is fair and can be an effective reward for quality performance. This arrangement is equitable providing all employees are within the same salary range.

An employer can also use a graduated bonus percentage plan for a designated group of employees. The bonus can be a percentage of the employee's annual salary. The closer an employer gets to the company's operating sales objectives, the higher the bonus percentage is.

Profit-sharing plans are tax deductible. The Internal Revenue Service requires that an approved plan (1) cover a majority of all employees, (2) stipulate a management commitment of periodic contributions to the fund based on profits (annual employer contributions are not required), (3) be communicated to all covered employees, and (4) specify a definite, predetermined formula for allocating employer contributions to individual employees and for establishing benefit payments.

## Example 1

Corbin Textiles uses the Scanlon plan for employee motivational purposes. The ratio of 40 percent was established for the production year 20x7, computed as follows:

| | |
|---|---:|
| Average sales value of production for 20x7 | $800,000 |
| Actual sales value of production | 3200,000 |
| Average payroll costs for 20x7 | 40% |
| Scanlon ratio ($320,000/$800,000) | |
| Bonus money for distribution in Jan. 20x8: | $800,000 |
| Anticipated payroll costs for $800,000 in sales value | 320,000 |
| Actual payroll costs for $800,000 in sales value | 240,000 |
| Labor cost savings ($320,000 - $240,000) | 80,000 |
| Distribution of labor cost savings of $80,000: | |
| 25% to company for production improvement | $20,000 |
| 75% to employees | 60,000 |
| 20% x $60,000 to reserve account | 12,000 |
| 80% x $60,000 for immediate distribution | 48,000 |
| *Bonus to each employee (determined as a percentage of present pay):* | |
| Bonus money available | $48,000 |
| Actual payroll cost | 240,000 |
| Bonus to each employee | 20% |

Thus, an employee who earns $6,000 in January 20x7 will receive a $1,200 bonus ($6,000 x 20%), making her total compensation for January 20x7 $7,200 ($6,000 + $1200).

## Example 2

Fantasy Gifts agreed to give any sales personnel who had been with the business for at least one year 5 percent of any sales that exceed the targeted amount of $2,000,000 for 20x7. All employees earn approximately the same annual compensation. The 5 percent is to be shared equally. For 20x7, Fantasy had sales of $2,500,000. Ten salespersons had been with the company for the entire year. Each salesperson receives $2,500 in January 20x7, calculated as follows:

| | |
|---|---:|
| Total 20x7 sales | $2,500,000 |
| Targeted sales | 2,000,000 |
| Excess sales subject to 5% bonus | $  500,000 |
| x 5% | 25,000 |
| Bonus to each salesperson ($25,000/10) | $     2,500 |

## Example 3

The Danforth Corporation agreed to pay its chief executive a 10 percent bonus based on income before deducting the bonus and taxes. The executive earned $100,000 for 20x8, and corporate taxes for 20x8 were 30 percent. The bonus is:

$$Bonus = 0.10(\$100,000)$$
$$= \$10,000$$

## Example 4

The Danforth Corporation agreed to pay its chief executive a 10 percent bonus based on income after deducting the bonus but before deducting taxes. The executive earned $100,000 for 20x8, and corporate taxes for 20x8 were 30 percent.

$$Bonus = 0.10(\$100,000 - bonus)$$
$$= \$10,000 - 0.10(bonus)$$
$$1.10(bonus) = \$10,000$$
$$Bonus = \$9,090.91$$

## Example 5

The Danforth Corporation agreed to pay its chief executive a 10 percent bonus based on income before deducting the bonus but after deducting taxes. The executive earned $100,000 for 20x8, and corporate taxes for 20x8 were 30 percent.

Bonus   = 0.10($100,000 - taxes)

          = 0.10($100,000 - taxes)

Taxes   = 0.30($100,000 - bonus)

Substituting for taxes in the bonus equation and solving for the bonus:

Bonus   = 0.10[$100,000 - 0.30($100,000 - bonus)]

          = 0.10[$100,000 - $30,000 + 0.30(bonus)]

          = $10,000 - $3,000 + 0.03(bonus)

0.97(bonus) = $10,000

Bonus   = $10,309.28

## Example 6

The Danforth Corporation agreed to pay its chief executive a 10 percent bonus based on income after deducting the bonus and taxes. The executive earned $100,000 for 20x8, and corporate taxes for 20x8 were 30 percent.

Bonus   = 0.10($100,000 - bonus - taxes)

Taxes   = 0.30($100,000 - bonus)

Substituting for taxes in the bonus equation and solving for the bonus:

Bonus   = 0.10[$100,000 - bonus - 0.30($100,000 - bonus)]

          = 0.10[$100,000 - bonus - $30,000 + 0.30(bonus)]

          = $10,000 - 0.10(bonus) - $3,000 + 0.03(bonus)

1.07(bonus) = $7,000

Bonus   = $6,542.06

## Example 7

Silver Ridge Discounters agreed to pay its chief executive a graduated bonus percentage on her annual compensation. The plan scale is based on a percentage of the sales target for the business year. The scale is as follows:

| Volume objective (% of sales) | Bonus (% of sales) |
| :---: | :---: |
| Below 90 | 0 |
| 90 | 1 |
| 90 | 2 |
| 91 | 3 |
| 92 | 4 |
| 93 | 5 |
| 94 | 6 |
| 95 | 7 |
| 96 | 8 |
| 97 | 9 |
| 98 | 10 |
| 99 | 15 |
| 100 | 20 |
| Over 100 | 25 |

For the year 20x8, the business achieved 93 percent of its targeted sales goal. If the executive's annual compensation for 20x8 was $100,000, her bonus would be $4,000 ($100,000 x 4%).

## How is it Used and Applied?

Employee profit-sharing plans are useful compensation techniques that are adaptable to the financial goals of businesses. Basically, a profit-sharing plan is an agreement by which the employees receive a share, fixed in advance, of the profits. Though the term "profit sharing" is not used precisely by many, a true plan generally involves a definite commitment on the part of the owner to pay, over and above a fair wage, extra compensation that bears a defined percentage relationship to profits.

Among the advantages claimed for profit sharing are that it (1) results in an increase in productive efficiency by reducing costs and increasing output; (2) improves employee morale; (3) provides for employee security in the event of death, retirement, or disability; (4) reduces turnover; and (5) improves public relations. A business owner can also use profit sharing as a means of drawing labor and management closer together, thus inhibiting the development of a labor union. Other specific objectives can be incorporated through the mechanics of a plan. For example, one firm distributes profit shares solely on the basis of attendance, to reduce absenteeism. The administration of an employee profit-sharing plan is sometimes difficult to effect. Many businesses go through the mechanics of computing and distributing profit shares, but receive little return. The employees must see a relationship between their efforts and the success of the enterprise. If high profits are paid to employees during profitable periods, it will generate a more favorable reaction on the part of employees during unprofitable periods. If a company is especially fearful of possible adverse effects during nonprofit periods, it should adopt a deferred-distribution type of plan.

# 137. Employee Efficiency

## Introduction

Employee salaries, fringe benefits, and related costs (unemployment insurance, employment taxes) are for many businesses the most significant cost. It is important to control these expenditures in order to maintain profits.

A determination must be made as to whether employees are efficient in carrying out their duties. The revenue obtained should be sufficient considering the size of the force.

The personnel manager is interested in employee turnover because it may be a sign of worker discontent. Further, a significant amount of money and time is wasted in recruiting, training, and developing staff.

The average wage rate is taken into account in hiring decisions, bidding on jobs and contracts, and negotiating union agreements.

## How is it Computed?

Sales dollars to average number of employees (work force). The average number of employees should be expressed in terms of full-time equivalents when the staff includes part-time employees.

Sales volume to average number of employees.

Profit to average number of employees.

Sales to employee salaries. The value of employee fringe benefits may be added to salaries.

Profit to employee salaries.

Number of transactions to average number of employees.

Tangible assets to average number of employees. If assets have changed significantly during the year, average assets should be used.

Employee turnover: number of employees leaving/average number of employees.

Employees leaving include those quitting, laid off, and fired.

Wage growth (adjusted for inflation):

(Average wages (current year) x [CPI (prior year)/CPI (current year)] - average wages (prior year))/average wages (prior year)

where CPI is the Consumer Price Index.

## Example 1

A business experienced the following for the years 20x7 and 20x8:

|  | 20x7 | 20x8 |
|---|---|---|
| Net income | $60,000 | $200,000 |
| Number of employees | 50 | 60 |

Worker efficiency has improved sharply, since profit generated per employee increased from $1200 per employee ($60,000/50) to $3333 per employee ($200,000/60). This is a very positive productivity trend.

## Example 2

A business' performance for year 1 is:

| Unit sales | 100,000 |
|---|---|
| Dollar sales | $2,000,000 |
| Number of employees | 500 |
| Salaries expense | $800,000 |

This year's ratios are:

$$\frac{\text{Sales}}{\text{Number of employees}} = \frac{\$2,000,000}{500} = \$4,000$$

$$\frac{\text{Sales volume}}{\text{Work force}} = \frac{\$100,000}{500} = 200$$

$$\frac{\text{Sales}}{\text{Salaries expense}} = \frac{\$2,000,000}{\$800,000} = \$1,600$$

Last year's figures were:

$$\frac{\text{Sales}}{\text{Number of employees}} = \$3,600$$

$$\frac{\text{Sales volume}}{\text{Work force}} = 180$$

$$\frac{\text{Sales}}{\text{Salaries expense}} = \$1,500$$

All the productivity ratios for employees have improved this year relative to last year- a favorable sign because greater revenue is being derived from employee efforts.

## How is it Used and Applied?

Efficiency measures can be used to see how productive the employees have been. The more revenue is generated per employee, the more profitable the business will be. High productivity ratios indicate good employee morale, training, and on-the-job performance. Are salary payments generating an acceptable level of sales and profits?

An increase in the ratio of sales to staff indicates better efficiency. The ratio may be improved through automation and other labor-saving devices. On the other hand, a decrease in the ratio may mean that there are too many employees relative to revenue, and that layoffs may be necessary. Sometimes this ratio is too low because union contracts prohibit the firing of workers, or contracts require too many workers per operation. If this is the case, renegotiate the union contract or, the next time the contract is up for renewal, insist that it be modified. In general, labor-intensive businesses have lower ratios than capital-intensive ones because the former emphasizes human resources rather than capital assets.

When the number of employees fluctuates significantly during the year, such as in the case of a cyclical or growth business, the average number of employees should be used in calculating the sales-to-number of employees ratio.

An increasing trend in profitability versus number of employees indicates greater productivity. In general, automated and high-technology businesses have higher ratios. Labor-intensive businesses typically have lower ratios.

Revenue and profit ratios versus the number of employees assist in computing profit sharing and bonuses, and wage rates in new contracts.

The number of transactions to the number of employees indicates the productivity of clerks in processing orders, delivery personnel in making shipments, and jobs completed by factory workers. This ratio can be used to test whether newly installed equipment, or modifications to work procedures and schedules, result in better employee efficiency.

It is a negative sign when the rate of growth in salaries exceeds the rate of growth in sales. Further, the ratio of profit to employees' salaries indicates whether the expenditure on human resources has been justified in the form of profitability. If labor costs are "eating into profits", there is a problem.

Tangible assets represent support to workers to improve efficiency. A higher ratio may mean greater productivity because additional resources such as labor-saving devices are being used. However, if these new assets do not generate greater earnings, the effort has not been worthwhile.

If high employee turnover is due to their quitting, the reasons should be found and corrective steps taken. Some possible reasons might be inadequate training, poor salaries and/or fringe benefits, unreasonable working hours, poor supervision and treatment, and a feeling that management does not care about them.

See Sec. 77, Efficiency Measurements.

# Part 15
# Buying or Selling a Business

## 138. Determining How Much Your Business Is Worth

### Introduction

In determining the value of your business, consider the nature of the business and its principal activities, the age of the firm, industry conditions, the economic environment, competition, marketing status, customer base, risk, past and potential profitability, growth rate, cash flow, and overall financial position.

### How is it Computed?

The business valuation methods to be covered include gross revenue multiplier, simple earnings, weighted-average earnings, capitalization of excess earnings, capitalization of cash flow, present value of future cash flows, book value of net assets, fair market value of net assets, and integration of methods.

### *Valuation Based on Profitability*

A major emphasis should be placed on profit in valuing a business. An evaluation of past earnings is typically a good start. Historical earnings are a barometer of future profitability.

The value of the small business may be determined by multiplying net income by a multiplier indicating what the owner could sell the business for.

Net income should be adjusted for unusual income statement items. For example, personal expenses which are not business-related, such as personal auto, travel, entertainment, and fringe benefits (e.g., health plan, pension, life insurance). Further, excessive salary equal to the difference between the owner's salary and a reasonable salary, should be added back. The entire compensation package should be taken into account, including "perks." For example, if the owner's salary is $250,000 and an equivalent qualified worker would receive $200,000, then $50,000 should be added back to profit. Interest expense should also be added back to net income because it is a financial rather than an operating expense.

If rental payments arise from a low-cost lease, net income should be adjusted to arrive at a fair rental charge. Extraordinary items (e.g., a gain on the sale of property) should be removed from profit to derive typical earnings.

If business assets are being depreciated at an accelerated pace, profit should be adjusted upward by an amount equal to the difference between the straight-line method and the accelerated depreciation method being used.

Net income should be reduced for investment income so as to obtain income from operations.

Adjust net income for business valuation purposes as follows:

Net income

Adjustments:

Add

Subtract

Restated net income

An illustration of the adjustment of historical net income follows:

| | |
|---|---|
| Reported net income | $325,000 |
| Adjustments: | |
| Personal expenses | 50,000 |
| Fringe benefits | 10,000 |
| Excessive owner's salary relative to a reasonable salary | 20,000 |
| Interest expense | 5,000 |
| Restated net income | $410,000 |

The adjusted net income should be multiplied by a multiplier to estimate the business' value. The multiplier should be higher for a low-risk business and lower for a high-risk one. For example, the multiplier for a high-risk business might be 2, while that for a low-risk business might be 4. A 5-year average restated historical earnings figure is representative of earning power. The computation is:

Average adjusted earnings (5 years) x multiplier = valuation

Simple average earnings is the total earnings for each of the years divided by the number of years. An illustration is:

| | |
|---|---|
| 20x1 | $ 80,000 |
| 20x2 | 60,000 |
| 20x3 | 100,000 |
| 20x4 | 125,000 |
| 20x5 | 115,000 |
| Total | $480,000 |

Average earnings (5 years) = $480,000/5 = $96,000

The multiplier depends on many variables, including stability, risk, growth rate, earning potential, financial health, industry conditions, and economic environment.

Weighted-average adjusted historical earnings gives greater weight to the most recent years, and is more representative than a simple average. Current earnings take into account current prices and recent business activity. For a 5-year weighted average, the current year is given a weight of 5 while the initial year is assigned a weight of 1. The multiplier is then applied to the weighted-average 5-year restated historical earnings to come up with the valuation. An example follows.

| Year | Net Income | x | Weight | =Total |
|---|---|---|---|---|
| 20x4 | $100,000 | x | 5 | $500,000 |
| 20x3 | 90,000 | x | 4 | 360,000 |
| 20x2 | 80,000 | x | 3 | 240,000 |
| 20x1 | 110,000 | x | 2 | 220,000 |
| 20x0 | 70,000 | x | 1 | 70,000 |
| | | | 15 | $1,390,000 |

Weighted-Average 5-year earnings:

$1,390,000/15 = $92,667

Weighted-average 5-year earnings x Multiplier Valuation = Capitalization-of-Earnings

$92,667 x 4* = $370,668

* The multiple may be based on such factors as earnings stability, risk, anticipated growth, or liquidity.

Another approach is the capitalization of excess earnings, computed as follows:

Weighted-average restated profit (5 years)

Less:     Normal return rate of weighted-average tangible net assets

Excess earnings

x          multiplier

Goodwill

Add:      Fair market value of net tangible assets

Business valuation

Capitalization of cash flow involves multiplying adjusted cash earnings by an appropriate factor and then subtracting liabilities as follows:

Restated cash earnings

x          multiplier

Capitalization of cash flow

Less:     Liabilities

Business valuation

## Valuation Based on Present Value of Future Cash Flows

A business may be valued at the present value of future cash earnings and the present value of the expected selling price. The growth rate in cash earnings may be based on prior growth and future expectations. The discount rate should be the return rate earned by the business. Refer to the present-value tables in the Appendix.

The format is:

      Present value (discounted) of future cash earnings

Add:      Present value of expected selling price

      Value of business

*Step 1: Present value of cash earnings.* Once the future earnings are determined, they should be discounted. Future earnings may be based on prior years' earnings and the current profit margin applied to sales.

*Step 2: Present value of sales price.* The present value of the expected selling price of the business at the date of sale should be determined.

# Valuation Based on Book Value (Net Worth)

The business may be valued at the book value of the net assets at the most current balance sheet date. Net assets equals total assets less total liabilities. However, this method is unrealistic because it does not take into account current values. It may be appropriate only when it is impossible to determine the fair value of net assets anchor goodwill.

# Valuation Based on Fair Market Value of Net Assets

The fair market value of the net tangible assets of a small business may be determined through independent appraisal. Expert appraisers for different types of tangible assets may be used, such as specialized appraisers for real estate, equipment, and trucks. Further, reference may be made to published values for particular assets, such as the "blue book" for business automobiles. Typically, the fair value of the net tangible assets (assets less liabilities) is higher than book value. To this, add the value of the goodwill (if any). Note that goodwill applies to such aspects as reputation of the business, customer base, and quality of merchandise or services.

A business broker, who facilitates the sale of small businesses, may be retained to perform an appraisal of property, plant, and equipment. According to *Equitable Business Brokers*, about 25 percent of businesses that change hands are sold through business brokers.

The general practice is to value inventory at a maximum value of cost.

Unrecognized and unrecorded liabilities should be considered when determining the fair market value of net assets, since such off-balance-sheet liabilities represent future commitments and contingencies. An example is an unrecorded lawsuit.

Off-balance-sheet assets, such as tax loss carryforward benefits, represent unrecorded assets that will increase the value of the business.

# Gross Revenue Multiplier

A business value may be computed by multiplying sales by a revenue multiplier typical in the line of business. For example, if revenue is $3 million and the multiplier is 0.2, the valuation is $3,000,000 x 0.2 = $600,000.

# Values of Similar Businesses

Recent sales prices of similar businesses may be used. While a perfect match will usually not exist, the businesses should be reasonably similar (e.g., size, product line, location). Sources of industry data include Dun & Bradstreet, trade association reports, and on-line databases. For example, assume that a competing business was sold 6 months ago for $3,000,000. If you believe that your business is worth 80 percent of the competing business, the valuation is $2,400,000.

## Integration of Methods

The value of the business may be estimated by determining the average value by two or more methods. For example, assume that the fair market value of net assets method provides a value of $3,000,000 and the capitalization of excess earnings method provides a value of $2,750,000. The value of the business is the simple average of these two methods, or $2,875,000 [($3,000,000 + $2,750,000)/2]. It is even better to value the small business using a weighted-average value of several approaches. The most weight should be placed on the earnings methods and the least weight on the asset approaches.

## Example 1

Assume that the fair market value using the net assets method provides a value of $3 million and the earnings method gives a value of $2.4 million. If the earnings method is assigned a weight of 2 and the fair market value of net assets method is assigned a weight of 1, the business valuation is computed as follows:

| Method | Amount | Weight | Total |
|---|---|---|---|
| Fair market value of net assets | $3,000,000 | 1 | $3,000,000 |
| Capitalization-of-excess earnings | 2,400,000 | 2 | 4,800,000 |
| | | 3 | $7,800,000 |
| Valuation ($7,800,000/3) | | | $2,600,000 |

## Example 2

This example is based on the capitalization~of-earning valuation.

| Year | Net income | Weight | Total |
|---|---|---|---|
| 20x4 | $120,000 | 5 | $600,000 |
| 20x3 | 100,000 | 4 | 400,000 |
| 20x2 | 110,000 | 3 | 330,000 |
| 20x1 | 90,000 | 2 | 180,000 |
| 20x0 | 115,000 | 1 | 115,000 |
| | | 15 | $1,625,000 |
| Weighted average 5 year earnings ($1,625,000/15) | | | $108,333 |
| x capitalization factor | | | x 5 |
| Capitalization-of-earnings valuation | | | $541,665 |

## Example 3

In this example, valuation using weighted-average net tangible assets is computed.

| Year | Amount | Weight | Total |
|------|--------|--------|-------|
| 20x0 | $ 950,000 | 1 | $ 950,000 |
| 20x1 | 1,000,000 | 2 | 2,000,000 |
| 20x2 | 1,200,000 | 3 | 3,600,000 |
| 20x3 | 1,400,000 | 4 | 5,600,000 |
| 20x4 | 1,500,000 | 5 | 7,500,000 |
| | | 15 | $19,650,000 |
| Weighted average tangible assets $19,650,000/15 | | | $1,310,000 |
| Weighted average adjusted net income (5 years) ---Assumed | | | $ 200,000 |
| Minus Reasonable rate of return on weighted-average | | | |
|    tangible net assets ($1,310,000 x 10%) | | | 131,000 |
| Excess earnings | | | $ 69,000 |
| x multiplier | | | x5 |
| Valuation of intangibles | | | $ 345,000 |
| Plus fair market value of net tangible assets | | | 3,000,000 |
|   Capitalization-of-excess-earnings valuation | | | $3,345,000 |

## Example 4

In 20x4, net income is $200,000. Earnings are expected to grow at 8 percent per year. The discount rate is 10 percent. You estimate that the business is worth the discounted value of future earnings. The valuation is computed as follows:

| Year | Net income | Present Value (PV) Factor at a 10% discount rate* | Total PV |
|------|-----------|--------------------------------------------------|----------|
| 20x4 | $ 200,000 | 0.909 | $181,800 |
| 20x5 | 216,000 | 0.826 | 178,416 |
| 20x6 | 233,280 | 0.751 | 175,193 |
| 20x7 | 251,942 | 0.683 | 172.076 |
| 20x8 | 272,098 | 0.621 | 168,973 |
| Present value of future earnings | | | $876,458 |

* From Table 3 in the Appendix.

If the anticipated selling price at the end of year 20x8 is $600,000, the valuation of the business equals:

| | |
|---|---:|
| Present value of future earnings | $ 876,458 |
| Present value of selling price ($600,000 x 0.621) | 372,600 |
| Valuation | $1,249,058 |

## How is it Used and Applied?

The owner may want to value his or her business to determine a potential selling price. The owner may also want to value a targeted small business to determine an offering price for the acquisition. In a lawsuit between parties, a business valuation may be required as a basis on which to settle the claim. If a business wants to expand its credit line, the bank will likely require a business valuation. Valuations are required in some tax situations, such as to determine the tax liability associated with a business liquidation.

A business may also be valued in a divorce action for equitable distribution between spouses.

Partners may want to value a partnership if there is an admission or withdrawal of a partner, a dispute between the parties requiring a settlement, or to establish a selling price.

# 139. Valuing a Franchise

## Introduction

If you are thinking of buying a franchise (e.g., Baskin and Robbins), you will want to determine how much it is worth to you. Can you earn enough money from the franchise to justify its initial and recurring franchise fees?

In valuing a franchise, consideration has to be given to the franchise tax. Many states have such a tax, which may be based on the net worth of the franchise. A franchise in a state imposing a high tax should be assigned a lower value by the franchisee.

## How is it Computed?

To determine whether to buy a franchise, perform the following computation:

Add: Present value of future cash earnings to be derived from the franchise

(excluding franchise fees)

Less:    Initial franchise fee

Less:    Present value of future franchise fees and franchise taxes

## Advantage or disadvantage of the franchise

A franchise with a long track record and reputation will have a higher value than an emerging or problem franchise. The franchise value depends on many factors, including territorial rights, length of agreement, exclusiveness, restrictions, and what must be supplied by the franchisor. A long-term agreement is worth more in the case of a lucrative franchise.

## Example

You are considering buying a Burger King franchise. The initial fee for the right to open up the store is $300,000. You plan to operate the store for 10 years. The annual year-end franchise fee is $100,000, payable to Burger King. You estimate the following stream of cash earnings (cash revenue less cash expenses) for the next 10 years:

| | |
|---|---|
| 1 | $ 90,000 |
| 2 | 125,000 |
| 3 | 140,000 |
| 4 | 150,000 |
| 5 | 165,000 |
| 6 | 170,000 |
| 7 | 180,000 |
| 8 | 200,000 |
| 9 | 210,000 |
| 10 | 225,000 |
| Total | $1,655,000 |

Your desired rate of return is 6 percent.

The franchise should be bought because it results in a net positive present value of $136,900 as computed below:

| Year | | Amount | x Present value factor (at 6%) | = Present value |
|------|-----|---------|--------------|---------------|
| 0 | $ + | 300,000 | 1.00 | $- 300,000 |
| 1-10 | − | 100,000 | 7.36* | - 736,000 |
| 1 | + | 90,000 | 0.94** | + 84,600 |
| 2 | + | 125,000 | 0.89 | + 111,250 |
| 3 | + | 140,000 | 0.84 | + 117,600 |
| 4 | + | 150,000 | 0.79 | + 118,500 |
| 5 | + | 165,000 | 0.75 | + 123,750 |
| 6 | + | 170,000 | 0.71 | + 120,700 |
| 7 | + | 180,000 | 0.67 | + 120,600 |
| 8 | + | 200,000 | 0.63 | + 126,000 |
| 9 | + | 210,000 | 0.59 | + 123,900 |
| 10 | + | 225,000 | 0.56 | + 126,000 |
| Net present value | | | | $+ 136,900 |

\* using the present value of ordinary annuity table for n = 10, i = 6%.
See Appendix Table 4.

\*\*Using the present value of $1 table. See Appendix Table 3.

## How is it Used and Applied?

By calculating the value of a franchise, the potential franchisee can determine whether it is worth the price he or she will have to pay the franchisor for the franchise. Further, an existing franchisee may need to determine what the franchise may be worth if he or she now wants to sell it to another individual, assuming the franchise contract so permits.

# Appendix

## Table 1: The Future Value of $1 (Compound Amount of $1) $= (1 + i)^n = T_1(i, n)$

| Periods | 4% | 6% | 8% | 10% | 12% | 14% | 20% |
|---|---|---|---|---|---|---|---|
| 1 | 1.040 | 1.060 | 1.080 | 1.100 | 1.120 | 1.140 | 1.200 |
| 2 | 1.082 | 1.124 | 1.166 | 1.210 | 1.254 | 1.300 | 1.440 |
| 3 | 1.125 | 1.191 | 1.260 | 1.331 | 1.405 | 1.482 | 1.728 |
| 4 | 1.170 | 1.263 | 1.361 | 1.464 | 1.574 | 1.689 | 2.074 |
| 5 | 1.217 | 1.338 | 1.469 | 1.611 | 1.762 | 1.925 | 2.488 |
| 6 | 1.265 | 1.419 | 1.587 | 1.772 | 1.974 | 2.195 | 2.986 |
| 7 | 1.316 | 1.504 | 1.714 | 1.949 | 2.211 | 2.502 | 3.583 |
| 8 | 1.369 | 1.594 | 1.851 | 2.144 | 2.476 | 2.853 | 4.300 |
| 9 | 1.423 | 1.690 | 1.999 | 2.359 | 2.773 | 3.252 | 5.160 |
| 10 | 1.480 | 1.791 | 2.159 | 2.594 | 3.106 | 3.707 | 6.192 |
| 11 | 1.540 | 1.898 | 2.332 | 2.853 | 3.479 | 4.226 | 7.430 |
| 12 | 1.601 | 2.012 | 2.518 | 3.139 | 3.896 | 4.818 | 8.916 |
| 13 | 1.665 | 2.133 | 2.720 | 3.452 | 4.364 | 5.492 | 10.699 |
| 14 | 1.732 | 2.261 | 2.937 | 3.798 | 4.887 | 6.261 | 12.839 |
| 15 | 1.801 | 2.397 | 3.172 | 4.177 | 5.474 | 7.138 | 15.407 |
| 16 | 1.873 | 2.540 | 3.426 | 4.595 | 6.130 | 8.137 | 18.488 |
| 17 | 1.948 | 2.693 | 3.700 | 5.055 | 6.866 | 9.277 | 22.186 |
| 18 | 2.026 | 2.854 | 3.996 | 5.560 | 7.690 | 10.575 | 26.623 |
| 19 | 2.107 | 3.026 | 4.316 | 6.116 | 8.613 | 12.056 | 31.948 |
| 20 | 2.191 | 3.207 | 4.661 | 5.728 | 9.646 | 13.743 | 38.338 |
| 30 | 3.243 | 5.744 | 10.063 | 17.450 | 29.960 | 50.950 | 237.380 |
| 40 | 4.801 | 10.286 | 21.725 | 45.260 | 93.051 | 188.880 | 1469.800 |

# Table 2: The Future Value of an Annuity of $1 (Compound Amount of an Annuity of $1) = $T_2(i,n)$

| Periods | 4% | 6% | 8% | 10% | 12% | 14% | 20% |
|---|---|---|---|---|---|---|---|
| 1 | 1.000 | 1.000 | 1.000 | 1.000 | 1.000 | 1.000 | 1.000 |
| 2 | 2.040 | 2.060 | 2.080 | 2.100 | 2.120 | 2.140 | 2.200 |
| 3 | 3.122 | 3.184 | 3.246 | 3.310 | 3.374 | 3.440 | 3.640 |
| 4 | 4.247 | 4.375 | 4.506 | 4.641 | 4.779 | 4.921 | 5.368 |
| 5 | 5.416 | 5.637 | 5.867 | 6.105 | 6.353 | 6.610 | 7.442 |
| 6 | 6.633 | 6.975 | 7.336 | 7.716 | 8.115 | 8.536 | 9.930 |
| 7 | 7.898 | 8.394 | 8.923 | 9.487 | 10.089 | 10.730 | 12.916 |
| 8 | 9.214 | 9.898 | 10.637 | 11.436 | 12.300 | 13.233 | 16.499 |
| 9 | 10.583 | 11.491 | 12.488 | 13.580 | 14.776 | 16.085 | 20.799 |
| 10 | 12.006 | 13.181 | 14.487 | 15.938 | 17.549 | 19.337 | 25.959 |
| 11 | 13.486 | 14.972 | 16.646 | 18.531 | 20.655 | 23.045 | 32.150 |
| 12 | 15.026 | 16.870 | 18.977 | 21.385 | 24.133 | 37.271 | 39.580 |
| 13 | 16.627 | 18.882 | 21.495 | 24.523 | 28.029 | 32.089 | 48.497 |
| 14 | 18.292 | 21.015 | 24.215 | 27.976 | 32.393 | 37.581 | 59.196 |
| 15 | 20.024 | 23.276 | 27.152 | 31.773 | 37.280 | 43.842 | 72.035 |
| 16 | 21.825 | 25.673 | 30.324 | 35.950 | 42.753 | 50.980 | 87.442 |
| 17 | 23.698 | 28.213 | 33.750 | 40.546 | 48.884 | 59.118 | 105.930 |
| 18 | 25.645 | 30.906 | 37.450 | 45.600 | 55.750 | 68.394 | 128.120 |
| 19 | 27.671 | 33.760 | 41.446 | 51.160 | 63.440 | 78.969 | 154.740 |
| 20 | 29.778 | 36.778 | 45.762 | 57.276 | 75.052 | 91.025 | 186.690 |
| 30 | 56.085 | 79.058 | 113.283 | 164.496 | 241.330 | 356.790 | 1181.900 |
| 40 | 95.026 | 154.762 | 259.057 | 442.597 | 767.090 | 1342.000 | 7343.900 |

*Payments (or receipts) at the *end* of each period.

# Table 3: The Present Value of $1 = T$_3$ (i, n)

| Periods | 4% | 5% | 6% | 8% | 10% | 12% | 14% | 16% | 18% | 20% |
|---|---|---|---|---|---|---|---|---|---|---|
| 1 | 0.962 | 0.952 | 0.943 | 0.926 | 0.909 | 0.893 | 0.877 | 0.862 | 0.847 | 0.833 |
| 2 | 0.925 | 0.907 | 0.890 | 0.857 | 0.826 | 0.797 | 0.769 | 0.743 | 0.718 | 0.694 |
| 3 | 0.889 | 0.864 | 0.840 | 0.794 | 0.751 | 0.712 | 0.675 | 0.641 | 0.609 | 0.579 |
| 4 | 0.855 | 0.823 | 0.792 | 0.735 | 0.683 | 0.636 | 0.592 | 0.552 | 0.516 | 0.482 |
| 5 | 0.822 | 0.784 | 0.747 | 0.681 | 0.621 | 0.567 | 0.519 | 0.476 | 0.437 | 0.402 |
| 6 | 0.790 | 0.746 | 0.705 | 0.630 | 0.564 | 0.507 | 0.456 | 0.410 | 0.370 | 0.335 |
| 7 | 0.760 | 0.711 | 0.665 | 0.583 | 0.513 | 0.452 | 0.400 | 0.354 | 0.314 | 0.279 |
| 8 | 0.731 | 0.677 | 0.627 | 0.540 | 0.467 | 0.404 | 0.351 | 0.305 | 0.266 | 0.233 |
| 9 | 0.703 | 0.645 | 0.592 | 0.500 | 0.424 | 0.361 | 0.308 | 0.263 | 0.255 | 0.194 |
| 10 | 0.676 | 0.614 | 0.558 | 0.463 | 0.386 | 0.322 | 0.270 | 0.227 | 0.191 | 0.162 |
| 11 | 0.650 | 0.585 | 0.527 | 0.429 | 0.350 | 0.287 | 0.237 | 0.195 | 0.162 | 0.135 |
| 12 | 0.625 | 0.557 | 0.497 | 0.397 | 0.319 | 0.257 | 0.208 | 0.168 | 0.137 | 0.112 |
| 13 | 0.601 | 0.530 | 0.469 | 0.368 | 0.290 | 0.229 | 0.182 | 0.145 | 0.116 | 0.093 |
| 14 | 0.577 | 0.505 | 0.442 | 0.340 | 0.263 | 0.205 | 0.160 | 0.125 | 0.099 | 0.078 |
| 15 | 0.555 | 0.481 | 0.417 | 0.315 | 0.239 | 0.183 | 0.140 | 0.108 | 0.084 | 0.065 |
| 16 | 0.534 | 0.458 | 0.394 | 0.292 | 0.218 | 0.163 | 0.123 | 0.093 | 0.071 | 0.054 |
| 17 | 0.513 | 0.436 | 0.371 | 0.270 | 0.198 | 0.146 | 0.108 | 0.080 | 0.060 | 0.045 |
| 18 | 0.494 | 0.416 | 0.350 | 0.250 | 0.180 | 0.130 | 0.095 | 0.069 | 0.051 | 0.038 |
| 19 | 0.475 | 0.396 | 0.331 | 0.232 | 0.164 | 0.116 | 0.083 | 0.060 | 0.043 | 0.031 |
| 20 | 0.456 | 0.377 | 0.312 | 0.215 | 0.149 | 0.104 | 0.073 | 0.051 | 0.037 | 0.026 |
| 21 | 0.439 | 0.359 | 0.294 | 0.199 | 0.135 | 0.093 | 0.064 | 0.044 | 0.031 | 0.022 |
| 22 | 0.422 | 0.342 | 0.278 | 0.184 | 0.123 | 0.083 | 0.056 | 0.038 | 0.026 | 0.018 |
| 23 | 0.406 | 0.326 | 0.262 | 0.170 | 0.112 | 0.074 | 0.049 | 0.033 | 0.022 | 0.015 |
| 24 | 0.390 | 0.310 | 0.247 | 0.158 | 0.102 | 0.066 | 0.043 | 0.028 | 0.019 | 0.013 |
| 25 | 0.375 | 0.295 | 0.233 | 0.146 | 0.092 | 0.059 | 0.038 | 0.024 | 0.016 | 0.010 |
| 26 | 0.361 | 0.281 | 0.220 | 0.135 | 0.084 | 0.053 | 0.033 | 0.021 | 0.014 | 0.009 |
| 27 | 0.347 | 0.268 | 0.207 | 0.125 | 0.076 | 0.047 | 0.029 | 0.018 | 0.011 | 0.007 |
| 28 | 0.333 | 0.255 | 0.196 | 0.116 | 0.069 | 0.042 | 0.026 | 0.016 | 0.010 | 0.006 |
| 29 | 0.321 | 0.243 | 0.185 | 0.107 | 0.063 | 0.037 | 0.022 | 0.014 | 0.008 | 0.005 |
| 30 | 0.308 | 0.231 | 0.174 | 0.099 | 0.057 | 0.033 | 0.020 | 0.012 | 0.007 | 0.004 |
| 40 | 0.208 | 0.142 | 0.097 | 0.046 | 0.022 | 0.011 | 0.005 | 0.003 | 0.001 | 0.001 |

# Table 4: The Present Value of an Annuity of $1 = T₄(i, n)

| Periods | 4% | 5% | 6% | 8% | 10% | 12% | 14% | 16% | 18% | 20% |
|---|---|---|---|---|---|---|---|---|---|---|
| 1 | 0.962 | 0.952 | 0.943 | 0.926 | 0.909 | 0.893 | 0.877 | 0.862 | 0.847 | 0.833 |
| 2 | 1.886 | 1.859 | 1.833 | 1.783 | 1.736 | 1.690 | 1.647 | 1.605 | 1.566 | 1.528 |
| 3 | 2.775 | 2.723 | 2.673 | 2.577 | 2.487 | 2.402 | 2.322 | 2.246 | 2.174 | 2.106 |
| 4 | 3.630 | 3.546 | 3.465 | 3.312 | 3.170 | 3.037 | 2.914 | 2.798 | 2.690 | 2.589 |
| 5 | 4.452 | 4.330 | 4.212 | 3.993 | 3.791 | 3.605 | 3.433 | 3.274 | 3.127 | 2.991 |
| 6 | 5.242 | 5.076 | 4.917 | 4.623 | 4.355 | 4.111 | 3.889 | 3.685 | 3.498 | 3.326 |
| 7 | 6.002 | 5.786 | 5.582 | 5.026 | 4.868 | 4.564 | 4.288 | 4.039 | 3.812 | 3.605 |
| 8 | 6.733 | 6.463 | 6.210 | 5.747 | 5.335 | 4.968 | 4.639 | 4.344 | 4.078 | 3.837 |
| 9 | 7.435 | 7.108 | 6.802 | 6.247 | 5.759 | 5.328 | 4.946 | 4.607 | 4.303 | 4.031 |
| 10 | 8.111 | 7.722 | 7.360 | 6.710 | 6.145 | 5.650 | 5.216 | 4.833 | 4.494 | 4.192 |
| 11 | 8.760 | 8.306 | 7.887 | 7.139 | 6.495 | 5.988 | 5.453 | 5.029 | 4.656 | 4.327 |
| 12 | 9.385 | 8.863 | 8.384 | 7.536 | 6.814 | 6.194 | 5.660 | 5.197 | 4.793 | 4.439 |
| 13 | 9.986 | 9.394 | 8.853 | 7.904 | 7.103 | 6.424 | 5.842 | 5.342 | 4.910 | 4.533 |
| 14 | 10.563 | 9.899 | 9.295 | 8.244 | 7.367 | 6.628 | 6.002 | 5.468 | 5.008 | 4.611 |
| 15 | 11.118 | 10.380 | 9.712 | 8.559 | 7.606 | 6.811 | 6.142 | 5.575 | 5.092 | 4.675 |
| 16 | 11.652 | 10.838 | 10.106 | 8.851 | 7.824 | 6.974 | 6.265 | 5.669 | 5.162 | 4.730 |
| 17 | 12.166 | 11.274 | 10.477 | 9.122 | 8.022 | 7.120 | 6.373 | 5.749 | 5.222 | 4.775 |
| 18 | 12.659 | 11.690 | 10.828 | 9.372 | 8.201 | 7.250 | 6.467 | 5.818 | 5.273 | 4.812 |
| 19 | 13.134 | 12.085 | 11.158 | 9.604 | 8.365 | 7.366 | 6.550 | 5.877 | 5.316 | 4.844 |
| 20 | 13.590 | 12.462 | 11.470 | 9.818 | 8.514 | 7.469 | 6.623 | 5.929 | 5.353 | 4.870 |
| 21 | 14.029 | 12.821 | 11.764 | 10.017 | 8.649 | 7.562 | 6.687 | 5.973 | 5.384 | 4.891 |
| 22 | 14.451 | 13.163 | 12.042 | 10.201 | 8.772 | 7.645 | 6.743 | 6.011 | 5.410 | 4.909 |
| 23 | 14.857 | 13.489 | 12.303 | 10.371 | 8.883 | 7.718 | 6.792 | 6.044 | 5.432 | 4.925 |
| 24 | 15.247 | 13.799 | 12.550 | 10.529 | 8.985 | 7.784 | 6.835 | 6.073 | 5.451 | 4.937 |
| 25 | 15.622 | 14.094 | 12.783 | 10.675 | 9.077 | 7.843 | 6.873 | 6.097 | 5.467 | 4.948 |
| 26 | 15.983 | 14.375 | 13.003 | 10.810 | 9.161 | 7.896 | 6.906 | 6.118 | 5.480 | 4.956 |
| 27 | 16.330 | 14.643 | 13.211 | 10.935 | 9.237 | 7.943 | 6.935 | 6.936 | 5.492 | 4.964 |
| 28 | 16.663 | 14.898 | 13.406 | 11.051 | 9.307 | 7.984 | 6.961 | 6.152 | 5.502 | 4.970 |
| 29 | 16.984 | 15.141 | 13.591 | 11.158 | 9.370 | 8.022 | 6.983 | 6.166 | 5.510 | 4.975 |
| 30 | 17.292 | 15.373 | 13.765 | 11.258 | 9.427 | 8.055 | 7.003 | 6.177 | 5.517 | 4.979 |
| 40 | 19.793 | 17.159 | 15.046 | 11.925 | 9.779 | 8.244 | 7.105 | 6.234 | 5.548 | 4.997 |

# Table 5: Monthly Installment Loan Payment (to Repay a $1,000, simple-interest Loan)

| Rate of interest | | | Loan term | | | |
|---|---|---|---|---|---|---|
| | 6 months | 12 months | 18 months | 24 months | 36 months | 48 month |
| $7^1{}_2\%$ | $170.33 | $86.76 | $58.92 | $45.00 | $31.11 | $24.18 |
| 8 | 170.58 | 86.99 | 59.15 | 45.23 | 31.34 | 24.42 |
| $8^1{}_2$ | 170.82 | 87.22 | 59.37 | 45.46 | 31.57 | 24.65 |
| 9 | 171.07 | 87.46 | 59.60 | 45.69 | 31.80 | 24.89 |
| $9^1{}_2$ | 171.32 | 87.69 | 59.83 | 45.92 | 32.04 | 25.13 |
| 10 | 171.56 | 87.92 | 60.06 | 46.15 | 32.27 | 25.37 |
| $10^1{}_2$ | 171.81 | 88.15 | 60.29 | 46.38 | 32.51 | 25.61 |
| 11 | 172.05 | 88.50 | 60.64 | 46.73 | 32.86 | 25.97 |
| $11^1{}_2$ | 172.30 | 88.62 | 60.76 | 46.85 | 32.98 | 26.09 |
| 12 | 172.55 | 88.85 | 60.99 | 47.08 | 33.22 | 26.34 |
| $12^1{}_2$ | 172.80 | 89.09 | 61.22 | 47.31 | 33.46 | 26.58 |
| 13 | 173.04 | 89.32 | 61.45 | 47.55 | 33.70 | 26.83 |
| 14 | 173.54 | 89.79 | 61.92 | 48.02 | 34.18 | 27.33 |
| 15 | 174.03 | 90.26 | 62.39 | 48.49 | 34.67 | 27.84 |
| 16 | 174.53 | 90.74 | 62.86 | 48.97 | 35.16 | 28.35 |
| 17 | 175.03 | 91.21 | 63.34 | 49.45 | 35.66 | 28.86 |
| 18 | 175.53 | 91.68 | 63.81 | 49.93 | 36.16 | 29.38 |

# Table 6: Area in the Right Tail of a Chi-Square ($\chi^2$) Distribution

0.20 of area

14.631

Value of $\chi^2$

*Example:* In a chi-square distribution with 11 degrees of freedom, find the appropriate chi-square value for 0.20 of the area under the curve (the shaded area in the right tail), look under the 0.20 column in the table, and proceed down to the 11 degrees of freedom row; the appropriate chi-square value there is 14.631.

| Degrees of freedom | Area in right tail | | | | |
|---|---|---|---|---|---|
| | 0.99 | 0.975 | 0.95 | 0.90 | 0.800 |
| 1 | 0.00016 | 0.00098 | 0.00398 | 0.0158 | 0.0642 |
| 2 | 0.0201 | 0.0506 | 0.103 | 0.211 | 0.446 |
| 3 | 0.115 | 0.216 | 0.352 | 0.584 | 1.005 |
| 4 | 0.297 | 0.484 | 0.711 | 1.064 | 1.649 |
| 5 | 0.554 | 0.831 | 1.145 | 1.610 | 2.343 |
| 6 | 0.872 | 1.237 | 1.635 | 2.204 | 3.070 |
| 7 | 1.239 | 1.690 | 2.167 | 2.833 | 3.822 |
| 8 | 1.646 | 2.180 | 2.733 | 3.490 | 4.594 |
| 9 | 2.088 | 2.700 | 3.325 | 4.168 | 5.380 |
| 10 | 2.558 | 3.247 | 3.940 | 4.865 | 6.179 |
| 11 | 3.053 | 3.816 | 4.575 | 5.578 | 6.989 |
| 12 | 3.571 | 4.404 | 5.226 | 6.304 | 7.807 |
| 13 | 4.107 | 5.009 | 5.892 | 7.042 | 8.634 |
| 14 | 4.660 | 5.629 | 6.571 | 7.790 | 9.467 |
| 15 | 5.229 | 6.262 | 7.261 | 8.547 | 10.307 |
| 16 | 5.812 | 6.908 | 7.962 | 9.312 | 11.152 |
| 17 | 6.408 | 7.564 | 8.672 | 10.085 | 12.002 |
| 18 | 7.015 | 8.231 | 9.390 | 10.865 | 12.857 |
| 19 | 7.633 | 8.907 | 10.117 | 11.651 | 13.716 |
| 20 | 8.260 | 9.591 | 10.851 | 12.443 | 14.578 |
| 21 | 8.897 | 10.283 | 11.591 | 13.240 | 15.445 |
| 22 | 9.542 | 10.982 | 12.338 | 14.041 | 16.314 |
| 23 | 10.196 | 11.689 | 13.091 | 14.848 | 17.187 |
| 24 | 10.856 | 12.401 | 13.848 | 15.658 | 18.062 |
| 25 | 11.524 | 13.120 | 14.611 | 16.473 | 18.940 |
| 26 | 12.198 | 13.844 | 15.379 | 17.292 | 19.820 |
| 27 | 12.879 | 14.753 | 16.151 | 18.114 | 20.703 |
| 28 | 13.565 | 15.308 | 16.928 | 18.939 | 21.588 |
| 29 | 14.256 | 16.047 | 17.708 | 19.768 | 22.475 |
| 30 | 14.953 | 16.791 | 18.493 | 20.599 | 23.364 |

# Table 7: Normal distribution table:
# Area under the normal curve

| Z | 0 | 1 | 2 | 3 | 4 | 5 | 6 | 7 | 8 | 9 |
|---|---|---|---|---|---|---|---|---|---|---|
| 0.0 | 0.5000 | 0.5040 | 0.5080 | 0.5120 | 0.5160 | 0.5199 | 0.5239 | 0.5279 | 0.5319 | 0.5359 |
| 0.1 | 0.5398 | 0.5438 | 0.5478 | 0.5517 | 0.5557 | 0.5596 | 0.5636 | 0.5675 | 0.5714 | 0.5753 |
| 0.2 | 0.5793 | 0.5832 | 0.5871 | 0.5910 | 0.5948 | 0.5987 | 0.6026 | 0.6064 | 0.6103 | 0.6141 |
| 0.3 | 0.6179 | 0.6217 | 0.6255 | 0.6293 | 0.6331 | 0.6368 | 0.6406 | 0.6443 | 0.6480 | 0.6517 |
| 0.4 | 0.6554 | 0.6591 | 0.6628 | 0.6664 | 0.6700 | 0.6736 | 0.6772 | 0.6808 | 0.6844 | 0.6879 |
| 0.5 | 0.6915 | 0.6950 | 0.6985 | 0.7019 | 0.7054 | 0.7088 | 0.7123 | 0.7157 | 0.7190 | 0.7224 |
| 0.6 | 0.7257 | 0.7291 | 0.7324 | 0.7357 | 0.7389 | 0.7422 | 0.7454 | 0.7486 | 0.7517 | 0.7549 |
| 0.7 | 0.7580 | 0.7611 | 0.7642 | 0.7673 | 0.7703 | 0.7734 | 0.7764 | 0.7794 | 0.7823 | 0.7852 |
| 0.8 | 0.7881 | 0.7910 | 0.7939 | 0.7967 | 0.7995 | 0.8023 | 0.8051 | 0.8078 | 0.8106 | 0.8133 |
| 0.9 | 0.8159 | 0.8186 | 0.8212 | 0.8238 | 0.8264 | 0.8289 | 0.8315 | 0.8340 | 0.8365 | 0.8389 |
| 1.0 | 0.8413 | 0.8438 | 0.8461 | 0.8485 | 0.8508 | 0.8531 | 0.8554 | 0.8577 | 0.8599 | 0.8621 |
| 1.1 | 0.8643 | 0.8665 | 0.8686 | 0.8708 | 0.8729 | 0.8749 | 0.8770 | 0.8790 | 0.8810 | 0.8830 |
| 1.2 | 0.8849 | 0.8869 | 0.8888 | 0.8907 | 0.8925 | 0.8944 | 0.8962 | 0.8980 | 0.8997 | 0.9015 |
| 1.3 | 0.9032 | 0.9049 | 0.9066 | 0.9082 | 0.9099 | 0.9115 | 0.9131 | 0.9147 | 0.9162 | 0.9177 |
| 1.4 | 0.9192 | 0.9207 | 0.9222 | 0.9236 | 0.9251 | 0.9265 | 0.9278 | 0.9292 | 0.9306 | 0.9319 |
| 1.5 | 0.9332 | 0.9345 | 0.9357 | 0.9370 | 0.9382 | 0.9394 | 0.9406 | 0.9418 | 0.9430 | 0.9441 |
| 1.6 | 0.9452 | 0.9463 | 0.9474 | 0.9484 | 0.9495 | 0.9505 | 0.9515 | 0.9525 | 0.9535 | 0.9545 |
| 1.7 | 0.9554 | 0.9564 | 0.9573 | 0.9582 | 0.9591 | 0.9599 | 0.9608 | 0.9616 | 0.9625 | 0.9633 |
| 1.8 | 0.9641 | 0.9648 | 0.9656 | 0.9664 | 0.9671 | 0.9678 | 0.9686 | 0.9693 | 0.9700 | 0.9706 |
| 1.9 | 0.9713 | 0.9719 | 0.9726 | 0.9732 | 0.9738 | 0.9744 | 0.9750 | 0.9756 | 0.9762 | 0.9767 |
| 2.0 | 0.9772 | 0.9778 | 0.9783 | 0.9788 | 0.9793 | 0.9798 | 0.9803 | 0.9808 | 0.9812 | 0.9817 |
| 2.1 | 0.9821 | 0.9826 | 0.9830 | 0.9834 | 0.9838 | 0.9842 | 0.9846 | 0.9850 | 0.9854 | 0.9857 |
| 2.2 | 0.9861 | 0.9864 | 0.9868 | 0.9871 | 0.9874 | 0.9878 | 0.9881 | 0.9884 | 0.9887 | 0.9890 |
| 2.3 | 0.9893 | 0.9896 | 0.9898 | 0.9901 | 0.9904 | 0.9906 | 0.9909 | 0.9911 | 0.9913 | 0.9916 |
| 2.4 | 0.9918 | 0.9920 | 0.9922 | 0.9925 | 0.9927 | 0.9929 | 0.9931 | 0.9932 | 0.9934 | 0.9936 |
| 2.5 | 0.9938 | 0.9940 | 0.9941 | 0.9943 | 0.9945 | 0.9946 | 0.9948 | 0.9949 | 0.9951 | 0.9952 |
| 2.6 | 0.9953 | 0.9955 | 0.9956 | 0.9957 | 0.9959 | 0.9960 | 0.9961 | 0.9962 | 0.9963 | 0.9964 |
| 2.7 | 0.9965 | 0.9966 | 0.9967 | 0.9968 | 0.9969 | 0.9970 | 0.9971 | 0.9972 | 0.9973 | 0.9974 |
| 2.8 | 0.9974 | 0.9975 | 0.9976 | 0.9977 | 0.9977 | 0.9978 | 0.9979 | 0.9979 | 0.9980 | 0.9981 |
| 2.9 | 0.9981 | 0.9982 | 0.9982 | 0.9983 | 0.9984 | 0.9984 | 0.9985 | 0.9985 | 0.9986 | 0.9986 |
| 3.0 | 0.9987 | 0.9990 | 0.9993 | 0.9995 | 0.9997 | 0.9998 | 0.9998 | 0.9999 | 0.9999 | 1.0000 |

# Table 8: t-Distribution Table: Value of t

| d.f. | t0.100 | t0.050 | t0.025 | t0.010 | t0.005 | d.f. |
|------|--------|--------|--------|--------|--------|------|
| 1 | 3.078 | 6.314 | 12.706 | 31.821 | 63.657 | 1 |
| 2 | 1.886 | 2.920 | 4.303 | 6.965 | 9.925 | 2 |
| 3 | 1.638 | 2.353 | 3.182 | 4.541 | 5.841 | 3 |
| 4 | 1.533 | 2.132 | 2.776 | 3.747 | 4.604 | 4 |
| 5 | 1.476 | 2.015 | 2.571 | 3.365 | 4.032 | 5 |
| 6 | 1.440 | 1.943 | 2.447 | 3.143 | 3.707 | 6 |
| 7 | 1.415 | 1.895 | 2.365 | 2.998 | 3.499 | 7 |
| 8 | 1.397 | 1.860 | 2.306 | 2.896 | 3.355 | 8 |
| 9 | 1.383 | 1.833 | 2.262 | 2.821 | 3.250 | 9 |
| 10 | 1.372 | 1.812 | 2.228 | 2.764 | 3.169 | 10 |
| 11 | 1.363 | 1.796 | 2.201 | 2.718 | 3.106 | 11 |
| 12 | 1.356 | 1.782 | 2.179 | 2.681 | 3.055 | 12 |
| 13 | 1.350 | 1.771 | 2.160 | 2.650 | 3.012 | 13 |
| 14 | 1.345 | 1.761 | 2.145 | 2.624 | 2.977 | 14 |
| 15 | 1.341 | 1.753 | 2.131 | 2.602 | 2.947 | 15 |
| 16 | 1.337 | 1.746 | 2.120 | 2.583 | 2.921 | 16 |
| 17 | 1.333 | 1.740 | 2.110 | 2.567 | 2.898 | 17 |
| 18 | 1.330 | 1.734 | 2.101 | 2.552 | 2.878 | 18 |
| 19 | 1.328 | 1.729 | 2.093 | 2.539 | 2.861 | 19 |
| 20 | 1.325 | 1.725 | 2.086 | 2.528 | 2.845 | 20 |
| 21 | 1.323 | 1.721 | 2.080 | 2.518 | 2.831 | 21 |
| 22 | 1.321 | 1.717 | 2.074 | 2.508 | 2.819 | 22 |
| 23 | 1.319 | 1.714 | 2.069 | 2.500 | 2.807 | 23 |
| 24 | 1.318 | 1.711 | 2.064 | 2.492 | 2.797 | 24 |
| 25 | 1.316 | 1.708 | 2.060 | 2.485 | 2.787 | 25 |
| 26 | 1.315 | 1.706 | 2.056 | 2.479 | 2.779 | 26 |
| 27 | 1.314 | 1.703 | 2.052 | 2.473 | 2.771 | 27 |
| 28 | 1.313 | 1.701 | 2.048 | 2.467 | 2.763 | 28 |
| 29 | 1.311 | 1.699 | 2.045 | 2.462 | 2.756 | 29 |
| Inf. | 1.282 | 1.645 | 1.960 | 2.326 | 2.576 | Inf. |

The $t$-value describes the sampling distribution of a deviation from a population value divided by the standard error.

Degrees of freedom (d.f.) are in the first column. The probabilities indicated as subvalues of $t$ in the heading refer to the sum of a one-tailed area under the curve that lies outside the point $t$.

For example, in the distribution of the means of samples of size $n = 10$, d.f. $= n - 2 = 8$; then 0.025 of the area under the curve falls in one tail outside the interval $t \pm 2.306$.

# Glossary

**ABC analysis** A selective classification and analysis of inventory SKUs according to annual dollar importance.

**Acceleration clause** A clause in a credit or loan agreement that states if the borrower does not meet the payment schedule, all remaining payments may become immediately due and payable at once at the demand of the creditor or lender.

**Accounts receivable turnover** Annual credit sales divided by average accounts receivable.

**Acid-test ratio** The most liquid current assets (cash, marketable securities, accounts receivable) divided by current liabilities.

**Accommodation** A loan without interest, collateral, or other consideration. An example might be a loan between members of the family or friends in order to start a business.

**Account** A record of the relationship and transactions between a business and another party (e.g., customer). The account balance is what is owed at the end of a reporting period.

**Action** A legal proceeding initiated by the business against another party such as for the nonpayment of a customer's account balance.

**Activity-based costing (ABC)** A costing system which first traces costs to activities and then to products. It separates overhead costs into overhead cost pools, where each cost pool is associated with a different cost driver. Then a predetermined overhead rate is computed for each cost pool and each cost driver. In consequence, this method has enhanced product costing accuracy.

**Additional paid-in capital** Excess received from stockholders over par value of the stock issued.

**Adjustment**

1. Changing an account balance because of some happening or occurrence, such as a product defect.

2. In insurance, the settlement of a claim.

**Advance**

1. Money given to an employee before it is earned, such as an advance against salary.

2. Payment received from customers in advance for work, goods, or services.

3. Money given by a banker to a borrower: in advance, usually short-term and in the form of an overdraft.

**After-tax cash flow**  Net cash flow (cash revenue less cash expenses) after taxes have been subtracted. It is the cash flow generated from operations.

**Allowance**  The reduction in price or increase in quantity of a good or service that the seller gives the buyer. Allowance may be given in special sale, damage, shrinkage, and spoilage situations.

**All risk/all peril**  A feature in an insurance policy that covers all risks/all perils unless specifically excluded by the policy.

**Amortized loan**  A loan that is paid off in periodic equal installments and includes varying portions of principal and interest during its term.

**Analysis of variances (Variance analysis)**  Analysis and investigation of causes for variances between standard costs and actual costs. A variance is considered favorable if actual costs are less than standard costs; it is unfavorable if actual costs exceed standard costs. Unfavorable variances are the ones that need further investigation for their causes.

**Annual report**  Evaluation prepared by companies at the end of the reporting year.

**Annuity**  Series of equal periodic payments or receipts.

**Approval sale**  A sale which is not finalized until the merchandise is accepted by the buyer. Title will pass only when approval is given or when the goods are retained by the buyer for a reasonable time period or that period specified in the agreement.

**As is**  A term for secondhand or damaged goods sold without either an express or implied warranty by the seller. The buyer is warned to inspect the items carefully since the burden of determining their condition falls on him or her.

**Asset turnover**  Sales divided by average total assets, revealing the efficiency of corporate assets in generating revenue.

**Average inventory** The average balance of inventory on hand; in the case of constant demand, average inventory is about half maximum inventory.

**Balloon clause** A provision in an installment sales agreement stating that the final payment by the customer will be substantially larger than all other payments.

**Bank reconciliation** A term used when reconciling the differences between the bank statement and the checkbook balance. The checkbook balance must be the same as the bank balance at the end of the period. Reconciling differences relate to (1) items shown on the checkbook but not on the bank statement (e.g., outstanding checks) and (2) items shown on the bank statement but not on the checkbook (e.g., bank service charges).

**Banker's acceptance** Time draft drawn by a business firm whose payment is guaranteed by the bank's "acceptance" of it. It is especially important in foreign trade, because it allows the seller of goods to be certain that the buyer's draft will actually have funds behind it.

**Bankruptcy** The inability to pay debts when due. A business is insolvent in a legal sense when its financial condition is such that total liabilities exceed the fair market value of its assets.

**Bargain basement** A physical location in a large retail store where merchandise can be bought at significant discounts.

**Beta** The variability in the price of a stock relative to the variability in a stock market index.

**Bill of sale** A receipt of money paid by the buyer to the seller.

**Billing cycle** The time period between periodic billings for merchandise or services rendered, typically one month. It could also be the periodic mailing of statements within a month to distribute the work load efficiently.

**Blanket rate** The same rate paid for transportation charges for a delivery of merchandise to buyers within a given geographic area.

**Boilerplate** Standard language found in contracts and agreements.

**Bond** Written promise by a company to pay the face amount at the maturity date.

**Book value per share** Worth of each share of stock per the books based on historical cost.

**Bounced check** A check that has been returned for insufficient funds.

**Breakeven analysis** A branch of cost-volume-profit (CVP) analysis that determines the break-even sales, which is the level of sales where total costs equal total revenue.

**Break-even point** The level of sales where total costs equal total revenue.

**Bridge loan** Short-term loan that is made in expectation of intermediate or long-term loans. The interest rate on a bridge loan is generally higher than that on the longer-term loans. An example is a temporary loan made to permit a closing on a building purchase prior to a closing on long-term mortgage financing.

**Budget** Quantitative plan of activities and programs expressed in terms of assets, liabilities, revenues, and expenses.

**Business cycle** Recurrence of periods of contracting and expanding economic conditions.

**Capital asset pricing model (CAPM)** Theory of asset pricing used to analyze the relationship between risk and rates of return in securities.

**Capital bond** Bond issue with a call (buy back) provision.

**Capital budget** A budget or plan of proposed acquisitions and replacements of long-term assets and their financing. A capital budget is developed using a variety of capital budgeting techniques such as the discount cash flow method.

**Capital budgeting** Process of making long-term planning decisions for capital investments.

**Capital rationing** Selecting the mix of acceptable projects that provides the highest overall *net present value* of future cash flows when a company has a limit on the budget for capital spending.

**Capital structure** Composition of common stock, preferred stock, retained earnings, and long-term debt maintained by the business entity in financing its assets.

**Carrying costs** The costs incurred in maintaining an inventory.

**Cash and carry** A requirement that a customer pay a retail store in cash for a good or service and either take immediate delivery or arrange for delivery (at a charge).

**Cash before delivery** A requirement by a seller that the buyer pay for goods before delivery. A discount may be given for immediate payment. The seller may do this when the buyer's ability to pay is questionable.

**Cash budget** A budget for cash planning and control that presents anticipated cash inflow and cash outflow for a specified time period. The cash budget helps the owner keep cash balances in reasonable relationship to needs. It assists in avoiding idle cash and possible cash shortages. The cash budget shows beginning cash, cash receipts, cash payments, and ending cash.

**Cash disbursement (payments) journal** Book used to record all payments made in cash such as for accounts payable, merchandise purchases, and operating expenses.

**Cash equivalent**

1. Immediate realizable money that can be obtained in exchange of goods or services.

2. Financial instruments of high liquidity and safety (e.g., Treasury bill, money-market fund).

**Cash flow**

1. cash receipts minus cash disbursements from a given operation or asset for a given period. Cash flow and cash inflow are often used interchangeably.

2. the monetary value of the expected benefits and costs of a project. It may be in the form of cash savings in operating costs or the difference between additional dollars received and additional dollars paid out for a given period.

**Cash flow statement** Statement showing from what sources cash has come into the business and on what the cash has been spent. Cash flow is broken down into operating, investing, and financing activities.

**Cash receipts journal** Book used to record all transactions involving the receipt of cash. Examples are cash sales, receipt of interest and dividend income, collections from customer accounts, and cash sale of assets. Typically, there are separate columns for the date, explanation, cash debit, sales discount debit, other debt, account credit, accounts receivable credit, and other credit.

**Cash shortage and overage** Situation in which the physical amount of cash on hand differs from the book recorded amount of cash. This is a particular problem with over-the counter cash receipts.

**Casualty insurance** Insurance that protects a business against property loss and damage.

**Certificate of deposit (CD)** Special type of time deposit. A CD is an investment instrument, available at financial institutions, that generally offers a fixed rate of return for a specified period. The depositor agree not to withdraw funds until the CD matures. If the funds are withdrawn, a significant penalty is charged. The fixed rate of return normally increase with the amount or the term of the investment.

**Certified check** Depositor's check that a bank guarantees to pay. The funds are precommitted.

**Closed corporation** A corporation in which shares are held by a few individuals, typically family members or management of the company. These shares are not available to the public.

**Coefficient of determination** A statistical measure of how good the estimated regression equation is. Simply put, it is a measure of "goodness of fit" in the regression.

**Collateral** Property that must be pledged as security for a loan. If the borrower defaults, the lender can usually seize the collateral.

**Collection period** Number of days it takes to collect accounts receivable. The Collection period can be compared to the terms of sale.

**Commencement of coverage** The date upon which insurance protection starts. Prior to that time, the risk of loss belongs to the owner of the business.

**Commercial paper** Short-term unsecured note issued by financially strong businesses.

**Common costs** Expense shared by different departments, products, jobs, also called joint costs or indirect costs

**Common Stock** A security which represents ownership in a company.

**Company car** An auto owned by the business but available to an employee for use.

**Compensating balance** The balance a borrower must maintain on deposit in a bank account, representing a given percentage of the loan. No interest is earned on this balance, which increases the effective interest rate on the loan.

**Concentration banking** Acceleration of cash collections from customers by having funds sent to several regional banks and transferred to a main concentration account in another bank. The transfer of funds can be accomplished electronically.

**Concession**

1. A reduction in the price a seller charges as an incentive for sales.

2. Any deviation from normal terms or previous conditions.

3. Permission, usually in the form of a lease, to conduct a particular type of business in a specific area or place.

**Contract of sale** A written agreement between seller and buyer in which the purchaser agrees to buy specified merchandise or services and the seller agrees to sell them upon the terms of the agreement.

**Contribution** Price per unit less variable cost per unit.

**Contribution margin (CM)** The difference between sales and the variable costs of the product or service, also called marginal income. It is the amount of money available to cover fixed costs and generate profits.

**Conversion costs** The sum of the costs of direct labor and factory overhead.

**Convertible security** Type of stock or bond that can be voluntarily converted into capital stock at a later date.

**Corporation** A form of business organized as a separate legal entity with ownership evidenced by shares of capital stock.

**Cost behavior analysis** Analysis of mixed costs. Mixed costs must be separated into the variable and fixed elements in order to be included in a variety of business planning analyses such as cost-volume-profit (CVP) analysis.

**Cost center** The unit within the organization in which the manager is responsible only for costs. A cost center has no control over sales or over the generating of revenue. An example is the production department of a manufacturing company.

**Cost driver** Direct labor that causes a cost item to be incurred (e.g., direct labor hours, number of setups, or number of inspections).

**Cost management** A system that measures the cost of significant activities, recognizes non-value-added costs, and identifies activities that will improve overall performance.

**Cost of accumulation** The collection of costs in an organized fashion by means of a cost accounting system. There are two primary approaches to cost accumulation: a job order system and process cost system.

**Cost of capital** Weighted average of the costs of debt and equity funds.

**Cost of production report** A summary of the unit and cost data of a production department in a process cost system.

**Cost pool** A group of related costs that are assigned together to a set of cost objectives (such as jobs, products, or activities).

**Cost-volume formula** A cost function in the form of $y = a + bx$.

For example, the cost-volume formula for factory overhead is $y = \$200 + \$10x$ where y=estimated factory overhead and x=direct labor hours, which means that the factory overhead is estimated to be $200 fixed, plus $10 per hour of direct labor. Cost analysts use the formula for cost prediction and flexible budgeting purposes.

**Cost-volume-profit (CVP) analysis** Analysis that deals with how profits and costs change with a change in volume. It looks at the effects on profits of changes in such factors as variables costs, fixed costs, selling prices, volume, and mix of products sold.

**Cost-volume-profit analysis** Sometimes referred to as breakeven analysis; the systematic analysis of the relationship of profit to changes in fixed costs, variable costs, and volume.

**Coupon rate** Interest rate on the face amount of a debt security.

**Credit** A loan extended to a business or individual payable at a later date.

**Credit analysis** Process of evaluating, before a line of credit is extended, whether a credit applicant meets the firm's credit standards.

**Credit application** A form used to record information regarding a credit applicant's ability to repay the debt.

**Credit bureau** An agency that gathers credit information about customers.

**Credit limit** A specified amount beyond which a credit customer may not buy on credit.

**Credit line** Specified amount of money available to a borrower from a bank, usually for one year. A credit line is a moral, not a contractual, commitment, and no commitment fee is charged.

**Credit memorandum** A form issued by a seller to a buyer indicating that the seller is reducing the amount the buyer owes.

**Credit rating** A rating to help the business determine if a credit applicant should be granted credit. It is based on factors such as the applicant's job history, income, assets owned, and credit history.

**Credit receipt** Written evidence of merchandise returned and the selling price.

**Creditor** Business or individual that has extended credit and is owed money.

**Current ration** Current assets divided by current liabilities.

**Debenture** Long-term debt instrument that is not secured by a mortgage or other lien on specific property.

**Debit memorandum** A form issued by a seller to a buyer indicating that the seller is increasing the amount the buyer owes.

**Debt-equity ratio** Total liabilities divided by total stockholders' equity.

**Decision tree** A pictorial representation of sequential decisions, states of nature, probabilities attached to the state of nature, and conditional benefits and losses.

**Deductible** The amount that an insured must pay on any insured loss before payment by the insurance company begins.

**Default** Failure to meet the conditions of a loan contract. It generally refers to the failure to meet interest and/or principal payments.

**Demand deposit** Deposit from which funds may be drawn on demand and from which funds may be transferred to another party by means of a check.

**Departmental rate** A predetermined factory overhead rate for each production department.

**Direct deposit of payroll** An agreement to utilize an automated clearing house to deposit worker paychecks automatically into employee accounts.

**Direct method** A method of allocating the costs of each service department directly to production departments on the basis of the relative portion of services rendered.

**Discharge of bankruptcy** An order in which the bankrupt debtor is relieved of responsibility to pay his or her obligations.

**Discount loan** A loan in which the whole interest charge is deducted in advance from the face value of a loan reducing the proceeds received. This increases the effective interest cost of the loan.

**Discretionary (fixed) costs** Those fixed costs that change because of managerial decisions, also called management (fixed) costs or programmed (fixed) costs. Examples of this type of fixed costs are advertising outlays, training costs, and research and development costs.

**Diversification** The spreading of risk such as by carrying different product lines.

**Dunning letter** Notices that insistently demand repayment of debts from customers.

**Economic order quantity (EOQ)** The order size that should be ordered at one time to minimize the sum of carrying and ordering costs.

**Effective date** The day a contract begins. After the effective date of the agreement, the parties are bound by it.

**Effective interest rate** Real rate of interest on a loan equal to the nominal interest divided by the proceeds of the loan.

**Electronic funds transfer** Paperless funds transfer.

**Employment contract** A legal agreement between the employer and employee specifying the particulars of the arrangement, such as employment terms and compensation.

**Entrepreneurial profit** The net income earned by the hard-working owner of a business.

**EOQ (Economic order quantity)** That particular quantity which, if ordered each time the inventory is replenished, will minimize the total annual cost of ordering and carrying the inventory.

**Equal credit opportunity act** A federal law making it illegal to discriminate when giving credit.

**Exchange** A customer returns merchandise and obtains merchandise of equal value in return.

**Expected value** A weighted average of the outcomes of an experiment.

**Exponential smoothing** A forecasting method involving a single weighing factor called alpha.

**Express warranty** A manufacturer's voluntary written warranty that accompanies its product.

**Extended coverage** Protection over and above that given by an insurance policy.

**Extended warranty** A service contract providing protection over and above that given by the warranty available with a new product.

**Face value** Nominal amount of a debt obligation or equity security as stated in the instrument.

**Factoring** Outright sale of a firm's accounts receivable to another party (the factor) *without recourse*, which means the factor must bear the risk of collection.

**Fee compensation** The payment to the bank to compensate it for services rendered.

**Financial leverage** Portion of a firm's assets financed with debt instead of equity.

**Financial statement** Report containing financial information about a company.

**Fixed cost** A cost that remains the same each period in the short run regardless of activity. Examples are rent, insurance, and property taxes.

**Fixed overhead spending (budget)variance** The difference between actual fixed overhead incurred and fixed overhead budgeted.

**Fixed overhead volume (denominator) variance** The difference between budgeted fixed overhead and the fixed overhead costs applied to products. It is used as a measure of utilization of plant facilities.

**Flexible budget** A budget based on cost-volume relationships and developed for the actual level of activity. It is an extremely useful tool for comparing the actual cost incurred to the cost allowable for the activity level achieved.

**Float**
1. Amount of funds represented by checks that have been issued but not yet collected.
2. Time between the deposit of checks in a bank and payment. Due to the time difference, many firms are able to "play the float," that is, to write checks against money not presently in the firm's bank account.

**Full warranty** A type of warranty that entitles consumers to full remedies for defective goods or services for a specified period of time.

**General partner** A partner who has unlimited liability for partnership debts in the event the partnership fails. The general partner manages the business.

**Gift certificate** A certificate generally paid for by the one person and entitling the recipient to obtain merchandise, food, or services at no charge up to the amount paid by the purchaser.

**Gross profit margin** Ratio of gross profit to net sales. A high gross profit margin is a positive sign since it shows the business is earning an attractive return over the cost of its merchandise sold.

**Holding company** Corporation owning enough voting stock in another company to control its policies and management.

**Illiquid**

1. Lacking enough liquid assets, like cash and marketable securities, to cover short-term obligations.
2. Current liabilities exceed current assets.

**Impaired credit** A reduction in credit given by a business to a customer who has experienced a determination in creditworthiness.

**Implied warranty** A warranty in effect whether expressed individually or not. It is mandated by state law. It provides the products sold are warranted to be suitable for sale and will work effectively whether there is an express warranty or not.

**Indenture** Legal document that specifically states the conditions under which a bond has been issued, the rights of the bondholders, and the duties of the issuing corporation.

**Insolvency** Failure of a company to meet its obligations as they become due. An analysis of insolvency concentrates on the operating and capital structure of the business. The proportion of long-term debt in the capital structure must also be considered.

**Installment credit** A type of consumer credit in which the consumer pays the amount in equal payments, usually monthly.

**Installment loan** A loan that is repaid in a series of periodic, fixed scheduled payments instead of in a lump sum.

**Installment sale** A sale in which periodic cash payments will be received over time.

**Internal rate of return (IRR)** The rate of interest that equates the initial investment with the present value of future cash inflows.

**Inventory turnover** The number of times inventory is sold during the year. It equals cost of goods sold divided by the average dollar balance. Average inventory equals the beginning and ending balances divided by two.

**Investment banker** Intermediary between an issuer of new securities and the investor.

**Investment center** A responsibility center within an organization that has control over revenue, cost and investment funds. It is a profit center whose performance is evaluated on the basis of the return earned on invested capital.

**Ironclad contract** A legal contract that will be very difficult to break.

**Job order costing** The accumulation of costs by specific jobs, contracts, or orders. This costing method is appropriate when direct costs can be identified with specific units of production. Job order costing is widely used by custom manufacturers such as printing, aircraft, construction, auto repair and professional services.

**Judgmental forecast**  Forecasting method that brings together in an organized way personal judgments about the process being analyzed.

**Just-in-time (JIT)**  A demand-pull system where demand for customer output (not plans for using input resources) triggers production. Production activities are "pulled", not "pushed," into action. JIT, in its purest sense, is buying and producing in very small quantities just in time for use.

**Keogh pension plan**  A tax-deferred retirement plan under which self-employed persons have the right to establish retirement plans for themselves and their employers. The contributions are tax deductible, and earnings are tax deferred until withdrawn. Self-employed individuals can contribute to their Keogh plan up to 25 percent of earnings, or a maximum of $30,000.

**Labor rate variance**  Any deviation from standard in the average hourly rate paid to workers.

**Labor efficiency variance**  The difference between the amount of labor time that should have been used and the labor that were actually used, multiplied by the standard rate.

**Lead time**  Time (usually measured in days) required for inventory to arrive after an order is placed.

**Learning curve**  A curve that represents the efficiencies gained from experience. It is based on the statistical findings that as the cumulative output doubles, the cumulative average labor input time required per unit will be reduced by some constant percentage, ranging between 10 and 40 percent.

**Lease**  A contract in which the lessee pays rent to the lessor in order to use real property for a designated time period.

**Least-squared method**  A method of fitting a trend line which minimizes the sum of the squares of the errors between the estimated points on the trend line and the actual observed points that were used to fit the line.

**Leverage**  The use of borrowed money to magnify potential returns from the business. It is hoped that the investment through leverage will earn a rate of return greater than the after-tax costs of borrowing.

**Leverage buyout**  Acquisition of one company by another, typically with borrowed funds.

**License**  A legal document given by a regulatory agency to a business to conduct some activity subject to prescribed terms. Typically, a fee is charged. An example is a liquor license.

**Lien**  A claim of a party, typically a creditor, to hold or control the property of another party to satisfy a debt. It permits the creditor to liquidate the property that serves as collateral in the event of default.

**Limited partner** A member of a partnership whose liability for the debts of the partnership is limited to the member's investment. A limited partner is not allowed to take active part in the management of a partnership.

**Line of credit** The maximum preapproved amount that a business may borrow.

**Linear programming (LP)** A technique used to find an optimal solution to the resource allocation problem under constrained conditions.

**Liquid** The state of having sufficient cash and near-cash assets to meet current debt.

**Liquid asset** Cash asset (e.g., cash or an unrestricted bank account) or readily marketable security. A liquid asset can be converted into cash in a short time without a material concession in price. Excluded from this definition are accounts receivable and inventory.

**Liquidation** Process of closing a business entity, including selling or disposing of the assets, paying the liabilities, and having whatever is left over returned to the owners.

**Liquidity** Ability of current assets to meet current liabilities when due.

**List price** The standard published price of a good or service.

**Lockbox** Box in a U.S. Postal Service facility, used to facilitate collection of customer remittances. The use of a lockbox reduces processing float. The recipient's local bank collects from these boxes periodically during the day and deposits the funds in the appropriate corporate account.

**Markdown** A reduction in the original retail selling price.

**Marketable security** Readily tradable equity or debt security with quoted prices.

**Markup**
1. An increase in the original selling price.
2. Adding a profit to cost to determine a selling price.

**Master account** Account from which funds are transferred to zero balance accounts when needed.

**Master (comprehensive) budget** A plan of activities expressed in monetary terms of the assets, equities, revenues, and costs which will be involved in carrying out the plans. It is a set of projected or planned financial statements.

**Material requirements planning (MRP)** System which recognizes the dependent nature of individual components in an inventory system and calculates quantities and schedule times accordingly.

**Materials price variance** The difference between what is paid for a given quantity of materials and what should have been paid, multiplied by actual quantity of materials used.

**Materials quantity (usage)** The difference between the actual quantity of materials used in production and the standard quantity of materials allowed for actual production, multiplied by the standard price per unit.

**Maturity value** Amount to be paid on the maturity date of a financial instrument.

**Mean** A measure of central tendency.

**Mechanic's lien** A lien placed against property by an unpaid service business in which the owner can hold on to the property until the customer pays for services rendered.

**Mixed costs** Costs that vary with changes in volume but, unlike variable costs, do not vary in direct proportion, also called semivariable costs.

**Money**

1. Cash.
2. Term broadly used to refer to a medium of exchange and unit of value.

**Money market** Market for short-term (less than one year) debt securities. Examples of money-market securities include U.S. Treasury bills and commercial paper.

**Money order** Check issued by a bank to a payee when an individual gives the bank funds in exchange. Payees sometimes require a money order since it is, in effect, guaranteed payment.

**Moving average** An average that is updated as new information becomes available.

**Multiple regression analysis** A statistical procedure that attempts to assess the relationship between the dependent variable and two or more independent variables. For example, total factory overhead is related to both labor hours and machine hours.

**Mutual fund** Portfolio of securities professionally managed by the sponsoring management company or investment company that issues shares to investors.

**Negative cash flow** A situation in which cash inflows are less than cash outflows. This is an unfavorable situation that may result in liquidity problems.

**Net worth** Total assets less total liabilities. This represents the owner's equity in the business.

**Net present value (NPV)** The difference between the present value of cash inflows generated by the project and the amount of the initial investment.

**Nominal interest rate** Stated interest rate on the face of a debt security or loan.

**Not-sufficient-funds (NSF) check** Check not covered by sufficient bank balance. In preparing its bank reconciliation the depositing entity must deduct the NSF check from the cash book balance.

**Offer**
1. A proposal to perform some activity or to pay some money. Once an offer is accepted, a contract exists.
2. To offer a good or service for sale.

**Open account**
1. An account having a balance, such as one in which a customer still owes the retail store money.
2. A credit relationship between seller and buyer.

**Operating cycle** Average time period between buying inventory and receiving cash proceeds from its eventual sale. It is determined by adding the number of days inventory is held and the collection period for accounts receivable.

**Opportunity cost** Revenue forfeited by rejecting an alternative use of time or facilities.

**Optimum production lot size** That particular quantity which, if produced in one production run, will minimize the total annual cost of setting up and carrying finished goods inventory.

**Ordering costs** The costs of getting an item into the inventory; these costs are incurred each time an order is placed.

**Out-of-pocket cost** Actual cash outlays made during the period for payroll, advertising, and other operating expenses. Depreciation is not an out-of-pocket cost, since it involves no current cash expenditure.

**Overdraft**
1. Negative balance in a checking account funds.
2. Situation where a borrower draws money against a previously established line of credit. The basic cost to the borrower is the interest rate levied on the daily overdraft balance.

**Payback period** The number of years it takes to recover your initial investment. The payback period equals the initial investment divided by the annual cash inflow.

**Payment plan** A plan specifying the dates and amounts of payments to be made under a financing agreement.

**Payroll withholding** The amount taken out of an employee's salary for taxes and other items (e.g., union dues) to be remitted to other parties (e.g., IRS).

**Petty cash fund** Minimal amount of money kept on hand by a business entity to meet small expenditures (e.g., postage, taxi fare).

**Portfolio** A group of securities held in order to reduce risk by diversification.

**Predetermined overhead rates** An overhead rate, based on budgeted factory overhead cost and budgeted activity, that is established before a period begins.

**Preferred stock** Class of capital stock that has preference over common stock in the event of corporate liquidation and in the distribution of earnings.

**Present value** Current worth of future sums of money.

**Prime interest rate** Interest rate charged by banks to their most financially sound customers.

**Prime rate** Interest rate charged by banks to their most financially sound customers.

**Probability** The chance that something will happen.

**Process costing** A cost accumulation method used to assign costs to units of a homogeneous product as the units passes through one of more processes.

**Professional liability insurance** An insurance policy taken out by a professional for malpractice coverage. The policy covers legal fees and possible damages.

**Profit margin** Ratio of net income to net sales. It reveals the entity's ability to generate profit at a given sales level. The ratio gives the owner an indicator of the operating efficiency and pricing strategy of the business.

**Profit-volume chart** A chart that determines how profits vary with changes in volume.

**Profitability index** The ratio of the total present value of future cash inflows to the initial investment.

**Program evaluation and review technique (PERT)** A useful management tool for planning, coordinating, and controlling large complex projects such as formulation of a master budget, construction of buildings, installation of computers, and scheduling the closing of books.

**Prospectus** Document that must accompany a new issue of securities.

**Quick asset** Current asset that can be converted into cash in a short time. Examples are cash, marketable securities, and accounts receivable. Certain current assets, such as inventory and prepaid expenses, are excluded.

**Rate of return on investment (ROI)**
1. For the company as a whole, net income after taxes divided by invested capital.
2. For the segment of an organization, net operating income divided by operating assets.
3. For capital budgeting purposes, also called simple, accounting, or unadjusted rate of return, expected future net income divided by initial (or average) investment.

**Reciprocal method** A method of allocating service department costs to production departments, where reciprocal services are allowed between service departments; also known as the linear algebra method, the matrix method, the double-distribution method, the cross-allocation method, and simultaneous equation method.

**Recourse** A business owner's right to recover from a customer payment for something sold or services performed.

**Refund** Amount paid back or credit given because of the return of merchandise.

**Regression analysis** A statistical procedure for estimating mathematically the average relationship between the dependent variable (sales, for example) and one or more independent variables (price and advertising, for example).

**Regression model** A forecasting model which relates the dependent variable (sales, for example) to one or more independent variables (GNP and Index of Economic Activity, for example).

**Relevant cost** The expected future cost that will differ between the alternatives being considered.

**Reorder point** Inventory level at which it is appropriate to replenish stock.

**Residual income (RI)** The operating income which an investment center is able to earn above some minimum return on its assets.

**Responsibility accounting** The collection, summarization, and reporting of financial information about various decision centers (responsibility centers) throughout an organization; also called activity accounting or profitability accounting.

**Responsibility center** A unit in the organization which has control over costs, revenues, or investment funds. For accounting purposes, responsibility centers are classified as cost centers, revenue centers, profit centers, and investment centers, depending on what each center is responsible for.

**Retail lockbox** A lockbox that collects numerous small-dollar remittances from consumers.

**Return** The reward for investing in a business in the form of earnings and appreciation in the value of the business.

**Risk**

1. Variability about income, returns, or other financial variable.

2. Possibility of losing value.

**Risk averse** Opposed to risk. It is a subjective attitude against risk taking.

**Risk management** The analysis of and planning for potential risk and their subsequent losses. The objective of risk management is to try to minimize the financial consequence of random losses.

**Risk reduction** An attempt by a business owner to minimize risk by taking some action such as diversifying and obtaining insurance coverage.

**Risk-return trade-off** A comparison of the expected return from an investment with the risk associated with it. The higher the risk undertaken, the more ample the return. Conversely, the lower the risk, the more modest the return.

**Safety stock** Extra units of inventory carried as protection against possible stockouts.

**Sales contract** An agreement between the seller and buyer specifying the terms of sale.

**Sales tax** A state or local tax based on a percentage of the selling price of a good or service that the buyer pays. The seller collects the tax and remits it to the sales tax agency.

**Seasonality** A fluctuation in business conditions that occur on a regular basis. It may be caused by such factors as weather and vacations. An example is the toy industry, which has its greatest sales in November and December.

**Secured loan** A loan requiring certain assets to be pledged as collateral.

**Segmented reporting** The process of reporting activities of various segments of an organization such as divisions, product lines, or sales territories.

**Self-employed income** The net taxable income of a self-employed person reported on Schedule C of IRS Form 1040. The self-employed individual pays a higher social security than a regular employee.

**Service contract** An agreement in which the seller or other third party will repair merchandise purchased by a buyer.

**Simple interest** The interest charge computed on the original principal.

**Simple regression** A regression analysis which involves one independent variable. For example, total factory overhead is related to one activity variable (either direct labor hours or machine hours).

**SKU** Stockkeeping unit; a specific different item in an inventory.

**Standard deviation** A measure of the spread of the data around the mean.

**Step method** The allocation of service department costs to other service departments as well as production departments in a sequential manner.

**Stock option** Right given the holder to buy a specified number of shares of stock at a certain price by a particular date.

**Stock right** Privilege giving current stockholders the first right to buy shares in a new offering, thus maintaining their proportionate ownership interest.

**Stock split** Issuance of substantial amount of additional shares, thus reducing the par value of the stock on a proportionate basis.

**Stop payment** Instruction to the bank not to honor a check when presented. As long as the check has not been cashed, the maker has up to six months to present a stop payment notice. However, a stop payment right does not apply to electronic funds transfers.

**Sweep account** A bank account in which excess funds are automatically transferred into an interest-earning account at the same bank.

**Target balance** Average collected balance to be maintained at the bank to compensate it for services provided to the small business.

**Temporary investments** Strategy of using seasonal excess of cash to invest in marketable securities that the company intends to convert back into cash within one year. The investments produce dividend and/or interest income as well as possible capital appreciations for the company.

**Tender offer** Bid to buy stock of a company at a specified price (usually at a premium over the market price) to gain control of the company.

**Term loan** Immediate to long-term secured loan granted to a business by a commercial bank, insurance company, or commercial finance company, usually to finance capital equipment or provide working capital. The loan is amortized over a fixed period.

**The Du Pont formula** The breakdown of return on investment (ROI) into profit margin and asset turnover.

**Tight money** A situation in which fewer funds are made available to borrowers by lending institutions and creditors. If available, the loans carry higher interest rates.

**Time deposit** Savings account at a financial institution that earns interest but is not legally subject to withdrawal on demand or transfer by check. The depositor can withdraw only by giving notice.

**Time value of money** Value of money at different time periods. As a rule, one dollar today is worth more than one dollar tomorrow. The time value of money is a critical consideration in financial decisions.

**Title** The legal right of an ownership interest in a property. It is evidence of ownership and lawful possession.

**Total quality control(TQC)** A quality program in which the goal is complete elimination of product defects.

**Total return** The return received over a specified time period from periodic income and capital gain on sale.

**Trade association** An organization representing the interests of businesses in the same industry.

**Treasury bill** Short-term obligation of the federal government, commonly called T-bill. Treasury bills carry on coupon but are sold on a discount basis. Denominations range from $10,000 to $1 million. The yields on T-bills are lower than those on any other marketable securities due to their virtually risk-free nature.

**Trend line** A line fitted to sets of data points which describes the relationship between time and the dependent variable.

**Truth in Lending Act** A federal law protecting credit purchases. The most important provision is the requirement that both the dollar amount of finance charges and the annual percentage rate charged be disclosed.

**Turnover** The number of times an asset, such as inventory, turns over during an accounting period.

**Unbundling** An approach in which the business only pays for bank services actually used.

**Underinsurance** The failure to carry sufficient insurance.

**Unlimited liability** Amount of risk borne by someone in a sole proprietorship or general partnership. Liability is not restricted to the capital investments, thus, if the business goes bankrupt, the owner risks his or her personal assets to meet creditor claims. In a corporation, however, the stockholder has limited liability up to his/her investment.

**Unsecured loan** A loan on which no collateral is required.

**Variance**

1. In statistics, the square of the standard deviation.

2. In cost analysis, the deviation between the actual cost and the standard cost.

**Volume-based cost driver** A cost driver that is based on production volume, such as machine hours or direct-labor hours.

**Zero-base budgeting** A method of budgeting in which cost and benefit estimates are built up from scratch, from the zero level, and must be justified.

# Index